MY LIFE AND TIMES

Tan Sri Dato' (Dr) Ramon V. Navaratnam is a distinguished former civil servant and corporate personality. A graduate in Economics from the University of Malaya in Singapore and a postgraduate from Harvard University, he was an economist with the Malaysian Treasury for 27 years, where he rose to become the deputy secretary-general. During that time, he also served as alternate director on the Board of Directors of the World Bank in Washington, D.C. For many years, he was involved in the preparation of the Malaysian annual budgets and five-year economic development plans. He then became the secretary-general of the Ministry of Transport in 1986.

After retiring from the civil service in 1989, Tan Sri Dato' (Dr) Navaratnam was appointed CEO of Bank Buruh for five years. He is now corporate adviser to the Sunway Group, executive director of Sunway College, a board member of the Monash University in Malaysia and the Monash International Advisory Panel, and a director of the Asian Strategy and Leadership Institute (ASLI).

He served the Malaysian government as vice-chairman of the Malaysian Business Council and as an independent member of the National Economic Consultative Council (1999). He was also on the Board of Directors of the Malaysia External Trade Development Corporation (Matrade) and served on the Board of the Malaysian Industry-Government Group for High Technology (Might). He is also a member of several National Economic Action Council (NEAC) Working Groups. He was a member of the Securities Commission.

He also serves on several voluntary organisations and was deputy president of the Malaysian Association of Private Colleges and Universities (MAPCU) and board member of the Malaysia-U.S. Business Council. He has also recently been appointed to serve as a Commissioner on Suhakam, the Malaysian Human Rights Commission and has been reappointed to the National Unity Panel. He was appointed to serve on the National Higher Education Advisory Panel in November 2004. He was recently conferred an Honorary Doctorate of Laws by Oxford Brookes University in the United Kingdom in recognition of his many contributions to public service and economic development in Malaysia.

Navaratnam is the author of *Managing the Malaysian Economy: Challenges & Prospects* (1997), *Strengthening the Malaysian Economy: Policy Changes & Reforms* (1998), *Healing the Wounded Tiger: How the Turmoil is Reshaping Malaysia* (1999), *Malaysia's Economic Recovery: Policy Reforms for Economic Sustainability* (2001), *Malaysia's Economic Sustainability: Confronting New Challenges Amidst Global Realitities* (2002), *Malaysia's Socioeconomic Challenges: Public Policy Issues Debated* (2003) and *Winds of Change: Malaysia's Socioeconomic Transition from Dr Mahathir Mohamad to Abdullah Ahmad Badawi* (2004).

He is married to Samaladevi and they have three sons.

Dear Roger & Sally Bamborough
With our admiration for
Your zest for life and Friendship

MY LIFE AND TIMES
A Memoir

Ramon V. Navaratnam

Khumpar
Feb. 5, 2011

Pelanduk
Publications
pelanduk.com

Published by
Pelanduk Publications (M) Sdn Bhd
(Co. No. 113307-W)
12 Jalan SS13/3E
Subang Jaya Industrial Estate
47500 Subang Jaya
Selangor Darul Ehsan, Malaysia

Address all correspondence to
Pelanduk Publications (M) Sdn Bhd
P.O. Box 8265, 46785 Kelana Jaya
Selangor Darul Ehsan, Malaysia

Check out our website at **www.pelanduk.com**
E-mail us at: **rusaone@tm.net.my**

Perpustakaan Negara Malaysia   Cataloguing-in-Publication Data

Navaratnam, Ramon V., Tan Sri, 1935-
    My life and times: a memoir / Ramon V. Navaratnam.
    Includes index
    ISBN 967-978-913-6
    1. Navaratnam, Ramon V., Tan Sri, 1935-
    2. Businessmen — Malaysia — Biography.
    3. Corporations — Malaysia — Biography.
    4. Civil service pensioners — Malaysia — Biography. I. Title.
    923.3595

Printed and bound in Malaysia

*For my dear late Father,
K.R. Navaratnam,
and my loving Mother,
Ruth Navaratnam,
who continue to inspire
me in countless ways*

Mum and Dad's wedding in 1934

On my graduation in 1959, BA (Hons) Economics,
University of Malaya in Singapore

CONTENTS

ACKNOWLEDGEMENTS

I WISH to express my sincerest gratitude to my dearest wife Samala, for her love and understanding and her quiet inspiration. To our three dear sons, Ravindran, Nahendran and Dharmendran, our lovely daughters-in-law, Premala and Angelina, and my darling grandchildren, Suhanya, Michael, Sunetra and Sarah, for their love and the joy they have given us.

My gratitude also goes to my dearest parents, sisters and brothers-in-law for their loving support, and to my many relatives and friends, for giving me the encouragement to pursue my goals.

I wish to also thank my secretary Haema for her patience, my persistent publisher, Dato' Ng Tieh Chuan, and Eric C. Forbes, for their help.

Our wedding day on December 9, 1961

PREFACE

I STARTED to use the word processor at home by typing the words, "I was born on January 6, 1935. ...", and then I felt the urge to carry on, which finally resulted in this volume of memoirs!

That was the origin of these memoirs — something unplanned, something which resulted from my attempt to learn how to use the personal computer at home. Initially, I did not think that I would pursue the writing of my memoirs to the end. However, as I progressed, I found the experience exhilarating. I would therefore recommend those who would like to have similar experiences to write their memoirs.

I wrote this book as a record of my life experiences for which I am most grateful, as well as to recall the highlights of my life for posterity. I hope my story will make a welcome addition to the rich family-memoir genre.

More importantly, I hope that this book will, in some small way, help to provide a little insight into the life and times that my generation went through. Having been born just before World War II, my generation had to struggle through and endure the trials and tribulations of the Japanese Occupation (1941-1945). Somehow we survived, to develop along with our country as we moved towards *Merdeka* (Independence) in 1957 and beyond.

We then progressed with our independent nation as the first generation of young Malayans and then Malaysians who gave our best to serve our newly independent country. We too progressed and prospered as a result of *Merdeka*. Those of us who became adults about the time of *Merdeka* were privileged to help lay the foundations of independent Malaya and modern Malaysia.

It is mainly to my family and my colleagues of my generation that I address this book with affection and fond memories. My admiration also goes to all those people who gave us so much to enable us to play our humble role in building our nation and our lives.

To my children and the forthcoming generations, I hope that this book will give them some flavour of our aspirations, concerns, problems and progress from the time before *Merdeka* to the post-*Merdeka* years, up to the present time (2005)!

Our family portrait.
From left to right: Dharmendran, Nahendran and Ravindran

1.
CHILDHOOD

I WAS BORN on January 6, 1935. Five years before World War II and 22 years before *Merdeka* (Independence), a six-pound baby boy was born to K.R. Navaratnam and Ruth Lee. They named him Ramon Veerasingam Navaratnam. I was born a blue baby at the General Hospital in Kuala Lumpur where my father worked for the colonial administration of the British government as an audit clerk. I was told that I did not have sufficient oxygen at birth, so my lungs were weak. Nevertheless, I did pretty well because of my doting mother and my caring father.

Soon after my birth, my father was promoted and transferred to Sungei Buloh as a chief clerk in the leperosarium, which was then the largest in Southeast Asia. At that time, Sungei Buloh was merely a little hospital town, nestled in a verdant valley about 15 miles from Kuala Lumpur, with a small community of doctors, nurses, administrators, clerks and other hospital-related staff, farmers and traders.

Life in Sungei Buloh was rustic and leisurely. The leperosarium was situated about two miles down a winding laterite road. A vendor on a three-wheeled motorcycle peddled meat and vegetables right to our doorstep daily without fail. Other provisions had to be obtained from the nearby township. Those who needed bigger items had no choice but travel to Kuala Lumpur.

Social life in Sungei Buloh was limited. The men would play badminton or football. At times, they would enjoy themselves with a drink at the local "pub" which was actually the coffeeshop of Ah Pey, an old Chinaman. Ah Pey sold beer, whisky and brandy. He also had plenty of multicoloured sweets and chocolates! Moreover, he also provided facilities for those who played poker and *mahjong*. But what mattered most to me and my chubby sister, Christina, was that whenever daddy came home late, he would bring us a big bundle of those colourful candies and *kannas* (pickled plums).

My childhood was made all the more exciting with the fraternity and fellowship of my cousins, who lived just up the road. My mother had five sisters and four brothers. My dear late aunt Agnes was the eldest. Uncle Charles Abraham, her husband, was a kind doctor who was dedicated to his profession. They had four lively boys — Sam, Collin,

Leslie and Robert—and a lovely daughter, Janet. Sam, the eldest, was serious and responsible. Collin was friendlier and more playful, but not when he had his bouts of asthma. Leslie was six months my senior, which naturally made him my closest peer and playmate. Janet, surrounded by her four boisterous and demanding brothers, developed a strong sisterly bond with my sister Tina. Robert, the youngest in the family, was certainly the most pampered and naughtiest!

My cousins and I got on well. We used to play rounders, hide-and-seek, marbles and catching, which were popular pastimes in those days. Occasionally, we went for long walks. However, we usually would not walk too far from our home, as our parents feared that we might unwittingly stray near or enter the leperosarium. It was believed at that time that leprosy was infectious and if anyone went too near a leper, he would become a leper too. Thus, if anyone of us fell and hurt ourselves, it would mean getting the excruciatingly painful "iodine treatment" from Dr Abraham.

When I was four, my parents felt that both Tina and I should join our older cousins to begin formal education. They felt that kindergarten would be more fun for us, and that we would certainly be able to learn something good along the way! Due to the fact that there was not a single school in the sleepy hollow of Sungei Buloh, I had to accompany my cousins and other children to Kuala Lumpur to attend preschool. We had to take a rickety old bus early in the morning, which meant that I had to wake up well before the break of dawn. Mum would lovingly dress me up in a warm Uvilla singlet and a sweater every school day to protect me from the chilly morning air, which often gave me coughs and colds. Furthermore, much to my displeasure, my strict mother would always insist that I swallow the last drop of porridge and a spoonful of cod-liver oil before packing me off to school at 6.30 in the morning.

The journey to school was fun. It would take more than an hour just to cover the 15 miles because the road was narrow, full of potholes, and had many curves and bends. We kids would enjoy ourselves being thrown from one side of the bus to the other on our bench seats. The kindergarten children were dropped at a girls' school—the St Mary's, as the boys' schools did not cater for preschoolers. As such, the older boys loved to tease all the younger ones by calling them "girlies"! My peers and I were often offended, and we yearned for the day when we would "graduate" to primary school and be accepted as "boys" once again.

Kindergarten was enjoyable. I had a gentle teacher by the name of Pearl Thuraisingam. I learnt the alphabet and nursery rhymes from her and made many friends among the boys and girls at the kindergarten. I recall that one day, we held hands in a small circle and went round and round a beautiful kingfisher which had been killed by one of the cats in the school. In unison, we sadly sang, "Who killed Cock Robin?" I also remember playing with the soft sand in a large, raised tin tray with many older sweet young girls who could not resist pinching and pulling my plump cheeks as well as ruffling my curly hair.

My parents had planned to send me to Pasar Road School and Victoria Institution which were among the premier schools in the country. They were also the schools that my dear late father was proud to attend in his days. But alas, it was not to be at that time.

As the dark clouds of war gathered in 1940, my dear mother was blessed with a sweet baby girl, Angelina. She was a source of great joy. However, she also brought a little anxiety. The question was, "Would there be any baby food for her, if war were to break out?"

Indeed, our worst fears were confirmed within the year when World War II broke out. My father was transferred to Ipoh, the hometown of my maternal grandfather, E. Foster Lee, an indomitable former headmaster, and his illustrious family. Though war was raging all over Europe and threatening the East and the Pacific region, Malaya had yet to feel its impact. Life went on as usual despite the frightening rumours which circulated around. We hoped that the cruel war would not reach Malaya. We prayed that we would be safe in the haven of the East, secure from the devastating war in the West.

Nevertheless, I still had to go to school. Due to the fact that I was not six years old on January 1, 1941 (my birthday was on January 6), I was denied admission to school! This caused concern to the Lee family. So, the grand patriarch, E. Foster Lee, was gingerly approached by my sweet, soft-spoken granny, after having served him his favourite steak.

"Dear," she gently addressed the old disciplinarian who was sipping and savouring his Cognac, "would you be able to persuade the authorities at the Education Department to admit Ramon to school?"

He replied that he would try to get me into Primary One at the Methodist Afternoon School provided "he knows the alphabets and is good at spelling!"

Grandpa sprang into action early the next morning. He walked with his walking-stick to the Education Department and worked things out with his old friends there. In his enthusiasm and confidence in his grandson, he caused a problem by proposing an early date for me to take the qualifying test!

Who would prepare poor Ramon for this critical test? My mother, who had been a schoolteacher, took on the challenge. She summoned her teaching skills and started coaching her little boy for the big test. Soon, she was joined by her three sisters — Muriel, Freda and Doris. These aunts of mine were zealous to fulfil their mission to equip their nephew with the necessary knowledge to pass the qualifying test. The Lee family's honour was also at stake. *The little preschool boy must make it. He must not fail! He could not afford to. It would be a shame to fail.*

I was drilled in spelling literally morning, noon and night. My mother and three aunts, with their well-meaning care and concern, were unable to coordinate their spelling reviews properly. They were testing me too frequently for my comfort, that was whenever they were free!

The day finally arrived. I was so over-taught that I came up top in my class. Naturally, I got lots of hugs and kisses from my much relieved mum, aunts and uncles, all of whom I am grateful to for my head start in school.

From then on, aunt Doris took over. She was teaching at the Methodist Afternoon School at Lahad Road which encroached on the premises of the Anglo-Chinese Boys' School. She was pretty and protective, and I was happy to be accompanied by her to class every afternoon. We went to school in a hand-pulled rickshaw, or occasionally in the trishaw, which was fun.

One day, aunt Doris and I had an unforgettable experience. We were ready for school and the *beca-man* had just lifted up his rickshaw to take us to school when there was a loud explosion. This stunned the poor *beca-man* so much that he dropped the two handle shafts, causing both of us to fall out from the rickshaw. We were badly shaken, but thankfully, only slightly bruised.

What was the cause of the explosion? Blasting was often done at the nearby limestone cliffs, and the sounds of explosions were not new.

But the *beca-man* was adamant. He insisted that it was a real bomb and that we should run for cover. Both of us started laughing at him until we saw the thick black smoke in the sky, followed by the shrill sound of the siren. We then realised the *beca-man* was right after all. Panic seized us. We ran to the bushes to hide. The *beca-man* fled elsewhere.

Yes, it was the first Japanese air raid! World War II had intruded upon us! We were being attacked by the dreaded Japanese Zero warplanes. In fear, we rushed home in the midst of a fleeing population that was seeking refuge. There were military trucks, rescue squads and confusion all over the roads with the traffic system in chaos. On reaching home, we found the entire Lee family hiding behind the house, visibly worried. They were waiting anxiously, wondering if aunt Doris and I would return home safely. When we finally got home, my mum and dad embraced me gratefully.

Some time later, someone shouted, "Where is daddy?" He was not in the large makeshift air-raid shelter under the huge mango tree with a low cement wall around it. We searched and finally found grandpa upstairs. He was standing coolly by the window, viewing the skies through his binoculars. He was watching the fierce aerial fight that was taking place between the Japanese Zeroes and the bulky British Royal Air Force fighters—the Bruster Buffaloes. We pleaded with him to take shelter but he brushed us aside with a harsh remark, "Damn it! Do you think I'm going to miss the sight of the British blasting these bloody Japs from the sky?"

Nothing could convince grandpa to leave the dangerous scene behind. We went back to our shelter and prayed for his safety. He was indeed a die-hard British supporter with his "Rule Brittania" and "Long Live the King!" sentiments. It was obvious that the British pilots were no match for the Japanese. In terms of skill, boldness and fire-power, the British were outdone by the *kamikaze* (sacrificial) fighters. The loss of many British planes was an ominous sign to the local population of the things to come. All the while, people had been led to believe that the Whites, i.e., the British, were superior and invincible. Watching the smaller Japanese planes giving the big British planes a beating was enough to dispel that belief. So, despite grandpa's fervour and his staunch support for the British, we all had to flee to the safety of the countryside.

Tears streamed down our eyes as we were sad to leave the grand old government house at Lorong Cheroh. The compound was vast and the large wooden structure, on squat white pillars supporting the house, was impressive. Moreover, the Lee family had stayed there for many years, and aunts and uncles had finished their schooling while they were living there comfortably. It held so many memories of family parties, of sentimental reunions, and of good and bad times. To many of us, it had become a part of our lives. Truly, it was a harrowing experience for us to leave this family house behind and to face the vagaries of war and the fearful future! We had to evacuate soon.

2.
THE EVACUATION

THERE was an acute sense of foreboding and fear when the whole Lee family carried their basic belongings to the waiting lorries. The plan was to rush to Teluk Anson (now Teluk Intan) where my mother's sister, aunt Violy lived. She was a kind, soft-spoken person with a sweet, enchanting smile. She was married to uncle Perimpanayagam, a technical assistant in the Telecommunications Department, who was amiable and generous, with a lovely daughter named Arul who was about my age. They were a loving and caring family who willingly opened their home to us as a sanctuary from the war.

Arul's father, the dear late uncle Perim (as he was fondly called) shared a room with my father in their bachelor days. They were thus good old friends. They even promised each other that they would try to marry two sisters. And so they did!

In the meantime, a war wedding was shaping up. It was an anxious and yet happy time when preparations were made for the wedding of aunt Muriel and dear late uncle Barr. Indeed, aunt Muriel was a beautiful bride while the late uncle Barr was equally impressive with his good looks and strong demeanour. We celebrated and rejoiced at the wedding, while the war raged on elsewhere.

At that time, my father had not joined the rest of the family. He had stayed back in Ipoh to pay the staff at his office their salaries. He wanted to pay everyone but many of the staff had fled from the bombing. As expected of this man of integrity, he placed the whole unpaid sum of 7,000 British Straits Settlement dollars into the strong safe in the office. He then cycled about 50 miles to join us in Teluk Anson!

After the Japanese occupied Malaya, dad returned to work under the Japanese. He surprised the Japanese military officers with his honesty when he reported the big sum of money that he had kept in the safe. However, instead of being thankful they were doubtful and ordered him to open the safe alone, fearing that the whole story was a trick and that a bomb was planted inside! He trembled for a few moments. Wild fleeting thoughts flashed across his mind. He asked himself: what if someone had opened the safe with a duplicate key and ransacked the money? The Japanese would never forgive him!

Nervously, under the cold watchful eyes of the Japanese who were cautiously standing at a safe distance away, dad turned the key of the safe. It was a great relief for him to find the brown packet of money intact! If the money had been missing, it was likely that his head would have literally rolled, as the Japanese had a strong inclination to cut off heads as a means of punishment. Many of my father's friends thought that he would have become a rich man had he walked away with the big booty in the midst of all the chaos when the British were retreating. He could have also hidden the money elsewhere instead of putting it into the safe. But, my father had no regrets. God rewarded him for his commendable trustworthiness as he was abundantly blessed throughout his life in so many ways.

One of the many blessings after the safe return of the $7,000 was the news that there was going to be an addition to the family. Though some people might have thought that it was not a good time to have a baby, my mother was more than ready to prove them wrong. With the help of uncle Perim and aunt Violy, there was no lack of nourishing food for her and the baby. The new addition, which was the fourth child, was another girl who became my third sister, Juliana (or Julie). She was a cute baby with an infectious smile that soothed our anxiety during the Japanese occupation.

After some time, the perceived safety of Teluk Anson was eroded. Along the coastal region of this small town, Japanese gunboats were sighted often enough to cause alarm to the locals. Almost everyone had heard of the atrocious Japanese raids, killings, looting and raping. As such, there was an exodus of the residents of Teluk Anson to the surrounding *kampungs* (villages) which were deemed safer.

Late one night, under the dim kerosene lamps, the elders in the family discussed the deteriorating war situation. They decided that the Lee family should seek refuge in the rural areas where they could be better insulated from the fighting and ravages of the coming conflict. Thus, the whole family packed and left at the crack of dawn the next day. First we went to a nearby *kampung*, and when the coast was clear, we ventured further to a smaller and more remote Malay *kampung* called Langkap, a small village with old thatched wooden houses that were widely dispersed. This *kampung* was situated near the jungle, and so it was hidden away from the trunk road. There were neither electricity nor tap water, but plenty of mosquitoes. Our main source of water was the deep well behind the house. It was sufficient to meet all our needs. Our limited lighting requirements were adequately met by the readily available kerosene and gas lamps.

Tapioca was the staple diet that was supplemented with sweet potatoes. Vegetables were cultivated in the backyard or bought from the villagers who sold them at high inflationary prices. The place abounded with fruit trees: jackfruit, *langsat*, rambutans and durians. The families in the *kampung* were quite self-sufficient and comfortable, but the most important consideration was that we felt secure, as we felt insulated from the war.

One day, however, the *kampung* was in a commotion because heavy bombing could be heard at a distance. This caused a flurry of fleeing villagers! The Japanese army was marching down the whole Malay peninsula towards Singapore. They were moving in trucks, on bicycles and on foot. To me, they all looked tough, rough and mean. They would stop at some *kampung* along the way to get young men to carry their equipment. They enjoyed getting some of the young locals to climb up the coconut trees, to pluck coconuts for them to quench their thirst. When they could not get the men to pluck the coconuts, they would simply cut the trees down! It was not uncommon for the Japanese military officers to demand young women to accompany them. Some of them later became the unfortunate "comfort women". It was also normal for the officers to haul up able-bodied men and conscript them into the Imperial Japanese Army on the spot.

Uncle Desmond and the late dear uncle Francis were the only two able-bodied young men with us at Langkap. Someone must have told the Japanese about them because one morning they came straight to the house and asked for them! When they did not get what they wanted, they began to make a search. It was then that uncle Desmond decided to come out from hiding. As soon as he was sighted, he was gallantly pounced upon and forced to join the soldiers outside. Helpless and grieved, uncle Desmond bade a tearful farewell to all of us. He was actually leaving the compound when uncle Perim whispered to him to slip away to hide in the jungle. The advice was heeded by uncle Desmond. If he had not slipped away, he could have been taken to the infamous Siamese Death Railway where so many Malayans, Australians, Britons and others perished.

After that frightening incident, the families gradually got adjusted to the serene *kampung* lifestyle. We soon received news that the Japanese Army had conquered Malaya completely in less than two months!

The mighty fortress of Singapore, with its gigantic 18-inch guns fell to the Japanese army, because the great guns were all placed in the wrong direction—facing the sea! The Japanese military strategists had brilliantly planned the invasion to start from the north at Kota Bharu instead of from the sea in the south as anticipated by the British defenders. So, despite being impressively armed, the "fire-power" was of no use to the British in the defence of Singapore. This wrong positioning of the formidable long-range guns due to the poor anticipation of the British military strategists must be one of Britain's biggest blunders in the war. We lost faith in the British! They were no longer invincible or superior! We stayed at Langkap in the *kampung* until it was safe to return to Telok Anson.

3.
THE JAPANESE OCCUPATION
(1941-1945)

THE time eventually came to return home. Thankfully, we gathered all our belongings and left for Teluk Anson by road. We found that most of the bridges had been partially or totally destroyed by the Japanese during the fighting. Without useable bridges, we had to travel by river. Two large *sampans* were hired—one for the extended Lee family, and the other for the Devadason family who had joined us at Langkap.

It was a long and tedious journey under the scorching sun by day and the eerie uncertainty of darkness at night. What was really nerve-racking was that there were crocodiles lurking all along the Perak River. Each time we children saw a floating log, we would think that it was a submerged crocodile, and we would scream! But there were indeed a few real crocodiles that passed by our *sampan*, and we saw some of them lazing along the muddy riverbanks. Fortunately, all of them were friendly and minded their own business! But little Ernest Devadason and his siblings and Tina and I, who were about the same age, were scared even when we saw anything floating down the river.

All of us reached Teluk Anson safely, and after a good rest, we made our journey back to Ipoh. Dad returned to his former job in the Ipoh Town Council, and as a result, all of us could stay in a decent wooden government house, at 755 Jalan Abdul Jalil in Greentown. It was semi-detached, and had a fairly big compound. All three of us, Tina, Angie and I, enjoyed ourselves playing in the open space and also with the neighbour's children.

However, playing around the house did not last long. The Japanese started their own schools, teaching in the Japanese language. I attended classes at the convent school in Greentown. The teachers were mostly locals. All of them had only been given crash courses in Japanese, and so, it was obvious that they were not proficient in the language. At any rate, most of the students and teachers did not take school seriously. They shared a secret conviction that the Japanese would not stay long because it was generally felt that the British and the Allied Forces would soon return.

Nevertheless, I carried on going to school where we learnt the basic alphabet called *katakana*, and some Japanese songs which were mainly military marching songs. It was also a normal practice every morning to sing the Japanese national anthem known as *kimigai-ayo-ohwa*. All the students were compelled to bow in the direction of Japan, the Land of the Rising Sun, and to the Japanese emperor. This routine did not last long.

I was only eight when I had to stop school in order to earn a living. The deprivation of wartime was felt severely at home. Food was scarce. Inflation was climbing higher each day and dad, being the sole breadwinner could not make ends meet. We tried growing tapioca, sweet potatoes and vegetables but still, there was insufficiency. The family income had to be supplemented.

Mum and Dad decided that opening up a small cigarette stall would be a good way to earn some income. There were hundreds of Indian National Army (INA) soldiers moving to and from their camp nearby. They frequently passed by the road in front of our house, and business was anticipated to be good. Using a big wooden box, Tina and I set up a "shop". Cigarettes were stacked on top of the box to which was attached a coconut coir rope which burnt slowly for customers to light up their cigarettes when they made their purchases.

Although the stall was placed directly under a huge shady raintree, the heat and glare became unbearable at around midday. What we normally did to overcome the heat was to take turns to stay inside the big box where it was much cooler. We often saw Rasamah Bhupalan and her sister Ponamah marching up the road, both of whom were adventurous volunteers in the Rani of Jansi Army under the great Indian fighter, Subbas Chandra Bose! They were training to 'liberate' India from the British!

The anticipated demand from the soldiers did not materialise. After a few weeks, the stall had to be closed down as business was bad. There were soldiers who did not pay, and there were those who promised to pay but did not. Some were nice enough to give us sweets. As two little children, we were in no position to argue or demand payment, and the little business therefore folded up prematurely. Boy, was I glad!

Due to the pressing need for a supplementary income, mum and dad hit on the idea of making and selling currypuffs. Mum would get up early in the morning to cook the curry, knead the pastry, and fry the currypuffs. After lunch, everything was ready for sale. Tina would help to pack the puffs into a basket which I would hang on the handle-bar of my oversized bicycle. I would then set off to find customers at tea time.

The currypuffs sold rather well, but in all honesty, I did not enjoy the job at all. It was tedious and tiring for an eight-year-old like me. Customers were sometimes nasty. They would bargain unreasonably or ask to sample the puffs. Some ate and refused to pay. Helpless and completely at their mercy, I could only wait and sometimes cry to be paid for my currypuffs! Of course, I did not tell my parents about all the hardship I had to go through. Otherwise, my mum who had worked so hard would be hurt, and my dad who thought that I was a strong and dependable child would be disappointed. Moreover, if I were to relate my problems to them, they would definitely want to protect me by stopping me from selling currypuffs. That would have meant a loss of additional income for the family. I just could not bring myself to let the whole family down. So, I just carried on doing what I was told to do to the best of my ability. Both these business experiences of my childhood made me unhappy about doing business. Later in life, I disdained doing business, considering it undignified.

One day, my dad called me and talked to me at length. He asked me whether I would prefer to continue selling currypuffs, or to begin working as a *peon* (office boy). I readily opted to start on the new job although my parents did not know why. They were merely impressed by my enthusiasm to work full time!

Dad cycled to work like most people in those days. There were few cars, and they belonged mainly to the senior Japanese officers. Bus services were non-existent. The best way for me to go to work was to ride pillion on dad's bicycle. So, every morning at 7.15am, dad would leave home with me sitting precariously behind him. We moved along Jalan Abdul Jalil, then Brewster Road, and then over the bridge and down the hill towards the Ipoh Club *padang*. Dad would then slowly apply the brakes to enable me to jump off the bike at the T-junction near the FMS Hotel. I would then walk about half a mile to my office at the Road Transport Department at St Michael's Institution. (This was my first salaried job and interestingly, the last job I held before my retirement was also in the civil service, as the Secretary-General of the Ministry of Transport of Malaysia!) That's life, I guess!

4.
MY FIRST JOB

MY job at the Japanese Road Transport Department was to run errands, dust the desks, sweep the floors, and dispatch letters to other government departments. I was given the use of the office bicycle whenever I had despatch work to do. I would have to cycle through crowded Ipoh town. Bicycles in those days were built to cater for adults only, and I had problems handling the bicycle because of my small body frame. However, the letters had to be dispatched. So, I held the left handle with my left hand, clutched the crossbar with my right hand, and pedalled with my legs below the crossbar. It was dangerous, as I often lost my balance and crashed into people and other vehicles. I managed not to lose a single file, and was therefore able to keep my job.

My job was a boon to the family. It was not the salary. After all, it was only $15 (Japanese) per month which was not much at all. What actually made everything worthwhile was the rice ration and the quota of Kuah cigarettes. The Japanese did not differentiate boys from men when it came to rations. As such, I was entitled to receive as much rice and cigarettes as my father.

The cigarettes which I obtained were often promptly sold in the thriving black market for a sum that was many times my meagre monthly salary. The additional ration of rice meant that our family members could have two square meals a day—when many others could only afford to have one. The availability of excess rice also meant that we could cater for our relatives whenever they visited us from Taiping, where the Lee family was staying with uncle Perim.

Life was hard. There was no childhood fun. There were no toys to play with. Clothes and shoes were scarce. The food we ate was almost the same day after day—rice or boiled tapioca with a little vegetable for lunch and dinner, with neither fish nor meat except on rare occasions such as birthdays.

On my ninth birthday, I remember my mother giving me a treat of yellow rice with meat curry. I enjoyed the meal immensely and wished that I could have more meat, but I dared not ask for any extra helping as I knew that my parents would be deprived of their share. Silently, I swore to myself that when I grew up I would earn enough to be able to have one whole piece of meat for every mouthful of rice! (I was able to achieve that little childhood ambition after the British liberated Malaya from the Japanese).

The depression, hardship, suffering and fears of wartime atrocities became more tolerable when clandestine radio-receivers spread the news that the tyrant, Adolf Hitler of Germany, was losing the war against the Allied Forces in Europe. We also rejoiced at hearing that the Japanese were getting a bashing from the Americans in the Pacific!

The deteriorating situation for the Japanese was felt even in my place of work. In the office, I could see the Japanese bosses becoming more impatient and sullen. The sweets I received occasionally as appreciation for my good work became few and far between.

One day, the boss was so upset over a small omission that he shouted at the chief clerk. The old man tried to explain in his poor Japanese, and all hell broke loose! The agitated red-faced Japanese boss started slapping the startled chief clerk repeatedly until the badly shaken old man could only manage to say "Saary! Saary!" before he slumped into his rattan chair.

This incident rattled me greatly. I had never seen anyone manhandled to that extent before. The days passed by more speedily with rising hopes and high expectations as more good news came through the grapevine. The Japanese were reported to be on the run. Then came the unbelievable news that the Americans had dropped the horrendous atomic bomb on Hiroshima! That was the *coup de grâce*. I could see that my fierce Japanese boss had become considerably subdued and upset. He was last seen in tears by the chief clerk himself and then he was never seen again. Apparently, the colonel had committed *hara-kiri* (suicide) but the truth never came to light.

A few days later, I was walking as usual across the field to share the tiffin-carrier lunch in dad's office at the Ipoh Town Council when I saw huge crowds of people milling around the field. Something strange was going on that day in mid-August 1945. There were many Japanese trucks, but they were controlled by Chinese-looking soldiers wearing three-star peaked caps and khaki uniforms. They were the members of the guerrilla "Malayan Anti-Japanese Army". They had come out of the jungles after four years of fierce fighting against the powerful Japanese Imperial Army. They were tormenting some of the Japanese soldiers who had surrendered and huddled in many parked lorries.

Obviously, the tide had changed. The order had now reversed. The much feared Japanese soldiers were the vanquished. The Allied Forces as well as the people of Malaya were the victors. The war was over! There was great rejoicing all over the country. Rations of canned food that had been stocked up were opened freely and big meals were served. There was no need to worry about the next meal.

Soon, the British, Australian, and Indian soldiers appeared on the scene. They had been on board the British warships anchored off Port Swettenham and were poised to attack if the Japanese did not surrender. The arrival of the soldiers was a most welcome sight. The civilian population treated them as saviours and friends. The children loved them because they were showered with lots of English sweets, biscuits, jam and cheese — delicacies that they had never tasted before. It was a wonderful time of our lives!

The transition from the Japanese occupation to British rule was administered by the British Military Administration (BMA). They restored law and order by rounding up all the Japanese and sending them to internment camps. Soon all essential services including hospitals and schools were restored. Everything was almost back to normal again. My short but eventful working life thus came to an end. Now I could go back to school!

5.
THE GROWING-UP YEARS

AT the age of 10, in 1945, just after the War, I was admitted to Primary One in Anderson School, Ipoh. I had to walk four miles to and from school daily. The school was in a chaotic state — the chairs and tables were broken, there were no blackboards, and the classrooms had been badly maintained. The teachers conducted tests to transfer the boys to different classes according to their proficiency in the 3Rs. I was soon sent to Primary Three as my reading and writing skills were pretty good. It was a kind of double promotion. My arithmetic was, however, not as good, as I had not been taught any arithmetic before.

My class was under the charge of Mr Krishnan, a stern teacher who also taught us arithmetic. He would call a weak student to his desk, poke one end of his big, blue pencil hard against the student's stomach, and give it a twist. At the same time, he would yell at the whole class, "You must study hard, eeerr!" as he gave the pencil another twist. The students thought he was crazy, and assumed that he must have been *shell-shocked* from the war!

Other than this menacing teacher, school was quite enjoyable. I made many friends in school, and I played hockey at Kilat Club *padang* (field). For hockey sticks, we had to improvise by cutting branches from the hibiscus plants. We would select those with a crooked end which could be used for hitting the ball. There were many other games that we played, for example, *Kavandy-Kavanda*, rubberband-throwing, marbles, and football. We also invented a variety of games that could be played with empty cigarette packets. We had a great time playing with spiders and fighting fish, too.

Kampar

Just as I was settling down and adjusting to student life, we had to move as my father was posted as a chief clerk to the District Office at Kampar. He was given a comfortable bungalow on a hill, at the base of which ran the main national trunk road through the small mining town of Kampar. The location of the house was ideal, as it was near to the shops, food stalls, market and police station.

Kampar was only 25 miles away from Ipoh by road. Thus, aunt Violy, aunt Doris, and Arul often travelled by bus to spend the weekends at our home. The proximity of the food stalls was a big boon. We would often stroll leisurely down the hill to the stalls for dinner. Tina, our cousin Arul, and I would look forward eagerly to enjoy Kampar's famous *ais kacang*!

When Arul's father passed away in Taiping, they moved to Ipoh where aunt Violy was teaching. Arul had no sisters or brothers, thus, Tina and I became close cousins to her.

As for schooling, the Anglo-Chinese school was the only English-medium school in Kampar. Since it was co-educational, Tina and I attended the same school. It was run by the Methodist Mission, and therefore, a strong content of Christian teaching and singing were included in the curricula. These characteristics together with the soft presence of the girls generally exerted a favourable and sobering influence on the boys. However, this affable atmosphere appeared to cramp the style of some of the tougher boys. Occasionally, there were bouts of bravado.

In one incident, a group of roughnecks rampaged through the school's open verandas, pushing all the boys and even the girls in their way. I happened to be in their path. The big bullies therefore carried me up and threw me down effortlessly. I fell on my face—and broke my two front teeth, even though it was not Christmas yet!

My parents felt that the dentists in Kampar could not be relied on to fix my teeth. I was taken to Ipoh where naturally, I stayed at aunt Violy's house. The Ipoh dentist really "fixed me up". He deadened the two front teeth by inserting a thin needle into my teeth and killed the nerves. Wow! It really hurt so much that at one stage I thought of jumping out of the dentist's chair and running away! It was my sweet cousin Arul who calmed me down. As a result of that bad experience, I always harboured a phobia for dentists. To this day, I think the Kampar dentists might have done a better and less painful job for me.

In the meantime, my mother was having another kind of pain. She was due to have her fifth and final child. We were already a family of one boy and three girls, and obviously, mum and dad were keen to round off the family with one more boy. But the new baby turned out to be yet another girl! Nevertheless, the baby was cute and cuddly. She was named Georgiana—perhaps just to have a more masculine name! Dad was particularly pleased with Georgie because, apparently, according to Tamil tradition, a female fifth child brings good luck. This new baby girl brought her doting daddy more blessings.

Taiping

About a year after Georgie's birth, dad was promoted and transferred again—this time to Taiping. The town was bigger than Kampar but smaller than Ipoh. However, it was certainly prettier, cooler and wetter than either of the two towns. It was situated at the foot of the high and majestic Maxwell Hills. Together with the waterfalls, the cool natural pools and the well-spread Lake Gardens, Taiping presented itself as a picturesque postcard.

Dad was posted to the Taiping Town Council as an Assessment Officer. He was given a semi-detached government house, which was near the Assam Kumbang *padang*. Our immediate neighbour was a Chinese family whose name was Lee Guan Seng. The other neighbour was the Jayasekara family. These three families had 12 children among them. Thus, Tina, Angie, Julie, Georgie and I found ourselves with many playmates along that little lane called Jalan Padang.

Taiping had two fine all-boys' schools—St George's and King Edward VII. I joined the Catholic Brothers' school, while Tina went to the Lady Treacher Methodist Girls' School. Every Sunday morning, Tina, Angie, Julie and I walked to attend Sunday School, which was held at Lady Treacher Methodist Girls' School. It was lovely to stroll along Museum Road which was lined with giant, old, and shady raintrees on which grew wild pigeon orchids—white and beautiful.

On our way, we would pass by a big wooden house on a big plot of land where uncle and aunt Chinniah stayed with their large family of five boys and three girls. They were all very sweet to us—the Navaratnam children. They would often invite us over as we returned from Sunday School or church, for a drink or some of the loving aunt's delicious sweets or *palaharams*. She was also talented in breeding turkeys, and mum would often persuade her to part with one of them for our Christmas roast!

Kamal, one of the many sons in the Chinniah family, was a tall and good-looking lad who was about my age. He used to eye Tina, but was too shy to approach her. (However, in later years, he made up for lost time at the Penang Teachers' College, where they fell in love and later got married.)

Taiping to Kuala Lumpur

In 1949, having served well at the Taiping Town Council, my father was now due for another promotion. As they say, if you want to get anywhere in your career in any country, you generally have to go to the capital of that country.

Thus dad was promoted to the Superscale Grade of the Government's Clerical Service and was transferred to the Public Works Department (PWD) in Kuala Lumpur as the Financial Assistant. That was a big promotion in those days before independence. While we were all happy for our father, it also meant uprooting ourselves, packing up and moving to a new place. For my sisters and I, it meant new schools again.

What was most worrying was that we had no place to stay in Kuala Lumpur as dad would have to wait for his turn to get government quarters in the crowded city of Kuala Lumpur.

However, dear aunt Agnes, who was the principal of Pasar Road School, kindly offered to put us up for the time being at her government quarters in Kampung Pandan.

The Victoria Institution

My cousins and I went to the Victoria Institution (VI). My father had also attended 'the old gray school' at High Street in Kuala Lumpur in the old days. It used to be a handsome and prominent building in the late 19th century. The students used to walk along the bunds of the Klang River, which flowed beside the old school and to look out for crocodiles. My father was fond of the school and admired the headmaster of his time, a Mr Shaw. Thus his peers called my father 'Shaw Navaratnam'! He felt strongly that I should also go to the VI And so I did.

The new VI was an impressive school. It is a big bold building which is well situated on a hill in the centre of Kuala Lumpur. It has first-rate science laboratories, a large and well-stocked library, a swimming pool which is quite unusual for a school and large playing fields, where several games can be played simultaneously.

In its heyday, it had the reputation for being one of the best (if not the best) schools in Malaysia. We students thought it was easily the best school in the country. The Penang Free School and the Raffles Institution in Singapore were regarded by us as worthy rivals but still not really up to our standards!

We had that great sense of pride, perhaps exaggerated, because our good teachers like Mr Lim Eng Thye and Mr Toh Boon Hwa used to tell us, "Just the chop of the VI on your leaving certificate will take you far in life". Many of us actually believed in it, although if all things were equal, there could have been some truth in the claim?

At the VI, I developed stronger leadership qualities. The opportunities for identification, recognition and the nurturing of innate and inherent talents were considerable. I realised quite easily that I was not a potential sportsman. I found that I enjoyed the extramural activities in the various clubs and societies that were available in the VI. I therefore took to debating, elocution and drama. I represented the VI in inter-school debates and in the historical quiz contests which were quite often won by the VI.

Although I had some initial problems in adjusting to the Victoria Institution, I gradually fitted in. The syllabi were wider, and the standards were higher than those at my previous school at the St George's Institution in Taiping.

From aunt Agnes' house we went to stay at uncle Rajasingam's house in Hale Road. He was my dad's cousin. Although we had a room to share, I would sleep in the hall while dad shared uncle Rajasingam's room. At least we were now all together as one family. Previously, dad had to stay separately with his other cousin, uncle Thalayasingham, at San Peng Road. Then we thankfully got our temporary government quarters at Imbi Road.

Our House at Hose Road

It was only after several months of waiting and moving around that dad was finally allocated a nice big wooden bungalow, with a large compound, at 435 Hose Road at Petaling Hill, near the present Dewan Bahasa dan Pustaka. It was spacious, with three rooms, a big hall and a wide veranda all round. Thus we could have many more relatives to stay with us if necessary. Moreover, the new house was near the Victoria Institution and it was also quite convenient for the girls as our house was near the bus stop, just down the hill.

We were able to have our cousins visit us and stay with us overnight without feeling crowded. Leslie used to come over and study with me. Janet often visited my sisters. Several of our relatives, like aunt Violy, Arul and Aunt Doris, Aunt Freda and others, who visited us from Ipoh and other places, stayed with us.

When uncle Barr left his job in Bahau estate, he and aunt Muriel and our cousins Sam and Ariam stayed with us for several months before they got their own accommodation.

What is important is the fact that there was this strong feeling of the 'extended family', whereby families opened their homes generously to each other during times of need and emergency, despite the inconveniences such arrangements would invariably cause. The spirit of togetherness and of sharing is important. But today, with more and more urbanisation, the family spirit, unfortunately, is weakening and breaking down slowly.

Once I had adjusted to the Victoria Institution, I enjoyed my schooling there. I had a group of good friends in school. We would meet every day during recess by the corner next to the library and spin yarns and compare our experiences in our respective classes. We were quite noisy during recess and also in the classrooms.

One day, I was sent to the detention class in absentia! I had the habit of often sneezing in class because of my bad hay fever. On one occasion when there was a lot of noise in class, the history teacher, Mr Rajadurai, shouted out from his desk, without looking up, "Navaratnam — get out of the class!"

The boys continued to make more noise and laugh loudly. Mr Rajadurai shouted out again for me to leave the class immediately, thinking that I was the person responsible for the laughter because the class would normally laugh every time I suddenly sneezed. The laughter continued. He looked up, to hear the class monitor and the boys say that I was absent from school that day as I was down with a bad cold! I suppose this story indicates the kind of reputation I had with my teachers — a noisy and playful fellow in class.

My Life at Home and School

As an old boy of the Victoria Institution, my father had many friends who were teachers at the VI, so he naturally checked on my performance in school. Invariably, I was described by the teachers as "noisy and playful"! I recall that he complained to my mother that he could not understand how I could be described as "noisy" at school, when I was in fact so "quiet" at home!

But I have to admit that I was somewhat different in school and at home. How else could it be? At school I was surrounded by boys. But at home I had all four sisters and no brothers to contend with. I could not possibly treat my sisters the way I treated the boys at school.

The Hose Road house had a servant's room beside the kitchen at the lower end of the house which was built on a slope. It was there that

I spent most of my time at home. Tina and I used the room as our study room, and it also became my private room and my retreat.

We did not have a car and so we went about town by bus, rickshaw, bicycle or just walked. As we grew up it became more difficult to keep the family going, what with the rising demands for school requirements, better clothes for my sisters, music lessons and the prospects of my going to college.

Dad was a senior officer in the clerical service but he was by no means paid that well. But mum was determined that we all had the best of everything possible though she had to rely only on his salary.

My father was an honest man. He was the Financial Assistant at the PWD, where temptation and the pressures would have been high to receive money on the side as many of his colleagues did. However, my dad was straight and upright, and this is one reason I believe that we all have been blessed. I have no doubt that I have been strongly influenced by his example of honesty and relative indifference to wealth and money *per se*. I have been in critical areas of government like the Treasury, dealing with confidential tax matters and the tenders and contracts in the Treasury and the Transport Ministry, but thank God I stayed clean.

It was hard work for our magnanimous mum while we were at school. She had no servant. She therefore had to get up early in the morning, prepare breakfast, and send the children to school. Then she had to cook lunch, clean the house, and then get ready for afternoon school where she taught.

As time went by, it became increasingly difficult to make ends meet. So, my mother became a temporary teacher in the Methodist Afternoon School in Brickfields. When she returned from school in the evening, she rested with her legs raised on a little bench, just long enough to have a cup of tea (which one of the daughters would make). Then, she would go back to work in the kitchen. When the girls offered to help, she would urge them to "leave it and go and study!" We still marvel at how she managed to do so much for so long!

Dad was a man of few words. He rarely raised his voice except if he had taken drinks, or if something had annoyed him. In any case, he was out at work for the whole day, and would usually return home only before dinner time or even later. Thus, he was not fully aware of what was going on at home. He was somewhat soft with the girls, though he was strict with me, being his eldest and only son.

He had a few house rules — his food had to be served hot, his personal belongings were not to be removed from his systematically laid-out dressing table, and he did not like many questions. He was not keen on visiting nor did he enjoy visitors easily. He was introverted and savoured his privacy and quiet moments. He would sit for hours in his big government issued chair at the corner of the veranda, and smoke in the dark — reflecting and pondering on things we never knew! He would occasionally come home late at night on his noisy motorcycle after a few drinks with his friends, but he would invariably be well balanced. Regardless of how late he retired to bed, he was always up early and well on time for work. He took his work seriously with a high sense of commitment and deep dedication. He had played football for the Tamil Physical and Cultural Association (TPCA), as well as badminton in his younger days. In his later years, he did not have other interests other than walking, just to keep himself fit.

By contrast, mum could be quite insistent and articulate when she wanted to, especially when the children were naughty. She would get upset when we idled away time, quarrelled, spoke rudely, talked back, or told lies. Tina and I would both be caned if we fought over little things.

She was quietly ambitious for her children. They were all expected to do well in school, and I was to go to college. If finance was a problem, she would work. That was exactly what she did, so that I did not have to work to help out the family — as had been suggested by some. She was a disciplinarian and all her children were made conscious of time. She would often say: "This minute will never come back again. So make the best of it!"

During the school holidays we were allowed to take a break and relax. On one occasion, I went to spend some time at Aunt Violy's house in Ipoh. Arul was a fine hostess. She introduced me to her many friends and admirers. In fact, she was pretty, and some of her admirers envied me.

One day, uncle Francis offered to drive Arul and me to Taiping to visit her father's (uncle Perim's) grave. Arul jumped at the idea, and aunt Violy was appreciative of the opportunity of going to the cemetery. Uncle drove well in his stylish Austin Coupe with its soft pullback hood. We placed flowers on the grave, tidied it up, prayed, and left. By the time we had visited some old friends, it was dark. We were all tired. Chelliah Navaratnam sat in front with uncle, while aunt Violy, Arul and myself dozed off behind. We had to rush back to beat the curfew that was enforced around Sungei Siput—the notorious hot spot during the Emergency. It was 1953, which was about the worst time in the life and death struggle between the armed communist terrorists and the government security forces in Malaya.

There were no cars on the dark, lonely, narrow, and winding road. The car was taking a sharp corner just past the high landmark hill before Sungei Siput town, when uncle Francis lost control and the car plunged down the steep slope on the side of the road. The car rolled at least three times on its sides, before it settled precariously on a soft grassy ledge on the side of the hill. Those of us behind screamed and thought we were going to die or become severely injured, but thank God, no one was badly hurt.

Every one of us gingerly scrambled out of the car for fear that it would topple, and painfully pulled ourselves up the hill to the road. We had to walk to town which was about four miles away, and through terrorist-infested territory! Just as we were contemplating our dangerous plight, a military armoured vehicle came down the road with its searing searchlights and machine-gun levelled at us! Obviously, the government soldiers thought we were terrorists or decoys, and so they were not taking any chances. One wrong move from any of us, and they would have opened fire. Uncle Francis was quick to raise his hands in surrender and urged the rest of us to do so. The British and Malay soldiers challenged all of us who were very frightened. We were shouting for help with our hands raised. When the soldiers recognised us as innocent civilians, they kindly helped us to get out of the dangerous area to the safety of the town, from whence we found our way home. It was indeed an eventful holiday.

Soon after I got back to Kuala Lumpur, anxiety began to build up in me over the expected examination results from the Cambridge Syndicate in the United Kingdom. In the meantime, I joined the sixth form, which I would have to leave if my results turned out to be poor. What would I do? My cousin and colleague Leslie, had joined the "Normal Class" to be trained as a teacher, and was slated to go to the Kirkby Teachers' College in England. In fact, my father was keen that I too should start working as a trainee teacher, and who knows—I might be able to go to the Kirkby as well! But my mother wanted me to go to university, and I was beginning to share that enthusiasm too. However, that was possible only if I got good results and if my family could afford to enrol me in university.

The examination results finally arrived. I did well with a few distinctions. I did equally well in the arts and the sciences, and faced the dilemma of whether to pursue an arts or science course.

I decided to join the sixth form arts class at the VI. Mrs Kemp taught me English and History, while Mr McCumsky taught me English Literature. Mrs Devadason, a talented and attractive Malaysian Ceylonese lady, who was my favourite teacher, taught me Geography. The class was mixed, with students from other secondary schools in Selangor that did not have post-School Certificate classes. The girls were hardworking, while the boys tended to take things in their stride. There was not much academic pressure, compared to the School Certificate year. The field of studies was narrower, the subjects were more interesting, and the teachers were more committed. All in all, sixth form was much more challenging and exciting.

There were also much more opportunities and time for extramural activities. Besides being active in many of the activities conducted by the various clubs and societies, I also took a keen interest in drama, which was under the charge of Mrs Devadason. One day, she called me aside and told me that she had been scouting for someone to play the role of Maria in Shakespeare's *Twelfth Night*, and that she was keen that I should take the part. My only problem was that I had to fix my broken front teeth before I could be selected for the role!

Fixing teeth cost money, and mum was contemplating on how to organise the monthly budget when Uncle Rajasingam, who was visiting, offered to help. So, I got my two new front teeth, and with heavy make-up, I looked like a pretty Maria!

The last few rehearsals were held in the Kuala Lumpur Town Hall. The cast had to cycle back home late at night. When we passed by the Kuala Lumpur Secretariat building, we would shout *"Api! Api!"* ("Fire! Fire!") loudly, and frighten the many vagrants sleeping along the corridors who would flee, only to find that it was a hoax! The Shakespearean play ran for a week, and it was a real success.

It was time for me to do some serious study when the final examinations were approaching. There was much to cover, but I did a fair stint and got through. In fact, I was one of the top scorers in history in the university entrance exam.

University term started in October, so there were only a few months to prepare to go to university. The Ministry of Education was holding interviews for scholarships and bursaries. I applied, and was called for an interview. At the interview, I was offered a teaching scholarship, but I explained that I preferred a non-teaching scholarship or bursary, as I wanted to get into the civil service. The panel was not too pleased.

The British government and especially its civil servants were more comfortable with providing financial aid to train teachers rather than potential administrators who would replace them when Malaya gained its independence in a few years! Why then should the senior British civil servants do anything to jeopardise their own future? The sooner Malayan graduates were available to fill the top civil service posts, the sooner the British positions would be "Malayanised", and the sooner they would have to leave Malaya. That would mean getting back to their small harsh homes and a rough period of resettlement in the United Kingdom.

It was therefore necessary for me to beat the system. I was determined to go to the university and to become an administrator in the civil service where my father and his father had worked so hard and long to reach the maximum in the General Clerical Service salary scale.

Prior to *Merdeka*, the British government had appointed some Malayan "Members to the Legislative Council". The "Member" or "Minister" of Education at that time was Dato' Clough Thuraisingam, whose wife, Pearl, was my first teacher at the kindergarten!

Collin, who was already at the university, kindly took me on his motorcycle one afternoon to visit the Minister to seek his advice and assistance regarding the scholarship. But Dato' Thuraisingam was resting at that time and "could not be disturbed"! So, I went home dejected. I had to see him to make sure that I received, at least some financial aid that my mother could then supplement — otherwise, I might not be able to go to the university. Then, the time spent in sixth form and my acceptance by the university would go to waste. Besides, my prospects in life would be jeopardised! I had to do something for myself and by myself, with the active encouragement from my mother.

I rang the private secretary to the Minister of Education to fix an appointment with the Minister to see him and to ask for help. The secretary was actually surprised by the request of this young schoolboy, and he was also quite curt. Despite the cold treatment, I refused to give up. I took a bus and walked to the Minister's office. I approached the secretary and told him that the Minister had promised my father that he would see me! This prompted him to inform the Minister accordingly. I waited anxiously and prayerfully. Sometime later, the Minister left his office to go to the washroom. He noticed me as I stood up to greet him, and he asked me, "Are you the boy waiting to see me?"

"Yes, sir!" I replied, and quickly explained that I preferred a general bursary and not a teaching scholarship. The busy Minister responded that he could only help if I had the required qualifications, and hurriedly moved to the washroom.

I returned home, satisfied that I had done my best.

6.
LIFE AT UNIVERSITY
(1954-1958)

AFTER having met the Minister of Education, the only thing to do then was to hope and pray that I would get a university scholarship. A few days later, I was informed that I had won a partial bursary that was not tied to teaching. It was a real blessing. Now, I could plan to go to the university!

But first I had to get suitable clothes, a good pair of shoes, and other essentials. Uncle Sam Lee was one of my mother's cousins who was keen that I should "dress like a college boy". He came home with aunt Claris and their sweet children, Girlie, Connie and Gerald, and gave me a branded set of tie, handkerchief and cravat. I had never possessed branded items before, and so I felt good. The fact that I still remember those loving gifts shows how important it is to practice small acts of kindness because such acts go a long way. Soon, I was all set to leave for college.

On the evening of my departure, Reverend Lundy was invited to have a prayer meeting at home. The Reverend prayed for God's guidance upon my life and exhorted, "May the bright lights of Singapore not distract Ramon from the true path". It was a prayer I could never forget. I also remember my mother, father, and four sisters kneeling in prayer in the hall for a long time. Right there itself, I decided to try hard to live up to their prayers and expectations, and resolved not to let my family down!

At the Kuala Lumpur Railway Station, I joined many of my friends who were also going to the University of Malaya in Singapore. Many of my uncles, aunts, and cousins were at the station to wish me well and to send me off. Going to college was a big deal in those days, because so few went for higher education. Watching the whole scene from the train, and from a distance on the railway platform, were many 'senior gentlemen', i.e., those senior students already in the university!

After the farewells, kisses, hugs, and some tears, the "freshmen" boarded the train. The third whistle sounded, and as the train pulled out, there was a loud clamour as hundreds of well-wishers collectively yelled their goodbyes. Then, there was quietness in the coaches as the new passengers settled down, either in their sleeping berths in the second class, or in their seats in the third class. All was calm except for the steady chug of the train.

It soon became obvious that it was the calm before the storm. A little while later, at the Kajang Railway Station, the "freshies" heard a big rumpus. They looked out and saw a group of "seniors" shouting loudly for the freshies to fall out on the railway platform! Most of the freshie-girls stayed in their berths with the curtains drawn. Several other freshies and I responded. The seniors made us do push-ups, and salute as they walked by on the platform. The train began to move, and we rushed back to the train. Once on the train, the 'seniors' went from coach to coach to rag us. The ragging lasted all night long! At the Johor Bahru railway station, some seniors from Singapore were waiting for us. They included the late Dato' Dr Arumugasamy and the late Dr Kumarapathy, my old schoolmates. They gave me a tough time.

At the Singapore railway station, the freshies alighted from the train with their heavy bags. The seniors, however, showed some consideration. They had hired a large lorry and herded the freshies into it and drove them to the hostels at Dunearn Road Hostels in Bukit Timah. On the way, they ordered the freshies to "take a deep breath to savour the smells of Singapore" as we crossed the Singapore River. The freshies did as instructed — and what a terrible stench it turned out to be! (Today, however, the Singapore river is clean!)

At Dunearn Hostels, all hell broke loose! The awaiting seniors picked and then pounced on their prey. They took them to their respective blocks and ragged them. Anyway, the seniors were not that bad, as they were also helpful. They showed us around the hostels, took us for our meals, and advised us about our studies and life at the university.

However, just when I thought that the seniors were satisfied and had had their fill of ragging, another group of them would come in from nowhere. But actually not all the seniors ragged, and not all were rough.

Most freshies were not ragged much, but as usual, a few were "blacklisted" for special treatment. These were the freshies who were regarded as interesting, argumentative, cheeky, defiant, and generally, hard to crack. I was regarded as one of them as I always had a smirk on my face, even after the toughest ragging. The seniors did not like it one bit. But I could not help that my facial structure was made such!

The tough seniors were extremely annoyed with me. They thought that I was taunting them and challenging their capacity to rag successfully. They felt that they had to break me, and so the roughest raggers came for me. The late Kasinathan, Vilvaratnam, Bob Nadarajah and Dr Teddy Leonard took me and a few others to the medical hostel at the Tan Tock Seng Hospital on their motorcycles. They purposely rode fast to scare the freshmen, and they succeeded in doing just that to me. I thought I would be flung off, judging from the way they weaved in and out of the traffic. I threatened to jump out for the love of my life. That scared Kasi. He said later, "This freshie's so desperate that he would do anything!"—and he actually slowed down, much to my relief. But I paid the price later!

At the Tan Tock Seng Hostel, they organised a stripping contest. The participants had to be fully dressed with long sleeved shirt, tie, socks and shoes. Then, they had to strip as fast as they could. I managed to develop stripping into a fine art, and repeatedly set a record of just 11 seconds flat! The late Dr Adisheshan was my closet rival. (That is why even today I need only 15 minutes to shave, shower and dress up for any function! It was good training. Ragging had some benefits!)

The ragging was getting too much of a strain. They kept trying to 'tame' me because I would not give in. Finally, I thought I would trick them. When some of the medical students went on night rounds, I took a snooze. When another batch returned, and roused me from my sleep, I feigned delirium! I mumbled and shouted, "I see bats! I see bats!" This put fear in the patient-sensitive medics who quickly conferred and decided that I had had too much. They decided that I was indeed suffering from delirium and delusions! Not wanting any responsibility on their heads, they quickly gave me a hot drink and promptly put me comfortably to bed!

I enjoyed a well-needed rest for at least a few hours. But my luck did not last long. Those medical students who knew me better returned and on being told what had happened, they realised the ruse and rudely awakened me. I was rushed to the bathtub which was empty and cold. They turned on the tap just enough to let the cold water drip on my head for an hour. Then, early the next morning, I was made to sit naked on the veranda, with my hands and legs thrusting through the trellis-like concrete wall. I was then asked to shout and wave to the nurses walking along the road below! Of course, the nurses did not know who it was, as they could not see my face. I hoped they did not see more than my hanging arms and legs! After all that, the medical seniors took me back to Dunearn Hostels — quite frustrated, as they could not wipe off that defiant smug smirk on my face!

It was now about four weeks since term had started, and I had not attended a single lecture! I was either being ragged during lecture time, or was just too tired to attend classes. When I finally went for my first history tutorial, Dr MacGreggor, the lecturer asked me where the Dutch exported their spices from. Vaguely, I replied "The East Indies". It was not good enough for this scholar. I was pushed to point out the exact location on the map. "Somewhere there!" I said and pointed generally at Southeast Asia on the world map. This annoyed the expert on Dutch history. He took the register and looked through it, mumbling "Navaratnam" and then asked mysteriously, "Are you related to S.T. Ratnam, K.T. Ratnam and K.J. Ratnam!?" All of them were my seniors whom the professor personally knew to be lackadaisical in their academic work! (They turned out to become a Permanent Secretary, an Ambassador and a Professor respectively later in life!) I felt like a hunted deer. I had obviously started on the wrong foot. Thus, it was the good history Professor who finally succeeded in wiping off the smug on my face! He said, "You could land outside "somewhere there"!

Then, the last day of ragging finally arrived. As tradition would have it, the freshies could "tub" the senior gentlemen who had ragged them. So my fellow freshies and I merrily went around getting the seniors into the tub or under the bath-showers. Ragging had its good points. It provided a bond between the raggers and the ragged. The rough edges of snobbery, arrogance and conceit were smoothened out. Cultural and ethnic constraints were reduced, and a common sense of identity and belonging emerged. This spirit of camaraderie was to last long into later life. It was a lot of good, clean fun.

Campus life then settled down after all that robust activity during the ragging period. But it was also in some ways an anti-climax. The lecturers required a lot of reading and research, and the tutorials kept us on our toes. Being the playful type, I hardly handed in my essays on time. Instead, I would be fooling around and would write my essay at the eleventh hour, sometimes throughout the night! Almost every hour, I would call out across the quadrangle to my fellow sufferer, Agos Salim (now Dr), to compare notes on the state of our progress in essay writing. (Those last-minute efforts helped me later in life to write speeches for Ministers quite speedily!)

After completing an assignment, a group of us would take a "green bus" to the city to celebrate. This would mean eating at Albert Street or somewhere cheaper, as any food was better than the hostel food. After that, we would see a movie, and then walk around the "Tekkar" area before returning to the hostels. Most of us did not have the means to go to nightclubs or bars, but just moving together noisily and playing a few pranks on the streets of Singapore, was a lot of fun.

The first year passed by quickly. The examinations were soon around the corner, and preparations proceeded at a feverish pace. I sat for History, Economics and English literature, and returned to Kuala Lumpur to wait anxiously for the results. Much to my surprise, I passed the examinations unconditionally. That meant that I had the whole three months holidays for myself. I passed every paper, (otherwise, a candidate had to return for a repeat, or re-examination).

I was now a full-fledged "senior gentlemen", one who was qualified to rag! I thus visited the Sixth Formers at the Victoria Institution, and instilled them with anxiety over ragging. There was T. Ananda Krishnan and Lalita Rajasooria whom I was waiting to rag. (Unfortunately, both of them left to study in Australia.) I then travelled to Ipoh to visit my old Anderson School. I accompanied some of the Ipoh seniors and waited at the canteen at interval time. We talked to a few potential freshies, Selvaratnam, Sockalingam, Jagadeva and my cousin (on my father's side) Ganambigai, somewhat condescendingly and left abruptly. But the story went around that the seniors were going around taking down the names of those they planned to rag!

I returned home after a good holiday, and spent the rest of the vacation in Kuala Lumpur. Browsing through the Radio Weekly one evening, I came across a picture of a Radio Singapore singer who took part in the Radio Schools' programme. Below the picture was a caption that indicated that the singer's name was Samaladevi, and that she was going to be admitted to the University of Malaya in Singapore! I made up my mind that I would look out for her—but only to rag her! That was a momentous decision in my personal life!

On the way back to Singapore, I found a good number of freshies on the train. I made them ask the Indian stationmasters along the way, if they had daughters to offer in marriage, and how much dowry they would give! This was done just before the train would depart. Thus, if the stationmasters took offence, the students would quickly jump on board the moving train.

On one occasion, we delayed the train by insisting that there was a cat under the train. The stationmaster had to give us the benefit of the doubt because it was a dark night, and the students were mewing away like cats! He delayed the train's departure until he realised that it was a ruse! He was being ragged!

Ragging

It was satisfying to get back to the university. I felt a great sense of freedom and fellowship. I shared a room with Ramanujam who was exceedingly tolerant of my frequent goings in and out, at odd times of the day and night. Indeed, I was hardly in my room as I enjoyed spending most of my time ragging and fraternising with my friends.

One day, I mistook a young-looking, small-built science lecturer, Professor Raisin Huang, for a freshie. I pulled his tie, and asked him loudly why he had walked by without greeting me! It was the quick intervention of a science student nearby that saved the day for me. The authorities frowned upon ragging, and I could have been hauled up for ragging and for trying to rag a professor to boot!

A few other seniors and I had often gone to the girls' hostel at Mount Rosie to rag as well. I would get all the girls together and get them to sing, or just to tease and verbally grill them, if they were cheeky. On the campus, the seniors would look out for other freshies who were non-hostelites, mostly Singaporeans.

One morning, I was sitting on the thick stone wall along the lecture hall veranda with some of my buddies (K.J. Ratnam, Rajan, Eugene, Boon Hooi and Donald Wyatt), waiting to rag some freshies. Two female freshies rushed past us to attend a lecture. We stopped them, but they insisted that they should be allowed to attend their lecture. That was their big mistake. Instantly, we knew that these non-hostelites were not aware of the "rules", and so did not realise that one should not "insist" with senior gentlemen—especially with those of us who had the reputation for being some of the most robust raggers! (In fact, a couple of seniors were later suspended from the hostels for their tough ragging. I believe I was spared because I was the official Chairman of the University Orientation Committee!)

The two girls were forced to give their names—one was Lucy Lim, and the other was Samaladevi—the girl whom I had noticed in the Singapore Radio Weekly in Kuala Lumpur!

It was lunch time when we had completed our interrogation. Lucy had a lunch appointment, and so we took Samala down to Dunearn Hostels for lunch! Samala was not entitled to eat at the hostels, but we soon solved the problem. She was given an empty plate, and was ordered to sing a song and to ask for food from the seniors around the table! In the end she had to sing several songs "for her supper" before she was allowed to go back for her lectures!

My ragging lifestyle continued, and I had a lot of fun. I took a few seniors to the Catholic Kingsmead Hostel where ragging was forbidden. The priest was persuaded to allow about 20 students, whom I had invited for tea, to go to Dunearn Hostels. We escorted the students, happily and casually down the hill. However, as soon as we turned round the bend and their hostel was out of sight, the situation changed. I started to shout at them to fall in line and marched them all the way to Dunearn Hostels. True to my word, I invited them to have tea. After tea, they were taken to the quadrangle, where I announced to all the hostelites around the quadrangle that I had a whole lot of freshies who could be ragged! The seniors, tired from a hard day's work and wanting some relief, converged on the fresh batch of freshies and enjoyed ragging them. After some hard ragging I allowed them to return. As I had promised, the priest got back his flock back in time for dinner!

The second year of the BA degree was what they called a "honeymoon year" because there was no examination to sit for. So I took it easy, skipping lectures often but making sure that my tutorials, which were compulsory, were well attended (though I did not prepare for them).

I was also deeply involved in the students' union activities. I stood for elections to the Students' Council, and obtained the highest votes from Dunearn Hostels! I did not offer myself for the Executive Council, but was on several executive committees.

This was in 1955 when Singapore was going through great political strife. The Labour Unions were flexing their muscles against British rule alongside the Labour Front, a political party led by Chief Minister David Marshall. Indeed, Singapore was in a state of serious unrest.

The students from the Chinese High School at Bukit Timah Road had barricaded themselves against the police. There was a real threat of violence. The university students' union sent a delegation to the students' rally at the Chinese High School at Bukit Timah to express its support, and to help prevent a confrontation with the Government. I was in that delegation. I came back highly impressed by their unity and determination to resist police action to break up the student barricades. Due to my involvement in the incident, my parents were told by some misinformed persons that I was a "communist"! They naturally got worried although they did not think that it was true.

I was thus having a fine education in organisation and leadership, but I was not doing much studying. I seriously thought that the whole purpose for not having any examinations in the second year was for students to play an active role in student activities! Unfortunately, the university authorities changed their minds, and decided to hold examinations. This was unprecedented for the second year arts students. I was caught off balance. I was grossly unprepared and thus failed my examinations! My dear cousin, the late Robert Abraham, who had also joined the university and had a great time, was in the same boat with me. Both of us went back during the vacation to stay at cheaper digs at Adams Road, to study and take the re-examinations. We had too much to catch up with and so we did not pass!

It was a severe blow to me. I had never failed any examination before, and it had dispelled my false notion that only those who were dull had to study hard!

I repeated my second year as a wiser and more sober student. I declined to stand for students' union elections. However, I realised that I still had to play a role in student corporate life. The opportunity arose when the Students' Council invited me to head the newly established Welfare Week Committee. I readily agreed to take the challenge because it was for a good cause, i.e., to raise funds for welfare homes and it would only be for about a month. It was the first major effort by university students to undertake charity work. It was also a kind of response to the public criticism that university students were self-centred and apathetic to the needs of society.

Welfare Week

This was in 1956—just one year before *Merdeka,* and the students wanted to identify themselves with the growing spirit of nationalism and to champion the cause of the people. I was given powers to co-opt members of my committee. I chose good organisers whom I felt could also work hard. One of those appointed was Samala! My reasons for choosing her were that, first, she was a non-hostelite and so could get the support of the Singaporean students. Secondly, she was president of the university's music society and could organise the concerts, and thirdly, she was a sympathetic supporter of the cause!

This special organising committee became known as the First Welfare Week Committee. Among those on the Welfare Committee were Donald Wyatt and Robert Abraham. We met often between and after lectures, and drew up an elaborate programme for the welfare week: (i) a Flag Day for the general public; (ii) a concert for the university students and staff; (iii) a fancy-dress football match; (iv) a special art exhibition at the university's new Art Museum; and (v) several other smaller events.

The then vice-chancellor, Professor Oppenheim, was requested to give his foreword in the souvenir programme, wherein he described the First Welfare Week as, "An acorn that will grow into a huge shady oak tree that will provide compassion and comfort to the poor and needy, in the years to come." Those were prophetic words, for this tradition has continued at the University of Singapore, the University of Malaya and many other universities in Malaysia which still organise "Welfare Weeks" and charity projects and programmes.

The most successful project was undoubtedly the Flag Day. Publicity was carefully organised. Radio Singapore and the press helped us a great deal. We supplemented this with our own brand of publicity. We hired a large lorry, fixed a public address system on it, and drove all round the city, blaring announcements of the Welfare Week. I enlisted our three pretty undergraduate friends—Carol Arumugam (now Mrs Selvarajah), Monica Daniels (now Mrs Moorthy), Lolitha Sreenivasan (now Mrs Mohan), Viji Nair and Robert Abraham to do the announcements. Together with Samala, they also sang over the public address system to attract the crowds' attention as we drove through the crowded streets of Singapore! Robert entertained the crowds with his humour each time we stopped to make the announcements.

The motto of the Welfare Week was "Help us to help our people". We chose this theme and were pleased with it because it crystallised the true purpose and meaning behind the whole Welfare Week. As students, we did not have the means to help the poor, so we needed the support of those who could afford to give to the poor. Furthermore, we were concerned with "our people" as opposed to a people belonging to a colonial government, as in the past.

We raised the largest amount of money from the Flag Day collections. We arranged for all the flag sellers to return their collection tills to the police station at Serangoon Road. A whole team of tellers counted all the collections, in the presence of policemen, who also offered to help. It was past midnight when we counted the proceeds of the last till. We raised about $17,000. This was a princely sum in those days.

The money was all donated to the various charitable organisations in Singapore within the next few days. We were all amply rewarded with the satisfaction that came from our sincere service to the less privileged. I think we all had also learnt from the rich experience of doing genuine charity for the poor.

The pioneering and overwhelming success of the first Welfare Week at the University of Malaya in Singapore was gratifying to me personally. I felt I had made a positive contribution, and I also got a better understanding of Samala's considerable sense of commitment. Moreover, I had, in the process, got closer to her.

University Pranks
We were up to other activities too. For instance, the students had to cross both the parallel roads of Dunearn and Bukit Timah on their way to lectures. The students' union had written several letters to the authorities requesting for a zebra crossing there, but to no avail. This prompted some enterprising students and myself to provide the zebra crossing!

One moonlit night during the Muslim fasting month of Ramadhan, a number of students, including the late Rajendra, Robert, Arumuga-masamy (now Dato' Dr) and I, bought some white paint and brushes, drew the outline of the zebra crossings on the road, and poured and dabbed the paint in the big outlined oblongs. While we were doing the job, our look-out men spotted an approaching police patrol car and quickly sounded the alarm to the students.

Then we bolted in the direction of the university's Ooi Tiong Ham Hall on the hill. We were in our *sarongs*, and thus could not run fast. The police alighted and gave chase, focusing their searchlights on the runaways. It was a frightening experience as the police searchlights made you feel that the police were literally at your heels, when in fact they were some distance behind. We students climbed up the upper floors of the building and watched the policemen scour the area below trying to find and arrest us. All of us were afraid of arrest. Our academic careers would have been spoilt. We waited for a few hours for the police to give up their search. Then, from a public phone, we rang up some of our Muslim friends in the hostels, who had risen at half past four in the morning to pray and to prepare for the fast. Only when they confirmed that the police had left did we return to the hostels!

Undoubtedly, our mission was accomplished! The zebra crossing, though partially done, was used all the time, and it was also given due recognition by the passing motorists!

Duke of Dunearn Road Hostels

At about the same time, the Duke of Edinburgh visited Singapore. The government had left the university students out of the celebrations. It was not that the exclusion bothered us, but we decided to have our own fun — at the government's expense.

A big welcoming reception and cultural shows were organised at the *padang* of the Singapore Cricket Club. Several clubs, societies and schools provided cultural and aerobic displays. The university students were in a group of about a hundred. We dressed up in white shorts and white shirts.

We assembled at the *padang* on the morning of the celebrations, and merged quietly into the large crowd. At the sound of a whistle, all of us converged onto the centre of the field, fell into proper formations and did our brief exercises quite professionally and then shabbily! The Duke was about 50 yards from the first line of us. He seemed to be concentrating with appreciation. The VIPs and organisers were seen referring to their programmes, trying to identify the participants. Soon, they discovered the "big hoax"! The police were alerted and their whistles were heard all around, as they charged into the *padang* to disperse the "disruptive" university students. All of us quickly bolted and disappeared into the crowd. The Duke was thrilled, and the officials were embarrassed, but we students had great fun! We had stolen the show!

Success went to our heads. We decided to plot another trick when we knew that the Duke would be visiting the War Memorial at Woodlands. He was to pass Dunearn Hostels. So we chose a fellow student, Earl Gow, to impersonate "The Duke". He was dressed up in khaki uniform with a military cap. Being tall, slim and fair-skinned, he did look like the real thing—from a distance.

On the day of the Duke's arrival, as soon as we saw the real Duke approaching way down the road, we sent off our fake Duke in an open jeep, with student motorcyclists in escort formation, on Dunearn Road. The hundreds of people who lined the road saw the impostor first, as his jeep was way ahead of the real Duke. The crowds waved enthusiastically at our impostor until they realised that they had been fooled, as the police outriders and grand entourage of the real Duke followed a few minutes later on the parallel Bukit Timah Road.

(Many years later, when I attended the Commonwealth Heads of Government Meeting in London as an official, I was also invited to a reception by Queen Elizabeth II. The Duke went around chatting with the guests quite casually, and when he came to my group, I related the incident of our prank. He did remember it and had a good laugh!)

Time passed rapidly, and I was seeing Samala more often. The only lecture we had in common was history. After lectures, we would go for tea together with Lucy and Cheang Hai Ding (later a Singapore Ambassador). Sometimes, I would accompany Samala home in the green bus, and return on the next bus. I found myself spending more time in the library mainly because Samala spent a lot of time there. Consequently, I studied more and thus both of us got through our second year examinations pretty well.

Christmas 1956

I went back home for the long vacation. I travelled to Kuala Lipis and Cameron Highlands with my cousin, Lloyd Thalayasingam, and another medical student, John Thambaya, for a fortnight. They were fine company and successful doctors now.

I returned home in time for Christmas. Tina had also come back from the Teachers' College, and together with Angie, Julie and Georgie, we all planned a lovely Christmas. I set out with Leslie Abraham to cut a big conical shaped Christmas tree, which I got from around Petaling Hill. In those days, there were no restrictions about cutting down any kind of tree. There were no environmental issues to talk about.

We planted it in a large pot, and the girls went about happily decorating it with mostly handmade decorations of all colours, shapes and sizes. The tree looked beautiful, and the house looked handsome.

Mum had "caponised" several cockerels, and fed them till they were now ready for the table. The only problem was that they had to be caught first. It was not an easy task because they had been trained to roost on a big tree beside the house in order to prevent them from being stolen. The way to catch them was to quietly get to the tree at night, surround the tree and then have someone to shake the tree branches vigorously so that the chickens would fall down to the ground in a daze. Then, those waiting around the tree would quickly pounce on the hapless chickens and proudly present them to mum, who would be waiting with her sharp knife.

Christmas eve was exciting. Tina and I joined the Methodist Tamil Church carollers. We travelled by bus and covered many houses, singing Tamil and English carols. I joined the group's practices late, because I had just returned from the university. So, Leslie gave me a romanised version of the Tamil carols to help me sing the Tamil words. When I found myself unable to keep up with the pronunciation, I just mumbled softly, mouthed the words at the crucial parts, and showed consistent vigour.

Christmas morning was a big rush. Having slept insufficiently the previous night on account of carolling, it was difficult for me to get up, dress in the new shirt and trousers, and dash off on the bicycle, or for the bus. After the church service, we wished our family and friends and hurried home to prepare for our guests. Some of them joined us for the Christmas lunch of roast turkey and the capons we had caught, red beetroot, chicken fillings, mashed potatoes with butter, and mutton curry of course. Mum cooked them all, and we still do not know how she managed it—without a maid.

The afternoon was kept aside to see a film at the cinema. My sisters, cousins and I walked down to the bus stop, hoping to get a bus, a taxi or even flag down a friendly car for a ride—as long as all of us could meet at the front of the cinema in time to go into the theatre together! Once inside the theatre, we relaxed, ate *keropok*, *kacang* and *kana*, chattered, laughed and enjoyed the show.

By the time we returned home, we were truly tired—but it was just impossible to rest on Christmas day! As night fell, we got ready for firing crackers and fireworks. We also had to receive our relatives or visit them. Cramming into a relative's car and driving around the town, singing carols and shouting out to friends and strangers added a lot of excitement. At the end of it all, we were all completely exhausted, hoarse, and ready to hit the hay!

We were now approaching independence. It was also a crucial time for me as I was approaching my final year for the BA degree. My performance in the examinations would determine whether I would qualify to do my honours degree. It had a far higher premium than a general degree such as the BA. There was no question that I had to work much harder than before if I wanted to qualify. I decided to do well enough to do my honours in either history or economics (I certainly preferred economics, which was considered a much tougher and more marketable subject.) Job opportunities after Independence would be much greater.

Samala

Samala was a tremendous help and a strong stabilising influence in my studies. She was much more studious and disciplined. She subtly provided me encouragement to compete. My pride would not allow me to do less favourably than her. In any case, I had to do well for my family and for my own future well-being. There was also the strong urge to prove that I was capable of success since some people fancied that I would not amount to much in life!

All these reasons motivated me to settle down to study hard although my carefree and playful spirit often took over. I spent more time in the library, took more trouble writing my essays, attended lectures more regularly and prepared better for my tutorials. Thus, when the examinations came, I was more prepared and less anxious than before, for that was the first time I took my student life seriously!

An important life-changing event occurred to me at this time. It was my decision to go steady with Samala. One late night, I was having a chat over *teh tarik* with the late Dr T. Selvarajah at Wahab's stall (Wahab was the favourite roadside tea stall owner opposite the Dunearn Hostels. He served tea, coffee, Milo, Horlicks and buns to the students for cash or credit, at virtually any time of the day or night!).

My good friend Selvarajah suggested that I should make a firm decision concerning Samala. He had heard from a reliable family source that someone else was interested in her. His advice was that pressure would mount, and she might relent if she found that I was not making any commitment. I thought about his advice. I realised that I had not yet formally committed myself to Samala for several reasons. I was only 22. I was the eldest and only son, with four sisters to whom I had responsibilities. I would have to support my parents soon as my father was going to retire. In any case, I was still a student, and I had to graduate first! So I had to postpone making the final decision, though the thought of marriage to Samala was on my mind.

The Bachelor of Arts final examinations were soon over and I had to return home. I wondered what would happen to my relationship with Samala if I failed my BA (or passed but failed to qualify for my honours degree), especially if Samala did. I felt that I could not face the possibility of Samala being better qualified than me! I had packed up all my things since I thought I might not be returning to the university. Who knows?, I mused. I was neither optimistic nor pessimistic, just neutral.

I returned to Kuala Lumpur. Back home I just waited patiently for the results. I hoped and prayed for good results, and kept corresponding regularly with Samala. "Tammy", a popular song that I liked at that time, reflected my feelings!

Merdeka

The wait for my results was made easy as there was a sense of excitement in the air with all the feverish preparations for *Merdeka*. The developments and events leading to independence were historical, and gave one a sense of the unfolding history. All this helped me to take my mind off the results of the examinations, and the worries of my future. The newspapers were full of reports of the British moves to prepare a smooth transition to the Malayan Government under the leadership of Tunku Abdul Rahman. I spent a lot of time reading and following these developments.

August 31, 1957 was set to be the date for Independence (*Merdeka*), and the days seemed to pass quickly towards that day. On the eve of independence, Leslie and I cycled to the Selangor Club *padang* (field) to witness the ceremony of the lowering of the Union Jack for the last time, and the raising of the new Malayan flag for the first time. As the Secretariat clock tower struck the midnight hour, the new Malayan flag reached the top of the flag pole after the Union Jack had been lowered to the ground. The large crowd went wild with excitement, cheering and shouting *"Merdeka! Merdeka!"* at the top of their voices. It was a thrilling moment of history in the making! I will never forget that historical moment. I was there!

On Merdeka Day itself, I got up early to go to the brand new Merdeka Stadium that had been specially constructed for the Independence ceremony. Tunku Abdul Rahman, the Chief Minister, had earlier given instructions that the grand stadium be completed in record time for the *Merdeka* ceremony.

However, my father forbade me to go to the Merdeka Stadium, fearing that there may be bloodshed as rumoured. I had to plead hard, and only when my mother interceded did my dad eventually agree to let me go to the Merdeka Stadium, but for a little while only.

The crowd at the stadium was huge. I had never seen such a multitude of people from so many diverse backgrounds. Thousands had come from the *kampungs*, the new villages, and the estates. They were all dressed in their best to celebrate and witness this great and historical ceremony of the handing over of the instrument of sovereignty and nationhood, to the newly independent Malaya by the British Crown.

I saw the Duke of Kent, with his high plumed cock hat, hand over the instrument to the Tunku, while the whole crowd held their breath as they witnessed this great moment of history. The solemnity and silence was suddenly shattered by the thunderous shouts of *"Merdeka! Merdeka!"* for 17 times, led by the Tunku with his raised right hand and open palms. The whole mass of jubilant people roared back the Tunku's shouts of *Merdeka* spontaneously. It was like an electrical impulse travelling round the stadium in waves. It was indeed heart-rending and a highly emotional experience that moved many to tears.

I went home inspired, determined that I would dedicate my life to the service of the new nationalist government of independent Malaya, where, like my father and my grandfather, I could serve my community and my country to the best of my ability.

Honours Year

The opportunity to serve seemed to come quickly when I was informed by the university that I was selected to do an honours degree in economics. I was thrilled, as that was my academic ambition, and I thanked God for it. I rang Samala from a public phone booth to tell her the good news and was in turn told that she too had qualified to do her honours in history. Now, we could both see the pleasant prospects of getting together again.

Time appeared to move slowly as I waited patiently to return to Singapore. At home, I looked forward to letters from Samala. I listened to her singing on the Singapore Schools Broadcasts, and spent much time with my sisters who were all growing up nicely into sweet, well-groomed and able young ladies. They were enthusiastic about my relationship with Samala. My mum and dad were understandably not so sure as I was only 23 years old, and I had to fulfil my responsibilities to my parents and my four sisters.

When I returned to university, I was given the choice of staying on at Dunearn Hostels, or transferring to the newly-built Raffles Hall. I told myself that I had already spent four years at Dunearn Hostels where I had my fun, and more than my fair share of youthful exuberance. This was a good opportunity for me to change my lifestyle and to improve on my image. I needed to shed the image of a rough, boisterous, student activist, to one who was preparing to leave university to start a career! I had to become more serious in my work and outlook — and I felt that Raffles Hall provided the answer.

Raffles Hall was different from Dunearn Hostels in many ways. It was built along the lines of a typical British-type university hall. We had long corridors, along which we had single and double rooms. As a final honours year student, I had the privilege of getting a single room. There was a comfortable bed, a cupboard for my clothes, a built-in writing desk and a ceiling fan. We had a washbasin with a mirror attached, but no individual toilet facilities. We had to go to the common bathroom facilities which were neat and clean, but cold!

I used to suffer from bad sinuses, and there was no hot water to bathe. So, I sneezed a lot because of the cold showers that I took early each morning. My loud sneezing disturbed many students from their sleep. One of those who complained about my loud sneezing was my classmate Salleh (later the Chief Secretary to the Government, Tan Sri Sallehuddin Mohamad). Thus I decided to imitate the antics of *The Three Stooges*, and would make a string of funny sounds after each sneeze, just to entertain my listeners. Eventually, those who were annoyed by my sneezing became amused, and even sympathised with me!

The honours year was less taxing than the bachelor's degree year. We concentrated only on economics, instead of having to cover other subjects as well. However, there was an academic exercise to be done. I chose "Prices in the Rubber Industry" for my subject. There was not much material on the subject at the university library. My supervisor,

Dr Charles Gambar, therefore advised me to see his old friend, Dr P.P. Narayanan, Secretary-General of the National Union of Plantation Workers (NUPW), to seek his advice.

When I returned home for the first-term holidays in March, I visited Dr P.P., as he was fondly called. He was helpful, gave me whatever material he had, and advised me to go to the Malayan Plantation Industries Employers Association, to get more information. So, using Dr Gambar's good offices, I visited the chief executive of the organisation, Mr Perera. He was just the opposite of Dr P.P. He had little time for me when I explained my purpose. He just told me that there was no need to do research into the wages of the rubber industry, because the estate workers were well-paid. He even refused to give me any published material! I thanked him anyway, but as I left the outer office, I picked up a whole set of annual reports that contained the wage scales—and disappeared fast!

I returned to the university for the final lap. I had to pass with a good honours degree. Although Economics was regarded as a premier subject. I also had to get a good academic class. Samala was there to help. She was a somewhat bright and disciplined student. On the other hand, I might be somewhat bright, but not so diligent. I was quite relaxed and maintained an active interest in political developments and students' affairs. I enjoyed discussion and debate with my friends late into the nights and did not spend much time on my studies.

After all, Malaya had just gained independence in 1957. My final year at the university in 1959 was a time of great excitement. There were a lot of debates and exchange of ideas as to how best our newly independent country should be managed!

In Singapore, the political feelings were high too. Singapore had self-government, but did not enjoy independence. The students from the Chinese school were high spirited and politically-conscious. Except for the Socialist Club members, most of the University of Malaya students were more establishment-orientated. At that time, the Socialist Club members were regarded as quite extreme. They were critical of the Government of the day, both of Malaya and Singapore.

Partly as a reaction to the extreme stance of the Socialist Club, the University Democratic Club was formed. David Marshall, the former Chief Minister of Singapore, was then opposed to the People's Action Party (PAP) led by Mr Lee Kuan Yew. The Socialist Club had close associations with the PAP, and shared many similar ideas. This made

some of us more comfortable with Marshall who did his best to cultivate the university students.

So, when he invited some of us to his home for lunch one Saturday,
we accepted. It was a good lunch of curry at his big breezy bungalow
on a hill in Changi overlooking the sea. We talked about the social and
political developments in Singapore and Malaya, and returned to the
hostels quite invigorated intellectually.

Sipping piping-hot *teh tarik* at Wahab's coffee stall, we all felt the
need to form another political club on the campus. There was Dr T. Selvarajah, Donald Wyatt, and I. We decided to call the proposed new political club, the University of Malaya Democratic Club. We also felt
that it was important to have a respected Malay student leader to lead
the club, and that it should be multiracial. The obvious choice for president would be Musa Hitam (later Deputy Prime Minister of Malaysia,
and Tan Sri). Musa was active in students' union affairs, and mixed
well with the other races. The only trouble was that he was hard to pin
down. He was constantly on the move. He cut lectures, visited his
friends in Geylang often, and, of course, frequently returned to his
hometown, Johor Bahru. So, the best way to get him was to catch him
in his room at night when he returned to sleep!

Selvarajah, Donald Wyatt, and I dropped in at Musa's room late
one night. We found him sleeping, but nevertheless decided to wake
him up. I tickled his nose with some thread, and he got up with a start,
somewhat annoyed. I explained to him our mission, and he was initially
reluctant to get involved with a political club. However, we won him
over with the argument that we needed to provide a forum for the students who were not leftist. He agreed to become the Democratic
Club's first president!

By now our friends had accepted the fact that Samala and I were
going steady. My friends ceased to insist that I go out with them. The
typical night out with my friends meant going to the late-night movie.
It was usually at the Rex Theatre at the Tekkar junction or the Cathay
cinema. We would take the green bus to town and have *kuay teow* at the
corner coffeeshop at Tekkar, or, if we had enough money to share
among us, we would have some more exotic food at Fatties at the notorious Bugis Street (Alas! This place has been cleaned up, and thus
robbed of its special charms, sights, smells and all.) We would walk
from Tekkar to the Cathay, and have fun all along the way. We would
tease the trishaw men, whistle at pretty girls, and thumb for lifts. Some-

times, we would have a little beer, pretend we were drunk, and sing along and be merry on the streets of Singapore.

At the cinema, we would sit in the third-class seats, and would talk and laugh among ourselves as if the whole hall was our private property. Often enough, we would inadvertently annoy the other moviegoers who would shout "Shut up!" This would encourage some of us to make more noise until, the audience gave up, or when an official threatened to throw us out! We would silence each other when the film started, but when there was a sad scene, we would pretend to sob. If there was a frightening ghost scene, we would shriek! That is how we had a lot of good clean fun in those days! There was little politicking.

By the time we got back to the hostels, it would be around 1am, and we would invariably adjourn to Wahab's coffee stall. There would be many others having a *teh tarik* or Wahab's famous *teh halia* (or ginger tea), which, apparently, was good for digestion and energy.

Commitment to Samala

When I was not with the boys, Samala and I used to take a break from the library and go for walks in the campus. Sometimes, she stayed for choir practices where she was the assistant choir director, helping that remarkable and gifted conductor, Mr Paul Abesheganandan. This meant that she had to work with choir members when Paul had other commitments. I was in fact in the choir, but I did not feel comfortable under her baton and direction. I thus dropped out of the choir. That was the end of my singing prospects! In retrospect, was it my pride, or male chauvinism, or both, that made me leave the choir? I still do not know.

Whenever Samala had to go home late, I would take her home by bus. We took the green bus to Middle Road, and then changed to a different bus to get to her house at 17 East Coast Road in Katong. It took about 45 minutes, but we used to enjoy those carefree rides back to her home. I usually did not have much time as the last bus would leave at 11pm. I could not afford to miss it. In fact, the bus service ceased by midnight, and I would be in trouble if I missed the last bus to the hostels from Middle Road as I could not afford to take the taxi.

On Returning Home

The 1958/1959 academic year was now drawing to a close. The examinations were drawing nigh. We had to get back to our studies in

MY LIFE AND TIMES

greater earnest. For what good would all our accomplishments amount to if we failed our examinations!

However, I felt a sense of quiet confidence and contentment. I had pretty well succeeded in achieving my modest aims at the university. I had had a lot of fun, attained considerable knowledge, a good training of the mind, and developed some leadership qualities. I had made many good friends and now, although not planned for, I had also gained a steady girlfriend!

So I had to do my best of what was left to be done. I began to study in earnest for my finals. With the encouragement of my parents, my sisters and Samala, I actually worked hard. The exams came and were soon over, much to my relief.

The last few days at the university were busy. There was a lot of packing to do. Books and notes borrowed were returned; bills had to be paid; and small loans (like Wahab's) were settled. All that having been done, it was sad to leave the campus where we had spent some of the best and happiest days of our lives.

Farewell to University

However, the most difficult part of the parting was with Samala. We met at her place on the eve of my departure, took a walk along the Katong Beach, and made our plans for the future. We had dinner at a cosy little delicatessen called the "Red House" along East Coast Road. I then took her home. With a heavy heart, I parted after wishing Samala and her family a fond farewell. I took the last bus back to the hostels for the last time. Early next morning, I hitched a ride home to Kuala Lumpur—and to a different life altogether!

Those days, it took about eight hours to drive to Kuala Lumpur! It was indeed a long ride, particularly when my feelings were mixed. I was sad to leave Samala and student life, and yet happy that I was now moving closer and closer to a new and exciting phase in my life. Will it be successful? Will it be rewarding? Those were the questions uppermost in my mind! At the same time, every mile brought me closer to home, but took me further away from Samala. I was going through an emotional conflict.

One of the popular songs in those days was "Que Sera Sera" and the following words and tune kept haunting my mind till I dozed off in the moving car: *Que sera sera, whatever will be, will be, The future's not ours to see, Que sera sera, What will be, will be. Que sera sera!*

A chip off the old block: my father and I when I was a year old in Sungei Buloh in 1936

At age 4 with my long curls!

When I was 6, at Lorong Cheroh, Ipoh, in 1941

In school uniform in Taiping, 1947

Mum (left), Aunty Agnes and the Abraham cousins in Sungai Buloh, 1940.
I am second from left, beside Tina

Grandpa, grandma and grandchildren in Ipoh, 1941. *From left to right*: Robert, me, Janet, Tina, Arul, Leslie and Collin. Angie is in grandpa's arms with Sam Abraham next to him

Uncles, aunties and cousins in Ipoh, 1941.
Kneeling from left: Robert, Collin, Janet, Arul, Leslie, Tina, me and Sam

Seated on the mat from left: Sam, Robert, Janet, Arul, Tina, Leslie, me and Collin.
(I shook my head when the camera clicked.)

My father, mother, Tina and me standing on the left, in Ipoh, 1941, with the whole Lee family

Our family with Granny at Jalan 5/10E in Petaling Jaya.
From left: Tina, Dad, Angie, Granny, Julie, Mum, me and Georgie in 1955

The extended family, with me standing second from the right in 1960

Tina and Kamal's wedding in 1962

Samala and me with mum and sisters in Petaling Jaya, 1962

Angie and Albert's wedding in 1967. Ravi is the little boy

Julie and James' wedding in 1969. Indran is on the extreme left

My sisters and brothers-in-law, James, Albert and Kamal, at our family home
at 5/10E Petaling Jaya in March 1970

A thorn among the roses! My four sisters and me at our Petaling Jaya family home in 1970

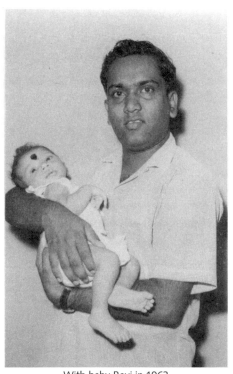

With baby Ravi in 1963

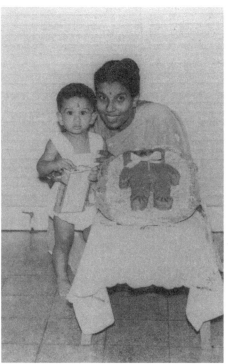

Ravi's first birthday in 1964 with Samala

My father with our nine-month-old son Ravi

My father-in-law, Mr Dharmalingam, Samala, Ravi and me
at Batu Caves, Selangor

I can vividly remember the long journey home. There was no air-conditioning in the car. It was uncomfortable as the day was hot and humid, with an overcast sky. We stopped at Yong Peng Road junction for lunch. We had *wantan mee* and sugarcane juice, and then drove on steadily to Kuala Lumpur in the rain. The rain beat heavily on the car screen, and the badly maintained roads got slippery. This delayed our journey, and we finally got into Kuala Lumpur at around 6pm. As we drove along the Federal Highway towards the Employees Provident Fund (EPF) building, the horizon ahead looked dark grey as the sun was setting. I was depressed and quietly asked myself whether the dark dusk was a forewarning. Would I have a dark or bright career ahead of me?

Mum, dad and my four sisters were delighted that their only son and brother was back home for good. It made a big difference to them that I would now be able to bear some of the responsibilities of running the home. Dad had retired, but was working part-time, while mum was still teaching on a temporary basis. She had sacrificially taken on the job to help out in the family budget, and to support me at college. Tina was teaching in Raub, Angie was taking a secretarial course, while Julie was doing her teacher training. Georgie was still studying. Now that I had come home, I would have to look for employment and help the family.

7.
SEEKING A CAREER

I felt that the responsibility of getting a job had suddenly settled down upon me. The carefree student days were finally over. Dad would not be able to work much longer, and I felt that mum should not carry on teaching because she was getting on in age and had so many other responsibilities at home. Thus, the family expectations were high for me to get a good job, and to help the Navaratnam family to move on to an even better quality of life.

I had to get a job soon. I certainly could not do much for myself or the family as an unemployed graduate. I started to look through *The Straits Times* and other newspapers every day, for job advertisements. I applied all over. There were vacancies mainly in the government. The private corporate sector was mainly in the hands of the British, who employed few locals at the senior levels. Although it was 1959, the British companies were still in no mood to recruit or train Malayan graduates to take over from them. In any case, there was some reluctance in those days to join the business sector which was regarded as "insecure" because there was no pension scheme as in the government. Furthermore, it was a tremendous prestige then to join the senior ranks of the civil service. This was particularly so because the British civil servants were being Malayanised, and their jobs were gradually taken over by Malayans.

I applied for several vacancies at the Customs Department, the Immigration Department, and even Radio Malaya. There was no Television Malaya then. Otherwise, I would have applied for any suitable vacancy there too! Then one day, I saw an advertisement for vacancies in the prestigious and premier echelon of the civil service — the Malayan Civil Service (MCS). There was another advertisement for the foreign service as well. I enthusiastically responded to both advertisements and waited.

But I could not be idle. So, I went to see dad's cousin, uncle Thalaysingam, for a temporary teaching job. He was the headmaster of the Methodist Afternoon School in Kuala Lumpur, and had helped me and many other university students and graduates with temporary jobs. "Uncle Singam" was a very considerate man. He offered me a job straight away. I was to receive $150 a month. This amount would look after my needs. I gave $100 to mum, and kept $50 for myself. Since I was staying at home, I really did not need much money. However, when I wanted more, I would go to mum rather than dad, and mum would give me what I needed.

I received many acknowledgement letters to my applications. I just had to wait to be called for the interviews. Then one fine day, I received a letter from the Public Services Commission, calling me for an interview for the MCS! This was what I was waiting for. It was about the best job interview anyone could get at that time.

The MCS was almost completely dominated by the British colonial officials. However, they were slowly but surely being Malayanised, i.e., they were being paid attractive compensation terms and phased out from the MCS. Their jobs were highly coveted by young Malayan graduates like me. It was a great privilege to be selected to join the MCS. Most of my colleagues applied to join the MCS in order to step into the White men's shoes and help our own government manage our newly independent country!

Moreover, the private sector at that time was quite small and relatively insignificant in terms of prestige and salaries. The large business houses were primarily owned and managed by the British. They had hardly any need for Asian graduate staff. Anyway, Asians were generally employed at the lowest levels. The rest of the private sector was mainly composed of small traders and retail businessmen who were largely Chinese. They too did not require graduates to run their small scale businesses.

The employment market in those days was therefore restricted for Malayan graduates, especially in the field of management. So, what were the options for ambitious young graduates? Invariably, they applied for government jobs because the government was easily the best employer at that time. There was much prestige in working with the British and for the new independent Malayan government. There were also all kinds of privileges like housing, free medical services, car loans and generous vacation leave. These comfortable terms and conditions were designed by the British colonial office at Whitehall in the United Kingdom, for their own British officers. Now, we Malayans were inheriting all these privileges that went with government jobs.

The jobs were available for arts degree holders in, *inter alia*, the teaching profession, the Customs and the Immigration departments, the Postal department, and Radio Malaya. The police force had for the first time opened its recruitment to graduates, and Hanif Omar (later Tun Hanif Omar), Dato' Ahmad Maulana (deceased) and Richard Gow were some of the first graduates to join the police force as graduate cadet Assistant Superintendents of Police (ASPs).

The MCS Interview

The MCS interview was for both the administrative cadre at home and the foreign service. The government was particularly interested to build up its diplomatic core, since as a newly independent country, it was necessary to establish the foreign service as a matter of high priority. I went for the MCS interview filled with anxiety and hope, but with low expectations. The government had a quota for recruitment. For every four Malays, only one non-Malay would get the job. (The quota system now is even less favourable for non-Malays).

I recall Wong Kum Choon (now Tan Sri) coming from Taiping to my dad's house to go together with me for the interview. We compared notes on the documents required for the interview, and I noticed that he did not have an envelope to neatly pack all his documents into. I had an extra envelope but was not sure whether I should give it to a friend who was also my competitor! But my better side prevailed, and I gave him my spare envelope. I felt all the better for it, and we both set out by bus for the interview at the Public Services Commission near the Tanglin Hospital, behind the present National Mosque.

There we met our classmate Sulaiman Abdullah (now Dato'), who looked almost funny with a large *songkok* on his head which practically covered his ears. When I asked him why he wore an oversized *songkok*, he replied that he had been told that since he looked a little like a Chinese, he had hurriedly bought a *songkok* on his way to the interview!

I must say that it struck me for the first time that the Malay quota system was pervasive, and that even the Malays had to show that they were "more Malay" than the other Malays in order to ensure they got their "special privileges". This theme of wanting to show that one was "more Malay than thou" was to recur repeatedly along the way of my long career ahead!

The MCS interview itself went off quite well. The public service commissioners were courteous and made us comfortable. I prayed before being called in, and I felt a quiet confidence. I was determined to put my best foot forward, without wanting to put it in my mouth! I did my best to draw the commissioners' questions to my strong points.

For instance, when they asked me what sports I played (since I was no sportsman), I quickly referred to my preference for students' union activities and my work as chairman of the Welfare Week Committee. They seemed to show keen interest, and this encouraged me to project my positive points of leadership and managerial abilities. It was a long and interesting discourse that I had with the commissioners. At the end of the 45 minutes, they asked me whether I would be interested to join the Foreign Service — if I was given a chance. I replied that I would strongly prefer the Home Service because of my family commitments, but would accept the Foreign Service as an alternative — if I was selected! This caused a laugh from the commissioners, and I was excused on this rather pleasant note.

Again, I just had to wait and see. It was a difficult period. Some of my friends had begun to get letters of offer, and some had even started on their jobs. However, those of us called for the MCS interview, had to wait longer because it entailed a longer period to process. I wondered what I would do if I did not get the MCS appointment or get called to serve in any other branch of government. Given my limited and unpleasant experience in doing my little business during the Japanese occupation, I was not keen at all to apply for the jobs in the private sector. I could have applied for jobs in the banking and insurance industries where my honours degree in economics was in demand, but I did not.

Appointed to the MCS

After several weeks, I came home after teaching at the Methodist Afternoon School and found a letter marked "On Government Service" waiting for me. I felt nervous as I opened and read its contents. I had been selected to the MCS! I was overjoyed, and said a silent prayer of gratitude. Mum, dad, and my sisters were delighted that I had been offered the prestigious and coveted appointment to the MCS.

I informed my cousin Leslie who had come to visit me at home. He was happy, and asked if he could tell others about the news, and I agreed. He then rode off on his bicycle to inform our uncle Victor Lee. He initially did not believe that I could have been selected to the MCS. I can understand his reaction, as it was difficult for him to accept that his nephew, who is non-Malay, could become a member of the MCS (which was dominated by the British), and so soon after independence.

My appointment letter stated that I was to report for duty on August 4, 1959 at the Federal Establishment Office at the Federal House. It was a real relief and indeed a great joy to be able to look forward to a prestigious job in the MCS and to dream of a distinguished career ahead!

8.
MY CAREER BEGINS

I WAS posted to the Ministry of Health and Social Welfare as a cadet MCS officer, with the impressive title of Assistant Secretary to the Permanent Secretary of the Ministry of Health and Social Welfare. I worked under the Permanent Secretary, Tunku Mohamed Burhanuddin (later Tan Sri and Chief Secretary to the government). He was from the royal household of Negri Sembilan. He had a princely bearing and was very able, having been trained by the British civil servants in the proud Whitehall tradition.

My First Day at Work

I was given my letter of appointment to the Ministry of Health and Social Welfare by an old friend, Susheela Vethavanam, or "Twinkle" (now Datin R.S. McCoy). She was the first lady to be appointed to the administrative cadre of the civil service of the MCS, as it was respectfully then called. In those days, ladies were not admitted to the MCS. So, she served as a "temporary officer"!

At that time, most government ministries and departments were housed in the Federal House at Jalan Raja. It was a specially designed building to accommodate the major ministries, and was officially opened for *Merdeka*. It was then regarded as a magnificent and impressive edifice and centre of the government administration. The other centres of power were the Ministry of Finance ("The Treasury") at the Secretariat Building, and the Prime Minister's Department which was at Jalan Dato' Onn, next to the residence of the Prime Minister (Tunku Abdul Rahman) called "The Residency".

The Ministry of Health was also at the Federal House. So I just took the elevator to the Ministry of Health from the Establishment Office — and to my first job. My job responsibilities at the Ministry related to establishment and service matters, covering both the Health and Welfare Departments. There were several competent and experienced clerks under me on whom I could depend upon for assistance and advice. Among them were T. Tharumagnyanam (later Tan Sri), and M. Mahalingham (later Tan Sri and Deputy Minister of Health). They were both studying for their Higher School Certificate and external law examinations. I recall being liberal with their leave to study for their examinations. It is a matter of pride that they have done so well in their careers.

It was also gratifying that both my first cousins, Dr Sam Abraham (now Dato') and Dr Collin Abraham (PhD) came under the jurisdiction of the same Ministry. Sam was in the Medical Department while Collin was in the Social Welfare Department of the Ministry. Some friends called us the little Mafia!

Cadet MCS Training

Cadet MCS officers like me had our own compulsory examinations to take. We were on probation for three years or longer, until we passed several examinations. We could only be confirmed in our appointments after passing all our examinations. We had about seven papers to take. I was exempted from the Malay-language papers since I had taken Malay Studies as my subsidiary subject at the university. That left me with papers on the General Orders (GOs), the Financial General Orders (FGOs), and papers on legal subjects such as Evidence, the Criminal Procedure Code and the Land Code. I suppose we were required to acquire this legal knowledge, as some of my colleagues were posted to the districts under the State Governments where they had to act as Magistrates in the lower courts. Those of us posted to the ministries did not need to use our legal knowledge, but what we learnt from the GOs and the FGOs were indispensable in our administrative duties.

The British MCS officers were retiring and leaving the country at a rapid pace. We actually had to do the job "hands on" despite our lack of professional experience and training. The government recognised the weakness of the system and the heavy burden of responsibilities imposed on us. Thus, it organised "administrative crash courses" for us, so that we would be better prepared to perform our duties, and at the same time, to pass our examinations on time—i.e., within the probationary period of three years.

An intensive training programme was also organised at the Staff Training Centre at Port Dickson. There were about 30 of us (made up of the Federal and State Government officers). The Federal officers were, of course, all my colleagues at the university. Most of us had our own cars by then, and we drove to Port Dickson from all parts of the country.

However, I did not own a car at that time as I was reluctant to take a car loan, since I would then have to pay the monthly instalments. It would mean that I would not be able to give more of my salary to the family. Thus, I took a ride with the late Badruddin Samad (later Dato') in his brand new, green German Opel Record. The journey was long as the road to Port Dickson was narrow and winding.

The gathering at Port Dickson was a grand reunion for all of us. We were given a single room each in a long hostel-like building facing the sea. It was like old times in the university campus again. We were looking forward to a good time ahead, as the course was to last for one whole month. But alas, this was not to be. Mr Chapman and Dato' Shariff turned out to be serious hostel wardens cum lecturers. They started on a strict schedule of studies from 8.30am to 4.30pm for five days in the week, and until 1pm on Saturdays. We kept the office hours!

These lectures were heavygoing so that we had little time for recreation. We could only go for a swim after tea, or play badminton, or just go for a walk along the beach. However, on weekends we would invariably visit Seremban, or more probably, Kuala Lumpur.

Theft at the Training Centre

Early one morning, we were all awakened by the shouts of our colleagues, who woke up to find that some of their belongings were stolen! I found that my old watch had disappeared. Others had lost cash and other more expensive possessions. We compared notes and discovered that everyone of us had lost something or other. We also found that there was human excreta at several places around the hostel. The locals told us that this was the sign that the notorious *pukau* gang had struck again. Apparently, their *modus operandi* was to pass motion around their target area. Apparently, this caused the intended victims to fall into a deep sleep. During that time, they would enter the rooms with impunity, and would take whatever they wanted, without fear of being found out. They had used some kind of charm. From then on, we bolted our doors and windows and slept restlessly, as the rooms were not air-conditioned, and we could not enjoy the fresh sea breeze.

The training course was most useful. We thus returned to our jobs a month later, better prepared to face the challenges in our work and our examinations. It was altogether a rewarding experience. I got through my examinations at every sitting. This meant that I did not have to repeat any papers and therefore managed to pass my examinations during the probationary period. Soon after that, I was confirmed as an MCS officer. From then, I had to plan for the next important stage of my life.

My First Car

By now, I realised that I had to buy a car. I used to get lifts from my good friend Alwi Jantan (now Tan Sri) to and from work. However, it was sometimes inconvenient as I had to walk down to the main road, i.e., Jalan Gasing, from Jalan 5/10E, where mum and dad lived. I therefore made arrangements with Mr Anthony Gomes and his warm-hearted wife, Winnie, to take me to work. He lived a few doors away from us, and he worked at the Chartered Bank, which was just next to the Federal House, where I worked. Thus, this arrangement was certainly convenient.

My specifications for my car were quite simple. It had to be relatively low priced, medium sized, able to take the whole family, and durable. I made enquiries of my colleagues.

Several car agents then approached me. One evening, I was test driving a Ford when I passed an old classmate, Wong Tuck Peng. He was so surprised to see me driving that he followed me home. (I had only recently passed my driving test and dad did not have a car—hence Wong's surprise and interest as to what was actually happening.) Wong came home and I told him my plans to buy the car. He strongly advised me to buy a Fiat 1100 instead, on the grounds that it would better meet my requirements. After much discussion, I decided to get a Fiat 1100. It was a compact, light green car that turned out to be ideal for the family. We enjoyed it a great deal, particularly because we had not enjoyed the luxury of a family car before. Now with the car, I was able to take the family for drives. However, I was badly disappointed when I wanted to drive down to Singapore for Samala's graduation.

Attending Samala's Graduation

Samala was graduating with a Diploma in Education after an honours degree in history. I was therefore anxious to attend her convocation, and to show my new car to her. So, I asked my understanding Permanent Secretary for leave, and he readily agreed. I had only applied for the Saturday, which was actually half a working day. However, since I was heavily involved in providing the data for the Development

Budgets for the Five-Year Plan (1961-1965), my good boss, the late Toh' Muda Abdullah informed the Minister that he had given me the Saturday off. The Minister was not told why I was taking leave, as my boss thought that it was unnecessary to tell him about my fiance's convocation. The Minister was unhappy with the fact that I was taking leave when he himself was anxious about the pace of preparation of the Ministry's Five-Year Plan. So, he overruled my boss' approval of my leave!

My boss kindly suggested that I should appeal to the Minister because I was not just taking a day off, but I was going down to Singapore for my fiance's convocation. However, I did not feel like going back to the Minister. So, I stayed back in Kuala Lumpur, much to Samala's and my disappointment.

The Minister later learnt the reason why I wanted take leave, and regretted his decision to reject my application. The Minister was Dato' Ong Yoke Lin (now Tun Omar)! But to be fair to him, he was unaware of the reason for my taking leave. He was gentlemanly, and apologised to both Samala and I, when he was the ambassador in Washington, D.C. and I was the Malaysian representative on the Board of Directors of the World Bank between 1971 and 1972. I believe that the good Tun would have given me leave if I had only given him the reason. But I was too dutiful, or maybe just plain scared. I still do not know. Perhaps, it was a bit of both!

By now, Tina was going steady with Kamal whom she had got to know better at the Penang Teachers' College. Since Tina and Kamal had decided to get married in April 1962, I realised that it was time to make my own plans for wedlock. I discussed this matter with my mum and dad, who showed much understanding.

My Friends and the Abraham Cousins
My good old friend from school days at the Victoria Institution, T. Ananda Krishnan (now a business tycoon) drove me down to Singapore in his fast, red sports car. We chatted and joked all the way. It was my last carefree ride as a bachelor.

Among the many issues we discussed were our future plans. I was in the civil service, and Ananda was in the commercial world at the old British company called Guthries. While I mentioned that I was all set to advance my career in the civil service, Ananda clearly indicated that he was keen on getting into big business. Besides his exhilarating company and adventurous driving style, I naturally got more elated as we whizzed past every milestone, since I was getting nearer to Singapore, closer to Samala and to our wedding!

We arrived at the house of our old friend, S.T. Ratnam, in Singapore. S.T. is a close friend of Collin Abraham, and I actually got to know him well through Collin. S.T. was one of the first locals to get into the top echelons of the Singapore Civil Service. His elder brother, Dr S.S. Ratnam (later Professor of Obstetrics and Gynaecology) had a big government bungalow at the Kandang Kerbau Hospital in Singapore. He generously made his house available to all the Abraham cousins, to Ananda, and to me. In many ways, it was also a good reunion among old friends.

Since it was on the eve of my wedding, it was unanimously decided that they would organise a bachelor's stag party for me. I was not much of a drinker then (or even now for that matter.) I did not know how to handle myself with the heavy drinking. But I felt that I wanted to let myself go. The result was that I broke down and felt sick.

I recall Sam, Collin and Leslie (the Abraham brothers) comforting me. They were like brothers to me, as I did not have any. They have always been close to me. Our destinies have intertwined at many stages in our lives. We had grown up together in Sungei Buloh, and were the earliest relatives and friends that I could remember. They knew my drinking capacity and limitations, and put me to bed.

The Wedding Day

The next day was my wedding day, but I got up with a heavy head. I took some Alkaseltzer pills for my bad hangover, had a good cold shower, and got ready to fetch Samala to go to the Registry of Marriages.

Samala looked beautiful in her short white veil and her green *saree*. Her thick black hair was set in an elegant bun, making her look dignified and poised. I had made a new suit, and wore it with comfort and some pride as it was my first suit. The wedding registration went off smoothly. After the formalities, we all went to Samala's place for lunch. It was a small house, and so we took turns to sit on the floor, as was the custom, to eat the excellent home-cooked curries from the neatly laid-out banana leaves.

In the evening, we were driven in Sam's new car to St Patrick's school in Katong for the reception. My sisters and my late cousin,

Janet Abraham, had rallied together and decorated the school hall with flowers (generously provided by our good friend S.T. Ratnam). Practically all my close relatives from Malaya were there to give their loving support. Both Samala and I felt grateful and blessed. I made my speech in a relaxed and jocular fashion. I remember inviting the guests to visit us in Kuala Lumpur, but that they should give us about a month's grace period, i.e., after our honeymoon!

The next morning, we all set off early for Kuala Lumpur. On the way back, we stopped for lunch at uncle Barr's and aunt Muriel's friend's home, Mr Nadarajah's place at Segamat. It was a pleasant lunch for which a goat had been slaughtered to feed the large family clan. Having recharged ourselves, we pushed on to Kuala Lumpur, which we reached late in the evening, tired but happy. We spent the next day at my parent's place in Petaling Jaya, and then we drove off for our honeymoon in Penang.

Our Honeymoon

It was a long but relaxing journey to Penang. Time was on our hands, as we were booked to check in late in the evening the next day, at a government bungalow on Penang Hill. We stayed at aunt Violy's house on the way. Aunt and uncle Francis made us feel very comfortable, and we set off for Penang early the next morning full of great expectations. The late Dato' Jegathesan was then the state financial officer, and he kindly agreed to book me a big beautiful government bungalow called *The Edgecliff*. We parked our car at the base of the Penang Hill, and took the railcar up to *The Edgecliff*. It was a very spacious house at the edge of the hill with a wonderful view of Penang City and the wide-open sea. The view at night was particularly breathtaking, with the whole city lit up below us. But we had little time for views up there. Instead, we had a lovely time on our honeymoon. The meals were very good. The walks around Penang Hill were invigorating. It was really so relaxed, quiet, peaceful and fulfilling. How wonderful it would be if life is one long honeymoon!

But all good things must come to an end. After a week, we drove back to Kuala Lumpur. On our way, we stopped at Kamal's place at Taiping. Uncle and aunt Chinniah, and everyone at home were most hospitable. We had a sumptuous lunch. Aunt Chinniah was indeed a great chef and very warm.

The road from Taiping to Ipoh was quite tedious. Although it was only about 40 miles, it took about 90 minutes. The road was narrow, winding and slippery. However, my Fiat 1100 had good road holding, and did not let me down. We got into Ipoh and headed straight for aunt Violy's house at Pearl Gardens in Fair Park. Unfortunately, no one was at home!

It was getting late. We could either look out for a decent hotel (which were few in those days), or think of a friend whom we could stay with for the night. Samala and I thought hard.

In those days, we had only one university for Malaya and Singapore. Therefore, we as alumni of the University Malaya, had good friends all over the country. It was not long before we recalled that Yang Amri (now Dato') and Putih Rahimi were married and living in Ipoh. We traced him through the telephone directory, and rang them up. He had a large government house as the Assistant State Secretary and they were delighted to have us stay the night with them. We had a long chat with our university colleagues, a good dinner, and a restful night. The next morning, bright and early, we set off for Kuala Lumpur and our new life.

The spontaneous hospitality that Amri and Putih showed us was typical of the times. We were a closely-knit group at the University of Malaya in Singapore. There were no racial hang-ups. We did not think of each other as Malays, Chinese, Indians, or Ibans—but just as Malayans. Race, religion, and culture did not come between us in our strong bonds of friendship. It is unfortunately somewhat different today!

Our Old House at Kampar

We had an easy drive to Kuala Lumpur. On the way from Ipoh, I showed Samala our old house at Kampar. It brought back old memories. I walked round the wooden house that was built on stumpy concrete columns. After *Merdeka*, the *penghulus* or village heads were promoted and given bigger roles in community development. So, a *penghulu* now stayed at our former house. He had kept the place clean. The old mango tree that I used to climb and spend time watching the birds was still there, but it somehow looked much smaller.

As I gazed at the high hills behind, I recalled going behind the house and hiking around the foothills looking for relics left by the Japanese military. I had found dented helmets and broken gun pieces. The story went that the Japanese military police used to shoot captured anti-Japanese Malayans and the British jungle fighters, up in those foothills. But I never found the skulls and bones that I sought to find! However, the Battle for Kampar was fought there.

There is now a new hospital at the foothills. The old hospital near the railway station was demolished as it was found to be sitting on rich deposits of tin ore. It was worth building a new hospital with some of the high profits obtained from tin-mining in those days. That must have been one of the earliest privatisation projects!

We left Kampar on our way to Kuala Lumpur. When we were approaching Bidor, I decided to give Samala a treat of the famous "duck mee" at a coffeeshop in this small town. I do not know of any other place in Malaysia that serves duck noodles the way they do in Bidor. It is simply delicious even if you do not care to dine on duck!

Having tucked in on duck meat, we drove onto Tanjung Malim. You had to pass through the Selangor-Perak border town of Tanjung Malim in those days. But it was worth passing through Tanjung Malim. Samala had not enjoyed the duck noodles as I did. So she was a little hungry and liked the idea of stopping again for the good coffee and tasty currypuffs at Tanjung Malim.

It was only about 50 miles to Kuala Lumpur, but it took us nearly two hours. Driving along the narrow, winding roads of the Kanching Pass and through Templer's Park took a long while. It would definitely have been longer for any driver who had to follow a long and laden lorry at that time!

Soon, however, we saw the low skyline of Kuala Lumpur and we were grateful that we were then reaching home safe and sound. It was altogether a lovely drive, but we were ready for a cold shower and a good rest. Mum, dad and my sisters were all happy to welcome us back home, as the newly married couple.

9.
SETTLING DOWN IN THE EARLY YEARS
(1961-1965)

AFTER our honeymoon we stayed at my parents' home for several weeks. It was good that we did so, as my family and Samala got to know each other better. We stayed in the room which I occupied as a bachelor, while we looked for a house of our own.

At that time, the government would either provide a housing allowance of $250, or a government house. Since I was on the long waiting list, I opted to rent a house. We decided to stay near my parents, since that would be mutually beneficial—they would not feel that I had left them, and we could visit them often to keep close.

Fortunately, we found a nice little bungalow at Jalan Chantek in Petaling Jaya, less than a mile from mum and dad. The landlord, a retired Punjabi government clerk, obviously knew the government regulations, as he charged me exactly my rental eligibility, i.e., $250 per month. (For that amount, one could only get a room today!)

I recall that he would come to the house at about 6pm on the last day of every month to collect his rental. He would knock on the front door soon after I had changed my clothes for tea. I suspected that he laid in wait in some neighbour's house, watching my movements. Otherwise, there was no reason for his timing to be so uncannily precise! His style was irritating, particularly due to the fact that he always made a big fuss over expenses incurred for repairs. One day, I got so annoyed with his bad attitude that I told him that his one dollar was as large as a "bullock-cart wheel"! After that remark, he was more casual about his rental collections!

It was a friendly neighbourhood. Our immediate neighbour was Baharuddin Musa (now Dato'). Baha was a university mate of ours, and we got on well. Often, we would have mutual friends visiting either of us. When they were told who our neighbours were, they would pop over to the neighbours' house as well.

That was the close neighbourliness that we enjoyed at that time. Now, the houses of the middle and upper-middle classes are bigger and separated by larger compounds, so much so that we have to practically fix appointments before visiting each other.

Samala's Career in Kuala Lumpur
Samala had taught in the Anglo-Chinese School in Singapore for about two years after graduating. She wanted to carry on teaching. Every government school was on the Unified Teachers' Scheme, and was allowed to hire their own teachers. So, I advised Samala to look up the telephone directory and ring up any school of her choice, to ask if there were vacancies. Then, I would help by following up with the Ministry of Education.

Samala got in touch with Convent Bukit Nanas (CBN) which offered her a place straight away. She taught history, English, and music, and she liked the job. That was her first experience teaching in a girls' school, and working with the dedicated and kind-hearted nuns. She enjoyed the culture and environment of the Catholic school.

Samala taught at CBN for practically her whole career. Hundreds of students passed through her, among them are some very prominent personalities today. Many VIPs sent their children to CBN, since it was a "designated" school. Good schools like CBN, which previously had disproportionately more Chinese and Indian students, were designated so that more *bumiputera* students could be posted to these schools, since the government wanted to have better racial balance.

Samala's teaching career is best remembered for the contribution she made to music and the CBN Choir! As the choir mistress, she sent her choir for many interschool choir competitions at state and national levels, and won many prizes. That is why I think she is fondly associated with singing by many of her past students.

But without bias, it is fair for me to say that, with her professionally trained voice, she was also a well-known singer. She took part in a Royal Command Performance for the King and the Queen. During the course of her singing career, Samala has sung over Radio Malaya, TV Malaysia, and has taken part in several public concerts. Most of her singing, however, has been with the Wesley Church choir. I, of course, do not take part but would encourage her by sitting comfortably and enjoying it all!

Samala's salary helped to supplement my starting salary which was about $700 per month. Together, we were able to rent a house, maintain the car, send some money to Samala's parents and my parents, keep our faithful old servant, and throw parties. Even then, we still could save some money! This shows how much more the value of our currency was in those days.

It was fun furnishing our house. We bought many of our kitchen utensils from the inexpensive and colourful night market or *pasar malam*, in Petaling Jaya. Marketing for fresh food like vegetables, meat and provisions, was also very convenient at the big wet market in Petaling Jaya. There was plenty of parking space, and driving was a pleasure, with no traffic jams at all, but it is not so today.

My First Job

At the Ministry of Health, I worked under Mr G. Edmunds, an expatriate British officer from the Colonial Office in London. He was in charge of the financial matters in the Ministry. I was to assist him, and at the same time get some experience in financial administration. This background was supposed to help me pass my examinations in Financial General Orders, before I could be confirmed after a minimum of three years of probation.

Mr Edmunds was to be my mentor. However, he was in no mood to teach. He was more interested in preparing to leave the country on the liberal "Malayanisation terms". He therefore hardly spent any time in the office. He was busy arranging for his passage back to England.

As part of the deal for independence, the British government persuaded the late Tunku Abdul Rahman, the then Chief Minister, to give generous compensation to the British civil servants who would gradually leave the country. Many of them were still quite young, and they were therefore compensated for the years they would forego in their service in Malaya. The Malayan civil servants had little say in the formulation of the liberal compensation, as the British colonial officers headed the Establishment Office and the Treasury. So, pretty packages were conveniently carved for themselves by themselves! That was the Colonial Government!

The Malayan political leaders were in no mood to argue with these British officers. They had to rely on them to prepare their briefs for the *Merdeka* negotiations with Whitehall in London. The priority was naturally to get independence first. Furthermore, it was important to earn goodwill from the British, so as to be able to part with peace and harmony, on both sides.

However, this liberal Malayanisation policy, although costly, nevertheless earned great dividends in the longer-term relations with Britain, and within the Commonwealth of Nations. Tunku Abdul Rahman had that magnanimity and foresight that paid off handsomely in later years.

Merely six years after independence, we were attacked by Indonesia in what was known as President Sukarno's "Confrontation" over the formation of "Malaysia"! I believe that if we had treated the British civil servants badly, like some other British colonies did, we would not have received the strong support that we had from the British. They readily responded to Malaysia's call for help to resist Sukarno's Confrontation and aggression against Malaysia. Furthermore, the British also persuaded some of the other Commonwealth countries to join our own troops in the war against Sukarno's soldiers. They came from Australia, Fiji, Nepal and New Zealand. Without the help of the Commonwealth forces we may not have been able to overcome the confrontation so soon or at all!

One day, Edmunds called me to his office. I thought it was about my work except that he looked too chirpy. He asked me to accompany him to the travel agents as he was going to book his air tickets back to the United Kingdom for good. He drove me in his Rover, and hinted that he wanted to sell it to me although it was beyond my income capacity. (He was responsible for approving my car loan!) We went to the Mansfield's Travel office, which was then at Campbell Road.

As we approached the entrance to the office, he stopped at the door and looked hard at me. I was not sure what he wanted. However, I soon sensed that he wanted me to open the door for him! I could not understand why he wanted me to do so—particularly since he was ahead of me. But the staff at the counter was waiting and watching. I thought I should break the stalemate and avoid any embarrassment. So, I stepped forward and opened the door!

He then bounced into the office with a big broad smile! He felt, I suppose, that he had made a point. He was the white boss and I was his junior Malayan officer. I never forgot that incident. It showed me how superior these expatriates thought they were. That was their colonial arrogance, which many still show!

Tina and Kamal Marry
In April 1962, my sister Tina married Kamal. They had been studying together at the Teachers' Training College in Penang, and then in Kota Bharu. I was grateful that they had decided to marry soon after our marriage. If not, it would have remained a prick on my conscience because I had married ahead of them!

Tina was meticulous, and I was impressed with her attention to detail in organising her wedding. She had a beautiful wedding. We drove in the bridal car to the Wesley Church in Kuala Lumpur. There was a "shower of blessings" at about 3.30pm, but then it cleared. Dad was in the car too, and we found ourselves early for the church service. Dad suggested that we park and wait at the Merdeka Stadium car park near the church, so that we would be able to arrive in church right on time.

The church was crowded with the members of the larger Lee family, and Kamal's family. As dad led the lovely bride down the aisle, I realised how worthwhile it was to have taken so much trouble to plan the wedding so carefully. The church looked all dressed up with the tasteful floral decorations arranged by our sisters, Angie, Julie and Georgie. The whole atmosphere was enchanting. Tina and Kamal made a handsome couple. The gratitude and happiness showed so clearly on the faces of our mum and dad. They actually reflected the joy of both families who were present to give their blessings.

From the Wesley Church, all of us adjourned to the Eastern Hotel where the wedding reception was held. Mum had made the wedding cake, while individual pieces were wrapped with the help of her sisters and some other members of the family. She also made her special grape juice punch, which was prepared in the hotel before the wedding. I really do not know how she had so much energy to do so much, but obviously it was all a labour of love for her. Dad too played his part well. He was always a man of few words, and so his speech was to the point and peppered with his special brand of dry humour. The whole reception went off very well indeed.

There were very few grand hotels in those days. One popular venue for holding wedding receptions was the Eastern Hotel in Campbell Road in Kuala Lumpur. It was a lovely, sprawling building of pre-war vintage architecture, with perhaps the largest banquet hall in town at that time. There was ample parking space, as the hotel was situated in the centre of extensive grounds and greenery. (Unfortunately, avaricious developers in the name of progress demolished that stately hotel.)

Joining the Treasury

After I had been confirmed, the Federal Establishment Office reviewed my next posting. At that time also, the World Bank was working on the Malayan Five-Year Plan (1961-1965). They needed staff with degrees in economics to work on the collation and analysis of socioeconomic data.

I recall that there were two senior economists from the World Bank who were attached to the Economic Planning Unit (EPU) in the Prime Minister's department to help us prepare the Second Malayan Plan. They were Dr Gilmartin and Dr Gulhati, and both of them were very diligent and knowledgeable. Oscar Spencer, a British expatriate, was the head of the EPU. Thong Yaw Hong (now Tan Sri) was the deputy at the EPU. Thong was highly motivated and close to the late Tun Abdul Razak, the then-Deputy Prime Minister.

The Treasury had just started a small section for financial planning under Malek Merican (now Dato'). Malek was an impressive Cambridge "blue", and a very able and dedicated officer. He was determined to build a strong economic research counterpart to the EPU in the Treasury. The Treasury was short-handed, and asked for me to be attached to the World Bank team at the Treasury, on a temporary basis! I think both the Treasury and the World Bank officials were trying me out. They did not want to risk getting me to the Treasury on a permanent basis! I understand that my boss at the Ministry of Health was also reluctant to let me go. There were insufficient local MCS officers in those days, especially with the exodus of the British expatriate officers.

In any case, I did my best. I had excellent guidance from Dato' Malek, the World Bank officials, and also from Tan Sri Thong. It was therefore not difficult to meet the exacting standards expected of me. Consequently, the Treasury made a strong bid for me and despite the objections from the Ministry of Health, the Federal Establishment Office posted me to the Treasury.

That transfer changed my whole career in the government service. I served in the Treasury for almost my whole career. I must be still holding the record for having worked in the Treasury continuously for 27 years! I only had a short break of two years when I was posted to the World Bank as an Alternate Director on its Board of Directors—but then, I was actually seconded from the Treasury itself. So technically, I was nevertheless, still a Treasury officer. Despite my different assignments in later life, I still regarded myself, first and foremost, as a Treasury officer!

My initial posting in the Treasury was to the Administration Division, as an Assistant Secretary. That was the first level in the MCS. The head of the Division or the Under-Secretary, was the late Mr William Fernando. He was one of the first non-Malay Malayans to be admitted to the MCS. He was able, tough, and a strong disciplinarian. He was the ideal kind of Treasury officer—fair and firm, and very professional in his work and conduct. He was my model and I learnt a lot from him.

I had to deal with staff and personnel matters, the rates of fees charged by the government, as well as government tenders and contracts. As such, I represented the Treasury on several Tender Boards of ministries and government departments. It was a great learning process as decisions had to be made on behalf of the Treasury. It was a big responsibility for a young officer to have to deal with multimillion-dollar contracts, but that was the order of the day.

The British MCS officers had it much easier previously. They spent their initial three years of cadetship just studying for the law examinations, the General Orders, and the Financial General Orders. They were also posted on attachment to District Offices where they neither did much work nor shouldered much responsibility. They had a good time indeed! It was a kind of paid holiday for them. But we were required to sit for the same examinations and take on full administrative responsibilities from the very beginning. We were posted not only to District Offices as full-fledged Assistant District Officers, but also as Assistant State Secretaries in the State Secretariats of the State Governments, and as Assistant Secretaries in the Federal Government ministries, as I was. We were thrown in at the deep end, and had to swim or sink, though most of us swam and survived.

The Challenge Serving in the MCS

It was also a great challenge for all of us. Here we were—fresh young graduates who were given heavy responsibilities and told to prepare ourselves to take over from our colonial masters! We felt a great sense of excitement and destiny. There was a wonderful sense of humility and yet pride in trying our best to live up to the expectations of our communities, our people and indeed our newly independent country. Our pride and our duty were to serve God, king and country! I hope the same aspiration prevails, even today!

However, the situation is quite different today. When my generation joined the civil service, there was hardly any private sector to talk about. The only really large corporations and conglomerates were the British agencies and trading houses, like the old British companies such as Sime Darby, Guthrie, Whiteaways and Robinson! There was actually no big local company. So, Malaysian graduates had nowhere to go except the government service.

However, the Government Service was relatively attractive then. It was permanent and also pensionable! After all, people and especially parents remembered the deep world depression of the late 1930s, and the severe unemployment. They remembered the terrible times suffered especially by those who were self-employed, as well as those who worked for the private sector. Thus, many parents and grandparents discouraged their children and grandchildren from joining the business sector.

Furthermore, there was this pride in having your child serve in the higher ranks of the civil service or in the professions where you could be seen to have taken over the reins from the white man and the former colonial rulers. Also, the career prospects in the civil service were comparatively more attractive than the private sector. Thus, the best and brightest formed the top echelon of the civil service! It is not the same now!

Non-Attractiveness of the Public Service

Today, the situation is quite the reverse. The private sector is far more attractive than the government service in practically all aspects. The pay and the perquisites are even better, and the security of tenure is well secured by the revised labour laws of the country after independence. Even the prestige of working in the government has declined considerably with the politicians and even businessmen often calling the shots, especially under the concept of "Malaysia Incorporated".

So, why would bright young graduates, or for that matter, anyone, be motivated to join the civil service? A true test would be to ask the children of civil servants whether they would like to follow in the footsteps of their parents! Only those who are truly dedicated to serve the country, or those who cannot find suitable employment in the private sector will want to join the civil service today! Of course, there is another group that opts for the civil service, because they think that life will be less demanding and more comfortable with the government. But that would be mostly at the lower levels of the civil service, such as counter clerks.

Personally, I think that our government is making a grave mistake in not attracting the best brains into the civil service. Only time will tell! Today, we are definitely not getting the best people into the civil service as we did in the past. As a result, the standards in the public services will deteriorate—if they have not already declined.

The consequences to the government and the country can be quite serious! The public service, especially the elitist civil servants such as the "Pegawai Pentadbiran dan Diplomatik" (i.e., the former MCS officers), and the professional officers like the doctors, engineers, lawyers, academics at the universities, and even schoolteachers, will generally be second rate, or the less capable group. How will they be able to cope effectively with the increasingly competent bureaucracy in the private sector? Worse still, how will they be able to deal competently with the more sophisticated civil servants in international negotiations in the global village under the new world order or globalisation?

Even at home, the public will suffer if the quality of the public services declines and continues to drop further. The lower levels of the government are already weak. Counter services and general administrative services to the public are already quite poor.

So, it is not surprising if these poor standards deteriorate further, if the government does not act soon enough to improve the attractiveness of joining and staying in the public service. The decline would be disastrous, and could even adversely jeopardise the achievement of Vision 2020 on time.

The next generation would lose out. If we take a generation to mean about 20-25 years, then it will be the babies that are born around this time. If we take the average life span at about 70 years, then those born after 1950 would live to see the dawn of the year 2020. By then, most of my generation or contemporaries would have gone for good! Those in their 60s now would by then be in their late 80s, and God willing, that would not happen to most of us. So it is now appropriate to upgrade the public services for the next generation. Otherwise, Malaysia and our children and grandchildren will lose out.

Our First Child

As soon as Samala's mother heard that Samala had conceived, she enthusiastically came up to visit us with Appoo, Samala's father. It was comforting and convenient to have Samala's parents with us. "Mamee", as I called her, was a great cook and very caring, while Appoo was always kind and gentle with a quiet dignity of his own. We enjoyed their stay with us. It was also very reassuring for Samala.

We were also lucky to have an elderly servant whom we called Parti (meaning "granny" in Tamil). She was about 60 years old and was wiry, diligent, and loyal. She proved to be a real asset in looking after all our three sons when they were growing up from infancy. Those types of servants were a class of their own. They were inexpensive and yet committed. They are indeed a rare commodity today where it is so difficult to even get local servants. (Many of them are imported from Indonesia and the Philippines at high cost — and lots of hassles!)

Samala carried on driving to school. She would drop me at the Petaling Jaya Railway Station near the National Union of Plantation Workers (NUPW). I would take the train right up to the end of the railway line, beyond the Kuala Lumpur Railway Station and the old Bank Rakyat building near the Secretariat, or Sultan Abdul Samad building which housed the Treasury. It was a pleasant ride, and was so convenient. Then, she would take the car to school and fetch me after work at the railway station in the evening in Petaling Jaya.

As we approached the birth of the baby, I was told that I had to attend my first international conference in Manila. I was of two minds. It would be my first visit overseas on government duty. But then I might not be around for the birth of our first child. However, we realised it would be quite odd to excuse myself from official duty on the flimsy grounds that my wife was expecting a baby, unless she was suffering from some serious health problem. Since Samala was perfectly well, I left for the Economic Conference for Asia and the Far East (ECAFE) in the Philippines.

It was in March 1963, and the conference was scheduled to last for a week. It was to end just after the baby was due to be born! The timing was bad for me because I might miss the baby's birth. I was therefore quite uneasy at Manila, expecting news from home any time, and hoping and praying that all would be well.

The conference went on successfully and was nearing its end — but I had still not received news from home. On my return, I was expecting to receive the good news at the airport, but learnt that the baby had not been born. Anyway, I had this gratifying thought that it was good that the baby was overdue. It was as if the baby was waiting for me to return home before coming out to the world to welcome his daddy home!

A few days after my return, Samala went into labour and the nurse advised me to go home as it would take some time for the baby to be born.

I took her advice. We did not have a phone at our place; so I arranged for the hospital to contact dear uncle Eddie (deceased) as soon as there were some definite signs that the baby was on the way.

At about 5am the next day, the loud banging on the grill gate awakened me. (Electric doorbells were practically non-existent in those days.) I was sound asleep and poor uncle Eddie had to shout loud and long to wake me up. I fumbled for the switch in the dark with anxiety, recognising the voice. I opened the front door and saw uncle Eddie grinning widely. He gave me a hug and announced with tears of joy that both Samala and the baby were fine. It was a boy!

I thanked God for his great gift and blessings. Soon after sunrise, I rushed to give the good news to mum, dad, and my sisters, who lived just down the road. They were exhilarated, and all of us went to the hospital. Samala was exhausted but so happy and relieved that the de-livery was smooth.

We named our first-born Ravindran Navaratnam. Ravi was a big and beautiful baby. He was long and pinkish, with a puckish smile! Most important, we thanked God that he was a normal, healthy and heavy baby (weighing 8lb and 4oz). It was sheer delight to take him home after a few days.

Ravi brought us good luck. As soon as he was born, I was informed that I had earned enough points to qualify for a government house! The period of waiting for government housing was also steadily getting shorter as the British expatriate officers were now leaving the country at a faster pace. I was told that I could choose from a few houses that were falling vacant. Samala and I visited several empty houses. But we fell in love with a lovely, big bungalow at 2623 Jalan Damansara on Federal Hill and near the Lake Gardens. It had a large garden with lots of trees, and a whole tribe of monkeys! The house was beautifully set in a small valley, and had a rather picturesque air about it. We chose it and never regretted our decision.

Our early married life was spent there, and all our three children spent the first few years of their lives in that idyllic home. It is still there although many other houses were knocked down to build Prime Minister Dr Mahathir Mohamad's residence in Kuala Lumpur.

The Indonesian Confrontation

Malaysia was established on September 16, 1963. There had been a lot of consultations going on among the British, Malayan, Brunei, Sabah, Sarawak and Singapore governments on how to work out the constitutional arrangements to form Malaysia.

In the process, President Sukarno of Indonesia got very upset and did his best to sabotage the formation of Malaysia. The Cobbold Com-mission was appointed with international representation, to find out if the people of these territories actually and genuinely wanted to gain independence from the British through the formation of Malaysia. Wisma Putra, Malaysia's foreign office, was primarily involved in the consultations and negotiations to form Malaysia. However, we in the Treasury were also involved, in working out all the financial implications of these constitutional arrangements.

Moreover, Sukarno did not confine his opposition to mere rhetoric — he actually declared war in what he termed euphemistically as a "Confrontation". This meant that a large part of our budget expenditure had to be allocated for security and defence. Although the British helped militarily and financially, the Malaysian government had to bear the brunt of the battle to protect Malaysia from the Indonesian attacks.

However, the Indonesians did not make much headway either in the international diplomatic arena, or on the military front. After about two years of confrontation, the Indonesians under Sukarno were persuaded to cease hostilities. International opinion and the United Nation's put pressure on Sukarno to withdraw from his adventurous confrontation. Thus, the long standing traditional relations and goodwill between Indonesia and Malaysia soon normalised.

Malaysia Celebrations

Malaysia celebrated its birth and victory over the Indonesian confrontation in September 1965 in grand style. As in all major issues in Malaysia, the Treasury has a significant say in anything that has financial implications. And there is hardly anything of significance that does not have financial implications! Thus, it had to be involved in allocating funds for the planning and organisation of the celebrations.

The cabinet formed a national committee to oversee the Malaysia celebrations. The Prime Minister was the chairman while the Minister of Finance, Tun Tan Siew Sin was appointed as a member of the committee and chairman of the finance committee. The secretary to the Treasury was a member of both these high-powered committees, and I was appointed as his alternate representative. This virtually meant that I attended all the meetings with the permanent secretary himself. For those meetings that he could not attend, I had to be there all by myself as the sole Treasury representative.

It was not until this experience that I realised that a Treasury representative had special authority and power that was out of proportion to the representative's own personal status and standing in the hierarchy of the civil service. I could practically block and overrule decisions that were not in accordance with prudent policies of financial management. Of course, I had to be fair, reasonable, and also to be careful not to get carried away and abuse the power and responsibility entrusted to me. That learning experience was of tremendous value to me at that time, and served me well all through my career.

I had to be flexible and practical as the situation required. For instance, it was important that we had good weather during the celebrations. The organising committee therefore requested that we hire a *bomoh* or medicine man to pray for the absence of rain. But how was I to account for that kind of expenditure in the Budget? Dato' Shariff, the former deputy of the Port Dickson Training Centre, was the chairman of the organising committee. He advised that if the weather was good, there would be no problem, but if it turned out to be bad, then people would ask why we did not get a *bomoh*. Then I could not possibly defend myself by saying that the Treasury's regulations did not provide for hiring *bomohs*. So, we had to be innovative and we found a way out. We hired the *bomoh* at government expense under the title of "protocol officer"! We all felt justified, as it did not rain for a few days during the celebrations. But towards the end of the celebrations, it rained. When the *bomoh* was asked to explain what had gone wrong, he promptly but sadly explained that the Indonesian government had hired a *bomoh* who was more powerful than him. So, it appeared that we had won the "war of confrontation" with Indonesia, but lost the "war of the *bomohs*"!

Our Second Child

We decided to have a playmate for Ravi as we did not want too big an age gap between our children. So, about a year after Ravi was born, Samala began to expect our second child. Given our first experience, we were a bit more confident and relaxed, less anxious and less uncertain. This time I was determined to be at the hospital when the baby was born. Samala went for her check-ups to the same new maternity unit at the General Hospital. As soon as Samala went into labour, I rushed to the hospital. Mum and Samala's mother came along.

We did not have to wait long. Soon, the nurse came out to give us the good tidings that we were blessed—with another baby boy! The nurse brought the baby for us to see. He was big and strong with a thick set of hair! We were grateful to God for a healthy baby, and for

Samala's safe and easy delivery. We named the newborn Nahendran Navaratnam.

Indran brought me good luck, too. I was now being considered for promotion. This time it was a big promotion—from Time Scale to Superscale "H". The salary was almost twice my basic pay at $1,360 per month! With all the allowances, my salary went up to about $1,500 per month, which went a long way in those days.

I became the Principal Assistant Secretary to the Treasury. It was a great feeling and a real sense of achievement. We were also very lucky. Normally, this promotion would have taken longer. But with the rapid exodus of the British officers, the Malayan officers took over the senior positions faster. I had mine in about five years since I started work. Today, it takes at least 10 years to reach that stage. No wonder there is so much frustration in the civil service today.

First Trip to London

My promotion was preceded by more training. The British provided a training scheme for senior civil servants in the Commonwealth, the colonies, and some other developing countries. I had been confirmed, and was now considered suitable for more advanced training in preparation for higher responsibilities. The British had the Royal Institute for Public Administration in London like our government's training institute at Intan.

I was selected from Malaya and was told to leave for the winter programme at the end of 1964. It was my first trip to the United Kingdom, and I was excited at the prospects of going so far overseas, especially by plane. I had never travelled so far before. I recall the long journey with stops at Delhi, Dubai, and Frankfurt. Finally, I reached London! I was quite exhausted after an almost 20-hour flight.

I was obviously in a daze when the plane landed and I walked down the steps from the aircraft. It was cold and I got a fright when I suddenly felt that I was exhaling "smoke" from my mouth. Actually, it was vapour from my breath against the cold of the autumn morning! But I had not been to a cold, temperate country before, and hence my disorientation and surprise.

My next surprise came soon afterwards. While walking along the tarmac to the terminal building at Heathrow Airport, I was genuinely surprised to see white men digging drains! My colonial childhood had not prepared me to see Englishmen doing menial work. I had associated the white man with power, authority and wealth. My first immediate boss was also British, so my mind could not accept that white men could be labourers as well! It was only then that I realised what tricks colonialism could play on the mind. Indeed, there is still this colonial mentality among many people in the countries of the South.

An elderly British ex-MCS officer, Mr Heasman headed the section dealing with the trainees from the Third World at the Royal Institute of Public Administration in London. There were senior officials from Tanzania, Ghana, Nigeria, Thailand, Jordan and Sri Lanka in a class of around 30. Our lecturers were mostly senior British civil servants and professionals from the business sector in the city of London.

I found the course useful. Obviously, our Malaysian standards were high. I participated actively, and enjoyed it. The course covered subjects on fiscal policies, monetary issues, as well as general management problems and solutions. It was a very practical course, which was relevant to my work in the Treasury.

I shared a room at 155 Paddington Gardens with the participant from Sri Lanka. He was somewhat careful if not stingy with his small foreign exchange allowance. So, I found myself putting shillings in the electric heater most of the time during those cold nights in winter. Each time I hinted that it was his turn to put a coin into the heater, he would say that he was not feeling cold. In actual fact, he was shivering with cold in his bed. I could not stand it and since I could afford it, I gave in and put in the coins so that the room could be warmer. After that he too enjoyed a good sleep, but at my expense!

We had a two-week vacation for Christmas in 1964. Since this was a wonderful opportunity to see Europe for the first time, I made plans to utilise some of the available mileage on my air ticket to visit Paris, Copenhagen, and Berlin. It was a lovely experience altogether. I visited and enjoyed Montmartre, the Moulin Rouge, the Latin Quarter in Paris, and the Tivoli, as well as the Walking Street in Copenhagen, where I was surprised at the openness to pornography. I particularly enjoyed visiting the Berlin Wall, which was the centre of so much international political and security attention in those days.

Christmas Day in 1964 was spent in Berlin. However, I never felt more miserable on that cold, wet, snowing, white Christmas day. I had read in the newspaper about an invitation to a Christmas party for foreigners and all those away from home. I was happy to be able to celebrate Christmas away from home at this prayer meeting, and to have dinner at the YMCA! When I arrived at the YMCA, I found several African students and many wayward-looking Berliners. I realised then that they were stragglers who had no home, unlike me who was just away from home. The prayer also sounded so sorrowful as the priest prayed for "lost souls without homes". The Christmas dinner was as depressing. They served some strands of meat with lots of potatoes, and a dried-up piece of cake as the Christmas pudding.

I really felt lost and lonely, away from Samala, my sons, mum, dad, and my sisters. It was then that I realised how much family meant to me. I also learnt that I should in future check on who would be attending a function before I responded to any invitation. That was a good lesson for me. In fact, I felt much better and recovered after I left the "party"! That was the worst Christmas I ever had.

I went back to London, and at Waterloo station, I did a little recording in a kiosk for Samala, Ravi and Indran. I sang Christmas carols and sent loving messages to them. I then posted the recording home and felt good.

After the three-month course, I returned home via Cairo. It was wonderful to visit the Pyramids and to take a boat ride along the Nile. I stayed at the 25-storey Cairo Hilton at the airline's expense. From my balcony, I could view the vast desert below and up to the horizon ahead. It was awe-inspiring. I breathed in the cool evening desert air deeply. At night, however, I had a real problem. The minute dust particles of the desert had got into my lungs (or for whatever the cause, I do not really know), and I developed serious breathing difficulties. I could not sleep and kept gasping for breath. I even felt pressure on my throat and chest, and wondered whether the room was haunted!

The episode lasted for a long while, but after I had prayed, I felt less and less pressure. I then slowly fell into a deep sleep. I was exhausted the next morning, but was grateful and relieved to leave the hotel for the airport. When I complained to the hotel cashier that the room was suffocating, he confessed quietly that he thought the room was haunted by some ancient Egyptian spirit from the Pyramids across the desert! I was glad to go home.

As was the practice then, there was a large crowd to meet me at the Kuala Lumpur airport as travelling by air was still a relative novelty at that time. It was such a joy to see Ravi and Indran, and to find that they had changed so much. I was grateful to Samala for staying at home dutifully to look after them with so much loving care while I travelled abroad.

Throughout my career in the government service, I travelled extensively, and the arrangement where she faithfully stayed at home with the children had become quite typical. Often, even if there was a chance to accompany me, she still chose to stay at home with the children. I have always been grateful to her for this.

Singapore's Separation in 1965

Soon after I returned home, I sensed serious political and racial tensions in the air. The Malaysian Federation including Singapore lasted only for about two years—from 1963 to 1965! During the short time when Singapore was part of Malaysia, the sense of harmony and stability was constantly threatened to the point of disruption and even implosion.

Mr Lee Kuan Yew, the Chief Minister of Singapore led his campaign of "Malaysian Malaysia". He was very able, articulate, and aggressive in his substance and style. He spread his call for more equal rights for all races. The Chinese, Indians, and other minority races were excited by this "battle cry" for equality in this new concept of 'Malaysian Malaysia'. This meant that all Malaysians would have the same rights and privileges. This also implied that the "special position of the Malays" that was so carefully negotiated with the British, would be minimised or even abolished!

This was untenable for the Malays. It went against the very grain of the progress of the Malay race in Malaysia. It struck raw nerves and hit at the very heart of the Malay ethos. The Malay sensitivity was seriously hurt. The reaction grew until it became unbearable for the Malays.

As a civil servant, I had to attend Parliament sessions to take notes of interest to the Treasury, and sometimes to assist my Minister, Deputy Minister or Parliamentary Secretary, to respond to the questions and comments raised by members of the opposition. Mr Lee led one of the parties in the opposition, the People's Action Party (PAP) from Singapore.

I recall how uncomfortable it was to hear Mr Lee Kuan Yew criticising the Federal Government in strong and vitriolic terms. It was sometimes embarrassing to see Tunku Abdul Rahman (the then-Prime Minister) rising in Parliament, to reply to Mr Lee's onslaughts. The

Tunku was a prince, and could not get himself to show the same degree of rancour and vehemence that Mr Lee expressed in his parliamentary and public speeches. Mr Lee, though undoubtedly a powerful debater, was hard and blunt in his presentations, and apparently rubbed the government the wrong way with his rough and provocative remarks.

In fact, Mr Lee's election campaign speeches were even more emotional and taunting. I attended several political rallies, including those of the PAP, and found them unusual in their insensitivity and bluntness. The people attending these rallies were often stirred up in their emotions and sometimes became quite restless. The Malays generally did not like what was happening. They saw ominous trends and began to get very anxious.

Tunku Abdul Rahman very astutely sensed the growing fears, pain, and anger of the Malays. He realised that if this very difficult and dangerous situation continued for long, there would be dire consequences for the future peace and stability of the new Malaysian nation. He therefore took the eventful and sad decision to separate the two historically close territories. It was a traumatic experience for all.

I was in Singapore when the separation was announced. Samala, the children, and I had gone to Singapore to spend the school holidays with Samala's parents. I had plenty of time on my hands, and thus I visited my old University haunts and several of my former university friends. After all, I had spent about five years studying at the University of Malaya in Singapore and it was therefore a sentimental journey and visit for me.

I was visiting Mr Ngiam Tong Dow, my classmate in the economics (honours) class of 1959. (He later became the Permanent Secretary of the Treasury in Singapore). It was August 9, 1965. We were having a comfortable and friendly chat in his office over coffee. Then, the public address system began to crackle and a strong sombre voice came on the air to announce as follows: "Attention, please. Attention, please. This is a very important announcement. The Prime Minister of Singapore has just announced that Singapore has separated from Malaysia. You will be informed of further developments."

Ngiam Tong Dow and I stared at each other in shock. I broke the silence and expressed regretfully that the separation would be unfortunate for both sides. I was therefore very surprised when he coolly replied that perhaps it was best for both sides, and that "Singapore would nevertheless survive and prosper". I wondered later whether he was better prepared for the shock than I was, or in fact whether he might have already had more than an inkling of what had been coming!

I then realised that he would have much to do, following that fateful announcement. I bade him farewell and left his room. I myself had much to think about and do too. As I walked into the sunshine outside the Fullerton Building, I felt better. I also had a strong urge to return home to Kuala Lumpur and to my work, to see what I could do in my small way, to serve my own country's cause — without Singapore.

I believed that the relations between Malaysia and Singapore, and even between friends and relatives on both sides of the causeway would never be the same again! This was true then and even more so now. Many events have continued to remind our people from time to time that we are the same people from the same stock and the same history, but that we have unfortunately been moving slowly but surely, further and further apart.

After separation, the officials from Malaysia and Singapore often met to discuss many areas in the government where we had to separate the administrative systems. Many Federal Departments had to be split, as we were now two separate countries. One vital issue that had to be reviewed was the Malaysian currency.

Malaysian Currency Split

The Singapore dollar was split from the Malaysian dollar on June 21, 1967. This meant that both countries had to intervene in the markets to ensure that both currencies were on par. This aim of course became increasingly difficult to achieve as time went on. Malaysia and Singapore have been, and are two different economies. Essentially, Singapore is a small island-state of about 230 square miles, while Malaysia is a much larger country of about 150,000 square miles. One is a city-state with a population of about three million, and Malaysia has a huge rural economy with a total population of about 24 million today. So socioeconomic policies had to be drastically different and sometimes even radically opposed.

Thus, it soon became clear that the Malaysian dollar could not keep up with the stronger Singapore dollar unless we kept intervening in the currency market to maintain the parity between the Malaysian and Singapore currency units. But this was not in Malaysia's interest. We would have to intervene a great deal, and this operation would cause us to use foreign exchange in order to shore up the Malaysian dollar—just to keep up with the Singapore dollar. This would not do especially in the longer term.

Initially, the currency parity was maintained through currency intervention. Tun Tan Siew Sin, Malaysia's able Minister of Finance, regarded the strength of our currency as a matter of pride. Soon, it also became a matter of "face saving" as the Malaysian dollar dipped against the Singapore dollar. Since we could not use precious foreign exchange and reserves just to save our face, we began to let the parity principle weaken—and the currency values of both countries slowly widened.

Gradually, Malaysians and particularly the Johoreans got used to the different strengths of the two currencies. The weaker Malaysian dollar also helped to reduce the tendencies of Malaysians to shop in Singapore. Instead, Singaporeans began to come over to Johor Bahru to do some of their shopping. This had another side effect in that the prices of goods in Johor started to escalate as demand for fruits, vegetables, fish and other consumer items kept rising. But it also gave better business to Johor businessmen and more incentives to produce more and to become more productive.

Overall, the decision to split the two currencies was a wise one. At least it removed the potential cause of a lot of friction in the planning and implementation of socioeconomic, fiscal and monetary policies. With the split of the two currencies and the different developments and directions of the two currencies, the two economies and the two countries drifted more definitely apart. The strength of the ringgit has deteriorated considerably since then!

Our Third Child

About this time, Samala was expecting our third child. This time, I was hoping to be blessed with a baby girl, as we already had two boys. However, I did not feel strongly about the matter. We would be happy just to be blessed with a strong healthy baby.

When Samala experienced labour pains, we took her to the same maternity ward at the General Hospital. I was delighted when I called the hospital to enquire how Samala was doing and was told that she had delivered a baby girl. I rushed from my office to fetch my mother and Samala's mother who was staying at our place in Petaling Jaya. I drove fast to the hospital with a lot of excitement in the car. I parked the car and practically ran into Samala's ward, congratulated her, and asked to see the baby. But she replied, "What baby?" I then realised that the baby had not been born yet!

A few hours later, Dharmendran (Dharm) was born on November 29, 1967. He was a lovely and chubby baby boy, and we were grateful, for now we had three sons! Dharmendran means "charitable" after the Sanskrit word *dharma* and he was also named after Samala's father, Mr Dharmalingham.

Angie's Wedding to Albert

The next exciting event in the family was Angie's wedding. As the saying goes "marriages are made in heaven". I was concerned as the eldest brother that my second sister Angie was not married yet. Angie was a dutiful and homely girl, who did not enjoy going out for parties. In any case, mum and dad were also quite strict, and did not encourage their daughters to go out on dates — unless they were going out either with me, with Samala and I, or with a group of friends. It was not deemed proper then (at least in our family), to go out on single dates unless the couple was engaged.

One fine day, a marriage proposal came for Angie from Mrs Elierzer, the wife of Professor Elierzer who was the head of the Physics Department at the University of Malaya in Kuala Lumpur. But to be fair to Angie, she could not just accept the proposal without seeing who she was being matchmade to. So, it was suggested that we would have a meeting over tea at the professor's house at Jalan Universiti, Kuala Lumpur.

It was an interesting experience for me. I had heard of arranged marriages, but this was the first time that I was involved in an actual situation. In Angie's case, it was a good compromise between an "orthodox-arranged marriage", and a "modern-style love marriage".

However, according to the traditional mode, the prospective couple would be allowed to talk and get to know each other — as if it was a casual meeting. Thus, the pressure and any stress of meeting with a view to marriage would hopefully be reduced. The couple could meet again under similar circumstances for lunch or dinner on a few other occasions, but that would be all. If the couple felt attracted or serious enough, then they would want to pursue the relationship. They could go out in a group with other members of the family. They would not be encouraged to go out too much, unless both parties felt that they had decided to sincerely develop the relationship. Otherwise, it was considered to be unfair—especially to the lady—if after all those meetings, nothing positive was going to develop!

Angie and Albert began seeing more of each other. Soon, the date for the engagement was set. They could then go out on dates together on their own, without anyone accompanying them. Since a long engagement was not encouraged, a wedding date was subsequently discussed and fixed for 1967.

Albert had studied law in Belfast and took up journalism upon his return to Singapore. Angie gave up her job as a secretary and became a good full-time housewife and devoted mother. With Albert having to work late into the nights as a senior journalist, she bore the brunt of bringing up their two loving children (a son, Dayan, and a daughter, Ranita). Both of them have done well, with Dayan becoming the first theology graduate in the family, and Ranita, a graduate schoolteacher, who adores kids. They are now happily settled in Australia.

Julie Weds James

By contrast, my third sister Julie fell in love with James Ragunathan when they both met at the wedding of Angie and Albert. James was like a brother to Albert. They both grew up in Singapore. Their families were closely attached as very good friends, Albert and James used to spend a lot of time together in Albert's home. Thus, it was not at all surprising that James became Albert's bestman at his wedding. The bridesmaid had to be Julie, as Angie's closest sister. There were therefore plenty of opportunities for James and Julie to meet and talk during the preparation for Angie and Albert's marriage. That was where cupid shot his arrow, or we could say, "God brought them together", as marriages are made in Heaven!

Just about two years after Angie's marriage, Julie and James got married in 1969. It was after the May 13 racial riots, and thus the tensions had died down and the situation had returned to normal. They too got married in the Trinity Methodist Church in Petaling Jaya, where Angie and Albert were married, and by the same pastor—Reverend Goh.

The reception was held at the Jade Room at the Robinson's Shopping Centre, which at that time was the major shopping centre in town. It was conveniently situated at Mountbatten Road, which joins Jalan Pudu. Julie made a beautiful and radiant bride as she posed beside

James who was dashing in his black bow suit. The banquet hall was decorated with floral formations that reflected Julie's talented touch.

James and Julie too have been blessed with a happy marriage and two fine children. Their son, Roshan, studied computing, while Sasha did a secretarial course. She too fell in love like her parents and married a handsome, enterprising Australian, Michael Kennedy, in Melbourne in 1997. They have also settled in Australia after James retired from Singapore Airlines as a senior manager.

The UNCTAD Conference in 1968

In the meantime, my career was developing steadily. Our third son Dharm must have brought me some luck. Soon after his birth, I was informed that I would have to represent the Treasury, on a big Malaysian delegation at the United Nation's Conference on Trade and Development (UNCTAD) in Delhi in 1968.

The UNCTAD Conference lasted about two months! It was a very senior delegation, with some strong personalities. They were Tan Sri Rama Iyer, Dato' Lew Sip Hon, the late Tan Sri Jamil Jan (from the ministries), and Tan Sri B.C. Sekher, then the director of the Rubber Research Institute. The minister who led the delegation was Dr Lim Swee Aun, the Minister of Trade and Industry.

Several committees were formed to spread out the work of this huge world conference. Different regions had to provide nominees for the posts of chairman and vice chairman for the different committees. When it came to Malaysia's turn to suggest a name for vice chairman, our delegation offered my name. So I became vice chairman of the Committee on Shipping, Freight, and Insurance! That was my first big experience in holding a high post and taking on important responsibilities at an international conference. I learnt a lot and obtained tremendous exposure and experience at that UNCTAD conference.

It was also the first time that I was given the honour and opportunity to make speeches at an international forum, on behalf of Malaysia. The experience was exhilarating for me, especially at my age. I was then 32 years old, but brash or confident (I am not sure which). Nevertheless, I felt good for delivering speeches on behalf of our government and the developing countries. It was interesting when developed countries did not like what we said and angrily reacted to the views of the delegates of their erstwhile colonies.

Malaysia had a real head start in those days over many countries in terms of performance at these conferences. First, we had a good command of the English language. Secondly, we were more confident because of our competence in the English language, and because Malaysia was comparatively better off than most developing countries. Thirdly, we were not heavily obligated to the industrial countries for loans or financial aid as most other developing countries. Thus, we were able to build a tradition of independent action in our negotiating positions, unlike most other developing countries.

Malaysia's independent stance, even then, irritated many developed countries as we were different from the others in that the rich countries could not influence or bully us as they did to many Third World countries. Thus, Malaysia established credibility and won much respect from all sides from the beginning, particularly from the developing countries. This high respect has grown over the years, and especially under Prime Minister Mahathir Mohamad's leadership in later years.

This assessment is borne out by the following anecdote. The Nepalese had a small and somewhat weak delegation. The Indians tried to dominate them and tell them what to say at the conference. However, the Nepalese or the Ghurkas, as we know them, are a very proud and militant people. They resented the condescending attitude of the more sophisticated and intellectual Indian delegation. So, they could not go to the Indians for consultations and assistance in preparing their strategies and statements for the conference.

As a result, my counterpart in the Nepalese delegation, the late Mr Achariya, came to me for help. His Minister was coming to the conference to make the final speech for the Nepalese delegation. But the Nepalese delegation was not ready with its speech! So they asked me, a foreigner, to help draft their Minister's speech. They had faith in a Malaysian to help them, in what was regarded as a very sensitive sovereign responsibility, because of the high esteem they had for Malaysia. I did what I could for them.

Consequently, this Nepalese official was so grateful that he invited me to visit his home in Nepal. I was keen to take up this kind offer as I could use the extra mileage on my ticket without having to pay for the flight to Katmandu. Just after the long conference, I was all set to have a good holiday in the Himalayan Kingdom of Nepal!

However, I had to do a personal favour for a cousin and had to forgo the Nepalese holiday. I explained to my Nepalese friend Acharia, and he was very disappointed. He sincerely wanted to return my favour to him. But as fate would have it, he was able to do so a few years later in Washington, when he worked as my technical assistant at the World Bank!

A Visit to Ceylon

I took a flight by Air Ceylon to Colombo immediately after that long but rewarding UNCTAD conference. Strangely, I felt "at home" on the flight. The crew was all Ceylonese (or Sri Lankan); the food had a Ceylonese flavour; and the pilots and air stewards were not only friendly but jolly chaps. The air stewardesses were particularly pretty and winsome with their wide midriffs, which they carelessly tried to hide with their colourful and attractive *sarees*! I enjoyed the flight.

As we flew over the Jaffna Peninsular at the northern tip of Ceylon, my mind drifted to my forefathers who had lived in Ceylon in the distant past. My paternal grandfather (the late Mr C. Kunaratnam), maternal grandfather (the late Mr E. Foster Lee), and maternal grandmother (the late Muriel Nathaniel) had migrated to Malaya before the turn of the 19th century. They adopted Malaya as their country and made their homes and careers here. They gave their best to the service of Malaya, where they lived and died after leaving their motherland. I, of course was born in Kuala Lumpur, and had never visited Ceylon before.

I was therefore somewhat nostalgic as the plane flew south over the beautiful Kandian Mountain Range towards Colombo. I suppose any Malaysian Chinese, Indian or Malay would feel the same, if he is visiting the land of his ancestors for the first time. This feeling is only natural although this is not generally discussed in our multiracial and sometimes over sensitive Malaysian society.

I kept thinking that I was returning to the land of my roots and the land of my forefathers. I realised that what I am was the result of my heritage and my ancestry, which I could not ignore or forget. For this was the reality. Being Malaysian does not mean that I have to deny my birthright or my origins. That was not being weak in my loyalty to Malaysia, but on the contrary, I would be able to contribute even more positively and purposefully to nation-building in the country of my birth — Malaysia, if I could understand my heritage.

Professor Chinappa and his lively wife Ranee Acca met me at the Katanayake Airport in Colombo. Immediate impressions of neglect and the slow pace of development in Ceylon struck me. The airport was very poorly maintained. The road from the airport to the city was narrow and full of potholes. There was hardly any development along the road that was flanked by wide spaces of underdeveloped land. I thought to myself, What has become of this country that was once known as "The Pearl of the Orient" and even "King Solomon's Island" and the Garden of Eden? I learnt to my dismay that my initial judgment was neither hasty nor rash.

As we approached the city of Colombo, I had to regretfully admit to myself but not to my enthusiastic hosts that my judgment was indeed quite right. Ceylon had deteriorated! In many ways, it could have been better for its people before and during its colonial era, as compared to after independence. What a shame! They had won independence, but then lost much of it through irresponsible political leadership, poor government and bad economic management.

I thought to myself that we in Malaysia had definitely managed our economy much better. I then vowed silently to myself that I would do my best, with God's help, to contribute in a small way towards the greater progress and stability in my own homeland, Malaysia! In fact, I can say with confidence that my visit to Ceylon was an important milestone along the way of my life, and a turning point in my nationalistic spirit and commitment to my career and my country Malaysia. I also saw for myself the bankruptcy of severe racial intolerance.

I visited the Chinappas in Kandy. It is the sacred city to the Buddhists who claim that they have the "holy tooth of Lord Buddha" in the magnificent temple that they have built in the beautiful Kandian Mountains.

I enjoyed Rani Acca and Chandran's warm hospitality and travelled to the higher and colder Nurailya mountains. The highlands were covered with vast tea plantations that looked very pleasant and pleasing to the eyes. The high craggy mountains with sheer drops were awesome and inspiring, as they tower high above the luscious undulating fields of green tea of varying shades. Here and there were little houses, like English cottages and groups of women in colourful Kandian *sarees*, picking tea leaves for their large wicker baskets strapped on their backs. It was altogether very picturesque and delightful to behold. One wondered at God's wonderful creation and I often asked what had gone wrong in that lovely country? Were there lessons for us in Malaysia? I would think so.

Lessons from Ceylon

So, what are the lessons that we can learn from the decline in Ceylon, and the desolation in the same country with a different name — Sri Lanka?

At the time of its independence in 1947, Sri Lanka was known as Ceylon. But the country seemed to be plagued with such bad luck and so many problems that the Buddhist priests and soothsayers decided that the misfortune was actually due to the wrong name for the country. The government was advised that the country's name must be changed to the ancient name of Sri Lanka, so that peace and progress would return to the country. So, the government which is strongly influenced by the Buddhist priests and Buddhism, changed the country's name to Sri Lanka. Unfortunately, the situation did not change; instead, things got worse. Good governance does not come with a change in name. We have to work at it, like in everything else.

The lessons for us, from the Sri Lankan tragic experience, I think, are that the past success of a country is no guarantee for its future progress. We have to continue to endeavour to promote national unity and good governance. The interests of the minorities have to be given fair and reasonable care and consideration. Never push minorities to the wall. They may be small, but if they perceive that they have been severely persecuted, they will react with such vehemence that cannot be anticipated nor imagined, as illustrated by the "tigers" of Sri Lanka. Never allow a bad racial situation to fester and get out of hand. Try hard to compromise before the situation gets too rigid and entrenched. Recognise that there is no winner in any racial or religious conflict. The tragically glaring examples can be seen in Sri Lanka, Bosnia, Ireland and many other places where racial and religious strifes can become deep-rooted and persist for generations.

With these thoughts in my mind, I flew back home, grateful to God that Malaysia indeed is a really blessed country despite our own relatively smaller weaknesses. But which person or what country is without weaknesses? It is our human frailty to have weaknesses. The real challenge is to strive to ensure that these frailties do not get out of hand and destroy the peace and progress that we have sought to build upon.

After 45 years of independence, Malaysia has become the most successful developing country. It is certainly the most modern, progressive and democratic Islamic country. However, we must be vigilant at all times against extremism and pursue moderation and pragmatism in a complex, multiracial and multireligious nation such as Malaysia.

10.
AT HARVARD

SOON after I returned from the UNCTAD conference in Delhi, I was told that my name had been submitted to Harvard University for admission to the Masters Programme in Public Administration. This was a specially designed academic programme named after Professor Mason of Harvard University as a tribute to his scholarship. It focused on economic development and public policy for senior officials from the public sectors of the U.S. and from developing countries.

I stood a good chance since I was in fact dealing with economic policy in the Treasury. Tan Sri Thong Yaw Hong and Tan Sri Rama Iyer had gone before me. Dato' Malek Merican was my boss at the Economics Division, and I am sure that he pushed my case strongly. He was a brilliant economics graduate from Cambridge and a far-sighted and first-rate manager. I learnt much from him and enjoyed working under him as his deputy.

The good news came through that I was selected for Harvard. I felt privileged and a bit apprehensive. After all, I had left academic studies about 10 years. The question arose as to whether Samala and the children should accompany me. The scholarship allowed me to take the whole family. I would also be on paid study leave. It was an attractive proposition and we consulted members of the Harvard Advisory Group in Kuala Lumpur about taking the family along. They advised strongly that it would be very cold in Boston, and that it would be ill-advised to take Dharm along, as he was only eight months old then. So, we left him in the loving care of Samala's mother, who took him to Singapore.

We sold our new Peugeot 404 and asked my cousin Leslie to stay in and look after our house, which the government had considerably allowed us to retain. We travelled to the U.S. via the "Big Island" of Hilo in the Hawaiian islands, where I was asked to give a lecture on the Malaysian economy to a Peace Corp Group on an orientation programme. It was on the way to Boston, and, convenient for me. It was also nice to have a break in Hawaii.

Hawaii

We stayed at a small hotel near Waikiki beach. I was quite excited about visiting Hawaii. Soon after we settled down, I took Samala, Ravi and Indran for a walk along the famous Waikiki beach. It was evening and the sunset was really beautiful against the bright blue sea. As the sun set, hundreds of torches were lit along the hotels and beach resorts, which also had many thatched huts along the white beach. It was lovely and reminiscent of the many rustic and romantic scenes I had seen on the screen and on pretty postcards. We spent the rest of the evening walking around the exotic "international market", had dinner, and returned to the hotel to have a good rest.

We then flew to the verdant volcanic island called "Hilo". We waited long at the airport because of some miscommunication. I was anxious, as this was my first experience travelling with the family so far away from home. Besides, Indran was having a fever. Finally, after a few phone calls, our hosts came to fetch us to the Peace Corp camp. The faculty staff were at hand to greet us. To our pleasant surprise, someone called out my name and rushed forward to greet me. It was my old friend, the late T. Thangadurai, who was referred to as "Professor Thanga"!

It was a real boon to meet Thanga whom we used to call "Bones" in school at the Victoria Institution because of his thin and tall frame.

From Hilo we travelled straight to Boston. We were given a small but convenient apartment in the highrise Peabody Terrace at Harvard. It was self-contained, with its own kitchenette, toilets and a small balcony. But it was bare, and we had to get our own furniture. It was a trying experience. We did not even have electric bulbs. So, on that first night, we slept on the cold floor in the dark, on the curtains they had provided! We were demoralised. We had expected at least some bulbs and some basic bedding, but the rooms were totally empty. Here we were in the U.S., at Harvard apartments and literally, "camping" in them! The next day we went shopping around to get some basic furniture, crockery and kitchen utensils—the bare essentials for a simple home!

We managed to settle down after a few days of discomfort. But I was under some pressure, as I had to start attending classes. Samala was a great source of strength to me. She organised the home, did the shopping and cooking as well as looked after the children, within the confines of a small apartment. This was the first time we lived in an apartment. It must have been hard on her, having to cope with so much, after having a comfortable life at home, with two servants. She never grumbled. Instead, she dutifully made the best of the situation, although she had not been keen to leave Malaysia.

Ravi and Indran at School in Boston

Ravi and Indran were only about three and five years old respectively, but they were ready for kindergarten school at Peabody Terrace, near Harvard University. It was efficiently run by the wives of the academic staff who were well-trained. The boys enjoyed going to school, which was in the same compound, and therefore very close by. Samala also did some voluntary work in the school, so that she would be able to follow their progress. The teachers were nice to our boys, but it was a bit different with some of the other boys.

One day, Indran came back home from school with a ripe tomato splashed across the back of his neck and white shirt. I tried to ignore his complaint and dismissed the incident as a child's prank. But I became concerned when he returned home very upset the next day. Ravi explained to us that there was a group of older boys who were going after Indran. They had ignored his protests against their bad conduct. They threw lighted matchsticks at Indran when the teacher was not looking. Indran began to cry as he related his story. It was then that I noticed that there were burnt holes at the back of his shirt. I got him to take off his shirt, and was shocked to see that he had burnt marks on his skin!

Apparently, some of the white boys had picked on Indran. I got angry as I realised how racist these white children could get even at their tender age. I went over to the school and complained to the teachers, who apologised profusely and promised to keep a close eye on those rough rednecks.

After that incident, I realised that I should not tell our sons not to fight, but that they should now learn to fight back if provoked, particularly if they were threatened or attacked. I began to teach them how to wrestle and punch anyone who attacked them. We had great fun wrestling on the bed.

Several weeks later, Ravi and Indran came home smiling. They excitedly told me that this time the teacher had to pull Indran away from one of the bullies. The bully had punched Indran but Indran did not take it lying down this time. Instead, Indran retaliated by giving the bully a black eye! The bullying stopped, and the teacher quietly told me that she was happy with the outcome, although this time, the other parents had complained! The boys enjoyed their schooling even more after that episode.

My studies at Harvard were intellectually stimulating but trying. We were in the Mason Fellowship Programme where middle career people like me, were put together with a whole lot of much younger post-graduate American students.

Their culture was different. They were cocky and somewhat disrespectful from my point of view. They would interrupt their lecturers and address the lecturers flippantly by their first names. They dressed shabbily, sometimes dirtily. This was the time of the infamous Vietnam War. Students at Harvard and right across the country were protesting against that terrible war where the communist Vietcong were killing thousands of young American troops.

However, the lectures were interesting and useful for my future work. I took courses in economics, public finance, and management, which were all enjoyable. Professor Papanick gave us two courses on development economics based on the famous 'Harvard case study' style. He was the Head of Harvard Advisory Group in Malaysia and at the Kennedy School of Government in Harvard. We had a lot of reading to do for the preparation for our tutorials where 'case studies' were discussed in detail. At the same time, there were other assignments to prepare too. Thus, I had little time for the family, except on weekends when I tried to take Samala and the boys out.

We used to go to Boston, which is just across the scenic Charles River. Filenes, the popular departmental store, was a favourite with us. We bought most of our warm clothing from Filenes because they had a unique marketing system. Selected items would be put on sale in a special section where the prices would be marked down every week by about 20 per cent. It was possible to get an item for almost a song if the item was not grabbed earlier by customers who dared not wait longer for the price to go down further.

Boston Green was a lovely park that was another favourite with us. There was also a good children's park where Ravi and Indran spent much time enjoying themselves. As we settled down, Samala felt more comfortable and confident to leave the children at home, to join the Harvard choir. We asked the boys if they could stay alone at home, and they said they could do so without any problem.

My examinations were drawing near and I had to give even more time to my studies. We did not quite like some of the colleagues on our programme. Most of them came to Harvard without their wives and children. Our best friend in the course was Phisit Pakkasem, a senior Thai official who warmed up to us and especially to the boys.

Soon the intense period of preparation for the examinations, and the actual examinations were over. I got my masters degree from Harvard, with gratitude and some pride! We were now happy to leave Harvard for home with a sense of accomplishment for me.

The Racial Riots of May 13, 1969

Before we returned home, however, the 1969 racial riots broke out. The American press was full of their own news so there was little news of Malaysia. In that sense, the Americans are insular! Nevertheless, I made it a point to read the *Boston Globe* every morning before going for my lectures.

One morning, I saw a large column highlighted as "Race Riots in Malaysia". I could not believe my eyes. I called out to Samala to show her the scary article. We immediately feared for our relatives, our friends, and of course, our country. What had happened in our peaceful and beautiful Malaysia? What had gone wrong? I believed that there was something really critical, otherwise the self-centred American press would not have covered the news so prominently. In desperation, we tried to ring home but to no avail. Communications had broken down. This made us even more restless and fearful of the worst. Our anxieties and our worries increased as no one could tell us what had really happened. We had learnt not to trust the press entirely, because of its tendency to sensationalise.

The next best thing to do was to call Dato' K.T. Ratnam for information. He was the councillor in the Malaysian Embassy in Washington, and would be able to give us the actual position. He explained that there was nothing to worry about.

I accepted the explanation and we all felt better. But I wondered whether it was possible that even K.T. was told this story from Kuala Lumpur initially to avoid anxiety and confusion? There must also have been some real hope in Kuala Lumpur at official levels, that the situation was incidental and would settle down.

But that was not to be. The following day's television and newspapers and the subsequent issues kept reporting about the riots. It was not a simple quarrel between two little groups at the marketplace, but a dangerous racial riot that was threatening the very survival of Malaysia as a nation.

When I spoke to K.T. again, he conceded that the situation at home was serious, but that he was confident that it was under control. Soon we read of the declaration of a state of emergency. The sensational stories in the press receded as other more dramatic incidents around the globe took centre stage. Then, we were convinced that some kind of normalcy had returned—and we thanked God for peace in our country once again.

Going Back Home

By August 1969, the situation at home was well under control. We were happily looking forward to going back home. But we also needed a good break. So we decided to take a holiday on our way back home. We visited Madrid, Lisbon and Colombo on our way back.

Madrid and Lisbon were fascinating because they were not Anglo-Saxon, and because they were less developed industrial countries. They were also interesting from the historical point of view, since both countries had been colonial countries in Asia. Portugal had special significance for Samala, as a history teacher, given its strong influence on Malacca.

But we also enjoyed Ceylon very much. This was because we met and stayed with many of Samala's relatives in Jaffna, where both our forefathers came from. We spent a few days in Colombo, and saw the sites of the city. But there was not much that was impressive. It was like Ipoh or Taiping during the postwar years.

From Colombo, we took the train to Jaffna, mainly because the boys would enjoy the ride. Since we were told that the trains in Ceylon were not very comfortable, I asked the stationmaster to give us seats in an air-conditioned coach. But thinking perhaps that I was a local who should know better, he promptly rejected my bookings for the air-conditioned coach. When I asked him why, he gave me a funny reply. He said, "Don't you know that I can only sell you an air-conditioned ticket, on condition that the air-conditioner is in condition!"

But I was determined not to be browbeaten, so I explained that I was a foreigner and asked politely, "When would I know that the air-conditioner will be in condition" and he replied, "When the train rings me from the previous station. Wait until then, I'll call you — but don't call me!"

With that he turned away. He had the final say and I just had to wait. After some time, he called out to me. He then looked at me with glee as he politely asked for my simple ballpoint pen. I handed it to him and he began to write down my particulars and then sold me the tickets. Next he admired the ballpoint pen and casually clipped it onto his shirt pocket with considerable satisfaction.

He looked so satisfied that I dared not ask him to return my pen. I also feared that if I did, he would find some reasons to deny me the tickets to the air-conditioned coach! So, I returned his smile understandingly, thanked him and disappeared into the crowded platform. On the train, the air-conditioner worked sporadically — and I got annoyed thinking of the stationmaster and the loss of my ballpoint pen!

In Jaffna, we visited several villages where our parents had relatives. I had heard names like "Udduvile" and "Thunavi" and I had imagined that they were big towns. However, they turned out to be little villages in a linear development all along Jaffna Road. They were more closely connected than our *kampungs* in rural Malaysia. The standard of living was low and the facilities were poor. But it was fun drawing water from the deep well and bathing behind thatched walls surrounding the well.

One day, we went to a nice place by the beach called "Kankesuaram" or KKS as they called it for short. I was walking along the beach when I noticed a man following me. He caught up with me and then quite boldly told me in Tamil that he fancied my "Singapore *sarong*", I got worried as I thought he could be a queer! I quickly walked away.

But the moral of the story: Ceylon was experiencing severe balance of payments problems for a long time. It had imposed foreign exchange restrictions and import controls. Therefore, this poor chap apparently had not seen a good imported *sarong* for a long time and therefore fancied only my *sarong* and thankfully not the owner too! Despite our own occasional balance of payments problems, I hope we would never get into this kind of situation, where we would go after foreigners for their *sarongs*!

11.
BACK HOME AFTER THE
MAY 13 RIOTS (1969)

I WENT BACK to the Economics Division under Dato' Malek's sound leadership. However, it was not long before he was selected to represent Malaysia and the Southeast Asia Voting Group on the Board of Directors of the International Monetary Fund in Washington. That left his deputy, Jegathesan, to act in Malek's position as acting head of department.

Unfortunately, Jegathesan had had a very bad experience during the May 13 racial riots. Some members of his family had been seriously injured, and he and his immediate family were terribly traumatised. He therefore decided to migrate to Australia. Tun Raja Mohar Badiozaman was then the Secretary-General of the Treasury. He was as he has always been—a very able, kind, and understanding gentleman of the highest order. He called Jega to his room and advised him to retract his resignation. Raja Mohar believed that Jega's trauma would wear off in time and that he would settle down. But Jega was determined to migrate. So the good Tun graciously accepted the letter of resignation, but put it into his desk drawer instead of sending it to the registry for official record. He then advised Jega to go to Australia as he planned and find out for himself whether he liked settling down there. If he ever changed his mind, Raja Mohar indicated that he would then treat his departure as leave of absence. If, however, Jega decided to stay in Australia, then Raja Mohar would regretfully accept Jega's resignation formally. It is indeed difficult to find people of Raja Mohar's magnanimity and wisdom in the civil service today!

Jega wrote back from Australia to say that he had decided to stay there, although he did not get a good job. He subsequently told me that he started his life in Australia as a taxi driver, then a postal clerk, and slowly rose to become an executive in the civil service. They did not recognise his experience in the Malaysian civil service.

His unfortunate experience was shared by many, although it was not typical. There were others who did very well. Some of those who went into business did exceptionally well. But most of the migrants will tell you that they went to Australia or other places for the sake of their children. They believed that their children would get a better education and have a better deal and future in Australia. I do not know about that and I am still not sure!

But after Jega left the Treasury, I became deputy head of the Economics Division. It was a real challenge. Furthermore, being just back from Harvard, much more was expected of me. We were lucky to have a member of the Harvard Advisory Group as the adviser in the Economics Division. He was Dr Anders Olgard from Denmark who later became one of Denmark's "three wise men". Anders was a professor and a sound economist. He not only gave us the benefit of his advice but also second opinions that helped us to formulate policy recommendations on a firm theoretical and pragmatic basis.

The head of the whole Harvard advisory mission in Malaysia was a Norwegian, Dr Just Faaland. He was positioned in the Economic Planning Unit (EPU) of the Prime Minister's department, with his team of about 10 Harvard economists. Their role was to provide research inputs into the economic planning process of the EPU. Dr Faaland was the counterpart of Tan Sri Thong Yaw Hong who was the first Malaysian to head the EPU after the British expatriate, Dr Oscar Spencer left.

It became clear that Dr Faaland was actually a very ambitious man. He was intelligent, sharp and tenacious. Tan Sri Thong found it difficult dealing with him because Dr Faaland was politically-inclined. Dr Faaland sensed the deep desire among some Malays in the civil service to rectify the mistakes of history and often gave advice, regardless of the consequences on the Chinese, Indians and other races. I believe that he therefore seized the opportunity to further his own agenda.

Planning the New Economic Policy (NEP)

Tun Abdul Razak succeeded Prime Minister Tunku Abdul Rahman al-Haj after the 1969 racial riots. The new Prime Minister had to set new directions in economic planning which would be more in keeping with the aspirations of the majority of the people of Malaysia, i.e., the Malays.

Here it is useful to give some background on the socioeconomic situation in Malaysia at that time, so as to appreciate the rationale for the NEP.

The Malays had been frustrated with the socioeconomic development in the country especially after *Merdeka*. They could understand the reasons for their relative neglect by the British colonial government. Countries that were colonised were exploited by the foreign colonial governments. Such was the nature of colonialists, and the British therefore did what other colonialists did, though perhaps with less vengeance.

Naturally, after *Merdeka* when the British left, the Malays expected their lot and their lives to improve and change for the better. They also expected big improvements to come fast. *Merdeka*, as in all former colonies, had given rise to high expectations. The Malays believed that they were not gaining much from independence. They had won political power from the British but they could see all around them that, it was mainly the Chinese who were gaining the wealth from the country. Thus, the Malays felt that they were losing out to the Chinese and other races from the considerable progress taking place in the country after *Merdeka*.

There was much justification for this feeling of being alienated in their homeland. It is true that the majority of the poor were Malays. It was also true that the Malays had the smallest proportion of the corporate wealth of the country. In fact, the Malays owned only about 2 per cent of the corporate capital in Malaysia at that time. The so-called "commanding sites" of the economy were almost entirely in the hands of foreign investors—mainly British, and the Malaysian Chinese. Even the Malaysian Indians were proportionately better off than the Malays, with a small slice of about 1 per cent of the total corporate sector.

Generally, the Malays were primarily employed in the agricultural sector as farmers and fishermen, and as smallholders and rubber-tappers in the commercial estates in rural Malaysia. In the urban sector, the Malays were mainly in the employment of the Government. Here again, the Malays occupied the lower levels of the Government service, except at the very top echelons at the (Malaysian Civil Service) MCS level, where they took over from the British colonial civil servants. The professional services, like the doctors, engineers, lawyers, and the graduate teachers were mainly made up of non-Malays. The graduate element in the public services was indeed very small and definitely well out of proportion to the population of the Malays in the country.

This adverse situation caused considerable resentment among the Malays. This resentment kept growing and simmering.

On the other hand, the Chinese in Peninsular Malaysia, were comparatively much better off. They were largely in the urban areas. They were in commerce and small scale manufacturing, wholesale and retail trade, construction, transport, and the export and import trade. They were, in other words, practically in every sphere of business activities. In the rural areas, the Chinese were mainly in tin mining and vegetable gardening and shopkeepers. Many Chinese were also professionals and corporate managers.

Most Malaysian Indians found employment in the rubber estates. They had come out from India as indentured labour and provided the British rubber estates owners and large British agency houses cheap labour. Housing in the remote estates was woefully inadequate; good drinking water and electricity were rarely provided, and the general welfare conditions were often well below decent human standards. Thousands died of malnutrition and malaria during early colonial times, especially in the opening of jungles for estates and building the railways. A small proportion was in the lower levels of the government service and in the professions.

While the Chinese and Indians acknowledged that they were immigrants, the Malays regarded themselves as "sons of the soil". They had in fact immigrated to Malaya in waves of traders and adventurers from Java, Sumatra, as well as sailors and tradesmen from as far as coastal India and southern China. But most of the earlier settlers came from the Malay Archipelago. So, it was natural for the Malays to believe and feel strongly that they ruled this country from the time of the Malacca Sultanate.

The aborigines can claim to be the original natives of the Malay Peninsular. However, they were scattered tribes who were nomadic and were not united or organised as large groups that could claim to have ruled the country. When the British negotiated the treaties for the protection of the rulers, it was with the Malay rulers, and not the aborigines. The Malays had therefore reasonably asserted that they had the sovereignty of the land. This is why the name "Malaya" is "Tanah Melayu" in Malay!

Given this scenario, the Malays developed some sense of insecurity and foreboding for their future. The poor showing in some electoral areas during the 1969 Elections added to this feeling of insecurity. There was a strong feeling among the Malays that the Government had not done enough for them. They wanted change, the kind of socioeconomic changes that would improve their situation and future prospects in (what they felt as) their own and only country. This fear, suspicion and frustration they vented on the other races whom they felt were the cause of their poverty and poor prospects to progress. This was the major cause of the 1969 racial riots.

The government was therefore expected to restore Malay dignity, pride and progress. The EPU was commissioned by the Government to draw up an appropriate socioeconomic plan. It was an onerous task. This tremendous challenge was made even more awesome, given the serious racial, emotional, political, and social undercurrents that underlined the whole socioeconomic environment.

The planning process was further aggravated by the divisiveness that was growing in the EPU. Tan Sri Thong, Dr Cosmos Robless, Dato' Sulaiman Abdullah, and the late Dato' K. Pathmanaban, were the senior Malaysians and mainstays in the EPU. Many other Malaysians were able and promising economists, but they were relatively younger and inexperienced. Collectively they were unevenly matched against the intellectual strength of the whole Harvard Advisory Group.

Fortunately, the Harvard group as well were divided in their approach to the planning process. Dr Faaland did not have full support from among the Harvard group. Most of them were American academics who were brought up and trained under the liberal economic tradition. They were less inclined to push for Government intervention, except on a moderate scale. However, Dr Faaland had very strong support from the Malay officials in the powerful Implementation and Coordination Unit that was also under the Prime Minister's Department. Dr Faaland jumped on that bandwagon with his own personal drive. Some would argue that Dr Faaland actually believed in strong interventionist policies. Others regarded Dr Faaland as an opportunist who was cashing in on the emotional shock and trauma of many politicians and especially the civil servants after the 1969 riots, who were responsible for the formulation of the NEP.

Tan Sri Mohd Sharif was the Secretary-General, while Tan Sri Chong Hon Nyan was the deputy Secretary-General of the Treasury at that time. Dato' Toh Ah Bah was the head of the Economics Division. Ah Bah was a bright economist but he did not feel inclined to get involved in any official debate. Chong Hon Nyan was undoubtedly able, but too diplomatic and cautious. Tan Sri Sharif was getting ready for retirement and in any case, he was not in any mood to take on the younger overzealous civil servants and economists. They felt that they had a special responsibility and even a real mission to raise the standards and well-being of the Malays. Tan Sri Sharif tried but it was understandably difficult and sensitive for him to intervene and moderate some of the strong views and actions of the "Young Turks" in the senior levels of the civil service.

For me it was more difficult as a non-*bumiputera*. I felt that I was becoming increasingly isolated. One day, when Tan Sri Sharif called me to his room for some clarification of the five-year plan projections, I took the opportunity to unburden my nagging concerns and anxieties. I explained my sense of isolation and asked whether my moderate views had the full support of the Treasury. I pointed out that unless I had the full support of the Treasury, I would get into trouble sometime. If the Treasury was not prepared to back me up, I asked that I be removed from my responsibility of representing the Treasury at these highly sensitive planning meetings.

Tan Sri Mohd Sharif was a civil servant of the highest traditions. I remember his smile as he told me that I would already have been removed if the Treasury found my views unacceptable. He said that he had faith in my judgment and objectivity, but that I should continue to be always polite in my presentation, and that whatever my views were, they would be acceptable provided that they were also fair, sincere and professional. This was a wonderful piece of advice, which I have tried to observe always. In the predominantly Malay civil service that I worked in, this good advice stood me in good stead and helped me in my career advancement in later years.

I gained considerable confidence from my discussion with Tan Sri Mohd Sharif. I also continued to represent the Treasury at these sensitive and arduous meetings at the EPU. However, I regretted that Dato' Malek was not around at that time. He was then representing the Southeast Asia Voting Group as our alternate director on the Board of Directors at the International Monetary Fund in Washington, D.C.

Malek was a man of conviction and courage. He would have been able to argue effectively as an intellectual and as a *bumiputera*, against the excesses pushed forward by some *bumiputera* officials, who were aided by some of the foreign Harvard advisers. But non-*bumiputeras* like me had a very tough time. We were often regarded with suspicion. Even when we were heard, there were some emotional individuals, who tried to be more pious than the Pope himself.

Thus, many of the non-*bumiputera* officials soon gave up, from a feeling of isolation, frustration or exhaustion. There were so few non-*bumiputeras* at the top levels of the government planning processes, and it was very difficult to counter the united and strong stand taken by some determined *bumiputera* officials at all these meetings. In any case, they were the more senior officers in the civil service, and no one can differ too much with one's seniors for too long!

Although I had the backing of the Treasury to say my piece at the EPU meetings, I realised that unless my senior officers in the Treasury carried forth my economic arguments at the higher levels of decision-making, all my strenuous efforts would be in vain. I felt that some of the policies and projections that were then propounded were far too radical for the Chinese, Indian and other non-*bumiputera* communities to accept, without serious reactions and implications on national unity. I was convinced that the inspiration for many of these radical ideas was coming from Dr Faaland (the head of the Harvard Advisory Group), who appeared to be backed up by some political force. At our meetings, he would act with much confidence that some senior *bumiputera* officers would take his cue!

At one EPU meeting, I clashed with him in an argument on the projected unemployment for the whole economy. These projections were made for the purpose of determining different alternatives or models for the Malaysian economy, in formulating the NEP.

Many Malaysian officials at the EPU and some members of the Harvard Advisory Group opposed some of the projections, while many others either supported Dr Faaland's or just remained supportively silent. But they dared not oppose Faaland openly at meetings but would encourage me to voice my criticism and objections against unreasonable issues.

At that time, Tan Sri Ghazali Shaffie had strong influence as a minister. He was a thinker and a leader in organising intellectual discussions at the political level on the socioeconomic future of the *bumiputeras*. This was the time of the National Operations Council (NOC) when Parliament was suspended during the Emergency that was declared at the time of the May 13 riots.

Some of the senior EPU officials were quite uneasy about the way Dr Just Faaland was conducting himself. He would often work with some of his own Harvard and other Malay officials and go over the heads of the senior officials, therefore effectively bypassing them. Tan

Sri Thong Yaw Hong, the Head of the EPU, used to feel very uncomfortable. He paid a heavy price later, as I did too, when he underwent open-heart surgery after his retirement from the government. Only God knows the tremendous anxiety and strain a few of us non-*bumiputeras* went through! I have no regrets, though.

We did what was best in accordance with our conscience, our faith and our loyalty to God, king and country—and that satisfaction is reward enough!

The Role of the Treasury

In view of these developments, I found myself in a bind. I was trying my best to be objective and professional but I could see that there were many who were prepared to play politics. I found therefore that I had to raise these matters at a political level myself, and then leave the political leaders to settle the serious issues at hand. But I was not sure whether my Minister Tun Tan Siew Sin was aware of the developments of the NEP. Knowing the Minister's thinking to some extent, I was not convinced in my own mind that he was fully aware of what was going on. I did not want him to tell me at a later stage (when it was too late) that I had let him down for not briefing him as my Minister earlier!

I also believed that even if my senior officers had informed him of the NEP, the Minister could not have been fully appraised. Otherwise, I believed that he would have reacted. In any case, I was full of doubts and deeply troubled. My health began to suffer and I began to get asthma for the first time in my life. I had many sleepless nights. I felt a rising urge within me to get my message to my Minister.

But how should I go about it. The opportunity came one day when I was having coffee with Tan Chye Mian, the private secretary to the Minister. We used to meet during coffee break at the old canteen that was in a zinc-roofed shed behind the Secretariat (clock tower) Buildings. I explained to Chye Mian my concerns that our Minister may not be fully aware of the formulation of the NEP. As it turned out, Chye Mian did not have a clue. However, he pointed out that it was possible that the Minister could have been given the papers confidentially, as a member of the Cabinet Committee on Economics. But that would be unlikely since Chye Mian had to record and file all Tun Tan's papers. Yet he could not recall seeing anything of the nature that I had mentioned. However, he promised to find out discreetly from Tun Tan, if he was aware of the NEP and the latest developments.

I was relieved. The responsibility had now passed on to Chye Mian. I did not have to bear the burden of doubt and concern as much as before. If the Minister was fully aware, then who was I to question whether he had or had not reacted? He was the Chinese political leader and if he felt in his judgment that the NEP in that original form was acceptable to the Chinese and other non-Malays, then who was I, as a middle-level government official, to question the emerging policies even in their extreme forms at that early stage. After all, that was the way the civil service had to operate. We only did the research, provided the alternatives, and made the recommendations. But it was the politicians, as the duly elected representatives of the people, who had to make the decisions and be answerable to the electorate for the decisions they took on behalf of the society.

Chye Mian briefed the Minister and I was summoned to see Tun Tan. Tun Tan looked serious and then characteristically went straight to the point and asked me, "What's all this about? A new economic policy?" So I explained what it was all about and showed him some of the more startling projections. He showed real surprise and then asked Tan Sri Chong Hon Nyan, my senior officer, whether he knew about this matter and asked for his views. Tan Sri Chong admitted that he was aware that various studies were being made on how to improve the living standards of the Malays and how to involve them more in the socioeconomic mainstream. However, no decisions had been taken as yet.

The consequence of all this was that Tun Tan realised that new and radical thinking was now being contemplated to change the very structure of the Malaysian economy. He then decided that he should get directly involved in all further developments from then on. He felt that these structural socioeconomic changes had significant political implications, which were far too sensitive and important to be left to the civil service. He instructed Chong to give him all the relevant papers and asked us to brief him on important developments on a regular basis from then on!

My intentions were honest and sincere. I had done my duty as a professional civil servant and thanked God for it. I often wonder what would have happened if Tun Tan got to know of the initial radical NEP, much later?

I felt that the discussions at the EPU on the formulation of the NEP began to become more moderate. I assume that Tun Tan had discussed the data that I had given him with Tun Abdul Razak and that the message had gone down to some of the overzealous officials, to be more cautious and realistic, given our multiracial society.

Right through this experience I had as my professional friend, Professor Anders Olgaard, who was the adviser of the Harvard group in the Economics Division of the Treasury. He was a prominent economics professor from Denmark who later became an economic adviser to the Danish Government. Being a Dane, he did not have much to do with the American economists at the EPU or with Dr Faaland who was Norwegian. We got on well and Anders would freely give his advice on economic matters and in my difficult relations with Dr Faaland. Anders was a true professional. He did not get involved in any personal or political matters and always observed the discipline of not interfering where and when he thought there was local sensitivity and responsibility. Anders was also great company. He enjoyed his Carlsberg, sang loudly, and laughed heartily.

Anders was followed by another sound economic adviser who was also a Dane called Professor Niels Tieggeson. He had a more serious disposition but was also very helpful and loyal to the Treasury and worked well with us as part of the Treasury team. They were not pushy, unlike their Norwegian compatriot, Dr Faaland.

We were lucky at the Treasury with our foreign advisers. Niels was followed by Dr Wolfgang Kaspar, a German who also got on well with the Treasury officials. He helped us start the Treasury Economic Report in 1971 and gave us good economic advice.

Money from the Trees

Although Tun Tan had considerable confidence in Toh Ah Bah and myself, he had an inherent scepticism about economics, as he trusted his business instincts better. We were engaged with the EPU in setting targets for government development expenditures for economic planning purposes. We had worked out that to achieve higher economic growth rates, we had to borrow more funds from abroad to finance the higher investment targets.

We therefore made recommendations to Tun Tan that the Treasury was conservative and should borrow more. Soon after Tun Tan had read our paper, he summoned us to his office. He also called in the Secretary-General Tan Sri Sharif. Tun Tan demanded to know why we wanted him to approve more borrowing. We explained that the EPU wanted a higher economic growth rate and since we do not have sufficient savings, the only way to find more financing was to borrow more from within the country and abroad—especially since our credit-worthiness was high. We soon found out that our confident presentation did not convince him. On the contrary, our recommendations irritated him badly. We carried on briefing him at our peril. Suddenly he yelled at us, "Do you think this is your grandfather's money? Do you think money grows on trees?" Silence followed.

We got up, excused ourselves and quietly left the Minister's room. Tan Sri Sharif stayed on. We were upset, especially since we had given our professional advice honestly. Ah Bah was more sensitive than I was. He felt ill and took the rest of the morning off. We could see that Tan Sri Sharif was also upset and sympathised with us.

In the afternoon, I was in Ah Bah's room trying to figure out the situation over the phone with the EPU officials. They had depended on us to clear the financial proposals with the Minister of Finance. They knew that if the Minister of Finance took a tough stand, it would be very difficult for even Tun Abdul Razak as Prime Minister to overrule Tun Tan Siew Sin. Such was Tun Tan's stature and standing with Tun Abdul Razak. Such was also the strength of the Treasury in those days!

The buzzer on Ah Bah's intercom rang. It was the Minister who summoned both of us. We thought we had had it. Ah Bah was quite distraught. I was concerned but insisted that I was not going to be upset. After all, we meant well. We gathered our courage and went into Tun Tan's office. As we walked in, the unusual happened. Tun Tan actually stood up, with a wide smile across his face. He extended his hand warmly in a kind gesture of welcome. He said that he was sorry if he had upset us earlier, but he felt strongly that the government should not borrow so much. He added that he would speak to Tun Abdul Razak about this important issue. We saw Tan Sri Sharif smiling too and then realised that he had told the Minister that we had been hurt by his harsh remarks. The matter was thus settled. Tun Tan was wise, tough, and at the same time, compassionate.

I now began to feel much more comfortable at the EPU meetings as they were more reasonable. I felt that I was given more attention and did not feel as much antagonism against me. Maybe, some of the Harvard group realised that they could not just push their ideas, as I would be keeping my Minister advised on the developments in the EPU discussions. Of course, they also knew that the Minister of Finance was a strong member of the cabinet and an effective leader of the Malaysian Chinese Association (MCA). Malaysia could have done much better with more ministers with the calibre of the late Tun Tan.

12.
SECONDMENT TO THE WORLD BANK
(1971-1972)

THE Southeast Asia Voting Group (SEA Voting Group), which was made up of 12 countries, had a representational rotation system at the World Bank Board of Directors. The system enabled every member of the group to represent the group as the director, the alternate director and the technical assistant on the Board of Directors of the World Bank (IBRD) and the International Monetary Fund (IMF).

It was Malaysia's turn to send someone to the World Bank in 1971. It was decided that a middle-level officer from the Treasury or Bank Negara would be seconded. Somehow or other, the Economic Planning Unit (EPU) was not considered for these prestigious and rewarding posts.

One day, Dato' Malek Merican called me to his room and told me that I had been nominated by the Treasury to represent Malaysia and the SEA Voting Group at the World Bank as an Alternate Director! I was very surprised, as I did not expect it. Furthermore, it was the Finance Division that dealt with the World Bank, and so it was assumed that the representative would be from that Division. I was taken aback. It was a big decision. I responded that I was highly honoured, but I would have to consult Samala and the family.

I was given short notice of about a month to leave for Washington, D.C. This made it even more difficult to decide. We had returned from the U.S. in 1969, and had settled down nicely. Ravi and Indran had adjusted well at the Garden School. Dharm was also quite secure with us after his traumatic separation from us, when we went to Harvard earlier. We would be uprooted again, if we had to go to the United States for the second time so soon. These were the thoughts that ran through my mind as I drove home that evening after work, to tell Samala the "good news". It was of course a big challenge and opportunity for my future career.

The next day, I told Malek in the office that I had some reservations about taking up the assignment at the World Bank. He was surprised that I should want to turn down what he considered a golden opportunity for my career advancement, since it would provide me excellent exposure and experience.

Malek's wife, Gaik, mentioned that living in Washington would be very different from living as a student in Harvard, Massachusetts. The World Bank would provide excellent housing and schooling for the children, and Samala would enjoy the facilities offered by the World Bank to the wives of its directors.

However, the meeting made me realise how much importance the Treasury attached to my going on duty to Washington. I learnt later that the government had in fact already decided to send a Malaysian to the board of directors of the World Bank, and that the Minister of Finance, Tun Tan Siew Sin, had agreed that I was to be the representative. Malek was actually being kind and considerate, which is characteristic of him. I spoke to Samala further about what we should do. She said that she would abide by whatever decision I finally made. In many ways, she made it easier for me to arrive at a decision.

I considered all the views and decided that I had to do my duty and take up the appointment in Washington. Malek was delighted to hear that I had decided to accept the new appointment and so was the new secretary-general, the late Tun Raja Mohar Badiozaman, who had been kept informed of the developments. I was thus the first Treasury official to be appointed to the board of directors of the World Bank.

Now we had to prepare to leave for Washington, D.C. It was not easy. We were advised to bring along Malaysian furniture. It was cheaper and it would give our home a Malaysian identity. So we ordered a whole household of it, from a furniture shop in Old Klang Road. Then, we looked around for a maid, and Tharumer, my helpful brother-in-law, helped us to find one from Banting. I had just bought a Peugeot 403 about a month earlier, but had to sell that car as well as Samala's car, in a hurry. Then there was all the packing to do. In the mean time, I had to be briefed by several government agencies that were borrowing from the World Bank and to get prepared for my new responsibilities.

We left Subang Airport in style. I was now the government's official representative at the World Bank. Nevertheless, the airport manager who knew me very well did not think it proper for me to use the exclusive airport VIP Lounge. The Treasury which allocates funds to all government agencies, however, overruled him. I was thus able to have a farewell party at the VIP Lounge for mum, dad, and the many relatives and friends, who kindly came to see us off. I recall with fond memories, uncle Chinniah (my eldest brother-in-law Kamal's dear father), who at the ripe old age of about 80, came all the way from Taiping to bid us farewell. That kind of affection and loyalty is hard to find today.

We flew to Bangkok on the first leg of our journey to Washington. I had to meet my new boss, the newly appointed director of the World Bank to whom I was to be the alternate director. She was the Deputy Governor of the Central Bank of Thailand, and was well known as Khunhing Suparb Yosandara. She was a very impressive lady — charming, sharp, and highly competent, with a flair for good public relations. I subsequently learnt a lot from her. We got on well and she liked Samala too. The Thais we met were also impressed by the good behaviour and polite conduct of Ravi, Indran, and Dharm who addressed them as "uncle" or "aunt".

Serving in Washington, D.C.

From Bangkok, we flew to Washington, D.C., via San Francisco. Our Malaysian Embassy officials and the protocol officers from the World Bank met us at Dulles Airport. We put up temporarily at the Georgetown hotel, which was near the World Bank. We had a whole suite with two floors and an elegant spiral staircase from the living quarters to the hall below.

Now the problem was to find a suitable house. We wanted a house in the suburbs where we could also send the boys to good schools. This was not as simple as it sounds. Washington was a beautiful city but not quite safe to live in. Beyond 14th Street, it was quite dangerous to walk or even drive around. The residential areas there were mostly black ghettos which were quite neglected by the authorities. They were worse than our slum areas!

In contrast, the suburbs were clean, safe and well-planned with lovely lawns and gardens as well as attractive shopping malls. The school systems varied widely in standards and performance, depending on how rich their local authorities were. The wealth of the local authorities of course depended on the level of incomes of the residents in the suburbs. These rich suburbs were invariably "white", and were a sharp contrast to the black ghettos!

This was where we had a problem! The World Bank property agents were very helpful but they had to persuade the suburb resident associations that we should be "accepted", although we were not white. There was this theory then that if non-whites moved into a white residential area, then the property values would go down, since the rich white people would then want to move out to "exclusively white areas".

So we were shown several nice houses that we liked but found that the prospective neighbours did not like our intrusion into their exclusivity because of our colour. Finally, after a lot of searching, we were shown a nice house where the neighbourhood was agreeable to having a coloured neighbour "from a foreign country and from the World Bank". I got to know of this problem after I had pressed the housing agent as to why it was taking so long to get a house.

Samala and the boys were getting impatient. The hotel suite was large but we were used to large government houses with large compounds. The boys were therefore getting restless. Furthermore, they were losing out on their schooling. We were therefore getting frustrated. I was feeling the strain particularly because I had to cope with establishing the new office at the World Bank before the director, Khunhing Suparb, arrived in Washington. I was also attending the board meetings twice a week and had little time to spare as there was much reading to do and to prepare for important meetings, and then to send reports back to the countries that I represented.

Thus, it was a real relief to move into our house in Annandale, Virginia. It was a pretty place. We had a warm family den in the basement where we had a TV and plenty of space for the boys to play with their toys. The hall and the dining room were at ground level while the three bedrooms were situated upstairs. The compound was also large enough for the boys to play their games. It was altogether a very pleasant house, which we would call home for the next two years.

Our furniture from Malaysia had arrived. We now felt more at home with our Malaysian furniture all around us. The Chinese round table with its "Lazy Suzy" was a real hit with our American guests. The red Meranti wood was a novelty. In fact, when we left for home, we were able to sell the furniture "dollar for ringgit". The house was deliberately made to look Malaysian. All our visitors saw it that way. It was a home away from home.

The usual government delegation came up to Washington for the annual World Bank/IMF meetings. As the Malaysian representative, it was only proper for me to invite the delegation over for dinner. So, Samala spent several hours preparing a nice Malaysian dinner. However, the dinner started off on the wrong foot when the delegation lost its way searching for our house, which was about a 45-minute drive from Washington.

The dinner party went off well. It was really good to entertain Tun Raja Mohar. He was so affable and relaxed as were the other colleagues and friends.

My role as alternate director at the World Bank was to assist my director, Madame Suparb, as I was the alternate director. I complemented and supplemented her role, and acted for her in her absence. I also had to represent her at meetings and had a lot of travelling to do. We had to travel to all the 12 Southeast Asian countries to brief their officials on developments in World Bank policies and especially on the progress of their applications for bank loans. My main concern, however, was to look after Malaysia's own interests.

Thus I kept closely in touch with the Malaysian Embassy. The Ambassador at that time was Tun Omar Ong Yoke Lin and the Councillor was Dato' K.T. Ratnam. We enjoyed working closely with them as they not only gave me good advice but they were also warmly supportive of my work. After all, Tun Omar was the very first Minister whom I had worked under, in the Ministry of Health and Social Welfare, and K.T. was my old university friend and Samala's cousin. 'Ben' Haroun (Mohd bin Haroun) was also at the embassy as the first secretary. We all got on well, and so it was a nice family working together to promote Malaysian interests in Washington.

McNamara's Operations Manual

Mr Robert McNamara was the president of the World Bank, with Burke Knap as the vice-president and Maude Mendels as the founder secretary of the Bank. It was quite a formidable team. The bank's staff was top class, and the directors on the board had to prepare themselves very well before they could ask the right questions or make fair comments. Otherwise, they ran the risk of being embarrassed by the very professional and sometimes 'clever' responses and retorts from the president and his highly competent staff.

There were some Bank staff whom I got to know well. They used to deal with me when I was in the Treasury. From them, I had learnt that the bank staff had guidelines for lending that were compiled as the "Operations Manual" of the World Bank. I realised that if I got hold of a copy, I would be able to better understand the full criteria for lending. This knowledge would also help me to question the bank when I thought that the bank was being political rather than professional.

The management of the bank also realised this, and therefore did not make this confidential document readily available to all members of the board. It must be realised that the board was made up of representatives from both the rich "lender" and poor "borrower" countries. There were, therefore, double standards often practised in the provision of information and the decision-making process in the bank. Furthermore, some of the richest donor countries wielded greater authority because their votes were weighted according to the amount of contributions they made to the share capital of the bank. They also had the advantage of having more of their nationals serving as bank staff (from whom many directors quietly obtained privileged information). They could get confidential documents, including the Operations Manual. But those of us from the developing countries, who were all borrowers, did not have any of those privileges. We simply had to live and survive on our wits!

I myself had to use my wits in dealing with the management in the World Bank. I decided that I had to get the bank's Operations Manual to enhance my effectiveness as a member of the board. I asked the staff whether I could borrow it. But they told me in hushed tones (as if they would be in trouble if they told me) that it was highly confidential and was exclusively made available only to the professional staff of the bank.

Under the circumstances, I decided to ask the secretary of the bank, Mr Mendels. He said that it was for the staff, and not for the directors. However, he promised to try to get me a copy of the manual. I waited but nothing came. I reminded him again but still he did not respond. So I realised that I had to be more assertive. Mendels had pushed me to the wall!

At the next board meeting, I happened to sit in the director's chair as the director was travelling abroad. I asked the president, Mr Robert McNamara, for the Operations Manual. I explained innocently that I understood that there was such a document and that I would be grateful to get a copy in order to learn more about the Bank's operations, so that I could play a more meaningful role on the Board! McNamara was taken aback. It was embarrassing for him to consult his advisers who flanked him at the board meetings. So he bravely agreed that I could have the manual and instructed Mendels to send it to me! Mendels was flabbergasted but could not say anything. He just glared at me as he nodded his head in agreement to McNamara.

The next day, he came to my room with the manual. He explained that an exception had been made in my case because of my request at the board meeting, but that I could keep the copy only for the day. He would come back in the evening to collect it back. I took the copy, thanked him for it and told him that I would return it to him only when I had finished with it. He said that it was not possible because the president did not say that I could keep it for long. I replied that since the president had not stated that I could only keep it for a day, I needed much more time to go through the important and bulky document.

I then opened my drawer, placed the manual in it and told him that only he and I knew where the manual was kept. Therefore, if the document went missing, then either he or I would be responsible! Mendels' face flushed. He then got up abruptly and left my room in a huff. I had put him in a spot. I thought I was firm but fair!

I learnt then that we have to be tough in dealing with the white men who are unreasonable and those who are arrogant bullies. I have held that attitude right through my career!

I have taken that stance ever since, especially when I negotiated with the representatives of the industrial countries after that experience — and it has paid off well. Of course, there are some reasonable white men who are not arrogant and condescending. These are the ones I would treat differently, i.e., with courtesy and humility. I realised that I had to make a judgment of character and attitude, at the start of a negotiation. However, I learnt that it was also useful to give the benefit of the doubt to the white man first, although there were disadvantages in that stance too, as sometimes they would misconstrue humility for weakness and incompetence! The best approach would be to adopt our "Asian style", i.e., to be polite, fair, reasonable, and open-minded to the other person's point of view, but firm and steadfast when we have to.

Those who take us for granted, however, should be promptly put in their place. To do that, we must be competent and confident. Good examples include the Malaysian Prime Ministers and some other cabinet ministers who brook no nonsense from westerners!

I gained a lot of respect from many of my more senior colleagues on the board after that intervention. Some of the representatives of the powerful rich countries of course, had already been given copies of the manual quietly, long before. But as a result of my request, many representatives of the developing countries also asked and received copies of that sensitive Operations Manual. I have no doubt that the quality of, and the balance in the discussions between the representatives of the rich North and the poor South countries, improved considerably as a result of my small initiative!

Lessons in Negotiation

My experience at the World Bank was invaluable. I was thus more able to interact with some of the top economists, financiers and planners at the World Bank. The board itself was made up of former ministers of finance, governors of central banks and other senior officials. The discussions and debates that took place at the board meetings were of a very high standard. It was a wonderful experience just to follow the quality of the exchanges and to observe the dynamics of the discussions and the shifts in the power play between the representatives of the developing countries and the industrialised nations. It was especially fascinating to observe the subtle interaction between the rich "lender" countries and the poor "borrower" countries in a board that was supposed to be made up of "equal" shareholders, but which was dominated by the rich countries. (That is why World Bank and IMF policies have often been skewed. We saw the IMF being used as a tool of the West in the currency turmoil in Asia even in 1998!)

McNamara and his Visit to Malaysia

But it was Robert McNamara who impressed me the most. He had an outstanding personality. His presence was powerful, as he had a tall big frame, and a strong deep voice. He was also physically fit and intellectually powerful. When he spoke, he was very precise and deliberate, as if he wanted to make his point and get away quickly. His concentration and memory were legendary. He remembered names, and even minute details. It was awesome talking to him. As president of the bank, he had to read hundreds of economic reports covering so many different countries, but he would often be able to correct his staff and others about facts or figures that they had given him some time back. He had an analytical mind, capable of assembling all the data that he had accumulated in his brainy head, and would give his assessment, which frequently differed from his top advisers. I found that he made people uneasy with his computer-like mind and his tremendous sense of discipline.

McNamara was almost like a "robot" to many people. He was fascinated with numbers. Anybody who could give him numbers to back his argument made a mark on him and carried the day. He was also cold and somewhat calculative. After all, he was the former secretary for defense in the US government who conducted the bloody war in Vietnam. He was obsessed with the so-called "body count" of Vietnamese killed — so the US army included soldiers, civilians and even little children in their body counts! This was the partial cause of his downfall in Vietnam. This weakness could recur in Iraq too!

As chairman of the board of directors of the World Bank, he would listen intently to our submissions, and always very shrewdly rephrase our many questions in a way that would elicit the kind of answers that he wanted his professional staff to give to the board. I had on occasion tried to further clarify that I had meant something else, but he would rephrase my question again and still have his own way. Any staff who answered the question as it was raised by the board members, would be pulled up, unless of course the answer was up to the ideological expectations of the bank. The Westerners dominated the World Bank, led by the U.S.! They still do — to their advantage!

It was with some reservations, therefore, that I received the news that McNamara wished to visit Malaysia. I was told that he would be able to see how well Malaysia was doing in socioeconomic development. I was somewhat concerned as to how this tough and apparently "soulless" man would adjust to the people and environment in Malaysia.

I approached our embassy on the matter, and they agreed to liaise with our authorities in Kuala Lumpur on the purpose, protocol and programme, and the leaders that he should meet. I also made sure that McNamara was fully briefed on the latest socioeconomic developments in Malaysia. The bank staff prepared good briefs for their president and his delegation — but they did not have the "feel" for Malaysia as Malaysians would have. I tried to fill the gaps.

Madame Suparb, my director, advised that I, rather than she, should go to Malaysia to prepare the way and accompany McNamara on his visit, since it was my country that he was visiting. I readily agreed, as I would have a chance to visit home, as well as to update myself on the latest socioeconomic developments back home.

My return home was a joy. The Malaysian Treasury had prepared an excellent programme in conjunction with the visit of the World Bank officials, so I really did not have much to worry about. That was great as I had more time to spend with mum, dad and my sisters.

Felda Projects

McNamara was keen to visit the World Bank-financed projects. The large land development schemes under the Federal Land Development Authority (Felda) impressed him greatly. At that time, we had considerable rural poverty with about half the population below the poverty line. The main reason for such a high rate of poverty was that the population was largely agrarian, the land they worked on was fragmented and relatively neglected by a century of so-called British "protectionism" and colonialism.

The traditional agriculture plots were small, dispersed, and overworked, and therefore not sufficiently productive. Consequently, the farmers' incomes were low. Large rural families compounded the poverty problems. The past neglect of the British colonial administration further aggravated the poverty conditions. The solution was to provide new land as Malaysia was fortunately blessed with a favourably "population to land ratio". Therefore, there was no need to introduce radical land reforms or tough laws on the redistribution of land. This would have caused considerable reaction and even resentment from the landowning class. Land reforms were considered to be socially disruptive and politically unacceptable. The solution therefore was to provide about 10 acres of land to each selected farmer and his family. They were then encouraged to plant rubber and oil palm trees. They were also urged to use some portion of the land to plant vegetables and to rear poultry for domestic consumption and even for sale.

These Felda projects helped a great deal to alleviate poverty. Farmers felt a strong vested interest in increasing their productivity, as their produce was no longer forced to be shared with the many unscrupulous landowners. The government provided all the necessary tools to assist them to build their standardised *kampung*-style wooden houses. They were provided with the implements and supplies to till the land, and to plant and fertilise their farm plots. These Felda farmers thus developed a sense of belonging and ownership, which enabled them to give of their best to make the land prosper and flourish on a sustainable basis.

How I wish that our employers in the industrial sector had given stronger vested interests to our workers. This would have enhanced productivity, increased incomes, and the standard of living much faster!

The World Bank's experience in Latin America, South Asia, and especially in Africa, on agrarian reform and poverty alleviation programmes had been disappointing, if not dismal. However, the story in Malaysia was different. It was a success story. It was an experience that was rewarding to the bank and a partnership that the bank could be proud of. Amid all those horror stories of failed development projects and programmes elsewhere, here was a massive land development programme that the World Bank could showcase to the world as part of its own success! No wonder McNamara and his senior staff were so enthusiastic right through their visit to Malaysia.

I accompanied McNamara on most of his visits in Malaysia. His wife also accompanied him on his inspection trips. She was a charming lady who I felt, had a tough time keeping pace with her husband's hectic life. While our officials concentrated on looking after and briefing McNamara, she was sometimes left out. So, I would go up to her to keep her company and brief her myself, for she was a highly intelligent lady in her own right.

From Mrs McNamara, I got to learn the softer side of that stern man—McNamara. According to his wife, he was a very private person. He enjoyed reading. He would read at least a book a month, and would make a presentation of his assessment of the book at a monthly meeting of a close circle of friends. He had a great passion for tennis, which he played twice a week despite his heavy schedule. He was a fitness freak who walked up the 12 floors of the World Bank building at 1818H Street in Washington every morning at almost a gallop!

There was, however, as in all success stories, a sad part to it. Their grownup son, one would have expected, would follow his father's footsteps or make his own impressive mark of his own choice. But this was their sad regret. He may have found it difficult to cope with his out-standing father's international reputation. Also, there was at that time a great reaction on the American campuses and among American youth, against the terrible Vietnam War — so perhaps that was one reason why the young McNamara took to drugs. He became difficult at home and dropped out of college like many "hippies" at that time. Then he went to California to start a little farm. He had obviously opted out of the American dream and the US system of severe competition.

McNamara's visit to Malaysia was a big success. They had seen at first hand how carefully we planned and implemented our socioeco-nomic projects and programmes. The World Bank was most impressed with the single-minded and dedicated drive of our Prime Minister Tun Abdul Razak.

The late Tun was highly committed to eradicating poverty and rais-ing the standard of living and the quality of life, especially among the agricultural and rural population of the country. McNamara was also highly impressed with our implementation capacity that was due to the high competency of our civil service. He said he had not seen many ex-amples of good governance in most of the other developing countries.

The World Bank was now prepared to do more for Malaysia as they had established that Malaysia was a sound borrower that was well worth investing in, as the lending risks were almost negligible. Further-more, the country obviously benefited from bank lending. Malaysia did show that it appreciated the World Bank's contribution to its rapid socioeconomic development and progress, and the World Bank was gratified.

I was indeed elated by McNamara's successful visit, and I felt that I deserved to be given leave to spend time with my family in Kuala Lumpur.

Collin's and Nancy's Weddings

I was fortunate to be able to attend two weddings during the times I visited Kuala Lumpur. One was Samala's longtime friend, Nancy Fer-nando, who taught with her at Bukit Nanas. The other was my cousin Collin's wedding to lovely Dharshini.

Nancy had become a good friend of mine due to our association over time. I was therefore glad to attend her wedding to a fine-looking Sri Lankan called Herman Perera. For company, I took my sister

Georgie along. Nancy was happy that the husband of her good friend Samala was able to attend her wedding and mentioned to the master of ceremonies that I had come from Washington. The emcee thought that I had come down from Washington especially for her wedding and made a public announcement of it, much to our amusement and some surprise on the part of some guests.

Collin's wedding was of particular significance to me. His wedding reception was appropriately held at the Royal Selangor Club where Collin had spent many happy hours. The reception was informal, with much singing and dancing. The many friends that Collin invited to his reception were also my friends. Hence, it was a lovely reunion and a jolly occasion.

It was now time to get back to Samala and the boys in Washington. I was very much looking forward to my return "home"—where my family was. I was so keen to get back as soon as I could that I remember taking a flight straight to Washington without the usual overnight stop in Tokyo or Los Angeles! It was a punishing flight, but it was worth getting back in a hurry.

Madame Suparb's Passing

It was back to hard work in Washington. My director Madame Suparb had not been keeping well, with a prolonged deep cough. Her illness persisted despite the best medical attention that was provided in the U.S. She was not able to attend many board meetings because of her painful cough and frequent spells of dizziness. This meant that I had to take on more responsibilities.

Besides attending the board meetings and other related committee meetings of the board, I had to meet several of our constituent delegations and looked after the operations of the office as well. I also had to prepare all the reports that had to be sent to all our 12 member countries every week. It was onerous and very demanding work, but it was wonderful exposure and a great experience. I was also anxious to do as much as I could to reduce the burden of responsibility and pressure on poor Madame Suparb. As her illness deteriorated, we were told that she was suffering from cancer! Before long, she returned to Thailand. After several months, she passed away peacefully in the land of smiles that she loved so much and which she had served so lovingly.

We were all very grieved. But life had to go on, as she would have expected us to carry on the good work she had been doing. I was greatly assisted by my old friend Acharia from Nepal whom I had met in 1968 at the UNCTAD meeting in Delhi. He was now my technical assistant. He would help me at least with the preparation of the minutes of the board meetings that we sent out to our members to highlight the main issues of the board discussions pertaining to their national loan projects.

Samala's Father's Demise
At about this time, Samala's dear father, Mr Dharmalingham, passed away suddenly in 1972 in Singapore. It was a severe blow to poor Samala. She took a long time to recover from her father's death. Soon, I also had to travel on duty to visit our constituencies in the Southeast Asia Voting Group. This time I had to visit Singapore and Fiji. I flew straight to Kuala Lumpur to spend a day at home before hopping over to Singapore.

Official Visit to Singapore
My visit to Singapore was fortuitous, as it was soon after Samala's father's demise. The Hindus have this custom of throwing the deceased person's ashes into the sea at religious ceremonies that are held about a month after the cremation of the body.

Though a Christian, I considered it my duty to take part in the ceremonies as far as I thought it appropriate. After all, I did this for my father-in-law whom I loved and respected. Sometimes, some religions are so intolerant that they do not even allow passive participation in the ceremonies of other religions. How can we preach love and tolerance, yet not practise them? If each religion taught more understanding, tolerance and acceptance of other religions, this would be a better world.

So, like a dutiful son-in-law, I wore the traditional Indian white robe or *dhoti* and witnessed the Hindu priest perform the ceremonies at the seaside at Changi Beach in Singapore. Then, we waded through the sea and prayerfully laid the ashes of my late father-in-law, which were in a decorated split coconut, on the calm blue waters, to be immersed with the universe for eternity. I felt grateful and blessed for having had the privilege of performing my last duties and for having paid my last respects to my kind and loving father-in-law.

Then, I felt relieved and ready to carry out my official duties for which I had come from Washington to Singapore. I made an appointment to see the permanent secretary of the Singapore Treasury, the late

Mr George Bogars. He was about the most senior civil servant in the Singapore government, and a very distinguished and brilliant official. He received me with all courtesies and heard me out intently as I briefed him on the World Bank's projects for the Singapore Port development and expansion.

The Singapore government already had a good reputation for sound financial management, and did not really need World Bank financing like some other countries did. So, the World Bank had to handle the Singapore authorities more carefully and discreetly. Some bank officials of course tended to treat some heavy borrowing countries quite indifferently. But they could not do so with countries like Singapore and Malaysia. These countries often found borrowing from World Bank more cumbersome and even more expensive than the market loans.

My role was to better understand the Singapore position and to reconcile any differences that might exist between the World Bank and the Singapore authorities, to ensure continuing good relations. We had some very fruitful discussions after some difficult times!

I well recall that Mr Bogars had a young, tall and good-looking gentleman at the meeting, busily taking notes and making sharp observations from time to time. I got to know him and he kindly helped me arrange for other meetings with the Singapore officials. He was very mature for his age and very impressive. He was introduced to me as Mr Goh Chok Tong (later the Prime Minister of Singapore!)

He has come a long way, but whenever I met him since then, he has always been polite and warm. It is that kind of spirit, and not condescension and arrogance, that will no doubt improve relations further between Malaysia and Singapore in the years ahead.

Visit to Fiji

From Singapore, I flew to Fiji which was also one of the members of the Southeast Asia Voting Group, that I represented. Their officials met me at the airport and took me to a pleasant hotel by the sea. On my way to the hotel, I could see that Fiji was indeed a beautiful tropical island romantically positioned in the Pacific Ocean.

Fiji appeared similar to postwar Malaysia. It was relatively underdeveloped, and depended largely on sugarcane plantations and the export of sugar. There was a great deal the World Bank could do for Fiji, and I was keen to assist the Fijians gain as much as possible from their relationship with the World Bank. However, I had the impression that the grassroot native Fijians were not so keen on rapid change and too much economic development. The following story would make my point.

A Fijian Fisherman's Wisdom

On the Sunday morning after I had arrived, I took a stroll on their lovely clean white beach. The sky was a bright blue. The sea was calm, cool and crystal clear and I was enjoying my lonely walk. Soon, I noticed a young Fijian fishing along the seashore. I stopped under the shade of a tall pine tree to have a chat with him. He spoke pretty good English although he had spent only a few years in school because, as he put it, "he loved loafing".

I asked him where he worked, and he replied that he found that there was no need to work permanently as he did not need much money. He explained in fractured English that he could live on the fish he caught and there was plenty of yam for him to dig up when he felt hungry. I asked him how he obtained his other needs like shelter, transport, and other items such as razor blades and the cigarettes which he was smoking. "Oh!" he added, "I make small jobs and buy small things. I use bicycle to move." He had built himself a little canoe and a nice conical-shaped traditional thatched hut. So he had everything he wanted, and did not need more. He was happy with his simple lifestyle.

I tried to be provocative and asked him whether he did not need more money to have a good time, like going to some kind of pub or disco with his friends. His answer was again quite down to earth. He replied that when he wanted some fun, he would "take canoe to see friends in outside island." There he could have a good local brew to drink and dance all he wanted with many of his girlfriends who wore grass skirts!

He was a happy man and I wondered seriously then whether he or I had a better quality of life. And here I was, trying to help the Fijian authorities to develop their economy with World Bank loans! The lesson I learnt was that if our major objective in life is to be happy and to enjoy a good quality of life, then there are many models we can choose from to meet the special needs and circumstances of different cultures and societies. We need not closely follow the World Bank model, or the Western ideals and values of socioeconomic development and so-called progress. The simple wisdom and logic of that humble young Fijian fisherman had taught me a lesson which I will always bear in mind: to lead a simple and happy life and make the best of what we have.

There is much to be learnt from the wisdom of our farmers, fishermen and workers. Sometimes, we modernise too rapidly at our own peril and too many basic values are sacrificed in the process! I wonder whether we in Malaysia have gone too far, too soon? (See what happened to Fiji later.) Rapid globalisation could also be disruptive. That is why we have all these international protests!

Our Sons in Washington

Back in Washington, my official duties kept me very busy. Samala did some voluntary teaching at the Belvedere School, where Ravi and Indran were attending. They enjoyed the school, the friends, and the very polite and caring teachers. When I could, I would take Samala and the boys to the several beautiful children's parks. Ravi, Indran, and Dharm used to enjoy themselves thoroughly at the playgrounds, the splash pools and the large shopping malls. We also used to visit "Giffords", which catered specially for small children, with all the goodies, especially the 33 flavours of ice cream!

There were good tour books for the children to visit places of interest. These books were written exclusively for children's interests, and dissuaded us from visiting places that we wanted to go to as adults. We had earlier made the mistake of taking them to enjoy scenic areas and art galleries that we liked and which we thought might interest them. But we soon realised that they got bored. Therefore, we discussed the places that we planned to take them, and always consulted the boys before taking them out. We took them to the Smithsonian Museum, the Washington Monument, the Jefferson and Lincoln Memorials, Arlington Cemetery, President Kennedy's Memorial, and the many pleasant and well-organised parks and playgrounds around Washington.

We also often travelled out of Washington to places like Boston Park and a town called Concorde, where "the first shot was fired that rang around the world" to announce the American War of Independence from the British. We also visited the very scenic West Virginian Mountain "sky drive", and drove through the battlegrounds of Gettysburg. Ravi, Indran and Dharm enjoyed these drives and visits very much. I have no doubt that they were enriched with lively curiosity and a spirit of inquiry from all these excursions—which helped them develop in a holistic way, later in life.

13.
EUROPEAN TOUR

AS the time drew near for my two-year term at the World Bank to end, we prepared to leave for home. It meant another major change, but we were looking forward to going home after two hectic years in Washington. The office work posed no problems. I had good staff, and they helped me in packing my things. I prepared suitable "handing over" notes and felt fulfilled. I had set up the first Southeast Asia Voting Group Office, and we had built a reputation for professionalism in our contributions to the board, and in our dealings with the World Bank staff. I was not easy or pliable like some other officials, particularly those from the less-developed countries that depended on aid. But there was a healthy and mutual respect that we all enjoyed.

The real hard work had to be done by Samala. The children had to wind down from school; farewell parties had to be attended and given; and all the shopping, selling and packing had to be done. We sold our good teak and *meranti* furniture that we had brought from Malaysia, and bought some American furniture, a big fridge, a cooker, a washing machine, and several other items that were either cheaper or not available in Malaysia.

Our good friend at the Malaysian Embassy, 'Ben' Haroun, had told me that it would be worthwhile to buy a Mercedes from Germany before going back to Malaysia. So we decided to collect it in Germany and tour Europe on our way home!

Family Visits London
London was our first stop. Our old friend, Bertie Tallala (now Dato'), was a diplomat at the Malaysian High Commission. I wrote to him to say that we would be passing through and would appreciate if he could book us our accommodation. However, he cabled back immediately inviting us to stay at his apartment. He fetched us from London's Heathrow Airport and settled us in his spacious apartment, where he lived alone as a bachelor.

Bertie was very kind and insisted on showing us around London after he came back from work on the day we arrived from Washington. As it was summer time, the evenings were still very bright and we were able to enjoy the sights and sounds of London. It was Samala's and the boys' first visit to London and they all enjoyed the tour tremendously. However, we were all tired as a result of the long flight.

We had a pleasant stay in London—thanks to Bertie. We had managed to see most of the favourite tourist spots such as the Buckingham Palace, the House of Commons, the Tower of London, the British Museum, St Paul's Cathedral, Trafalgar Square, and many other fascinating sights. A few days later, we flew to gay Paris.

Paris Visit

We landed at Charles de Gaulle Airport and booked in at a neat little pension along the River Seine. We were lucky to have another good friend at the Malaysian High Commission. He was Emile Morais. He had known me as a boy in Ipoh. He was married and had his family with him. When they heard that we were in Paris, they got in touch with us and invited us over to their place for dinner. They suggested that we leave the boys with them while we went to the grand show at the famous Lido theatre. It was well worth the pricey tickets. The colour, talent and extravaganza were quite remarkable.

The next few days were spent visiting the impressive French monuments and taking in the charms of Paris. We took a coach tour and then a short boat tour of the beautiful city. We also took the boys to the Tuileries Gardens, the celebrated Louvre to see among others, the Mona Lisa, Notre-Dame, Montmartre, the historic neighbourhood of the Latin Quarter with its labyrinthine side streets, and the famous Moulin Rouge. The boys were wonderful walkers and were very good in that they did not complain about having to walk so much.

My New Mercedes in Europe

From Paris, we travelled to Luxembourg to collect my new Mercedes 220. It was an interesting experience. I was asked exactly what I wanted in the car—should it have powered-steering, automatic drive, leather seats, and white-walled tyres? Mercedes catered for all tastes and practically custom-made their cars for their clients. The car was in a pleasant sea-blue, and it was a real pleasure driving it out from the Mercedes factory. It was my first Mercedes, and since then, I have preferred and been lucky to have had Mercedes cars since then. They have been reliable, durable, comfortable and stylish, and I have enjoyed them immensely.

We drove from Germany to Switzerland. At the foot of the snow-capped Matterhorn, we found a pretty little traditional Swiss inn where we spent several days. I took the boys climbing the low slopes at the foothills. They played with the snow and thoroughly enjoyed themselves. Then we drove through the long Simplon tunnel and on to Rome.

In Rome, we again visited the main tourist sights. We took a tour of the Vatican and the Catacombs and then drove south to Venice. We found Venice fascinating. The gondola rides were exciting and the little restaurants were most attractive for their ambience and tasty meals.

We then boarded a luxury boat and spent about a week on a cruise around the Aegean Islands of the Mediterranean Sea. That was an excellent break for all of us. I shipped the Mercedes to Port Klang, and from then on, I was freed of the responsibility of driving.

The boat was called *The Bernina*. It called at many small fishing ports and little towns along the Aegean Coast. We would disembark and spend a few hours at each small port and village, to observe the way of life of the Greek farmers and fishermen. We also did some shopping of attractive souvenirs and native crafts as we spent our time casually in these picturesque places. The time spent on board this luxury yacht was itself very comfortable and rewarding. The sailors liked our children a great deal. We played games with them on the open deck, ate a lot of fresh seafood, and had a whale of a time on board.

We soon docked at the port in Beirut, where we were scheduled to take a flight home. Beirut was relatively peaceful in those days, and very prosperous. The city was well laid out and quite elegant. It was perched on a hill overlooking the Mediterranean and therefore very picturesque.

14.
RETURNING HOME

WE took a direct flight from Beirut, and arrived safely in Subang International Airport. All of us were grateful to be back in our own homeland. We had a good experience in Washington, and had enjoyed the holidays on the way back, but home is still the best!

Samala's sister Shantha and her husband Tharumer kindly invited us to stay at their home in Klang for a few weeks. Samala wanted to spend some time with her sister and mother, as this was the first time she was seeing them after her father's death. This arrangement worked out well, as our boys were able to spend time with their cousins, Nalini, Malini, and Shalini with whom they got on very well. We also had to wait for our government quarters, and, of course, our new Mercedes.

Government Housing

Before long, we were allocated our government quarters at 17 Jalan Selangor on Federal Hill in Kuala Lumpur. It was a nice one-storey house with two big bedrooms upstairs and a study room downstairs.

We also had a large compound where the boys played football, cricket, hockey, badminton, and ping-pong. While we played, we could often observe a whole tribe of monkeys watching us. There were lots of them around. Most houses were specially fitted with metal grilles to keep them from entering. In fact, there were cases where these monkeys had attacked little children outside as well as inside the homes that had no window grilles. We thus never fed the monkeys. Like some humans, they often bite the hands that feed them!

It was fun living in government quarters in those days. The rental was nominal as it was highly subsidised. The garden was maintained by the PWD, which also undertook the repairs of the house. The Federal Hill area was really green with old trees all around. Many of these fine trees and forested areas have since been cleared to build new housing estates! But our old house still remains. Federal Hill is an excellent residential area, but I wonder for how long more before it is also filled up with concrete condominiums? Already I see intrusions from developers!

Preparing Budget Speeches

On my return from Washington, I was promoted as the head of the Economics Division of the Treasury. Dato' Malek was then promoted to Deputy Secretary-General of the Treasury. We also had Dr Wolfgang Kaspar as our economic adviser. Dato' Dr M. Shanmugalingam and Tengku Malek became my deputies. We had a very good team with Dato' Mustapa Mohamed (later Minister of Entrepreneur Development and in the Prime Minister's Office) and his wife Datin

Kamarazan, Dato' Isham Mohd, Dato' Tik Mustapha, Dato' Dr Aziz Yacob, and Dato' Nik Siddique, as some of our stalwarts.

The draft budget speeches had always been prepared by Bank Negara Malaysia in the past. Their Economics Division, under the able leadership of Tan Sri Dr Lin See Yan and Dato' Fong Weng Pak (later Deputy Governors of Bank Negara), produced the drafts that we in the Treasury had to review. We would make the necessary amendments and submit them to the Minister of Finance for consideration. The Minister would make changes, which we had to check, review or revise with Bank Negara for resubmission to the Minister.

This arrangement was not very efficient nor practical. It was useful when the budget was less ambitious and more straightforward — and when the Treasury had few economists. But over time, the budget speech evolved into a major policy instrument that expressed the government's overall socioeconomic policies, priorities and directions. The Budget Speeches became even more important in giving substance to the Five-Year Economic Plans and the long-term Outline Perspective Plans. They also contained some political flavour which was necessary in managing the complex Malaysian political economy. The Treasury Economics Division had been built up strongly by Dato' Malek Merican.

Thus, it became clear that the Budget Speech should be prepared in the Treasury. By now, we had built up our capacity in the Economics Division to write an Economic Report that would accompany the Budget Speech. We also had our adviser, Dr Kaspar, to help us out. The Budget Speech would now have to be written entirely by Treasury officials. Bank Negara would provide only the small portion pertaining to the monetary policy.

Actually, I still do not understand why the draft budget speeches had to be written by Bank Negara earlier. After all, the secret new tax proposals and the secret new custom duties were all prepared by the Treasury, the Inland Revenue, and the Customs Departments. "The International and Domestic Economic Situation and Prospects" was done by Bank Negara earlier, but now the Treasury was capable of writing it. Furthermore, we had the advantage of being physically closer to our Minister of Finance Tun Tan Siew Sin whose thinking we also understood better.

Bank Negara would have liked to carry on with the old arrangement, because it gave them stronger influence with the Minister of Finance and the management of the economy. They could even use their power to persuade the Treasury to do more fiscal planning, like cutting down expenditures and raising more taxes, rather than Bank Negara having to do more on monetary policy. But the Treasury now got the upper hand with the strengthening of its Economics Division and our responsibility in preparing Budget Speeches and publishing the Treasury's Economic Reports. The Treasury's predominant position in the government now continues.

Treasury Economic Report

Bank Negara did not quite like the competition that our new Economic Report would give to their well-established Bank Negara's Annual Report. But we managed to convince our senior officials and especially the Minister of Finance that we could deliver. So, we went ahead to produce the first Treasury Economic Report in October 1972, for the 1973 Budget.

We also prepared the Minister's draft Budget Speech all by ourselves for the first time in the history of the Treasury! It was indeed an achievement that all of us in the Treasury were proud about. We had proven ourselves worthy of the trust placed on us by our very meticulous and demanding Minister, Tun Tan Siew Sin. We had also proved some sceptics wrong.

The Treasury Economic Report was well received by our Minister and the Cabinet. We also managed to persuade him to table it in the Parliament as a Supplement to his Budget Speech, and it turned out to be a big hit in Parliament. It considerably improved the quality of the debates on the Malaysian economy in Parliament!

I believe that he was somewhat unenthusiastic initially about the Economic Report, as he felt that he would have to defend the views of economists at the Parliament meetings, when he privately did not quite appreciate economists. He had always been more of a sharp businessman and an astute political leader.

Malek Merican Leaves the Treasury

The Southeast Asia Voting Group had Annual Meetings in each of the member countries. Malek and I therefore had to attend one of those meetings in Jakarta in early 1973. Malek's wife Gaik accompanied him. One evening, the three of us went out for dinner, when Malek broke the news to me that he was contemplating leaving the civil service for the lucrative banking sector. I was taken aback. To me, Malek was the ideal professional civil servant, and a first rate Treasury officer. And now he was thinking of leaving us. I protested. How could he let us in the Economics Division down? How could he let the Treasury down? I tried to explain my views while Malek listened calmly. But he had made his decision.

Malek's sudden departure left a vacuum in the Treasury. In many ways, Malek was irreplaceable. Wong Yoke Meng (the late Tan Sri) took over Malek's place as Deputy Secretary of the Treasury, but he had a different style. Yoke Meng was bright, able and a good friend, with pretty strong views that he tenaciously adhered to. But we got on well together. There were times when we wanted to have quiet chats over lunch. So we would go down to the Chinese coffeeshops down the road from the Treasury (in the Segambut area) to have a bowl of good *wantan mee*!

Yoke Meng and I worked very closely on several important issues. One of these vital matters was in regard to Malaysia's membership of the Sterling Area. As Malaysia developed her trade relations with other countries, apart from Britain and the rest of the Commonwealth countries, our trade volumes and value with the Commonwealth countries declined, while our reserves in non-Sterling currencies, especially in US dollars, increased. Furthermore, there was no need to have any special relations with Britain as in the past. In fact, it was considered wise to show our independence from Britain even in the field of finance. Thus, the Treasury and Bank Negara officials worked together and recommended that Malaysia should break away from the Sterling Area. Malaysia thus ceased to be a member of the Sterling Area on June 23, 1972.

15.
COMMONWEALTH MEETING IN OTTAWA, CANADA

AS head of the Economics Division of the Treasury, I often had to accompany the Prime Minister and the Minister of Finance to the Commonwealth Heads of Government Meetings (CHOGM).

The CHOGM of July 1973 was held in Ottawa, Canada. Tun Abdul Razak led the delegation, with Tengku Ahmad Rithauddeen (who was the Foreign Minister) and several officials from other ministries.

Tun Razak was happy with the delegation's performance, and was therefore quite relaxed. But the casual mood among the Malaysian delegates was suddenly shattered, when we received the sad news that the Deputy Prime Minister, Tun Dr Ismail, had passed away in Kuala Lumpur on August 2, 1973.

Tun Razak was shocked and he took the news very badly. He decided to leave the meeting immediately on the next available flight. But in the meantime, he had to be sedated to enable him to rest. Such was the strong fraternal friendship that Tun Razak felt for Tun Dr Ismail. I recall seeing him off at the airport, and was surprised at how shaken and frail he appeared. In retrospect, that was just about $2\frac{1}{2}$ years before Tun Razak himself passed away on January 14, 1976. I presume he would have known that he was quite ill at that time.

Kuala Lumpur as Federal Capital

Back in Kuala Lumpur, the hot issue of the day was the on-going negotiations between the Ministry of Finance and the Selangor state government regarding the compensation offered for the transfer of Kuala Lumpur to the Federal Government. The question was how much should the state government be paid for agreeing give up Kuala Lumpur to the Federal Government. It was a thorny problem which was difficult to settle at official levels since the Sultan of Selangor was himself very concerned over the historical decision to part with Selangor's sovereign land forever.

The most appropriate person to discuss with the Sultan of Selangor at that time was Tengku Razaleigh Hamzah, the Minister of Finance. He was well respected, had great appeal, and perhaps just as importantly, had the necessary royal rapport as a "Tengku". The discussions with the Sultan were polite, proper and prolonged. But the Tengku's charm and the Sultan's strong sense of national pride prevailed, and a mutually acceptable arrangement was arrived at. A reasonable compensation was paid to the Selangor State Treasury to develop the new township of Shah Alam and, of course, the "Marble Arch" which marks the border between the new Federal Capital of Kuala Lumpur and Selangor.

On Being Conferred the Datoship

I had a hand in preparing the briefs for the "royal discussions", and so, I think our Minister, Tengku Razaleigh, recommended that, as a subject of the Sultan of Selangor, the title of "Dato" be conferred on me. I heard about the award under interesting circumstances.

I was in Seattle, Washington, with the MAS delegation to witness the handover of the new Boeing 747. We were all seated at a formal lunch hosted by Boeing when I found that my name card on the dining table had the title "Dato" prefixed to my name for the first time. As soon as I looked up for clarification, I saw Risham Singh and Sitham from MAS, coming forward to congratulate me warmly. They had got a cable from their chief executive officer, my university mate Tan Sri Aziz Rahman in Kuala Lumpur, who had advised them to give me that pleasant surprise. Mariam Lisut, my secretary of 17 years, also sent me a cable to congratulate me on behalf of my staff. I was very surprised.

My Datoship was a tribute to the whole Economics Division as well. We had worked as a professional team, and the award was in recognition of the Economics Division's contribution to economic and financial planning and management in our country and I felt gratified.

16.
SERVING TUN TAN SIEW SIN
AND TUN ABDUL RAZAK

TUN Tan Siew Sin served the government and the nation with great distinction, from the earliest days leading to our independence and well beyond *Merdeka*. He succeeded his illustrious father, Tun Tan Cheng Lock as the leader of the Malayan Chinese Association (MCA), and a member of the cabinet.

Tun Tan Siew Sin was also the Minister of Trade before he became the Minister of Finance. As a Minister, he gave great confidence to the business community, both domestic and foreign, especially after independence. There had been concerns as to whether Malaya would follow the way of many other developing socialist-type economies that nationalised their industries and economies, and eventually went down the drain. But Tun Tan overcame all these doubts.

He had many British officers working under him in the civil service. I think he realised that the British officers found it somewhat difficult to promote local trade and industry, because they had been trained to think and act mainly to protect the interests of their motherland — Great Britain. Thus, Tun Tan must have been quite frustrated when he made his now famous pronouncement that his senior British officials who were members of the "Malaysian Civil Service", were neither "Malaysian" nor "civil" nor did they provide real "service" to the nation! Of course, the British civil servants reacted angrily to this critical ministerial statement. But then, they were already on their way out, and therefore their protests fell on deaf ears! But we Malaysian civil servants truly liked Tun Tan's remarks!

Tun Tan's brilliance showed through when he was the Minister of Finance. He was the most senior finance minister in the Commonwealth when he retired before the general elections in August 1974. He had been Minister of Finance for about 15 years and was regarded with a great deal of reverence by his peers in the World Bank, the International Monetary Fund, and indeed among bankers and financiers all over the world.

We in Malaysia owe a great deal of gratitude to Tun Tan for his leadership in the Treasury, and for his deep dedication to serve the country with impeccable integrity and high standards of financial discipline. He truly had a rare resolve to act in the national interest first and always, even if it adversely affected his personal or political interests.

Tun Tan had a flair for details without losing sight of the long-term strategy. He could go through voluminous documents rapidly, and yet when you least expected, he could point out a wrong figure, an arithmetical error, and even a misplaced comma or colon. We had to be very careful before we sent Tun Tan any paper for approval. He would pull us up quite abruptly, and this was very embarrassing. Despite checking and rechecking, I was pulled up on several occasions as I worked closely with Tun Tan. My challenge and satisfaction was therefore to get my drafts back, without any red mark or correction. Indeed, I learnt a great deal from Tun Tan on how to write "clearly, comprehensively and concisely", as he put it. Tun Tan's great diligence and demanding pace took a toll on him. He had part of his lung removed when he was a young man. The medical problems relating to his lungs resurfaced. He needed medical attention and a great deal of rest. He therefore was finally persuaded to take a break from his heavy duties in the government and the MCA, to get medical attention.

Tun Razak, who succeeded Tunku Abdul Rahman as Prime Minister on September 22, 1970, then took over the duties of Minister of Finance as well. I had the privilege of preparing the draft Budget Speech for Tun Razak. His style was different from that of Tun Tan. Tun Razak empowered his officials and advisers more than most leaders that I have come across. Tun Razak was interested in the main issues and in the political implications of any new policies. He left the details to the officials. He did not say much. He just asked a few sharp questions and if he was satisfied with the answers, he gave his approval.

He had the habit of acknowledging the remarks of those who spoke or briefed him, by responding with a "hmm". But some officials were known to have taken his acknowledgement as an assent to their proposals, when in fact he was merely acknowledging that he was listening to their views. Some got into trouble as a result of this. But we in the Treasury had a different culture. We would always follow up with a memorandum to confirm our understanding and get a decision in writing. We had therefore no problems working under Tun Razak as he especially understood the style and system of the civil service—having been one of them before. Tun Razak was also a very decisive man because he had confidence that he had the full support of his cabinet.

We were also greatly assisted by one of our most outstanding civil servants of the day, who was Tun Razak's "special assistant". He was the late Tan Sri Zain Azraii. He was highly intellectual, polished, truly professional, and had the full confidence of the Prime Minister. So, when I had a problem of getting clearance for a budget policy proposal, I would consult my dear old school captain and friend, and he would get the decision for the Treasury. Zain was a fine diplomat and an excellent civil servant. It is such a pity that he is no longer with us.

Tun Hussein Onn as Minister of Finance
The fourth Malaysian general elections were held on August 24, 1974. The Barisan National government did outstandingly well once again. As expected after a general election, a cabinet reshuffle followed.

Fortunately, we were privileged to have as our new Minister of Finance, the Deputy Prime Minister, Tun Hussein Onn. He was previously the Minister of Education, with a reputation in the civil service as a tough and no-nonsense type. He was, after all, a former military officer trained at the famous Deradoon Military Academy in India, during World War II.

We in the Treasury were happy to hear that he was coming as our new boss. We had Tun H.S. Lee and Tun Tan Siew Sin as strict bosses, so we were not concerned when we heard through the civil service grapevine that Tun Hussein Onn was a hard taskmaster. We were used to it and liked the idea, as we had to have a strong minister in the Treasury to deal with other ministers who were always asking for more and more financial allocations. But we did not expect him to be that tough so early in his career as the Minister of Finance!

The first day Tun Hussein arrived in the Treasury, he summoned all the heads of divisions, heads of departments, and senior officials in the Treasury. We were all ready to brief the new Minister on the workings of the Treasury, but Tun Hussein had other ideas. Somehow, he had the impression that there was a lot of corruption in the Ministry of Finance. He might have been told that the Customs Department had a larger share of corrupt officials than in other places. I do not know the real reason, but as soon as he came into the conference room to address us, he lashed out at all of us.

Tun Hussein Onn was not one to mince his words. His main point was that he was unhappy to hear that there was corruption in the Treasury, and that he was determined to wipe it out. He believed that the Treasury, as the heart of the government's financial management, must be clean. He was right and all good Treasury officials agreed with him. But what they could not understand was why he had to be so severe with us—as if the Treasury was corrupt, and all of us, by implication, were also corrupt. Quite naturally, we all reacted against Tun Hussein's strong remarks which we considered unjustified. We wondered what his basis for the criticism was, particularly since he was so new to the Treasury.

We also realised that he would not tolerate open contradiction. When someone asked him whether he could elaborate on why he thought there was corruption in the Treasury, he did not quite like the suggestion that he was being unfair.

We all went back to our rooms quite concerned that our new Minister had such an unfavourable impression of us. Many of us were quite justifiably discouraged. But we soon also learnt that our initial misgivings were quite baseless.

Tun Hussein turned out to be a firm, fair, kind, and considerate gentleman, and also a distinguished leader. His inspiration, I believe, came from his high integrity. His strong values were inherited from his illustrious father, the late Dato' Onn Jaafar, who was the first leader of the United Malays National Organisation (UMNO). He also derived his strong discipline from his military background.

I recall going to Tun Hussein's official residence at the Lake Gardens for a meeting, when he was not so well. As I waited for him to enter his study, I noticed on the wall, a framed inscription that read like a military code of conduct from Deradoon. It read something like this: "The children and their mothers come first, my soldiers come second, my officers come next, and I come last." I believe that he lived up to the spirit of that doctrine and the motto "I come last". Indeed, Tun Hussein was a very selfless person. He worked very hard and took his files home regularly. He did not give himself much time to rest or relax. His guards would carry several red boxes of files every day when he returned home, and we often wondered how many files he could clear, with all the official functions he had to attend at night. But he nevertheless observed the daily ritual.

He had an inclination to laugh loudly and quite suddenly over a funny remark during a serious discussion. We sometimes wondered whether it was his way of unwinding or taking a break from the heavy discussions at hand. When he relaxed, he was very warm and friendly.

But Tun Hussein also had a temper. Fortunately, it was not a short temper, and we could often see it develop. However, we also learnt the art of watching the signs. Thus, when Tun Hussein did not like something and got irritated with the way some tactless officials presented their cases, his temper would slowly rise. We could literally see it rise as his right hand would close at the tips of all five fingers and his hand would gradually rise higher and higher with a clenched fist. When we saw his right hand begin to rise, we would try to distract him with other matters or discourage the official concerned from pursuing with his unproductive briefing. Most times, our tactic worked!

However, despite my care and vigilance, I got into trouble with Tun Hussein on one occasion when I was briefing him on the draft Budget Speech. Tun had wanted to include the proposal to build the new Senai airport at Johor Bahru. But at that time in the early 1970s, the air traffic from Johor Bahru to Kuala Lumpur and to Singapore was relatively low. So, the civil aviation officials were not prepared to give the project high priority. They preferred to use the funds for what they thought (from a technical point of view) were often more urgent airport projects.

My role was to put all the tax, expenditure and financial proposals together in a coherent manner to make economic sense. So I frankly told the Tun that I had problems with the proposed Senai airport, as the civil aviation officials had strong reservations about this proposal. I did not know that he had heard about these reservations before, and had overruled the objections earlier. So when he heard my views, he thought that I was also opposing the project. I saw the fingers of his right hand tighten, and then his hand began to rise. Quickly, I tried to distract him. I even suggested that after all it was the Finance Minister's prerogative to provide funding, and that we could overrule the Department of Civil Aviation. But it was too late. His tension had been building up previously. He finally exploded at me. I just kept quiet.

He was in no mood to listen and I realised that I would only make matters worse if I tried to defend myself. So, I let him carry on until he slowly simmered down. Then in a calm voice he asked me to explain myself. I did so and to my great surprise, he laughed in a very paternal and affectionate way and asked me why I did not explain myself earlier. I told him that I was taken aback by his outburst, and we then both laughed together! He told me to forget about it and to put the Senai Airport project in the Budget Speech. After that episode, we got on very well. Even when he became Prime Minister, he would always have time to have a few words with me whenever we met.

There were times when there would be some professional differences of view between the Treasury and the Economic Planning Unit of the Prime Minister's Department, which also came under Tun Hussein as Prime Minister. However, most times we won the argument because Tun Hussein knew the Treasury officials better and trusted their judgment. In the final analysis, Tun Hussein was by nature, and by his military and legal training, a very meticulous and careful person. The relatively conservative and cautious approach of the Treasury officials therefore appealed to his philosophy. He became a strong champion of Treasury policies even after he became Prime Minister. Tun Hussein further consolidated the financial discipline and high standards of prudence set by Tun H.S. Lee, Tun Tan Siew Sin, and Tun Razak, who was also Finance Minister for a short time.

I believe that earlier Ministers of Finance like Tun Lee, Tun Tan and Tun Hussein laid the solid foundation for Malaysia's financial management, strength and stability. That is why the Malaysian experience in socioeconomic progress and prosperity has been so successful and also so different from most developing countries.

But Tun Tan and Tun Hussein could not have been such strong Ministers of Finance if not for the firm support that they received from both Tunku Abdul Rahman and Tun Razak. It was quite remarkable that they all worked so closely together and allowed their Ministers of

Finance so much freedom to manage the country's resources independently. I cannot recall any time, when the Prime Minister overruled the Minister of Finance. Even in the case of the budget proposals, it was rare for the Treasury not to have its way. The only time there might have been some disagreement was when there was a political basis for changing or deferring a Treasury Budget proposal, especially in the area of new taxes. This harmonious relationship between the Prime Ministers and their Ministers of Finance was strong and beneficial to the nation.

Tun Razak as Prime Minister

Tun Razak became the Prime Minister on September 22, 1970, after holding the chairmanship of the National Operations Council (NOC) for more than a year. He had been Deputy Prime Minister and Minister of National and Rural Development for many years earlier. As Deputy Prime Minister, he served Tunku Abdul Rahman, the first Prime Minister, with great loyalty and dedication.

With his *Red Book* strategy, he transformed the rural economy of Malaysia from widespread poverty to a much-reduced level of poverty, and indeed raised the standards of living of the country. The *Red Book* was based on the concept of the planned and strategic war against militant communists in the jungles of Malaysia. Every district in the country was under a District Officer who would have a series of maps in literally a red-covered book. Each map covered important aspects of the topography, geography, population, agriculture, income distribution and employment patterns in the area.

Tun Razak would visit every district to review the progress made in the implementation of the various *Red Book* plans. He would meet the rural folk and discuss their problems, hopes, and aspirations. He would advise them and encourage them to work closely with the government and its numerous policies and programmes to fight and overcome poverty. Tun Razak genuinely cared for the poor in our country. He approached the fight against poverty with missionary zeal, and was very successful at it.

He pushed hard to expand the land development schemes. The Federal Land Development Authority (Felda) opened up thousands of hectares of jungle land for new land settlement for farmers, who were caught in the grips of poverty, mainly due to inadequate land to cultivate economically. I think that it was because of his deep dedication to help the poor, that the masses rallied round the leaders in resisting the communist terrorists. Tun Razak's identification with the aspirations of the masses also gave them a strong sense of identity and pride in upholding democracy and independence. This is one reason why Malaysia did not develop the culture of military rule and dictatorship as in many developing countries. Tun Razak spent a great deal of time with the common people and did not travel much abroad. His priority was at home.

Tun Razak had been responsible for the national education policy that was based on his report called "The Razak Report". This report laid the foundations for the education policies in Malaysia after independence. It still remains the basis for our education system and reform — that has been implemented with great skill and style by his worthy son and heir, Dato' Sri Najib Razak, who has also served as Minister of Education.

New Economic Policy (NEP)
Of all the great contributions made by Tun Razak towards building Malaysia into a strong and stable nation, his formulation of the NEP stands out as a monument to his illustrious career as an outstanding leader.

The NEP, which was Tun Razak's brainchild, was the main policy instrument that saved Malaysia from disunity and deterioration after the shocking and traumatic racial violence of May 13, 1969. It was Tun Razak's genius that made it possible for the Malays, Chinese, Indians, Sri Lankans, Kadazans, Dayaks, as well as other minority races to accept the political and socioeconomic compromises in good faith. More importantly, it was the confidence and trust that the people of Malaysia had in his sincerity of purpose that led the diverse peoples of our country, to accept the NEP.

The NEP was built on two pillars: to alleviate and eradicate poverty regardless of race and to remove the identification of race with occupation.

In retrospect, these two aims saved the country and safeguarded the sovereignty and integrity of Malaysia. This claim might sound hollow to many Malaysians and especially to the youths of today — but I believe this thesis to be true. I also believe that time will prove that this policy has stood the test of time and brought continued peace and prosperity to the country.

Those of us who lived and worked during those tumultuous times know how sensitive and uncertain the future of the country was at that crucial time. Most Malays felt that enough was enough, and that the bloodshed on May 13, 1969 should not be in vain. That was the time of the National Operations Council, when Parliament was suspended. As chairman of the NOC, Tun Razak had almost absolute power. The government of the day could have usurped power permanently as indeed has been quite common in many countries. Some of these countries are quite close to us and could have provided attractive models to follow. But Tun Razak stood firm against some extremist views and demands by even some respected intellectuals who felt it was now or never. They were keen for power and wealth and did not want the opportunity to pass. They felt that they had to strike while the iron was hot.

The Chinese and, to a lesser extent, the Indians felt a great sense of insecurity. Would there be large-scale nationalisation? Would the non-Malays have a chance to survive or have a fair place under the Malaysian sun? What would be the fate of our children? Would they be severely discriminated against in education opportunities, employment opportunities in the government, and later, in the private sector as well? Would the government use its absolute emergency powers, the military troops and the police force, to suppress the non-Malays and rule by decree?

These were some of the deep concerns and fears of many non-Malays that were not openly expressed or articulated. But these fears, whether justified or not, were real and even contagious. That is why so many non-Malays migrated to Australia, the United Kingdom, the U.S., and even to Singapore and many other places after the May 13 riots. That is why many parents, especially the richer ones, also sent their young children abroad, mainly to the United Kingdom and Australia for studies and to wait and see how it would all turn out, particularly after Bahasa Malaysia was introduced as the medium of instruction in Malaysian schools.

We should thank God that Malaysia actually turned around and grew from strength to strength as a united nation. Credit for this wonderful achievement must go largely to Tun Razak. It was he who decided to return the country to normalcy and the democratic path. He could have maintained his absolute power and Malaysia could have moved towards autocratic rule and anarchy, just like many other developing countries. History and all Malaysians therefore owe Tun Razak a special place in our national history and in our hearts.

Tun Razak's Passing

Tun Razak's toil, stress and sacrifice eventually took a silent toll on him. Outwardly he looked well, but because of his hectic schedule, hardly anyone knew that he was very ill. It was therefore a shock to the nation when he went to London for urgent medical treatment.

The whole country hoped and prayed that he would pull through. But, unfortunately, he passed away peacefully in London on January 14, 1976. His body was flown back to a nation shaken. They remembered him with deep gratitude for having pulled the nation through its darkest times. They remembered him for his great patriotism, his great honesty, integrity and his immense sacrifice to the nation.

I recall going to his funeral. It was a grand funeral. The magnitude of the mourning was widespread—for here was the passing of Malaysia's own true son, patriot and hero of the people. I was with Thong Yaw Hong, Cosmos Robless, Rama Iyer, Ramesh Chander, and Malek Merican at the Masjid Negara to witness the last rites. We had all worked for the great leader at one time or another. We were distressed and wondered what would be the implications of the untimely death of Tun Razak, on the future of our country.

The NEP, Tun Razak's legacy, is still with us, although in a somewhat modified form. The major difference is that whereas the NEP had a time frame of 20 years, the National Development Policy (NDP) has no time limit now. This can mean that the NDP can go on and on, and that the *bumiputeras* will enjoy government preferential treatment and patronage for a much longer time. On the other hand, it could mean that we need not rush to attain the NEP targets by rigid dates. Whether this policy is sound for the government and the people (the *bumiputeras* and the non-*bumiputeras*), only time will tell!

However, I believe that the NDP will continue to provide strength, stability, progress and prosperity, only if the policies are implemented in a fair and just manner—within the spirit of its founder—Tun Abdul Razak Hussein al-Haj. Already there are some signs of excesses, of increasing corruption and distortions. Some big businessmen are getting huge contracts that have made them multi-millionaires or even billionaires very quickly. Whether this is good for the country and the people, again only time will tell! But I see that some excesses are already causing strains on the economy. "Money politics" has been growing to the detriment of progress.

17.
TUN HUSSEIN ONN BECOMES PRIME MINISTER AND DR MAHATHIR MOHAMAD DEPUTY PRIME MINISTER

ON January 15, 1976, just a day after the demise of Tun Razak, Tun Hussein Onn, the Deputy Prime Minister, was sworn in as Malaysia's third Prime Minister. He was Tun Razak's brother-in-law and was regarded as a reluctant political leader. He agreed to become Prime Minister only because of his deep sense of duty in having to respond to the call to serve the country in its time of need. He was in reality a professional soldier and a lawyer — not so much a politician. He had given us all, his subordinates, the impression that he was not the political type, and it was obvious that he did not enjoy playing politics. He was as straight as an arrow, and scrupulously clean and transparent in his leadership and management.

Tun Hussein quickly settled down to the heavy responsibilities of leading the government. We knew that there would have to be a cabinet reshuffle under his leadership. He could not be the Prime Minister and the Minister of Finance at the same time for long. For us in the Treasury, that would be too good to be true. We waited without a full-time Minister in the Treasury which, in the meantime, was run mainly by the senior Treasury officials. However, we did not have to wait long.

On March 5, 1976, Prime Minister Tun Hussein Onn appointed Dato' Seri Dr Mahathir Mohamad as Deputy Prime Minister and Tengku Razaleigh as Minister of Finance. Dato' Richard Ho Ung Hun was appointed as Deputy Minister of Finance.

Tengku Razaleigh as Minister of Finance
I had met Tengku Razaleigh only once, before he became Minister. It was in London when I was on my way to a World Bank meeting in Washington around February 1976. My former schoolmate, Ananda Krishnan, had heard from our High Commission that I was in London with some Treasury officials and invited us for lunch. It was there that I first met Tengku Razaleigh. But I had heard a great deal about him since he was a prominent leader in Petronas, Pernas and Bank Bumiputra.

In his short period after graduation in Belfast, he had already built a formidable reputation as a bright and rising star who was destined for great things and top leadership in the country. Ananda could have guessed that Tengku Razaleigh was going to be appointed Minister of Finance — that was why, perhaps, he wanted Tengku to meet some of the Treasury officials who were going to work under him.

We had a pleasant lunch at a leading hotel. There was good wine and good company, lively discussion and a lot of good humour. We all enjoyed ourselves right through to tea-time, and then we had English tea and muffins as well! The Treasury officials present were highly impressed with Tengku's style and self-confidence. We, of course, were not aware that he would be our boss soon. Otherwise, I would have been more careful with the way I handled my discussions with him. I had argued a lot with him. He was provocative and I was cavalier!

Tengku Razaleigh was the first long-serving Malay Minister of Finance in the country and the youngest ever. He was also the first Malaysian minister with an economics degree. It did not take him long to get a good grasp of fiscal and monetary policies of the Treasury, as well as its relations with the rest of the government. We gave him a few briefings and soon realised that he knew his onions and that it was difficult to get anything past him without his knowledge, although he was new to the Treasury.

Tengku was really sharp, and he dressed sharply too. With his extraordinary princely charm, wit and warm personal relations, he quickly won the confidence, support and loyalty of the Treasury officers. He had a real flair for leadership and the cultivation of teamwork, camaraderie, and a family spirit in the Treasury. The officers and staff were happy in the Treasury under Tengku's leadership. Somehow, he did not have a harsh word for anyone. If someone was found wanting, he would make a joke of the lapse in a good humoured way and would subsequently give the person less onerous responsibilities. By the same token, if he found someone to be able, hardworking and responsible, then that person would be given more responsibility. It was as if he practiced the maxim of "from each according to his ability".

Thus, I was one of those who was given more responsibilities. The other senior officers who were loaded with more work and responsibilities were Tan Sri Sallehuddin Mohamad and the late Dato' Badruddin Samad. Salleh was the head of the Tax Division; Badruddin was the head of the Budget Division, while I headed the Economics Division of the Treasury. We were a good team. After all, we were all from the same economics class at the University of Malaya in Singapore, from which we graduated in 1959, when we also started our careers in the

Home and Foreign Service, or as it was known then, the elitist Malaysian Civil Service (MCS).

Being good friends, we were able to take greater advantage of the arrangements Tengku Razaleigh had introduced in the new Treasury building at Jalan Duta. Under this arrangement, all the heads of divisions in the Treasury were required to leave their respective divisions that were situated on different floors of the 16-storey tower building at Jalan Duta and to move to the 14th floor. The Minister, his staff and the secretary-general occupied the 15th floor. The Conference and Dining rooms were at the 16th floor.

Although most of the heads of division were reluctant to be situated on a different floor from their staff, for fear that they might lose contact and even leadership of their staff, Tengku Razaleigh insisted that there were more pros than cons to his proposal. So, we acquiesced and moved to the 14th floor. But we soon realised that the Tengku was right. This was his first move in changing the management style of the Treasury and in making it more orientated to corporate business management.

The advantage of this new proposal was that the consultation, co-operation, and coordination in the Treasury improved considerably. The Treasury had grown so big without our realising it. Obviously, the Tengku found that we were all working in our own worlds without the benefits of constant consultations that would better focus our thinking and planning to achieve the same vision and mission of the government and the Treasury.

What happened was that, instead of holding our planning close to our chests, we began to share our knowledge and to integrate our plans more meaningfully. This enabled the heads of divisions to interact more closely and to develop wholesome economic, fiscal and monetary policies, with the osmosis of ideas from all divisions into a composite Treasury view of the economy. In this way, we understood even better what had to be done to improve fiscal management.

We soon began to enjoy this new style in the culture of Treasury management. When we could, we would just drop into each other's office to discuss a problem that our own officials could not solve among themselves, perhaps because they had narrow tunnel views on the subject. But when we, as Heads of the Divisions put our heads together, we would have a different perspective and thus found it easier to resolve the different viewpoints. In this way we were able to put up agreed positions and specific recommendations to the Secretary-General and the Minister. Thus, the previous entrenched positions and controversies or conflicts were considerably reduced. This made it easier for Tengku Razaleigh to manage the large, strong and powerful Treasury more effectively.

Moral of the Shoes

Our frequent informal meetings on the 14th floor of the Treasury building strengthened our personal relationships too. We got to see the human side of each other much better because of our close rapport. One day, we were having an informal meeting on budget planning when we had a break for tea and then started comparing notes on our frequent travels. We talked about the good purchases we had made abroad.

Then, someone showed us the pair of good Italian shoes that he had recently bought overseas. Someone else soon took off his pair of shoes that he had bought in Paris and spoke highly of its fine quality. They both wore expensive shoes costing about RM300 a pair at that time. I was not going to be outdone. So, I took off my shoes, bent them as they had done, to show the softness and the shine of the leather. I explained that I had bought the pair in Venice where it was cheaper than in Rome or Paris at only RM200. I showed them the brand name that read "Tulsea" and pointed out that it was custom made especially for me. Salleh and Badruddin were impressed and commended me for getting such a good bargain.

I myself felt impressed that I had managed to convince them that I had bought such expensive shoes, although they knew that I was quite a frugal fellow. I smiled to myself and they got suspicious. I then felt compelled to tell them the truth (which I had intended to, anyway). They soon learnt that I had bought my pair of shoes which were indeed handmade from genuine calf leather with the Italian-sounding name of "Tulsea" in Kuala Lumpur, for only RM40!

To me, it proved a few things. We were (and many still are) very brand-conscious. We tend to ignore our own local products that may be as good or even better than the foreign ones. Anyway, I am still frugal, and am quite proud of it. I continued to use those shoes quite comfortably for many years.

Non-Malay Frugality

I think there is another moral to this story. I have found that many non-Malays in the same income bracket as our Malay colleagues tend to save more than some of our Malay friends do. I have asked myself for the reasons, some of which I list below:

First, I think that non-Malays generally earn their money through greater effort. They are less likely to get accelerated promotions in the civil service or win concessions and contracts in the private sector.

Second, non-Malays feel compelled to save more especially for their children's education, because they are less likely to get government scholarships.

Third, non-Malays have to save more as they are less likely to have their children admitted to the local universities because of the ethnic quota system for entry to the local universities. Thus, they need to save more to be able to send their children for twinning degree courses with foreign universities or to send them abroad for further studies. For instance, it can cost as much as half a million ringgit to educate a child in a good medical college overseas. How does one get that kind of money, unless one begs, borrows, steals or sacrificially saves from his meagre income? Of course, if he is wealthy or had inherited some properties, or was corrupt, it would be a different story.

Thus, the national policies virtually force some people—especially the non-Malays to save more. Maybe these were the reasons that unconsciously forced me to save, since Samala and I had three schoolgoing boys who, thank God, were able to benefit from good foreign university education, mainly through our relatively frugal and simple lifestyle. We rarely bought branded or foreign clothes!

18.
THE NATIONAL LANGUAGE IN EDUCATION

IN the 1970s, there was great concern about the future of our children, especially among the non-Malays. The Malay language was officially adopted as the medium of instruction in the national education system. This was a good move as it contributed a great deal towards the promotion of a national identity and stronger national unity. But it might have been overdone.

Unfortunately, the English language was given far less priority than previously. Thus, the standard of English began to decline steadily. Less time was given for the teaching of English and English literature. Teachers were given less time at the Teachers' Colleges for training in the teaching of the English language. The standard of communication and expression in the English language therefore deteriorated even further.

Middle-class parents, especially those in urban areas, became increasingly concerned about the future prospects of their children's education and careers. They were used to the former colonial system of education where the English language was given high priority, even (quite wrongly) much higher than that of the Malay language. Parents like us and even our parents have come a long way, mainly because of our education and proficiency in the English language. The concern for the future of our children's education was therefore genuine and with a sound basis. With more globalisation, one had to master the English language to prosper and progress.

The consequence was that many parents, especially those who had the money, were prepared to send their children (some at the tender age of 11) to the United Kingdom, Australia, and even the U.S. to study in the English language. They were sent to boarding schools or to live with relatives who had migrated earlier. They made many sacrifices so as to send their children abroad. It was traumatic.

Another unfortunate consequence of this downgrading of the English language was that it encouraged the many concerned parents to also migrate overseas. They did not mind the emphasis on the teaching of the national language, which they considered to be legitimate and fully justified. However, they were against the serious downgrading of the English language, which they could foresee would definitely affect their children's future prospects.

This grave concern was not only felt by the professional and middle classes. Several government ministers had also begun to send their children abroad to study. Their official and public justification at that time was that they were not too concerned about the relative neglect of the English language. However, some said that they felt obliged to send their children abroad because they did not want their children to be shown any preference locally or be seen to be given preferential treatment as children of ministers! Some of these ministers' children are now back home and are holding high official posts in the government, though not necessarily in the civil service. Some are big businessmen and multi-millionaires! This is what a good English education has given them! But a good education in English was denied to the masses. This alone set back the progress of the majority of the children and youth of this country. They now run the risk of marginalisation in the Digital Age! Now, thanks to Dr Mahathir and Pak Lah more English will be taught in schools, especially for Mathematics and Science.

Our Children's Education

Many of my relatives and friends sent their children abroad. Several asked me why I did not seem worried about the need to send our own children abroad. My answer was quite simple:

First, we could not bear to send our children abroad at such a tender age. What is the point of having children if we were going to send them to boarding school to be looked after by some strangers?

Second, our children were only in primary school, and I was confident that they would be able to learn Malay and at the same time remain pretty good in English. After all, we spoke English at home.

Thirdly, we believed that some parents were over-exaggerating the adverse effects of having Malay as the medium of instruction. We felt that we should not overreact and should give the new education system a chance. We were not prepared to be hasty in such an important matter. If the education system deteriorated badly, then we were prepared to send our children abroad, but not before we were convinced that the system was actually declining so rapidly that it would affect our children adversely. We had our children studying in the U.S. when I was at the World Bank, and we could appreciate the pros and cons of sending our children abroad at a young age.

However, much later, when Ravi and Indran were in lower secondary at the Victoria Institution (where my father and I had attended school), I asked them whether they wanted to study abroad. I explained that they could stay at home and go abroad to study later, but that if they wanted to study medicine, then they would need to seriously consider going to the United Kingdom to study earlier. We were told that it was easier to get into a British medical school from a British secondary school, and preferably from a British "public school"!

In fact, we were prepared for contingencies. As the children grew older, I applied to several public schools in Britain. I had actually got favourable replies from good schools like Oundle and Sevenoaks, but felt the decision should largely be based on how Ravi, Indran and Dharm, felt about studying abroad at a tender age.

We did not want to be in the position of some parents who were faced with the questions posed by their young children who had asked: "Mum and Dad, why did you have me if you wanted to send me away for someone else to look after me?" That was a terrible question. We did not want to give our children that trauma. Neither did we want to suffer the pain of separation, nor the inability to influence their development and to guide their precious lives during their growing-up years.

When we asked Ravi and Indran whether they were interested in doing medicine, they were quite clear that they were not. I was quite pleased with their decision because I still have strong views that medicine, like priesthood and teaching, are special callings and vocations, unlike most other jobs. Thus, I believe that those who choose to be doctors, teachers or priests, should be blessed with a high degree of commitment and dedication to serve the sick and the poor with compassion and not for profit! They should not become doctors merely to make money, as many of them do. I myself did not see any evidence of Ravi, Indran, or Dharm being interested in medicine. So that was a good decision, as they did not have to rush off to the United Kingdom or anywhere else, where they could get admission into a good medical school.

Ravi faired well at school consistently. He did not have to do all his subjects in Malay. The science subjects were still taught in English. So, he was able to cope in the new school system pretty well. His early education at the Garden School in Kuala Lumpur and in the U.S. gave him a good foundation in general and in English in particular.

Indran too coped pretty well at school, although he was in the first batch to face the full brunt of teaching in Malay. It would have been fine, except that the teachers themselves, especially the non-Malays, were really not well-prepared to teach the Malay language professionally and proficiently. Furthermore, most of the textbooks were not well written in Malay. Indeed, these Malay textbooks were often rush jobs. There were many gross errors, which were unacceptable to the teachers and students alike.

I therefore explained to the boys the differences between the school systems here and in the U.S. I pointed out that in the U.S., the classes were much smaller and the teachers had a lot of time for each child. They could give more individual attention and build up closer and warmer friendships with the pupils. Here in Malaysia, the classes were much bigger, with about 40 to 50 students per class. There was so much to teach in a short space of time, and so it was difficult for teachers to give personal attention.

Dharm Reads Early

Dharm had no problems adjusting to school. He was too young to attend school in the U.S. He was about two years old when we took him to the States where I was serving on the World Bank Board of Directors. Samala spent a lot of time with him.

Dharm was a keen student. He would spend a lot of time looking at the many interesting children's books that we had got for him in the States. I therefore started teaching him in a playful way to read the letters of the alphabet and then to read phonetically. For instance, I would teach him to read and to pronounce the word "at". Then I would draw up a whole list of words made up of "at". Thus, very soon Dharm could read words like *bat, cat, fat, hat, mat, pat, rat* and *sat*. Then I would join the words into a sentence such as: "The fat cat sat on the mat with a hat to get the rat!".

We thus had a lot of fun, for I would continue with the word "un" and have words like *bun, fun, gun, run*, and *sun*. Dharm picked up fast and it was most gratifying to watch him progress at a fast pace. Soon, he was reading phonetically for his own fun. Before long, he would read whole simple sentences from even the newspapers. So Dharm started to read at about the age of three and a half.

After we returned home, Dharm went to St John's Primary School. We were all at work or at school. We did not have a good servant after our old servant Parti passed away. Since 1974, it had been already difficult to get reliable servants.

Dharm had to attend the afternoon school for a short period. When he started school, since we had no servant and all of us were at work or at school, he was left alone at home. He was about six years old and was in standard one. Samala would cook his lunch before she went to school and he would have his lunch by himself after doing his homework. He also had to bathe and dress himself up for school. After that, he would go downstairs, unlock the door, let himself out, lock the door, and then throw the key into the house, instead of taking it to school. He would then walk down to the main road to take the school bus to St John's Institution at Bukit Nanas.

We were not happy with this arrangement, but could not do much about it. In any case, this was to last for half a year only, and so we thought we would make the best of a difficult situation. I felt that if I could work as a despatch office boy at the age of eight, surely Dharm would have the confidence to manage himself. He was an independent and self-reliant kid. I always assured Dharm that I would immediately come home anytime he felt that he needed me. He could ring me or if I was at a meeting, he could ring up my faithful secretary Mariam Lisut. She would then get in touch with me or Samala, and we would respond at once. We wanted him to know that we were just a phone call and a few minutes away from home, in those days of traffic-free driving!

Dharm's Episode

One fine day, however, the usual routine for Dharm was shattered. I was working intently on a draft speech for the Minister when Mariam rushed into my room. She told me that Dharm had rung her to say that "thieves" had entered the house! I was alarmed. I told her to call the police while I took my clerk and drove off in my Peugeot 403 to our home. I drove fast and even ignored the traffic lights to get home as soon as possible.

When I reached home, I called out to Dharm but there was no response. I imagined that he was muzzled and was being held hostage by the "thieves". So I went round the house, but found that the front and kitchen doors were locked. I started wondering how those "thieves" could have got into the house. Then, I went to Dharm's bedroom window with my clerk, and yelled his name repeatedly. Finally, he answered. I was relieved and asked him to open the kitchen door. I found him in tears and shaken. I asked him what had happened to the "thieves", and he replied, "No, papa, it's not thieves, but bees!" That was a real relief! Apparently Dharm had finished his lunch and was ready to go down the staircase to put on his shoes when he heard the buzzing of bees. Two big wasps were trapped by the glass door near the staircase, and were noisily banging themselves against the glass panes. This aggressive behaviour of the bees naturally terrified Dharm. He had to pass by the bees to get down to the ground floor in order to leave the house for school, and he was really scared!

When I had found out the facts, I quickly rang Mariam. She had learnt about the misunderstanding, as she was in conversation with Dharm while I was driving furiously back home. Hence, she had used her initiative and phoned back to the police to explain the confusion. All was well that ended well!

We learnt that it is difficult to strike a balance between allowing a child to grow up to be self-reliant and independent, and at the same time, ensure that we are not taking undue risks. Today, the task must be even greater. We do not want our children to be timid and lacking in confidence. We want them to be able to learn to take the knocks and to learn the lessons of life early in life. This is necessary so that they can acquire the skills of living, self-confidence and decision-making as part and parcel of developing their personalities.

But the environment has become far more hostile. Parents have to protect them against the reckless traffic, pornographic material and drugs that are readily available from their schoolmates. Too much protection from these scourges will make our children lose that cutting edge that is necessary for competition and entrepreneurial development.

On the other hand, too much freedom and an over-liberal outlook could inadvertently encourage them to become too independent, assertive, aggressive and defiant. They then would cease to listen to their parents and teachers. We could make things worse by giving in to their requests and sometimes even their demands. That is when trouble starts. They neglect their studies and could even drop out of school. Eventually, they could be involved in drugs and sex, and become anti-social elements.

Declining Social Values

I have no doubt that this is the way the phenomena of *lepak* and *bohsia* have developed. I would describe *lepak* as "excessive loitering" resulting from idleness and purposelessness. *Bohsia*, I would describe as "boredom that often leads to unhealthy social activities, including quiet sexual socialising".

These two social ills are interrelated and can adversely influence and undermine the tender and impressionable lives of our youth. Unfortunately, we do not have many opportunities in our society for school and social dropouts to get a second academic chance to break out from this downward social spiral. Thus, when they get into the mainstream of decline, they invariably sink further into the quagmire of social decay.

The social problems become more serious when we consider that they are happening despite the almost full employment in the country. Where there is unemployment, it is understandable that idleness alone can cause irresponsible youth to fall prey to hooliganism, crime, drugs and other antisocial behaviour. But it is not so easy to understand why youths who are fully employed should get involved in unhealthy activities. Is it because of the stress of urban living, the difficulties of coping with severe competition, ethnic tensions and odious comparisons, or poor parental care? Or is it due to an education system that adds so much pressure and so little pleasure during school life? It must be a combination of these and many other factors that have contributed to this undesirable situation. This is a threat to the nation's social stability.

One important area which sociologists must analyse is the positive and negative aspects of the NEP on social values, behaviour patterns and the conduct of the Malays. There is no doubt that the NEP has benefited millions of Malays, but there could also be adverse effects brought upon a large number of Malays who have not been able to cope with the rapid changes brought about by the NEP. In any case, the expectations of the Malays have been raised so high that many find it difficult to live up to the expectations of their parents and political leaders. These people have constantly urged them at home and in public to emulate the generally more hardworking Chinese, and this has been frustrating to many Malay youths.

There is also the concern that many *bumiputeras* have been disillusioned by the promise that they enjoy "special privileges" which, in reality are not easy to come by for most of the low-income Malays. Children at school could feel that the government would protect them and look after them. The government gives them what they need, without the need to work hard for scholarships and career advancement. They could develop a "dependency syndrome" or a subsidy mentality that really does not give them the emotional or psychological motivation to want to strive to excel. These values and attitudes, if not corrected early in their lives, will no doubt erode their will and determination to give their best in their endeavours at school and at work. Thus, the government may inadvertently be doing them a disservice!

The same argument applies in attempts by *bumiputeras* at starting up business ventures. They might be given licenses to start businesses quite easily but they have to find their own markets. Even when they have found ready captive markets, they may fail to prosper if they believe that the government will always be available to stand by to hold their hands. Even if this is not quite true, there is a strong perception that the government will not let them down and this is not conducive to their overall progress. Nevertheless, because their expectations are high, they can get terribly disappointed when their expectations turn sour. Then frustration sets in and that sometimes encourages indul-gence in antisocial practices.

The government had also over time become far more selective in the provision of scholarships and concessions. These privileges are now given to those *bumiputeras* who are thought to have the capacity to take full advantage of these privileges. Thus, more and more of the top academic scorers are getting the scholarships and study loans. More *bu-miputeras* with proven track records are also being given the responsi-bility to buy and run the huge corporate and privatised entities.

So there remains a large pool of *bumiputeras* who continue to have high expectations but lost ambitions. There is this growing gap be-tween hope and reality that is being unfulfilled. Fortunately, there are also some outstanding leaders among the *bumiputeras* but we need more of them for our country to progress on a more solid basis.

Tengku Razaleigh

Tengku Razaleigh was appointed a minister in March 1996. He was all set to take the centrestage and play a significant role in the Treasury, and in national and international economic affairs. On April 29, 1986, just a month after he became Minister of Finance, he was elected chairman of the board of governors at the 9th annual general meeting of the Asian Development Bank (ADB). He chaired the ses-sion with great distinction in Manila the following year.

A Civil Servant's Reward

I was on Tengku Razaleigh's delegation to the ADB meeting in Ma-nila, and it was quite inspiring to be led by a Minister of his calibre. He had both substance and style. He showed real flair in the conduct of the meetings and won the respect and admiration of the delegates. I helped to draft all of his many speeches and it was a real pleasure to en-joy the satisfaction of seeing him perform so well and to bring so much credit to our country.

In fact, that is perhaps the greatest reward for any civil servant — to know that he has done his best to serve his Minister and his country. It is a sense of exhilaration and reward, which is generally not understood in the private sector because they generally do not see beyond their money and the profits. But thank goodness, those values still remain, to a large extent, at least at the top echelons of the civil service.

If all the national contributions of the civil service were to be valued purely in monetary terms, then it would lead to poor priorities and bad national performance. Businessmen will need to increasingly realise that without civil servants of high calibre, the country will falter and lose out. Then the businessmen will not be able to prosper. There is so much good work done behind the scenes in the research for the preparation of sound policies at national and international levels. This cannot be quantified in only monetary terms, because nations are not managed only for profits. If that was the case, then it would be easy for governments to manage and govern effectively. But we are dealing with people's future, national pride and the progress of human welfare—all of which cannot be reduced simply to money in so crass a manner.

It is as unbecoming to equate the value of the national service of a soldier to his paltry salary, or compare the services of an *ulama* or priest to the spiritual welfare of a human being, to the low salary he would get, to keep body and soul together. But unless our society's values improve, we run the risk of going off the rails, in our path towards developed-nation status.

Rafidah as Deputy Finance Minister

Dato' Seri Rafidah Aziz was appointed Deputy Finance Minister on April 14, 1997. She was a young, bright academic who had been lecturing at the University of Malaya, and was also a charming lady. Her rise to high position in politics and government had been meteoric. She was full of enthusiasm and quite assertive. She was articulate, and was prone to lecturing us on economics, which was her field of teaching at the university. There was no doubt that she was meant for greater things in the future.

However, initially we in the Treasury felt her presence in the heart of the Treasury somewhat disconcerting. We had never had a Minister in the Treasury who was a lady. Some of us found that briefing Rafidah on Treasury matters was quite an uneasy experience. I think she may have sensed all this discomfort for she joked with us, called us by our first names and treated us as her colleagues. Soon we were all quite comfortable in her presence.

I used to sit next to her in our weekly "post-cabinet" meetings with the Minister, Tengku Razaleigh, and I enjoyed interacting intellectually with her. I learnt that she had strong feminist views but still maintained her feminine grace. We soon realised that we would get quick retorts if we cracked jokes that were distasteful or made remarks that had a male chauvinistic flavour.

The male domination in the Treasury had been eroded and the Treasury was never the same again. But Rafidah was definitely an asset to the Treasury for, among other things, we began to appreciate more the need to look after the interests of women and the implications of our budget tax and expenditure proposals on women.

19.
TUN HUSSEIN ONN PUSHES FOR THE COMMON FUND

MALAYSIA was strongly dependent on rubber production and especially the price of rubber as a major source of budget revenues and foreign exchange earnings. A fall of a few cents in the price of rubber had quite an impact on our capacity to balance the budget and to sustain our high investment in socioeconomic development at that time.

In mid-June 1977, the Commonwealth Heads of Government Meeting (CHOGM) was held in London. A major item on the agenda was the proposed establishment of the Common Fund. This fund was meant to provide a cushion against the wide fluctuations in the price of rubber in the international marketplace. These price fluctuations were often suspected by the developing countries to be subtly manipulated by some industrial countries. They were the major consumers of natural rubber and also producers of the competitive "synthetic rubber".

Furthermore, the U.S. operated a large strategic stockpile of natural rubber. This stockpile, run by the U.S. General Service Administration (GSA), caused serious problems to natural rubber-producing countries at that time. Any releases had a serious and damaging effect on the price of rubber. Malaysia, Indonesia, Sri Lanka, and several other developing countries used to be adversely affected by the operations of this US rubber stockpile.

We were therefore keen to get the Common Fund established. Some developing countries even suspected that the U.S. sometimes used the GSA stockpile as "Damocles' sword" over our heads. If we disagreed with any U.S. foreign policy, then we were and could be held to ransom by the U.S. to disrupt our economies through the manipulation of the GSA rubber stockpile.

The CHOGM in London, therefore, afforded Malaysia a good opportunity to press the Commonwealth countries to get the Common Fund established. The other developing countries in the Commonwealth looked up to us to take the lead since we were the biggest producer, and were in any case, the best equipped by virtue of our high standing, our track record of sound economic management, and the outstanding officials that we had in Tan Sri Rama Iyer, Dato' Lew Sip Hon, and Tan Sri B.C. Sekhar in our delegation. I was on the delegation as a younger official.

The Commonwealth Secretariat nominated our Prime Minister, Tun Hussein Onn, to present the case for the establishment of the Common Fund and to lead the way. We officials had done our homework. We had prepared the position papers, and had canvassed among the delegations of the Commonwealth member countries. We had also built up some consensus at the official levels in support of the Common Fund.

Now we needed our Prime Minister to raise this critical issue at the meeting of all the Prime Ministers from the Commonwealth countries. Metaphorically speaking, the rubber tree was ready to be tapped. We were all seated in the lounge outside the conference hall. Then we got a message that Tun Hussein would have to get ready to get into the conference hall, as his turn to speak would be coming up soon. We were therefore all set for our Prime Minister to leave the lounge for the conference room, when we found Tun Hussein looking all around him, as if he had lost something. But his speech was in his hand. What was so important as to cause him to look around in an anxious manner? It was not his reading glasses for he was wearing them. When we asked him what was the matter, he mentioned anxiously that he was missing his six-inch plastic ruler that he always carried with him to underline his notes and speeches!

We all started searching for his ruler. We looked under the chairs, on the thick colourful carpet, and under the cushions of the big leather chairs. We could not find any ruler.

Time was moving on and the conference officials came out again to invite Tun Hussein into the conference hall to deliver his important speech. When they found out our problem, they too joined the search for the Prime Minister's ruler. We were all now somewhat frantic. And then we found the transparent plastic ruler on the colourful carpet! We quickly gave Tun Hussein the ruler. He put it into his shirt pocket with joy, and then walked confidently into the conference hall, much to our relief. He was then in top form and delivered his speech with conviction and confidence.

Many of the Commonwealth Prime Ministers at the meeting were impressed with his speech, which provoked and promoted much fruitful discussion. The result was that our Prime Minister won a great deal of support for Malaysia's campaign to form the Common Fund. But many of us in the delegation often wondered what would have happened if we did not find that precious ruler in time for Tun Hussein. That little ruler ruled the day.

20.
TENGKU RAZALEIGH HAMZAH'S
ROLE IN INTERNATIONAL FINANCE

AT the 30th annual general meeting of the World Bank and the International Monetary Fund (IMF) in Washington in September 1977, Tengku Razaleigh Hamzah was elected as the chairman of the 31st Meeting to be held in the following year (1978). He was also appointed to serve as the representative of the Southeast Asia Voting Group (SEA Voting Group) of 11 countries, on the Interim Committee of the IMF. This Interim Committee consisted of 21 Ministers of Finance (who represented groups of countries, similar to our SEA Voting Group), from all over the world. Because of all these appointments, he was also asked to serve as the chairman of the joint committee of the World Bank and IMF for 1977/78. This committee was empowered with the responsibility to review all the salaries and conditions of service of the staff of both the international financial institutions.

It became clear, therefore, that both the financial leaders of the industrialised countries and the developing countries regarded the Tengku very highly. But all this entailed a great deal of work — for the reputation of Malaysia was at stake, including the personal standing of Malaysia's Minister of Finance. He had to perform well as the world's top financial leaders and experts would be watching him. Of course, as with all Ministers, he could not carry the whole responsibility and bear the brunt of the hard work all by himself. He had to rely on his staff for back-up, research and intellectual support. More importantly, all the ideas, thoughts and plans had to be analysed, organised and written up in a convincing manner. This was why the Minister had to take his staff along with him on his many trips abroad.

I therefore had to do a lot of travelling overseas. I had to accompany the Minister to meetings which were conducted by the World Bank, IMF, and many fora, including the Commonwealth of Nations. I was kept busy but I enjoyed the experiences of meeting top officials, intellectuals, thinkers and outstanding world leaders. The exposure and interaction with such high-calibre people proved to be a real treat and a source of inspiration for me.

I was able to travel extensively and participate actively at these high-level international conferences, mainly because I felt confident that Samala would look after the boys and the home with loving care. Whenever I came back from long overseas trips, I always returned to a home that was well run, harmonious and stable. The boys' educational and emotional needs were always well taken care of by Samala's love and dedication to her duties as a loving mother and a devoted wife.

My work was especially demanding when I followed Tengku Razaleigh. He had high standards and was very particular that we should get the right message across, with the correct tone and the appropriate subtleties. These requirements called for a great deal of drafting and redrafting, requiring lots of refinement in language and substance. The Tengku himself had a flair for the English language and it was quite exacting sometimes to get the right chord in a draft speech to achieve his high standards.

The Tengku used to read and reread his draft speeches, and I would then be asked to revise the text repeatedly and sometimes at odd times. One day, while we were travelling across the Atlantic to one of those many Washington meetings, he summoned me to his first-class compartment of the aircraft at 3am to go through a draft speech that I had prepared for him! I had enjoyed a good dinner with a few glasses of Don Perrignon and was fast asleep, when his faithful private secretary, Alias Ahmad, woke me up. He had not been sleeping but his mind was as clear as a bell. We went through the speech, and he made some amendments after some discussions with me. He also gave me a few points to consider for further inclusion in the draft.

We arrived in Washington the next morning. Tengku went straight to bed! But I had to go straight to the Malaysian Embassy to redraft some parts of the speech and to get it retyped. In those days, we did not have the luxury of personal computers. So, imagine how laborious it could be to have to retype everything just because of some amendments! I had a wash and a quick breakfast and started redrafting the speech. By noon, I was ready with my new draft, so I gave it to the typists and went out for lunch, with my friend Caesar Wellington and other officials.

The embassy staff were always very kind and obliging. They would look after our meals and even take us to do some shopping, if there was time. When I returned from shopping, the revised draft was neatly typed. It was evening and I returned to the hotel, gave Tengku the latest draft speech, and asked to be excused. I was really tired and needed a good bath and plenty of sleep. But Tengku, in his own way of showing his appreciation, characteristically advised me to have a short nap and to be ready in about two hours. He wanted to give me a well-earned dinner at a posh restaurant. That was the last thing on my mind, but it was always very difficult to refuse the well-meaning persuasions of Tengku. Anyway, that was his style. He always made sure that he took his staff to the best restaurants and discos in the world!

Brandt Commission Visits Malaysia

Soon after we returned from Washington, we had a big assignment. The Willy Brandt Commission was commissioned to write a report on the major development issues facing developing countries, with a view to enhancing human welfare.

Dato' Khartijah Ahmad was Malaysia's representative on the Commission, and this was a great honour to Malaysia and to Malaysian women in general. She is very bright, articulate, entrepreneurial and persuasive. She won support for Malaysia to be one of the few countries to be visited by the Commission since Malaysia was regarded (even then) as a promising developing country.

The Brandt Commission was to visit the Treasury to be briefed by the Minister of Finance. Of course, Tengku Razaleigh, as usual, wanted to do everything in style. Instead of the usual flip chart briefing, he wanted to introduce a new technique called a "multivision" slideshow. This programme which was computerised showed several slides at the same time in colour and proved to be very attractive and impressive.

Tengku asked me to be the scriptwriter for a commentator who would read the script that was to be incorporated in the slide show. It was a challenge. If the Minister thought I could do it, then I should try my best to deliver my best. So I started working on it (with the little time that I had) to the best of my ability.

Bangsa Malaysia

I recall that I had stated in the opening of the text of the multi-slide show that Malaysia is made up of many immigrant races. I explained that the Malays originally came from Indonesia, the Chinese from China and the Indians and Ceylonese from the Indian subcontinent. I pointed out that the original peoples were the aborigines in Peninsular Malaysia, and the Ibans, Dayaks, and other ethnic groups in Sabah and Sarawak in East Malaysia. However, my Secretary-General, Tan Sri Abdullah Ayub, asked me to change the draft. He pointed out that I should not mention that the Malays came from Indonesia since they are actually *bumiputeras* (or "sons of the soil").

I then realised the change in the trends. I sensed again how important it had become to stress the differences between the *bumiputeras* and the non-*bumiputeras*. Unfortunately, after about 45 years of independence, that cleavage remains on an even more pronounced scale! I wondered then and I continue to ask even now, when will we move more resolutely towards the establishment of a truly "Malaysian race" or "*Bangsa Malaysia*". We should move away from *Bangsa Melayu*, *Bangsa Cina*, *Bangsa India*, Ibans, Dayaks, and *Bangsa lain-lain*, to achieve the "*Bangsa Malaysia*" identity as soon as possible.

It will be necessary, as in many other societies, to take a long time to evolve as a united nation. But what is worrisome is that, at the rate we are going, it is going to take a much longer time than necessary. This is because there are many Malaysians who would want to delay the process of creating "*Bangsa Malaysia*" or a "Malaysian race". These people want to protect and perpetuate their own vested interests. Some of these people will accumulate wealth, hoard it, stash it, and enjoy it for generations to come.

All of us loyal Malaysians therefore have a moral, spiritual and patriotic duty to do our best within peaceful and legal means, to ensure that we move more purposely towards the creation of the "Malaysian race" or "*Bangsa Malaysia*", as envisaged in our Vision 2020. We owe it to our forefathers, ourselves, our children, and future generations to achieve the status of *Bangsa Malaysia* as soon as we can.

Finally, the script was completed well in time for the Brandt Commission briefing. The Minister was pleased. He received praises for a good presentation, and the Brandt Commission members themselves were most impressed with Malaysia's political style, socioeconomic progress and management techniques.

Their assessment was that if Malaysia carried out its sound policies as well as it had done in the past, then they had no doubt that Malaysia would perform even better in the future. They felt that Malaysia could be a model for many other countries to follow. In retrospect, their assessments have proved to be correct.

IMF Consultations

We also had economic assessments from the World Bank and the IMF. Unlike the World Bank, the IMF holds annual discussions with the government as well as the private sector leaders and officials on the state of the nation's economy and its future prospects. The IMF was certainly much more "macro-oriented" than the World Bank. The IMF examined the overall economic performance and was not "project oriented" as the World Bank. This was because of their different roles. We, in the Economics Division, and the economic planners in the macro division of the Economic Planning Unit, found that the IMF consultations were not only very useful, but also very intellectually stimulating.

I think that one of the main reasons why Malaysia is economically better off than most developing countries is that we did listen to the World Bank and the IMF, before making up our own minds on socioeconomic policies best suited to our country's needs and aspirations. We have also seen examples of IMF failures all over the world and recently some of its weaknesses in the Southeast Asian currency crisis, as well as those in Turkey and Argentina.

That is how many developing countries lost confidence in these two multilateral institutions. That is also how these two institutions got to lose their credibility. The situation has got so bad that many developing countries now blame the World Bank and the IMF for their present socioeconomic woes and even their political instability. But Malaysia has come out relatively well in our relations with the World Bank and the IMF because we are more discerning, and know how to handle them. But our experience with them has not been so smooth either. We have had real problems with the World Bank from time to time. At one stage, the World Bank staff, which was dominated by Americans and Europeans, were against our borrowing from the World Bank for financing our oil palm plantations. This was because our palm oil posed serious competition to the American farmers who produced soya bean oil.

During my days on the board of the World Bank, the American directors had to get instructions from their Treasury on every loan the World Bank made to the developing countries. Owning about 20 per cent of the World Bank share capital at that time, the American vote carried a great deal of weight.

21.
FIRST BUDGET DIALOGUE
(1976)

TENGKU Razaleigh had many friends in the private sector as he had come from the business community. He also had many friends among the academic community since he was quite gregarious and enjoyed discussions and debates.

On one occasion I accompanied him to address the Malaysian Economic Association's Convention at Universiti Sains Malaysia (USM) in Penang. He gave his speech and took several questions competently. Unfortunately, there was not enough time for more questions as the conference had to end in the evening as scheduled. After we adjourned, many of the Penang members of the Association indicated that they would have preferred a longer dialogue with the Minister.

I felt the same dissatisfaction too. Somehow, the dialogue with the Minister had ended quite abruptly. So, I went up to Tengku, explained the situation, and asked whether he could have an informal dialogue with them in the canteen. He agreed spontaneously when I told him that the response from the academics was overwhelming. The ensuing discussions were free, open and on the level, with no punches pulled.

Tengku liked the session. I then ventured to suggest that a similar open dialogue could be held with the academic and business community in Kuala Lumpur, and he responded favourably. That was therefore the beginning of the formulation of the policy to have the "Annual Budget Dialogue" between the Treasury and the business and social groups. Initiated by Tengku Razaleigh, that tradition continues to this day in the Treasury.

These open dialogues provided the origins for the Malaysia Incorporated Policy and now the Langkawi Dialogues and the concept of Smart Partnerships.

Treasury Secrecy

The Treasury became even more open and transparent under Tengku Razaleigh's leadership. Its "ivory tower" image was fading and rightly so. But the distance between the Treasury officials and the public remained. We civil servants were trained to keep away from being too close to the public. The main reason was that we were dealing with very sensitive matters like the awarding of large tenders and contracts, as well as the introduction of new taxes.

My own lifestyle was influenced by the fact that I worked on these sensitive issues in the Treasury. I refrained from mixing freely with my friends at the clubs and pubs. Although I had been one of the early members of the Lake Club, I would rarely go to its bar for a good drink because of my past bad experiences. For, if I visited the club or a pub before the Budget Day, friends and even strangers would crowd around me at the bar to ask questions about the budget preparation and the proposed new taxes. I would of course not tell them anything. But I knew that there were people there who would brag about having special information about the budget and wrongly attribute the source to me. So I just decided to have my peace of mind and keep out of trouble by keeping away from clubs.

As a result of this experience, I also advised Samala not to buy any major household item such as a refrigerator, a television or worse still, a car, during the later half of the year, as long as I was working in the Treasury.

We were aware that many of the vendors would be observing us. If any senior Treasury officer bought a major item of expenditure, the vendors would use that fact as "proof", and would spread the rumour that the taxes were going to be raised for that item. As a result, these unscrupulous businessmen would increase their sales. Thus, Samala would buy major items only at the beginning of the year, i.e., after the budget when the new taxes had been raised. Some of her friends thought she was silly, but that was just a small price to pay for working in the Treasury.

The Treasury has traditionally maintained a high degree of secrecy for the sole purpose of protecting the integrity of the budget. In fact, a few weeks before the annual budget, armed police were positioned at the entrances of a few floors of the Treasury buildings at Jalan Duta. Treasury officials would also be very reluctant to take phone calls for fear of being thought of collaborating with the press or the business-men by passing secret tax information. Everyone realised that just one phone call to the right person at the right time could cause someone to make a fortune. It is thus imperative that Treasury officials exercise care and be clean (and to be seen to be clean as well). All this explains why Treasury officials generally keep to themselves, as I did during my 27 years there.

Governors Tun Ismail Ali and Tan Sri Aziz Taha

If the Treasury and its officials had a reputation for being relatively aloof, then Bank Negara Malaysia, the Central Bank of Malaysia, were even more so. Bank Negara is the guardian of the monetary policy of the nation, and it reports to the Minister of Finance. It does not deal with the Budget's fiscal policy but recommends broad monetary policy for the government's decision. It would then implement these decisions on a day-to-day basis. Because it manages credit, interest rate and for-eign exchange policy, Bank Negara too has to maintain a high level of secrecy.

The first Malaysian governor of Bank Negara was Tun Ismail Mohd Ali, who actually laid the foundations and set the high standards and the strict style of Bank Negara. Tun Ismail was himself academi-cally outstanding. He was also a dedicated and highly committed mem-ber of the Malaysian Civil Service, and a person of exceedingly strong integrity.

Tun Ismail was also a very serious person who hardly smiled, let alone laughed. Though his stature was small, he had a solid presence, which was further reinforced by his severity. He brooked no nonsense and asked for no favours. He was thorough almost to a fault. Even the littlest of mistakes or apparent improprieties annoyed him. So, one had to be always guarded in his presence as you would never know when you would say or do something that would inadvertently earn his disap-proval.

It was under that kind of leadership that Bank Negara took shape and developed into a first rate financial institution. Consequently, the IMF, the World Bank, and the whole international financial community had high respect for the Central Bank of Malaysia.

We in the Treasury had to handle Bank Negara very carefully mainly because of Tun Ismail's style of management and tough personality. He was proper with all the Ministers of Finance and got on well with them. But many officials in the Treasury and the civil service felt uneasy in his company. There are many anecdotes about Tun Ismail and his tough disposition. There are many who enjoy a good story about Tun Ismail. They would regale themselves with "folklore" that was often based on their own personal experiences. It may not be fair to relate the stories regarding others but I can at least tell a little story about my own odd experience with Tun Ismail.

The Southeast Asia Group was meeting in Rangoon, Burma, in the 1970s. Burma (now called Myanmar) was even less developed. There was impressive greenery all over and the hotel where we stayed had beautiful plush verdant surroundings. I followed Tun Ismail with Tan Sri Dr Lin See Yan to the meetings, and we stayed at the same hotel.

After the meetings, we were all set to leave for the airport on a cool clear morning. See Yan and I waited dutifully at the entrance to the hotel for Tun Ismail. As he emerged from the hotel into the fresh open space, I tried to break the ice and politely greeted him with, "Good morning, Sir. It's a beautiful morning!" But to my great despair, Tun Ismail bluntly shot back "What's so good about the morning?"

What could I say? I was just flabbergasted. I looked at See Yan, and he simply shook his head at me in surprised sympathy. His message to me was not to say anything more, but to keep quiet. We all got into the car that took us to the airport. See Yan sat in the centre between the Tun and myself. No one said a word right through that long and uncomfortable journey. I knew then that I, like many many others, was not in the influential Tun's good books. It was indeed a relief to get into the business class of the plane and to have a strong drink to keep myself cool! That is a small example of Tun Ismail's flavour.

After many years of distinguished service to the nation, Tun Ismail retired and his worthy Deputy Tan Sri Aziz Taha took over on July 26, 1980. The change was noted with some relief in some quarters. Nevertheless, it must be said in all fairness that it was because of outstanding

At the Place de la Concord in Paris in 1963

My first international conference with Minister of Trade Dr Lim Swee Aun
at the ESCAP Meeting in Manila in 1963

With Malaysian High Commissioner Dato' Abdullah Ali, Tan Sri Thong Yaw Hong
and Inder Singh in London in 1965

Attending a dinner hosted by Tun Abdul Razak in honour of the
President of the World Bank, Robert McNamara,
in Kuala Lumpur in 1972

On being conferred the title "Dato" by the late
Sultan of Selangor in 1974

On being confered the title "Tan Sri" by the King in 1989

Tun Hussein Onn celebrating his birthday on board a MAS flight with me on the right

Tan Sri Sheriff Kassim, myself and Tan Sri Thong Yaw Hong facing criticism
at a Treasury Briefing in 1986

Leaving the Treasury on being transferred to the Ministry of Transport in 1986.
From left to right: Tan Sri Ali, Tan Sri Zain Azraii, me, Dato' Husseini, Tan Sri Shariff and
Dato' Mustapa Mohamed at the Jalan Duta Government Complex

Leading the Merdeka March Past as Secretary-General of the Ministry of Transport in 1988

With President Robert Mugabe of Zimbabwe and Tan Sri Jeffrey Cheah at Sunway College

With Tun Dr Ling Liong Sik and Dato' Bashir Ahmad of MAS at Layang-Layang in the
South China Sea in 1988

At our Class of 1954 reunion in Perth organised by Tan Sri Alwi Jantan (right) with
Tan Sri Musa Hitam (middle) chairing

With President Masire and the CPTM group in Botswana.
From left to right: Tan Sri Kishu Tirathrai, Ian Strachen, Dato' Dr Michaela Smith,
President Masire, Roger Bamborough and Tan Sri Dr Omar Rahman

With Dr Henry A. Kissinger and Dato' Sri Mohd Najib Razak at the residence of US Ambassador John Mallot in Kuala Lumpur

A word with Prime Minister Tun Dr Mahathir Mohamad in 1996.
(Hardev Kaur of the *New Straits Times* is in the background.)

Presenting one of my seven books to Tun Omar Ong Yoke Lin, my first ministerial boss, at Sunway College, with Tan Sri Jeffrey Cheah on the left, in 1998

With Dato' Michael Yeoh, Tan Sri Ghazali Shafie and Dato' Razman at an ASLI conference in 1999

Christmas with Samala, my mother Ruth Navaratnam and Tengku Razaleigh Hamzah
at our home at 9, Lorong Medang, Bangsar, in 1984

At the launching of my fifth book, *Malaysia's Economic Recovery: Policy Reforms for Economic Sustainability*, by the Deputy Prime Minister, Dato' Seri Abdullah Hj Ahmad Badawi in April 2001

financial leaders like Tun Ismail (and Tun Tan) that such strong foundations were laid in our economic and financial structures.

Tan Sri Aziz Taha was groomed by Tun Ismail in his own mould, but he had a different personality altogether. He was also very professional and strict, but certainly far more amiable and communicative. Like many other Treasury officials, I found it much easier to work with the new Governor who was also in our age group. The relationships between Treasury officials all down the line, also improved considerably. Discussions among the major economic agencies (that formed the famous Macro Group) like the Treasury, the Economic Planning Unit, the Ministry of Trade, the Ministry of Primary Industries, and the Statistics Department, also became more open and fruitful. The National Development Planning Committee that was represented by the Secretaries-General of the major economic agencies also lightened up with more lively debates—and even some laughter!

22.
WINDS OF CHANGE
IN THE 1980s

THE early part of the 1980s saw the political and economic environment change quite rapidly. Tun Hussein was not keeping good health. The pressure of work on him had been growing. He was more of a statesman than a politician. I do not think that he really enjoyed the power play and political manipulation that is typical of political life. He also did not have the political killer instinct although I have no doubt that as a good soldier, he would have had no scruples to order to kill on the battlefield. He was a soldier, a professional, and first and foremost—a real gentleman.

Tun Hussein had to go to London for medical treatment. Dato' Seri Dr Mahathir therefore had to take over as Acting Prime Minister on November 29, 1980.

Kuala Lumpur, besides being the national capital, like any other political capital, is also a capital for starting, spinning, and spreading rumours. Because Kuala Lumpur is only about 94 square miles (about half the size of Singapore), it is therefore just about the optimum size for a city, with the right economies of scale, for efficient rumour mongering!

As soon as the news got out that Tun Hussein was not well, the rumour-making machine was automatically switched on. The questions of the day naturally were: "How long will he be able to continue as Prime Minister?" and "Who will take over?"

It was sad, but I suppose that is the way of the world. When leaders or any other important personalities are on top, people generally look up to them and go to them for favours. They hope that the relevant leaders will stay in power, in order to gain from their friendships. But as soon as there is a doubt about their continuity, relations start to change and rumour mongers start to work full time.

The stories were therefore rife that Dr Mahathir would be taking over as Prime Minister. This theme gave rise to a lot of politicking and a fresh outburst of power play. All this also led to new political alignments and realignments.

The political jockeying for power was heightened by the onset of UMNO's general elections in the next few weeks. We in the civil service of course had no part in all these political activities. Only the very junior civil servants were allowed by the service regulations to take an active part in politics. The senior civil servants were barred from playing an active role in party politics. However, we were aware that several, especially senior Malay officials did play some role in UMNO politics, quietly behind the scenes.

Some of us got an inkling of the power shifts taking place in the Treasury itself during the period running up to the UMNO general elections. Tengku Razaleigh was spending less time with his Treasury policies and officials, but more time with his political advisers and supporters. He also spent more time travelling outside Kuala Lumpur, visiting his constituency in Kelantan and other places, for political support.

The Deputy Finance Minister, Rafidah Aziz, was also giving more priority to her political work.

The 32nd UMNO General Meeting was held and Tengku Razaleigh was very narrowly defeated by about 40 votes by Dr Mahathir to become the President of UMNO.

Tun Hussein who had been on medical leave now tendered his resignation, and Dr Mahathir Mohamad became Malaysia's 4th Prime Minister. He appointed Tan Sri Musa Hitam as the Deputy Prime Minister. As expected, a cabinet reshuffle soon followed.

Those of us in the Treasury were pleasantly surprised when Tengku Razaleigh was reappointed as the Minister of Finance despite having challenged Dr Mahathir. At the same time, Dato' Seri Rafidah Aziz was appointed as the Minister of Trade and Industry.

The Treasury was also changing. After Tengku Razaleigh had lost his election fight against Dr Mahathir, the Treasury was no longer the same. Some of us felt that the Treasury was beginning to lose its power and independence. In the past, the Finance Minister's say on financial matters was almost final, but now we found that our recommendations on fiscal and financial policies were being questioned more and more by other government agencies. It was possible that some ministers became bolder as the Minister of Finance was losing political ground and backing in the cabinet.

The Economic Recession in the 1980s

By 1980, the economy also began to slow down again. The Treasury had therefore been pushing hard for expenditure cutbacks in view of the difficult budgeting and the weakening of the overall financial position that had re-emerged as a result of the world economic slowdown.

The budget deficits were widening and the balance of payments was seriously under strain. There was a major dilemma in the Treasury as to whether the world economy would soon pick up or whether it would continue to slide into recession. The Malaysian economy is so open and relatively small that whatever happened in the industrial world would affect us significantly for better or worse. Thus, if the industrial countries were buoyant, we did even better. But if they faltered and weakened, Malaysia would also suffer adversely because so much of our international trade and investment depended on the fluctuating external demand for our goods and services.

The Treasury initially went along with the belief that the recession would be short, and that we therefore need not take pre-emptive action too early to slow down our development expenditures and investment. We needed to keep up the rapid pace of development and lay stronger foundations for infrastructure expansion, in order to fight poverty and to improve the standards of living of the *rakyat* or the mass of our people.

Our consultations with the World Bank and the International Monetary Fund as well as other international socioeconomic institutions, did not help much. They could not tell us for sure whether the worldwide recession would be ending soon or how long it would last. They however did preach caution. They suggested that since there was this great uncertainty, it would be preferable to give the benefit of the doubt to being more cautious and conservative in our economic management.

But each time the Treasury tried to cut back on government spending, it would be strongly resisted by the other government agencies that did not want to cut back on their well-planned and pet socioeconomic programmes and projects. This was understandable, but very difficult to handle, particularly when no one could be sure if the recession was going to continue for long. What if after undertaking the painful process of cutting back, we found that the world economy was actually picking up?

It would have been a pity to deny the poor the benefits of development and the fruits of the NEP and the rewards of independence that we had been enjoying. We also could not pursue "stop-go" economic policies that would disrupt the hard-won socioeconomic stability and strength. Furthermore, domestic and international confidence in our ability to manage the Malaysian economy prudently would suffer a serious setback.

Dr Mahathir Asserts his Leadership

There was this state of flux due to the political uncertainty as to how to deal with the recession without causing internal sociopolitical problems. From the Treasury's point of view, it was quite clear as to what had to be done. After some time, it became more apparent that the global recession this time was unusual. This recession was not following the normal pattern of lasting for a short period and then recovering. This recession was dragging on.

The Treasury realised that there was a limit to borrowing on the domestic and foreign markets while the recession burnt itself out. The budget revenues were also declining and the expenditures were at the same time rising. The export earnings were falling steadily, whereas the import bill was rising to meet essential requirements and continued government spending.

The economy was on a slide. Some tough policy decisions had to be made fast to save the situation. There was no time for politics anymore. The times called for tough political leadership and a strong will to adopt and effectively administer the bitter medicines that were necessary for the economy to recover from its ailments. We could not wait for the world economy to recover, for us to move up in tandem. We now had to pull ourselves by our own bootstraps.

Now that the UMNO general elections were over and the leadership had been established, the political problems had been removed from the scene. We had already worked out the economic solutions in the Treasury in conjunction with the Economic Planning Unit and Bank Negara.

We needed the political leaders to move and they did finally rise to the challenge posed by the economy. At a briefing that the Treasury gave to the new Prime Minister, Dr Mahathir, the decision was finally taken to accept the recommendations of the Minister of Finance to cut back the budget's expenditure allocations to all ministries. It was truly a bold decision on the part of Dr Mahathir, the Finance Minister Tengku Razaleigh and the whole cabinet. The Deputy Prime Minister, Dato' Musa Hitam, also saw the wisdom of having to take the tough remedial action. This made decision-making less complicated as he fully supported the drastic measures that were adopted to reduce government spending on all fronts.

On June 28, 1981, therefore, the Prime Minister, Dr Mahathir Mohamad, made the announcement to the nation of the cutback in national expenditure and a review of a package of fiscal policies to combat the recession even more resolutely. The Prime Minister had asserted his leadership.

From that point onwards, the economy began to slowly improve. What was significant was that the business confidence also strengthened as the private sector appreciated the tough and timely initiatives that were taken by the government to fight the recession. However, it was not an easy task. Several large infrastructure projects had to be phased out over a longer period so as to spread out the spending. This meant a lot of renegotiations of government contracts that had already been awarded. This could have caused the problem of infrastructure bottlenecks that the country faced later on. But at that time, it could not have been helped. We had to cut back or face the prospects of a serious financial deterioration.

The moral of the story is that we should not take the risk of trying to spend ourselves out of a recession unless we are sure that the recession will be for a very short period. But who can tell? So, the lesson to be learnt is either to build up large reserves to keep for a "rainy day", or to really act fast and decisively as soon as the economy is threatened.

The other lesson that was learnt was that government cannot and should not be expected to bear the full brunt of managing the economy nor even to rely on its own wisdom alone to do so. Thus, the idea dawned that maybe we should consult and coordinate more with the private sector and the businessmen. We should also learn from non-Western models, like Japan. Thus the "Look East Policy" was born.

The "Look East" Policy

Dr Mahathir drew inspiration from Japan's socioeconomic and the successful practice of "Japan Inc". He saw how Japan stirred itself from the ashes of defeat and rose to become one of the leading economies of the world. How did they do it? They had become the strongest economy in Asia and superseded the former colonial powers that had dominated Asia for centuries.

Colonialism had not only dominated the economies of the colonies, but more importantly, colonialism had eroded the self-respect, self-confidence and much of the cultural values of the colonised people. Even after independence, most people felt that the erstwhile colonialists were superior in so many ways, even if they did not deserve to qualify for that honour. The West was regarded as special, strong and way ahead of us in most areas of human endeavour. We tend to forget the greatness of our own ancestry, the richness of our traditions and religions, and the nobility of our own values. We had to restore confidence in ourselves. Our will to succeed had been deeply eroded by colonial exploitation and domination for many generations. Our mindset had been adversely affected!

We could not look to the West for inspiration. How could we when they continued to exploit the poorer countries for their own self-interest through international trade and often, even aid? The West has dominated the South countries or the developing world through colonialism and now neo-imperialism. They generally cannot accept that their erstwhile subjects can be at the same sovereign status as them, although we may not be in the same economic situation. So they try hard to maintain their dominating position in order to sustain their *status quo*. It is neo-colonialism and the practice of political and economic dominance of the North over the South that is now continuing through globalisation.

We find the Caucasian North generally arrogant, overbearing and condescending. It is therefore difficult to relate to them in a sincere and dignified relationship. But we also need to learn from their advanced technology in order to forge ahead and compete with them to get a fair share of world trade and prosperity. This is the global dilemma.

One way out was to look to a developed country that would be easier to deal with—a country that was less arrogant and not insensitive to the aspiration of developing countries such as Malaysia. Such a country was Japan, with which we could identify better as an Asian country.

Thus, Dr Mahathir created this new "Look East" policy. This meant that we should look more to Japan, the Koreans and even the Taiwanese for their great socioeconomic successes, their drive, discipline, and values. These values were often the antithesis of the Western and especially American social values of outright competition of market forces regardless of social inequalities.

The West believes in human rights that are carried to the extreme in that they show preference to protecting the rights of the individual at the expense of the society at large. On the contrary, Eastern or Asian values give higher priority to the rights of the whole society, even if it means that the rights of the individual are sometimes reduced. The Japanese are renowned for their values of hard work, filial piety, honesty, honour, thrift, humility and respect for the elders. These values have made the nation and the people great. They are an Asian nation and if they can do it then why can't we? If they can beat the white man in his own game in trade and technology, then why can't we try as well?

I believe that was the logic behind our Prime Minister's vision and the concept of his "Look East" policy. That's why the new Look East Policy was well received by Malaysians.

Malaysia, Inc

Prime Minister Dr Mahathir had visited Japan several times and had seen how closely the Japanese government, its officials and the business leaders had cooperated to build Japan into a powerful and rich nation. Japan had risen to become a world power within a decade after the Western powers destroyed it in 1945. The atomic bombs were dropped on Asian Japan and not on the enemy in Europe—Caucasian Germany! All this must have made a lasting impression on Dr Mahathir and his generation of leaders. These past experiences even had a serious impact on my generation—which is only about 10 years younger than Dr Mahathir's generation.

The strong bond between the government and the private sector in Japan helped to forge a sense of unity and purpose, in the interests of the government and business, the nation and the Japanese society as a whole. If the Japanese had gained so much from that kind of cooperation and collaboration, then why couldn't Malaysia do the same in our own way?

Dr Mahathir thus adopted the policy of "Malaysia Incorporated". This policy promoted the idea that the government would now encourage civil servants and businessmen to work together to advance national goals on a mutually beneficial basis—for the government and the private sector. Now the work force and the Labour Unions have also been included in what is called the "Smart Partnership".

Reaction to Malaysia, Inc

I have to say that the concept did not look as simple as it seems. Many of us in the civil service were quite surprised at the adoption of this policy. Under the British administration, we had been brought up not to trust the businessmen. They were supposed to be exploitative, greedy and out to cheat the government, the civil servants and of course the consumers and the people. They were supposed to only serve their selfish self-interests and to just make profits for themselves!

I recall the address by Tun Abdul Aziz Abdul Majid (the first Malaysian Chief Secretary to the Government) to us as fresh recruits into the Malaysian Civil Service, during the induction course at the Port Dickson Training Center. He made it very clear that he did not want to see us fraternise and get close to businessmen. He felt that we would be open to corruption and would get distracted from our duty to King and Country. The private sector was to be treated with courtesy but with propriety and firmness, since generally, it was thought, their motives were to make money without care or concern for the public interest.

It was thus the special role of the civil servants to look after the national and public interests. We were to have no vested interests, except the honour, privilege and pride of serving the nation. We would have to provide the professional advice and guidance to the duly elected representatives, to serve the people!

This was the philosophy of the British Civil Service whose role we had inherited. We were brought up on the model of Whitehall in London and the Colonial Civil Service whose role model was the ICS, i.e., the Indian Civil Service in India. They were regarded as the "gift of the gods" who were mandated to rule India under the British. That tradition took a long time to fade away.

Under these circumstances, it was not difficult to appreciate the suspicion, the indifference and even the initial resistance to this new concept of "Malaysia Incorporated". The discomfort with this policy became stronger when we realised that there was a growing sense of identity and affinity between the politicians and the businessmen in what some civil servants regarded as an "unholy alliance". Some individuals benefited unduly from this new policy, because of their close political connections with Government.

As the politicians became more entrenched in their power and influence, the business community became bolder, especially in the local authorities and state governments. Land alienation, which was conducted mainly by the land offices and the civil servants under the district officers, now came under more direct influence of the politicians and indirectly, the businessmen. It was felt that the land that was reserved or zoned for specific purposes was alienated for other purposes, thus benefiting some big businesses. Of course, as the economy grew, more land had to be converted for commercial use and alienated to developers. But the decision-making process was often dominated by the politicians often at the behest of their vested business interests. So, the role of the professional civil servants declined. All this did raise questions as to the rationale and validity for the introduction of "Malaysia Incorporated".

In retrospect it is clear that on balance, the "Malaysia Incorporated" policy contributed greatly to the rapid development of Malaysia. The government now listens and cooperates more closely with the private sector and seeks to understand the problems faced by the private sector in order to be able to assist it to overcome its problems, especially in dealing with the government itself.

23.
GEORGIE AND SOREN WED

WHILE I was caught up with all these fascinating policy changes in the government, and enjoying being part of it all, I was always aware of my responsibilities to my family. As the eldest and only son and the head of my own family, I felt that I had to be responsible for the welfare of every member.

Georgie, my youngest sister, had stayed with us in our home at Jalan Damansara during the year that she sat for her School Certificate at the Methodist Girls' School. I felt that I was responsible to see that she was well-married (as the other three sisters had been), without the family having to go through the unkind experience of raising funds for a suitable dowry.

Our parents were always comfortable, though certainly not rich. Our mother, particularly, always managed to save here and there although she did not have much to spare from the income that dad brought home. Nevertheless, she provided the daughters with sufficient gold and jewellery to make them presentable and confident.

Georgie had finished her schooling and began to look for suitable employment. She did not want to teach or do nursing or be bound to a desk job. She is adventurous and different from her more conservative sisters, as indeed is her generation. I also looked around to help her get employed. She impressed the interviewers with her vivacity and got a job in an advertising firm. She liked her work, and did well. She has a pleasant personality, speaks and writes well, and is quite extroverted. Because she is the youngest in the family, my parents were more relaxed with her. She had the opportunity to move around more easily, partly due to the fact that her work required her to socialise with a wider circle, outside her office work and the church.

One day, when I visited our parents' home in Petaling Jaya, I found a Caucasian gentleman sitting in the hall talking to dad. Georgie introduced him to me as Soren Beck. I wondered protectively as the elder brother, "Who is this Caucasian who has come to visit my youngest sister?" I guessed that would be a natural concern of any loving elder brother who had been taking care of his sister's welfare, especially in those conservative days!

Soren came more often to the house. He was seeing Georgie a lot and I began to realise that Georgie and Soren were getting serious in their relationship. I was relatively open to the idea of them going steady, but I was concerned that mum and dad might not like an inter-racial marriage. I was also concerned that Soren was a Dane, and if they got married, then Georgie would probably have to settle down in Denmark. In those days, we knew precious little about Denmark.

I spoke to mum about my concerns, and was pleasantly surprised that both my mum and dad were quite open to the prospect of an inter-racial marriage as long as they felt Georgie was sure that Soren was the right man for her. I was expecting all my sisters to marry Jaffna Tamil men, and so far all of them had done so. I also talked to Georgie and was satisfied that she was fully aware of all the implications of marry-ing a Caucasian.

Soon it was time for us to fix the wedding date. When that was done, preparations went full swing ahead. They had a lovely wedding at our parents' house for the extended family and close friends. Soren's parents, the late Poul and Inger Beck, came down from Denmark and it was remarkable how well they fitted into our family. Soren's parents were warm and friendly and were quite different from my notion of stiff and snooty Caucasians.

I must say with gratitude that Soren has become a fine brother-in-law, and has made Georgie very happy. They have two dear sons, Hans Anand and Carl Chandran, who are gentle, pleasant, bright and affec-tionate. They have noticeably both Danish and Tamil names, and have the best of both worlds in their good upbringing and cultural values. They have been fortunate in having been able to return to Malaysia often because of Soren's work as a consultant economist. Hans is now an economist in the British Civil Service and Carl is a doctor.

Dad's Demise in 1981

My dear father was getting on in age. In 1981, he was 77 years old and was getting frailer. Nevertheless, he observed his daily routine. He would be up at 7am, and would then get ready to walk down the road from our family house at 5 Jalan 5/10E in Petaling Jaya to the shops, or to take a bus to town.

My father felt the winds of change differently. His father, Mr Ku-naratnam, had come to Malaya from Ceylon to work in the British Co-lonial Civil Service. He did very well as chief clerk in the Chief Secretary's Office. My father was born in Malaya, and followed in his father's footsteps to join the clerical service where he also rose to the top ranks of the service. He retired as an Office Assistant in the Ministry of Works. His senior bosses were British, and he found them exemplary in their work and sense of fairness. He had seen the change in the administration. He retired at the age of 55 in 1960. Since he was still healthy and alert, it was difficult for him to adjust to the changes that were also brought about by his retirement and Independence.

There were limited opportunities for him to work after retirement. It is a pity that he did not have the opportunity to be more meaningfully occupied. He would read and do some light gardening. He was a good footballer for the Tamil Physical and Cultural Association in his younger days, and because of his daily walks, he kept good health.

But age was catching up with him. I used to see him and my mother at least once a week. He was a man of few words. Thank goodness that Tina and Kamal were living just across his home. Their children, Shari, Nava and Charmaine, gave him joy as they were often around him as "his neighbours". But as time passed, he became quieter.

On April 5, 1981, mum rang me up frantically. She screamed "Daddy has fallen down. He is unconscious. Please come now!" I rushed from our house at Federal Hill, which was only about a 10-minute drive from dad's place. Dr George Ananda had been called. As I rushed into the house, the doctor came out of the room with a sad face. I then sensed that my worst fears had been confirmed. Our dear father had passed away peacefully!

It seemed that earlier on, dad had walked up the gradual slope to his house. As he entered the house, mum offered to make him a cup of tea. He agreed and then went to his room to change into his *sarong*. As mum was preparing the tea, she heard him fall. She rushed into his room and found dad slumped on the floor. He had had a massive heart attack—and left to meet his Maker, peacefully and without any suffering of any kind. It was a wonderful blessing for him to go in such a quiet and sudden manner, but it was a great shock to our dear mother and all of his children and loved ones.

When I went into his room, his body was still warm. I was shaken to see him lifeless. His mouth was sunken and I then realised that he was without his dentures. He had changed into his *sarong* and taken out his dentures for the last time. I went to his bathroom, took his dentures, and placed them in his mouth. He looked calm and content, even more so with his kind and gentle smile. I thanked God for his life and said a silent prayer for his soul.

I then went out to the dining room to join Tina and Kamal in consoling our dear mum who was distraught with shock and grief. My sisters Angie, Julie and their families were informed and they made plans to come from Singapore immediately. Georgie was in Denmark and when we rang her, she pleaded that we should wait for her before we buried our dear dad. She had difficulties getting a flight home. So we postponed the burial for another day to enable all dad's children to pay their last respects to our very loving, kind and gentle father.

The funeral service at home was worshipful and dignified. My sisters and relatives sang hymns and prayed as dad's body lay sedately in the coffin in the hall. The Trinity Church was filled with floral decorations and melodious singing and rich tributes to our dear father for his quiet dignity, and his kind and private lifestyle. At the cemetery in Petaling Jaya, Indran played "The Last Post" solemnly with his clarinet as the priest and all of us prayed and dropped earth on dad's coffin — as a last tribute and farewell to our loving father.

Then we all went home, sad and forlorn, but grateful to God that dad had such a lovely passing and a beautiful farewell. Life had to go on. We resolved in our hearts that we should try to emulate his good ways and to follow the advice and the paths that he had set for each of his loving children.

We were concerned that mum would wilt under the severe strain of dad's passing. However, we underestimated her religious fervour and great faith in the Lord. Indeed, she was very depressed, but she slowly found solace in her prayers, in her Christian faith and her fellowship with the Lord and her church. She celebrated her 97th birthday on November 11, 2004. We are grateful to God for her presence. She has carried on to testify for the Lord in her own special way. We cherish dad's memory and his many fine qualities that have become our heritage.

24.
LEADERSHIP BY EXAMPLE

IN the meantime, the strong leadership exerted by Dr Mahathir Mohamad set the government moving at a much faster pace. Other political leaders had to keep up with the rapid progress made in so many fields under his dynamic leadership. I think he realised that many civil servants at grassroots level were unable to keep up with him and the many changes which were taking place. Neither could many politicians.

The continuing strength of the politicians in government tended to make some of them arrogant. This was a trend that had to be checked. Some political leaders who felt that they could urge the people to be hardworking and thrifty, must be willing to make sacrifices themselves. But at the same time some politicians themselves tended to think they were above the need to practice what they preached! This was also true of many civil servants who were somewhat aloof from the people. They needed to be reminded of their obligation to serve the people. But what would be the best way to get politicians and civil servants to be humble and to serve the country and people better?

Some businessmen too had become cocky with their wealth. They were mostly the *nouveau riche* who tended to flaunt their newfound wealth. Many of them had actually become rich almost overnight through the benevolence of the government. They had won concessions and contracts that they farmed out to others, and would collect the rents. They had become the modern-day rentier class.

Dr Mahathir provided a contrast to some other political leaders who spent little time with the people. He knew that it was neither proper nor politically healthy for the common people to be told one thing, while some politicians do something else. He must have realised that he must introduce a change in outlook and values. He thus introduced the concept of *Kepimpinan Melalui Teladan* ("Leadership by Example"). This slogan had many beneficial consequences.

First, it discouraged many politicians from preaching what they did not intend to practise. Second, the politicians became more sensitive about urging the people to attain high moral values that they themselves did not possess. Third, the people themselves became more aware of the need to check their leaders' performance against their public promises, especially before the elections. Finally, businessmen and civil servants got the message that they should also follow the high degree of hard work, dedication and the commitment to serve the people, as exemplified by some of our top leaders.

There were thus many beneficial effects resulting from the implementation of the concept "Leadership by Example". People did see the special qualities of sacrifice and the strong determination of some of our senior leaders and looked up to them. They tried to benchmark their own standards and performance against those set by these leaders.

Unfortunately, many politicians continued with their wayward ways (such as corruption), and their followers followed their bad examples literally according to the slogan — Leadership by Example! Many leaders in the government, the civil service and the private sector had gone the wrong way. They have become corrupt, arrogant and greedy. They were leaders but were not worthy examples to follow.

Thus, after some time, it became quite embarrassing to promote the concept of "Leadership by Example". This call therefore slowly faded away and ceased to be used. Many of us in the civil service, including myself, were relieved to see the demise of the concept for we realised that it was a concept that was idealistic and not necessarily pragmatic. In fact, it became the butt of jokes from time to time when different circumstances and incidents emerged and undermined the credibility of the slogan.

Dr Ling Resigns

On April 28, 1984, Dato' Seri Dr Ling Liong Sik who was Deputy Minister of Finance, resigned from the government and went on long leave to London. I was upset as I liked Dr Ling. I had found him to be sharp, deep in his analysis, eager to learn economic policy and most of all, I found him to be informal and quite relaxed in his relationship with his staff and me. I regarded him as a good friend and I think he regarded me as a close friend too.

After he resigned, he would occasionally give me a call and we would meet from time to time at the Merlin Hotel (or what is now called the Concorde Hotel) for a chat and a quiet drink. Dr Ling's wife, Datin Ena Ling, is a very charming, gracious and warm person with no airs, unlike the wives of some ministers. They have two good-looking and well-mannered sons, Ah Leong and Ah Kiat, who, like their parents, are likeable.

On one occasion when I was invited for a chat, I found, to my pleasant surprise, Datin Ena with Dr Ling at the coffee lounge. Dr Ling talked nostalgically of the good times he had when he was working in the Treasury. He spoke well of the high Treasury standards. He then abruptly turned to me and said: "If and when I get back to the gov-

ernment and become a minister, I would like you to become my Secretary-General."

Datin Ena was as surprised as I was and she quickly remarked to
him: "That would be nice, but how can you say this when no one can be
sure. Aren't you raising Ramon's hopes?" I was a bit embarrassed for
my former boss as I know that he meant well. So, I added that as a civil
servant I was fully aware that my career (especially as a non-*bumiputera*) depended on a lot of imponderables and that I was nevertheless grateful for his confidence in me.

I said that I would be honoured to serve under a minister of his calibre, hoped for the best and we all let the matter to rest. (Several years
later I became Dr Ling Liong Sik's Secretary-General at the Ministry
of Transport. He was indeed a man of his word.) He did such a good
job as Minister of Transport and leader of the MCA that he is now Tun
Ling Liong Sik!

Promotion to Deputy Secretary of the Treasury

I had gained considerable seniority since I joined the Treasury in
1961, and had been the head of the Economics Division since 1972. I
had already established a sort of record as the longest-serving officer in
the Treasury. I suppose one could say that I had become a kind of "specialist Treasury officer" since I was mainly serving as an economist and
not as an administrator or manager.

At a Treasury staff dinner, I received a note written on a paper ser-
viette addressed to me from my boss, the Minister of Finance, Tengku
Razaleigh, who was the host at the main table. The note read, "I am going to announce in my speech shortly, that I've received the OK to promote Salleh, Badruddin and you as the three new deputy secretaries-
general of the Treasury!"

I was overjoyed. I had not expected this important promotion at
that time in view of the difficulties for the promotion of non-*bumiputera*
officers. I was already on superscale B, and now, being promoted to superscale A! It was something to be really happy and grateful about. I
looked up towards the Minister after reading the note. Our eyes met
and he smiled in acknowledgement at my show of appreciation. That
was the kind of deep understanding and loyalty I enjoyed with Tengku
Razaleigh. I was given the responsibility to oversee the Economics,
Tax, Valuation and Insurance Divisions of the Ministry of Finance. I
was undoubtedly given some of the more important divisions of the

Treasury to manage. Fortunately, I had very able Heads of Division, and that made my heavy responsibilities relatively light.

The head of the tax division was Sheriff Kassim, who later became a Tan Sri and the Secretary-General of the Treasury. Ali Abul Hassan (also became a Tan Sri), then became the head of the economics division, and later the head of the Economic Planning Unit in the Prime Minister's Department, Governor of Bank Negara and now Special Adviser to the Prime Minister. Clifford Herbert also served under me and later became Tan Sri and Secretary-General to the Treasury. R. Dass was the able Chief Valuation Officer.

It was a challenging experience heading those Treasury divisions and being able to work with such fine officers who later made their mark as outstanding civil servants.

25.
THE PROTON SAGA

ON June 7, 1984, Dato' Khalil Yaacob, the Minister in the Prime Minister's Department, announced that the newly made-in-Malaysia car, would be named "Proton Saga". A competition was held nationwide, and hundreds of names had been sifted through before the judges finally recommended a few names for final selection. The Prime Minister, I think had the final say. The name was well received by the people as it had a definite Malaysian flavour in its concept and sound.

The saga is well known to most Malaysian children. We used to pick those beautiful, bright red saga seeds from under the big saga trees, to play with them. We even saved them as our own childhood perception of wealth. A whole pile of bright red saga seeds was indeed an attractive sight for a child. Alas! Today, the wealthier and urban children may not have even seen a saga seed, and even if they do, they may not attach the same childlike romance that we readily associated with those beautiful red saga seeds.

Furthermore, this small saga seed, which is the size of one's little fingertip, is very hard. This quality gives the right image of the new Malaysian car. The word "saga" also means "a long story". This suggests the story of Malaysia's graduation from an agricultural to a manufacturing country. It reflects our pride in making our own cars instead of having to import cars from all over the world, particularly from our former colonial masters—the British!

But the word "Proton" is even more significant as it indicates Malaysia's entry into the age of science and technology. Protons and neutrons are now familiar words to even ordinary Malaysians. To foreigners, proton is even more familiar, and thus "Proton" has an international flavour. This would help promote the brand name of the new Malaysian car in the international markets.

However, despite the soundness of the name of the new Malaysian car, there were many who seriously doubted the viability of this new Malaysian car! Some of the academic fraternity in particular raised serious doubts about the financial and business viability and sustainability of this daring, difficult and costly project.

On the technical side, there were many who even questioned the quality, capability and also the durability of this new Malaysian car. All this time, cars were either imported or assembled in Malaysia, There were, therefore, some strong vested business interests that were stoutly opposed to the manufacture and the protection given for the manufacture of a Malaysian car. Thus, we had vicious rumours circulating that the Proton Saga did not have enough power to even climb the road to the Genting Highlands Resort. It was suggested that one would be taking a big gamble by buying a Proton Saga. Car salesmen would advise that the Proton Saga was like a "tin can" as it could be crushed in a crash with any other car, including Japanese cars assembled locally!

Initially, it was difficult to fight these attempts to discredit the new Malaysian car. Many Malaysians also doubted the ability of Malaysians to produce a locally manufactured car, although the engine and many component parts were actually imported from Japan. Perhaps, this was a psychological problem resulting from the colonial hangover, derived from over a century of British rule. Many believed that we could not do what the former colonialists could do.

On the financial front, there were more genuine concerns as to the viability of the Proton project. The major international car manufacturers were primarily in the industrial countries. They had a tremendous head start in research and development, in enormous investment in plant and machinery, in backup capital, and in marketing. Most importantly, they had large world market shares and therefore enjoyed the real advantage of huge economies of scale. Of course, if we examined the new car project purely from a business point of view, I would agree with the academic critics myself.

Proton Saga: Benefits

But I think the academics missed the point. Government expenditure on infrastructure such as roads, railways, airports, shipping ports, schools, hospitals, etc, will never be considered viable if we simplistically use financial analysis, only because the benefits of these investments cannot be easily priced. How does one estimate the monetary value of the benefits of saving a life at a government hospital?

Similarly, it could be argued that there are considered practical benefits from manufacturing the Proton Saga, although the car may not be initially profitable. First of all, very few investments are profitable from the start, unless of course you are digging gold from just below the surface! Secondly, we have to consider the great benefits that accrue to the whole economy in the form of "spin-offs" from the investment in the production of the Proton Saga.

There is also the "transfer of technology" not only in the motor industry but in the many related support industries. Then there is a wide range of small and medium industries and small businessmen who would gain from the vast opportunities that are available for them to get involved in manufacturing activities. We could also take into account the "exposure value" of our workers and our society to the enormous potential for high end manufacturing, especially since we come from an agricultural tradition. When we take all these factors into account, then we are taking on "an economic assessment" and not necessarily a pure financial viability analysis.

Indeed, in economics, it is called "shadow pricing" which is the technique of giving economic or monetary value for the benefits derived from "spillover effects" of an investment! We do give preferential treatment to domestic and foreign investment in the initial period of investment. This is also the case with the Proton Saga, which is admittedly now given significant protection in the form of hefty import duties imposed on foreign cars.

The question is not, therefore, whether we should have started to manufacture our own Proton Saga, but whether the Malaysian-made Proton Saga can actually face international competition in the world markets, as they open up and free themselves from "protection" — under the new rules of the World Trade Organisation (WTO)?

This is a question, that is exceedingly difficult to answer. It depends on how efficient we are in bringing down costs to make our Proton cars more competitive with the foreign cars that will come into our Malaysian markets in increasing numbers under globalisation. This will happen once we are required to pull down our tariff protection walls, when the WTO free trade rules are fully implemented in the future. The best way out is to form strategic alliances with the big car manufacturers. Then the success of the Proton Saga will be sustained, even after the Asean Free Trade Area (AFTA) is fully operational for cars in 2005.

26.
CABINET RESHUFFLE
(1984)

IN 1984, the Prime Minister announced a major cabinet reshuffle. Tengku Razaleigh was transferred to the Ministry of Trade and Industry as its Minister and Daim Zainuddin (later Tun) was appointed the Minister of Finance. My career seemed threatened! I had been working closely with Tengku Razaleigh as my Minister. I had always been professional with my Ministers, as I became more senior and worked more closely with them. However, we were also close friends. This caused some misunderstanding even among some of my own colleagues.

I recall meeting the Deputy Prime Minister, Tan Sri Musa Hitam in the washroom of all places, after an important meeting at the Prime Minister's office. My colleague, Tan Sri Sallehuddin Mohamad, was with me. As we left the washroom, Musa, in his characteristic half-joking, half-serious tone, told us loudly, "Ah-hah, you two chaps are very close to Razaleigh eh! Ah! You guys watch out!" He half laughed again as he left us.

Salleh and I exchanged our thoughts on the matter, with some concern. After all, Musa was the Deputy Prime Minister, and we could not take him lightly. On the other hand, he was one of our oldest friends in high places in the government. He was our university mate. He could not have meant what he said. But, if he had, we would definitely have to "watch out".

Thus, when it was announced that Daim Zainuddin was coming to the Treasury, I was concerned. Some of my colleagues were already telling me that they had heard that some of Daim's friends were urging him to replace me and a few others who had been close to Tengku. We were to be transferred to the other ministries.

I was reconciled (as any civil servant had to be) to changes in postings. After all, I had already been in the Treasury for about 24 years! In any case, it was the prerogative of the minister concerned, to pick and choose his most senior officers and advisers. But I was also comfortable in my own conscience that I had always served loyally, and that I could not help it if others thought otherwise. However, despite all the rumours, I must say in fairness to Tun Daim, that he treated me with courtesy and professionalism. Never once did he even allude to my close working relationship with his predecessor and political rival, Tengku Razaleigh. For this and the fact that he was a very able Minister, I have a high respect for him. I served him with dedication and loyalty, as is the tradition of all good senior civil servants, for another three years in the Treasury, before I was promoted to become the Secretary-General in the Ministry of Transport in 1986.

New Investment Guidelines in 1985

The adverse effects of the world recession was still with us when Tun Daim took over the reins of the Ministry of Finance. The government budget was becoming strained. We could not borrow too much as the cost of debt services was already rising, and it was not known how long the world recession would continue. In a recession, it would also be damaging to economic growth to cut back too much on new expenditures in order to protect the integrity of the budget. Neither was it the right time to raise taxes to boost revenue. We were in a quandary with hardly any room to manoeuvre. We had to spend more to counter the depressive effects of the recession, but our resources to do so were limited. The Treasury was hard pressed to find a way out.

One way out of the economic malaise was to attract more foreign investments. However, foreign investment in Malaysia was slowing down because of the worldwide recession. More importantly, our foreign investment guidelines at that time had some definite requirements to limit foreign ownership. This was not acceptable to the foreign investors, but we could not keep the strict requirements and expect the foreign investors to change. If we wanted them badly enough, it was we who had to change.

Thus Daim Zainuddin, the new Minister of Finance, decided to beat the recession. On July 28, 1985, he courageously announced that Malaysia was changing its policy on its existing investment guidelines. This bold announcement improved the investment climate almost immediately. Enquiries started pouring in and the whole business atmosphere became clearer and brighter. It was a real fillip to the Malaysian economy. It went somewhat against the grain of the NEP, but Daim had the full backing of the PM himself, in a way that Tengku Razaleigh might not have received.

Foreign investments that were of special benefit to the economy from an employment, technology and especially from the point of view of actively promoting exports, were given special exemptions from the requirement to hold a maximum of only 30 per cent of the equity. The more they could export, the more they could own in equity capital — even up to 100 per cent foreign ownership.

The PM, at an investment seminar in New York on October 1, 1985, further strengthened Finance Minister Daim's breakthrough announcement. There, he clearly spelt out the "New Foreign Equity Guidelines". The response from American investors was enthusiastic.

The Malaysian economy began to turn around from that point onwards. The stronger capital inflows encouraged the domestic investors to undertake "joint enterprises" with the American and other foreign investors. The employment prospects and economic performance improved considerably. Incomes began to rise. Consumption also rose to create more demand for goods and services — and the whole economy began to move out of recession into a new stage of gradual recovery and faster growth.

We in the Treasury were not only seeing the light in the tunnel but were witnessing a bright recovery. We were also relieved to feel the exhilaration of economic progress once again. Indeed we had been at a loss as to what more could be done to fight the debilitating recession. We had recommended that foreign investment would help to give the economy the much needed economic stimulus, but it was a political decision to relax the almost sacred NEP-inspired foreign investment guidelines. Only the political leaders of the time could make that crucial decision — and they made it with courage and foresight. That is what we need to have always, particularly now with globalisation!

All this proves one thing: if there is a political will, an economy can pick up and prosper faster. It also shows that Malaysian political leaders are prepared to be pragmatic and to overrule "sensitivities" in the overall public and national interests. The only reservation some of us in the Treasury had at that time was to ask why this major political decision was not taken earlier. Maybe it was such a strategic decision that it had to be taken after great care and consultation—and that took time!

The 'Buy Malaysia' Campaign

Though the government had adopted tough measures to fight the recession, more had to be done. Thus, in 1985, Dr Mahathir Mohamad launched the "Buy Malaysia" campaign. We Malaysians had become spoilt and also prejudiced against our own goods. Goods and services provided by foreigners were deemed to be better, more durable and more "classy". They were even thought to give better value for money, although imported goods and services were not always as good as they were made out to be.

We had become too brand conscious regardless of the true value of these imports. For instance, many of the products that we imported were actually made in Malaysia, but we would buy them under a foreign brand name such as the shirts manufactured by Tan Sri Kishu Tirathrai's Globe Silk Store and Dato' G.S. Gill's golfballs. Dato' Gill's golfballs sold much better after he renamed them as *McGill's* golfballs (as if any Scotsman's golfballs were always better to play with!). There are many other interesting examples.

The "Buy Malaysia" campaign was the antithesis of the British policy under colonial times and even for a short period after independence, when we had not yet changed those British-inspired Treasury Instructors. At that time, those of us in the Treasury had to "show cause" as to why we had to authorise the allocation of funds and the purchase of any item from anywhere else other than Great Britain! We even had to import paper cups and toilet paper from Britain!

When the "Buy Malaysia" policy was introduced, I thought to myself: "Goodness! Gracious! What irony? What a reverse in policy?" Now I would be pulled up for authorising the purchase of goods and services from Britain and other foreign countries—unless the item could not be produced locally. The "Buy Malaysia" campaign helped greatly to draw public attention to the wide range of Malaysian products that had gradually emerged in the Malaysian market. We began to develop a sense of pride in Malaysian products. This was a source of strength to Malaysian manufacturers and it gave them a big boost in their confidence to expand production and exports. Partly due to the success of the "Buy Malaysian" campaign and the whole package of policy proposals that had been set in motion to counter the recession, the Malaysian economy continued to gain momentum.

The Economic Recovery and the North-South Expressway

I felt a great sense of fulfilment when the recession came to an end. Our long hard days of uncertainty, doubt and searching for solutions were coming to an end. The patience, policies, and strong political will to take tough decisions, were paying off.

Now we had to change our policies, shift gear in the economy and move forward faster once again. We had to do something big and bold to lift the economy, without causing further strain on the financial system that was strained by the persistent recession. The massive North-South Expressway (NSE) project that was launched about this time, provided part of the solution.

The NSE provided a real boost to the economy. This was the brainchild of the Prime Minister, Dr Mahathir, and the Minister of Finance, Daim Zainuddin. It was about the biggest privatisation project ever undertaken then and imposed no real strain on the government budget. The foreign exchange implications were also minimal since roadbuilding has a high local content as well as a large labour content. We had enough engineers and technicians who had been building roads for ages in the PWD. We also had a large pool of contractors and subcontractors who had been relatively idle and were most anxious to take on more work in this exciting project. Also, this huge project gave a wonderful opportunity to the government to fulfil its aspirations to assist the many *bumiputera* contractors, who had their fledgling contracting businesses damaged by the recession. The NSE was thus a real boon to all concerned. All this business activity helped to accelerate the pace of economic recovery.

We now had to consolidate the economic recovery and ensure that growth was maintained at a sustainable pace. We officials were now less stressed and could plan more purposefully for the future with greater confidence. Hopefully we had learnt our lessons and would try harder to steer away from any future recession or even economic slowdown. But that was not to be!

27.
COMMONWEALTH FINANCE MINISTERS'
MEETING IN THE MALDIVES

BY NOW I was working closely with Tun Daim Zainuddin, the new minister of finance. It was not difficult to win his confidence if you deliver on time. I was able to do so with the good team that I had and so there was really no problem. Therefore when it was time for Tun Daim to choose his team to attend the Commonwealth Finance Ministers' meeting in the Maldives, he selected me to join the delegation. As was Tun Daim's practice, we had a small team to minimise costs. But the consequence was that a few of us had to spread ourselves thin and move from one meeting to another to cover all the important discussions and to be able to brief the minister properly.

The Maldives — an island archipelago in the Indian Ocean — was a lovely place to relax after work, although there was hardly any time and hardly any nightclubs. The Maldives being a conservative Muslim country, the locals would not serve liquor with their own hands. But there were foreign workers who would serve quite readily in the bars of the fine tourist hotels that they had.

When we landed we found that the Boeing 747 began to pull back with its screeching brakes as soon as it landed. Then the aircraft slowed down considerably on the airfield and began to turn around, as if there was no more distance to go. I looked out and all I could see was the ocean all around us. I felt quite insecure — it was as if the plane had landed in the middle of the ocean.

When we disembarked and walked out of the small airport, we were taken along a narrow path and helped on to a motorboat. It was then that I realised that we had actually landed on a small atoll island. That was why the big Boeing 747 had a problem of inadequate space to manoeuvre! But the surprises continued!

The motorboat took us to another island where our hotel was situated. The journey on the high seas of the vast Indian Ocean was frightening. The waves were high and the motorboat "pilots" were like Japanese *kamikaze* pilots. They were certainly worse than the most daredevil taxi drivers that I had ever experienced. To them, it was fun, especially when they found out that we were quite scared of the rough seas. They turned up their throttles and went fast and headlong into the high waves. There were times when we were just "jumping" over the waves and this shook us up. So we had to appeal to those crazy pilots to go slow. They kindly obliged but could not help laughing at our fears.

We could see that the Maldives were really a whole atoll of pretty little islands. We could actually see all these islands forming a huge circle in the middle of the Indian Ocean.

The hotel was grand and modern in its design. The architecture captured the romance of the ocean and was built to take advantage of the beautiful sunrises and sunsets. Strong, cool breezes swept right through the hotel lobby, throughout the day and night.

The next day when we got down to the beach we found pristine beauty: the sands were white, shiny and clean and the sky was a bright blue, while the water was crystal clear. At the jetty by the hotel, we could see a wide variety of small fishes of every hue swimming carelessly around. They would crowd together every time we threw some bread at them. It was truly paradise, almost untouched by Man, as if it was at the beginning of Time.

The conference was a success. Malaysia had gained a reputation as a well-managed economy and we were thus in a position to provide knowledge of our experience in developing our economy. Tun Daim was businesslike. He did not mingle much among the other ministers and delegates at cocktail parties. He was somewhat more reticent than usual and we wondered why. One afternoon, we found out the reason.

The morning session of the conference was over and we had adjourned for lunch. The conference hall was nearer the chalets that were occupied by the officials. The ministers were provided with better accommodation at the hotel itself. But their rooms were at some distance from the conference hall. As I was relaxing in my chalet during the lunch break, I observed Minister Daim approach my chalet. He asked me whether he could rest in my quarters and of course I readily agreed. He came into my chalet and just lay on the concrete bunk. When I invited him to use my bed, he explained that he wanted to lie down on the hard bunk — as he had a bad back that was giving him trouble and severe pain! So that was why he had been even more quiet than usual. After about an hour's rest, he got up and went for the ministerial meeting — and he did well.

Tun Daim Consults Me About
Zain in Washington, D.C.

In April 1986, Tun Daim attended the Development Committee meeting of the World Bank in Washington, D.C. I followed him for that meeting. I enjoyed going to Washington, D.C. as I had many friends there, having worked at the World Bank for two years on the board of directors, about 15 years before.

Once when I was often visiting Washington, D.C. for World Bank and IMF meetings, the security guards asked me if I had just come back from a mission abroad since they had not seen me for a few months. They could not believe that I had returned home for good. The bank staff used to be away for long periods of time on overseas economic missions, covering several countries at a time. Hence the confusion and some doubt! However that turned out to be my last official trip to the World Bank and the International Monetary Fund.

After an official meeting one evening, Tun Daim called me aside for a private chat. This was an unusual gesture on his part and I wondered what he wanted to see me about. He was always straight to the point and so he looked straight into my eyes and asked me: "How well do you know Zain Azraii?" I replied without hesitation that he was one of my oldest and best friends and that I had the greatest respect for his exceptional good qualities and intellect.

Tun Daim, in his characteristic fashion, then looked down, twitched his moustache and asked his second question, "So you wouldn't mind working under him?"

I was taken aback that he should ask me such a question as I had never in my whole career been told who my boss would be and especially asked whether I would mind working under my new boss. In the civil service you only know who your new boss is only when you see him after reporting for duty! And you never are consulted on whether you would be able to work with the new boss. But I supposed that was Tun Daim with his corporate style.

I replied that Tan Sri Zain Azraii was someone I had always admired from the days he was my school captain at the Victoria Institution in Kuala Lumpur and that I would enjoy working under him as my new Secretary-General of the Treasury. That assurance was sufficient for Tun Daim. He added that Zain Azraii was being transferred back from his assignments in Washington, D.C. and New York to serve at home. He expressed the hope that I would give him my full support. I assured him that as a loyal civil servant, I would serve the country and my superiors in the best traditions of the MCS.

Soon after we returned home, Zain Azraii reported to the Treasury as the Secretary-General. I do not think that this new top job was his cup of tea. He was an outstanding diplomat and really did enjoy the world of diplomacy. That is why he excelled in his diplomatic career. But he was also a dedicated civil servant in the true traditions of the civil service that his illustrious father Dato' Zainal Abidin also belonged to. He had been sounded about serving as head of the Economic Planning Unit earlier but had graciously declined the offer.

The government recognised that Zain Azraii was doing a splendid job as ambassador to the U.S. and Permanent Representative to the U.N. and that it was only wise to let him continue to contribute his expert services to the nation in those capacities. But when the government called him at their time of need to return home to serve, he readily responded. I think it was also Tun Daim's persuasion that helped to tilt the balance of Zain's judgement.

We both worked together exceedingly well; I was, after all, his old schoolmate. He was quick to pick up the finer points of fiscal and monetary management since he was not that new to the subject of Economics and Economic Management. After all, he did take the prestigious Oxford degree, the PPE—Politics, Philosophy and Economics. Besides, he was a director of the World Bank while also being ambassador in Washington, D.C. He was thus well qualified for the highly prized post of Secretary-General of the Treasury. It was the second most senior post in the whole civil service after the Chief Secretary to the Government, who was then Tan Sri Sallehuddin Mohamad.

28.
LEAVING THE TREASURY
(1986-1989)

I ENJOYED working with Tan Sri Zain Azraii at the Treasury. We were making a fine partnership with my long experience and accumulated knowledge in the Treasury, and Zain Azraii's great flair, intelligence and diplomatic skills. But Tan Sri Sallehuddin, the Chief Secretary to the Government, had other plans.

Salleh, who was my former classmate at university and colleague in the Treasury, one day called me to his office in the Prime Minister's Department. After our usual friendly exchanges, he became serious. He told me that he planned to promote and transfer me to the Ministry of Transport as Secretary-General.

I was taken aback. I thanked him for his confidence in me but asked if I could be promoted within the Treasury since I still enjoyed my work there. Despite my record as the longest serving officer in the Treasury, Salleh insisted that he could not give me a promotion if I opted to stay in the Treasury. If I rejected this offer, he could not promise me further promotions since I was already 52 years old and had only 3 years more before retiring at 55. When I could not give him a definite answer, he advised me as a friend that there were many serious contenders for the prestigious post and that he would give me a few days to think it over.

I went back to my office quite disturbed, as I had not expected this new change of events. I had taken it for granted that I was a Treasury officer through and through. It was my professional calling. I had not regarded myself as anything else but a "specialist Treasury officer" in the MCS, which was really a generalist management service. When I told Zain Azraii about my meeting with Salleh, he was upset. How could I be transferred at this time so soon after he took over the Treasury. He needed all the help he could get to go forward with his plans to lead the Treasury? I could not offer him any advice but simply suggested that he consult Salleh himself.

I was trying to figure out whether I should tell Tun Daim or let my Secretary-General report to the Minister about the impending change of his second in command. But I was soon called in to see the Minister of Finance. Tun Daim was stern and he asked me quite abruptly whether I wanted to leave the Treasury because I did not want to work under Zain Azraii. This question troubled me and I told him politely that I was hurt by the implications of his question. He looked surprised and I asked him for his permission to be outspoken on this sensitive and personal matter. He then looked even more surprised and agreed to my request.

I explained to Tun Daim that Zain Azraii and I were close friends and that his late father Dato' Zainal Abidin and his mother Datin Putih Mariam had known me since I was a schoolboy when I was studying with their sons, Zain Azraii and his elder brother Zain Azahari, at the Victoria Institution. In fact, Dato' Zainal had been my referee when I applied to join the MCS. So how could it be suggested that I was reluctant to serve Zain Azraii?

Tun Daim was apparently moved. He noted what I said and told me that he would talk to the people who mattered.

A few days later he called me to his office again. He was not happy. He told me that he had taken up the matter of my transfer to the highest levels, but was advised to let the matter rest. Since the question of transfers was a matter for the civil service, he was also told that if I were retained in the Finance Ministry, my promotion would suffer. He said that under the circumstances, he would not stand in my way and would reluctantly let me go to the Ministry of Transport on promotion as Secretary-General.

I left the Treasury with mixed feelings. The Treasury had been my "home" in the civil service. It had been good to me. But I could not ask to stay, as it would jeopardise the rest of my career. I was on the horns of a painful dilemma for sometime. But I finally decided to accept the promotion and the transfer. I went up to Salleh, and conveyed my decision. He was glad and congratulated me. Now I had to make preparations to move to the Transport Ministry as soon as possible.

On the day I left the Treasury, we followed the Treasury tradition of bidding farewell to its senior officers who retire or go on transfer after long service in the Treasury. It was a sad and nostalgic occasion. The Treasury staff of a few hundred lined up at the entrance of the Treasury building at Jalan Duta to bid farewell to me. As I shook hands with each officer and staff, I recalled some incident or other that had bound our friendship. It was this fraternal spirit of working hard together under trying circumstances that had created the strong Treasury *esprit de corps*.

After bidding goodbye to all my colleagues, I went up to the cluster of the most senior officers: Zain Azraii, Sheriff Kassim, Ali Abul Hassan, Clifford Herbert and Mustapa Mohamed (who later became Second Minister of Finance). Together with a group of other senior officers they walked me down the stairs in front of the Treasury buildings to my waiting car. I felt my eyes dampen and tears rolled down my cheeks as I was driven off. I was leaving my "home" of 27 years ... for good.

29.
OUR SONS' EDUCATION

RAVI, Indran and Dharm were getting on well in school. They started their primary education at the St John's Primary School at Bukit Nanas in Kuala Lumpur. We chose St John's mainly because it was a good school which was also close to, and on the way to Samala's school, the Bukit Nanas Convent. It was convenient for her to just drop them on her way to school.

Often the boys would walk over to her school during the recess for a bowl of noodles and a drink. When they had afternoon school, they would take the school bus at about 11am and get to Samala's school canteen to have lunch before walking across the road to St John's. It was altogether a congenial arrangement.

Of course, we did not have the time-wasting traffic jams that we have today. Hence whether one took a car or a bus to school, there was not that much time wasted in going to and from school.

Those days you could choose your school for your children without trouble. Now you have to admit your child at the school nearest your home. However, some outstanding schools are "controlled" and reserved for students from special backgrounds. Thus you have a large number of children of prominent parents in schools like Victoria Institution, Bukit Nanas Convent, Bukit Bintang Girls' School, St Mary's and St John's Institution. Of course, those of us who went to the Victoria Institution believed that we belonged to the "best school in the country"!

St John's Primary School was a good primary school. It was on par or even better than Pasar Road School or Batu Road School that were the so called "feeder schools" to Victoria Institution. The discipline was better and the students of St John's Primary came from better family backgrounds and the middle-income group.

Ravi, Indran and Dharm therefore did enjoy St John's Primary School. They could have easily gone to St John's Institution secondary school. However, I was keen that they should attend VI where my late father and I had gone to school. Dad had attended the "old grey school where the winding water flows" at High Street. (This quote is taken from the old school song!) The old school was built of wood, by the Klang River near the High Street Police Station! My father used to tell me that when the Klang River rose after heavy rains, large crocodiles would emerge. The VI Headmaster would then take out his double-barrel gun and go hunting for the poor crocodiles—watched keenly by the VI boys. However, by the time I went to the VI, it was already relocated in the present school building, which was built in 1984 at Jalan Davison. Due to its long and illustrious history, there was always a strong *esprit de corps* among the VI students. Sometimes this sense of pride went a bit too far. I recall Mr Toh Boon Hwa, our tough Science teacher, once telling the class: "Don't worry if you are a good footballer but a weak student. All you need is the VI chop on your leaving certificate and you will surely get a good job anywhere!"

I am afraid one of my good friends took him seriously and literally too. He was a fine sportsman. He played most of the games for the school and neglected his studies. Consequently he failed his Cambridge School Certificate Examination and ended up becoming a junior clerk. Fortunately what his teacher said helped him to move up the ladder of life. But, unfortunately, he did not get very far without good academic qualifications.

I was influenced by this real-life story and when it came to our sons, it was quite clear in my mind that they should not spend too much time playing games in school. Indran for instance was keen on cricket. He wanted to give more time to it, but I discouraged him. I told him that he must ensure that he did well in his school studies and when he went to university he could find the right balance himself and play whatever games he wanted to.

I was quite strict with our boys during their schooldays. I encouraged them to play games but only in the neighbourhood and at home and that too only between 4pm and 7pm at the latest. At our government house at Jalan Selangor in Federal Hill, we were lucky to have a large compound. I would join the boys in playing football, badminton, hockey and cricket. Some children in the neighbourhood would join us and we would all have a good time. We also played table-tennis and Samala would join us—and often beat all of us! She had played table tennis for the university and was pretty good at it.

We were members of the Lake Club. There the boys took up tennis, squash and swimming. Samala would drive them for lessons and they would enjoy the wholesome sporting facilities at the club. I take special pleasure in the thought that although I did not do well in sports myself, I had spent time teaching the boys most of the sports and games they know today. Ravi plays hockey quite seriously; Indran has played for the Bar Council and Dharm played hockey and represented his Chisholm College in swimming and water polo.

We also started them on *tae-kwon-do*, the Japanese art of self-defence. Ravi and Indran took a few grades but it was Dharm who took the art more seriously and advanced to the higher grades. He was attempting the black belt when he discontinued. Samala and I would take them for lessons on Saturdays and it was great fun to watch them spar.

Tae-kwon-do requires a strong sense of discipline. The students of a higher grade have the right to pull up the students at the lower grades, when they are asked to supervise the junior students at training. When Ravi discontinued *tae-kwon-do* and had decided to go back for some brushing up, Dharm had overtaken him in seniority in the martial art and sometimes tried to order him around during *Tae-kwon-do* lessons!

I was keen that the boys cultivate the art of reading. I was particularly concerned that the boys were learning in Bahasa Malaysia or Malay as the medium of instruction. It bothered Samala and me that there was a distinct danger that they would lose out in their command of the English language. I therefore made it a point to take them to all the major libraries in town to expose them to the wonderful habit of reading and to improve their English as well. At that time there were mainly the Book Club, behind the Selangor Club, the American "Lincoln Centre", the British Council and the Lake Club libraries. We were members of all these libraries and would visit them almost every week. The boys started off reading Enid Blyton and graduated to Charles Dickens and other authors.

Today, it makes us feel good that they all have a healthy interest in reading. Our fears about their proficiency of the English language therefore turned out, fortunately, to be unfounded! But I believe that the situation would have been bad if we did not take the necessary counter measures to encourage them to read in English.

Malay as a Medium of Instruction

Unhappily this was not the case with a large number of children of our children's generation. The introduction of Malay as the official medium of instruction was a laudable policy. But it was carried too far and eroded the importance of English and caused many other problems. The use of Malay as the medium of instruction greatly helped to equalise opportunities in learning between the *bumiputeras* and the non-*bu-miputeras* and between the urban and the rural children. In many ways it did give the Malays a considerable advantage in learning and in educational advancement. This is because Bahasa Melayu is the "mother tongue of the Malays" and so unlike the non-Malays, the *bumiputeras* and Malays in particular, do not have to learn the Malay language from scratch. Thus the *bumiputera* students have a head start in education at the primary school level. It was like the advantage many of us had as students from the urban areas and those especially from English speaking homes or with parents who had been educated in English.

But a whole generation of Malaysian students lost out on the ability to read, write and communicate effectively in the English language. This is a pity as we need not have lost our comparative advantage in and through the English language, if we had not reduced the priority given to the teaching of English as a second language. Perhaps more time should have been given to the teaching of English. Unfortunately, those *bumiputera* students whom the government wanted to help to improve educationally and to give a better market value for their educational qualifications, did not gain as much as those who became proficient in both Bahasa Malaysia and the English language as well.

The situation is now being gradually rectified and improved. But the process has to be speeded up before we cause our children and their children to lose out even more in this highly competitive environment which is becoming increasingly globalised. In the new world of high technology and information technology, those who cannot communicate well in the world language (which is English) will lose out and not be able to catch up with the dynamic and rapid progress taking place.

Can we afford to neglect English? Shouldn't we care enough for our children to give them a better start in life? Of course, the middle and richer classes will be able to give their children a good education in both Malay and English, but what about the majority of our children who will have to attend the government school system? The wealthy will continue to send their children to "public schools" overseas and the many new private schools at home. But what about the vast majority of our children? Surely they need to do well in life too. I'm glad that after so many years, the policy on English is truly now being improved. But it's better late than never!

We made sure that our sons studied both Malay and English. I remember telling our boys repeatedly "Study Your MEMS", i.e., "Malay, English, Maths and Science". I believed that if they could master just these four subjects, then they could develop fast in their studies and take on any course of studies that they wanted to pursue. We gave them some tuition to strengthen their foundation in Malay. I felt that it was far better to spend money and give them a good education at home rather than send them abroad. In the first place we did not have that kind of money to spend, being an honest civil servant and not a professional in the private sector. But I think, more importantly, we strongly believed that our sons should be brought up in the country of their birth, with our own Asian values. We wanted them to be as Malaysian as possible.

The boys did well at Victoria Institution. I remember the pride I felt in driving them up the hill to VI on the first day of school for each of our three sons. I felt the presence of my father who was a proud product of the school. He had been so loyal to the school and proud of the VI and its headmaster, a Mr Shaw, so that his colleagues and relatives used to call him "Shaw"! I felt that sense of continuity and fulfilment and I hope my sons would feel the same, God willing, when they, in their time, decide to send their children to the VI too.

Choosing to Study Abroad

When the boys sat for their Malaysian Certificate of Education (MCE), we had to decide whether to admit them to the Higher School Certificate class at the VI. We were quite unsure as what to do. If we sent them to the HSC class, they would be committed to going to the local universities. That did not seem to be an attractive prospect because of the following uncertainties:

First, admission into our universities was based on a "quota system". The ratio was about 55 per cent *bumiputeras* to 45 per cent or less for non-*bumiputeras*. At that time the broad category of Indians, which included those of Sri Lankan origin like us, were given a quota of only about 6 per cent within the 45 per cent for non-*bumiputeras*. Second, there was no assurance that once selected, you could have a choice of the university or the faculty you wanted. Third, there was a growing perception that the academic standards in most of our universities were going down. Many of the political leaders themselves were not sending their children to our local universities. Fourth, the medium of instruction was largely in Malay, so I believed that the students' proficiency in the English language would further deteriorate. Fifth, I had heard that after the unfortunate racial riots of 1969, the local university campuses had become relatively polarised.

For these reasons, Samala and I regretfully decided not to send our children to the local universities. We would use our hard-earned savings from Samala's and my civil service salaries to send our children for the best education possible. We decided that if we could not afford it, then we would borrow to send our sons abroad for a good education.

The Boys Travel Abroad On Their Own

Our sons did not have to start at Taylor's College soon after their school-leaving examinations. The term at Taylor's College started only in April. Thus they had plenty of time at their disposal. So we decided to send them abroad for holidays, for the experience of travelling abroad on their own.

I was a member of the Board of Directors of the Malaysian Airline System (MAS) and so I qualified to get high discount tickets for the family and myself. Thus it was quite inexpensive to send the boys abroad. In fact we had used this privilege to travel to other counties during the school holidays. We had visited India, Thailand, the Philippines, Indonesia, Australia, New Zealand and Japan. We did not feel the urge to travel further afield because we had already lived in the U.S. and had visited Europe before.

We sent Ravi to London after his School Certificate examinations. We had made arrangements for Ravi to stay at my cousin Robert Abraham's place. Ravi arrived at Heathrow and waited for Robert. I had told Ravi to wait for Robert. But if Robert did not turn up, then I told Ravi to just rough it out on the cushioned seats at Heathrow for the night and then to get directions to the YMCA. I wanted Ravi to learn to be self-reliant and tough. If he had been a girl I would not have taken the risk, but, as a young resourceful lad, I thought he should take risks and be self-confident. Ravi was only about 16 years at that time and was happy to take the challenge and I was proud of his sense of independence.

At Heathrow, Robert's friend turned up after Ravi had waited a few hours. He identified himself and took Ravi to Robert's apartment. Robert looked after Ravi well. However he was quite busy with his "Tabernacle Project" which involved looking after the welfare of West

Indian immigrants. Ravi therefore went out on his own to explore and enjoy London by himself and in the process learnt a great deal.

We did the same for Indran after his MCE examination. He had been quite relaxed about his examinations and I was quite concerned. I used to advise him to study harder but he seemed to be taking things quite easy. But somehow, just about two months before the examinations, he began to study in earnest and he did very well. He accepted my suggestion to visit my sister Georgie and brother-in-law Soren in Copenhagen, and enjoyed his stay with Georgie, Hans and Carl. He too benefited greatly from the exposure of travel.

Dharm was not keen to travel soon after his examination. Instead he chose to travel when he went to Australia. He accompanied us to New Zealand during one of our several trips to Australia. We gave him plenty of space and he enjoyed the trip with us.

From Taylor's College to Australian Universities

Ravi, Indran and Dharm went to Taylor's College at Bangsar Road where it was then situated. It was convenient as Taylor's College was just over a mile from our new private house at 9, Lorong Medang in Bangsar. The boys could even walk to school. However, most of the time Samala or I would drop them at the College on our way to or from work.

Taylor's College then was just a means to an end. It did not provide a rounded education. The facilities were cramped and crowded. There were no playing fields and hardly even a garden. It was situated behind a petrol station and the environment was not so conducive to learning. But it served a purpose for us parents and the students. The boys made the best of what was available at Taylor's College and went on to study in Australia.

In 1980, Ravi was the first of our sons to study in Australia. He did well to get admitted to study the double major of Economics and Accounting at Monash University in Melbourne. It was the first time that any one of our children was going to be away from home for a long period. I was concerned about him and wanted to give him every encouragement to do well. In retrospect, I recalled my own experience leaving home for the University of Malaya in Singapore when I nearly went astray. I thus expressed my concern in the only way I could. I wrote to him practically every day for about a month before I slowly phased out!

I gradually got used to Ravi being away studying abroad and now looked forward to Indran and Dharm to follow him to make their way through college.

The following year, 1981, Indran left for Australia too. Fortunately he also went to Monash where he was admitted to study Science. He was keen to do Physics. However he did well enough in his first year to qualify to do two degrees at the same time. So he chose to do the exacting academic combination of Science and Law, and qualified as a lawyer.

Dharm soon followed to study engineering at the well-known Chisholm College, which is now part of Monash University in Melbourne. He too was active in student union affairs and completed his degree in mechanical engineering on time.

Saving for Education

The financing of the boys' education was always a concern to us. For that reason, Samala and I resolved to be careful with our expenses and to give high priority to our savings and investment. We were comfortable but definitely not wealthy. Samala in particular was not at all interested in spending on jewellery, expensive clothes or even expensive entertainment or vacations. I myself did not care for expensive lifestyles. We rarely ate at expensive restaurants. In any case we often had dinner in the best hotels in town because we were invited for official functions.

Our simple, private and unpretentious lifestyle thus enabled us to save a high proportion of our joint incomes. With this saving we bought properties and sold them when the price was right to make some profit and thus increase our savings. We never took an active part in the stockmarket except to try our luck at initial public share issues for which we were only occasionally lucky. My being in the Treasury discouraged me from participating in the stockmarket as I did not want anyone to be able to point an unfair finger at me or even Samala. Our prime motivation to save was to be able to finance our children's education.

This is where our values had to be very different from some of our Malay colleagues. They could afford to be quite relaxed about their spending because they were much more confident about their capacity to obtain government scholarships and subsidised loans to finance their children's education. Even if their children could not get into foreign universities, they had a better chance to get into higher education by going to the local universities or to the Mara Institute of Technology for diploma and professional courses.

Fortunately Tengku Razaleigh understood my predicament of having three sons to educate. He spoke to Tan Sri Abdullah Salleh, the chairman of Petronas who arranged for Ravi to get a study loan. Although this meant that Ravi was tied to serve with Petronas for seven years, it was good in the sense that he would be assured of a job on his return from his studies.

Indran too was fortunate. When his turn came to go to University, I approached my old university mate, Tengku Shariman who was head of Pernas. He was also kind to help me get a smaller study loan for Indran. However, we still had to supplement both these loans as they were not full loans.

When it was Dharm's turn to attend university in 1985, the late Tan Sri Lee Loy Seng (whom I got to know well through Tengku Razaleigh) also assisted me to get partial assistance from his foundation. I did not even ask him but he had asked me how our children were faring in school when he accompanied Tengku Razaleigh on one of our trips abroad at Hong Kong. That was the measure of the man. He was quiet, observant, caring and magnanimous. I recall being really touched by his concern when he expressed his admiration of how careful we were in saving for our sons' education. He himself had come up the hard way and appreciated sacrifice.

Study Loans for Children
of Government Servants?

Samala and I know what anxiety one has to go through in wanting to ensure that our children will be able to go for higher education if they have the ability to do so. Only those who are salaried workers understand the deep concerns of parents. Those of the upper middle-income class and the rich or wealthy will not be able to experience that feeling of uncertainty, anxiety and frustration. What if our children qualify for higher education but we do not have the funds to send them to college? Our professional peers and colleagues in the private sector did not have to go through that kind of pressure, at least to the same extent as those in the civil service. The managers, doctors, lawyers and engineers in the private sector, with the same or lesser qualifications and experience than their counterparts in the public service, enjoyed much higher salaries and perquisites and were therefore more able to send their children for higher education abroad when they could not get places locally.

This was the main source of grievance of most civil servants. They did not mind so much the wide differentials in the salaries and the perquisites between the government and private sectors. After all they chose the civil service as their careers and no one forced them into it, although at the time of joining the civil service, the salary differentials were not so wide. As time went on and the private sector expanded rapidly, obviously the disparity between the incomes in the public and private sectors widened considerably. The irony was that the public servants were serving the public and national interests, while their counterparts in the private sector were serving their own interests. Yet the public servants were often not able to send their children for higher studies because they could not afford to on their relatively low public service salaries.

I believe that the public servants could be much more motivated if the government could alleviate this heavy responsibility and burden of finding funds for their children's education. Indeed at this time when the attraction to serve in the public service has been declining steadily, it would be wise to introduce more incentives for those who want to serve the country and to work for the government.

One such incentive would be to introduce an attractive public service Study Loan Scheme for all those children of public servants, who qualify to benefit from tertiary education. The scheme should be based on the criteria of merit and a means test. Thus the brighter and especially poor children of public servants should get higher priority for larger loans, which of course should not exceed the minimum funds that are required to meet the cost of fees, accommodation, travel and other essentials.

The government will also benefit considerably from this student loan scheme in the following ways: (i) the retention rate in the civil service will be raised and the government will be able to keep the better qualified civil servants as well; (ii) since only the brighter students who gain admission to the institutions of higher learning would get the loans, the government does not have to allocate much funds for the loan scheme; (iii) the cost would largely be limited only to the subsidised element of the interest rate. Hence the cost will be quite small for the government to bear; (iv) the morale of the government servants would be raised and their children given hope and encouragement to do well in school. Otherwise, there would be less incentive to study — especially when they feel that all their academic efforts would lead to nothing, if their parents cannot afford to send them for higher studies; (v) the government could thus encourage the scholars to join government service on the completion of their studies. Some of them could take pride in continuing the tradition of their families in serving the nation as some of us did; (vi) this is certainly a laudable way for the government to express its appreciation to public servants regardless of race and it would also help to meet the manpower needs of the country.

I sincerely hope that in the future, the government in its wisdom will adopt loan schemes for all public servants, regardless of race and for all students who want to pursue higher education — not just the brightest students. This will have a salutary effect on the public service and the whole nation. However, the education loan scheme should be fair and reasonable. While some preference can be continued for the *bumiputera* students, in the interests of promoting overall balance and equity, the issue of a proper balance has to also apply to the non-*bumiputeras* as well. As time moves on there must be less of the preferential treatment — otherwise we will be causing disunity and even disloyalty!

Why Study in Australia?
When the funding for our sons' education was settled, the question of where they should study became an issue. Should they study in Britain, Australia or the U.S.?

We discussed the pros and cons and finally chose Australia. But what was our basis for choosing Australia? We had several reasons.

First, Australia was less expensive. The Australian government at that time still subsidised university education even for foreign students. The cost of studying in the U.K. or the U.S. was much higher. Second, Australia was closer to home. This meant that the cost of travel to and fro was much cheaper than travelling to the U.K. or the U.S. In an emergency, we could be there or the boys could come home in just seven hours of flying time. Third, the Australian weather was much more comfortable than the English weather. Fourth, Australia is more Asia-orientated and therefore racial discrimination is much lower. The boys would not be exposed to much bigotry as in many parts of the U.K. and the U.S. Fifth, the boys would enjoy sports and be able to follow all kinds of sports all round the year in Australia, which is a very sports-loving country. Sixth, the Australian system of education was regarded as far more modern and innovative than some of the tradition-bound educational institutions in the U.K., and the wide range of academic standards in the U.S. I believe that the Australian education system has the best of both worlds, i.e., the U.S. and the U.K.

For all these reasons we leaned towards sending our three sons to Australia to pursue their higher education.

The boys received a good rounded education in Australia. The academic standards were high. The intellectual environment was free and the scope for extra mural and sporting activities was exceedingly diverse and rich. We are grateful that our sons developed well and grew into well-rounded young professionals and gentlemen, partly through the sound education they had in Australia and of course because, if I may say so, their home upbringing!

On completion of his studies, Ravi joined Petronas. After about two years, he wanted to go to the U.K. to do Law. Ravi had wanted to do corporate finance at Petronas but they kept those challenging jobs for others and placed Ravi in the Audit Department instead. He did not find the job exciting.

But I could not afford to send him to the U.K. to do Law when the other two boys were at college. So I told him that he could do his London Law examinations externally if he really wanted to do law. I meant it also as a challenge and he took it. He studied part time with his good friend Siva. He used to come home from work, have a quick wash and then rush off to the Vanto Academy for his Law lectures—without even having a cup of tea.

It was, I thought, highly creditable that he had that kind of tough discipline that helped him to pass his examinations every year without dropping any subject any time. Once he got his LLB London, he wanted to go to London to do his bar finals. We decided that he deserved our full support, having worked so steadfastly to get his Law degree. On his own part, Ravi used his own savings from his earlier work at Petronas to go to the U.K. and to study there for one year. There again he passed his bar finals in the first attempt and then joined the well-established British Merchant Bankers of Klienwort & Benson. Later he returned home to work in corporate finance at KYM, a public listed company.

Indran's case was more straightforward. He finished with two degrees in Science and Law in five years. Soon after his studies, he returned home and started his chambering at the old law firm of Messrs Shearne & Delamore, and carried on working there. Later he moved on to Kadir Kassim.

Dharm worked as a graduate engineer in Australia for a while. He enjoyed the experience he gained working in the Australian environment, but he returned home to develop his career. He tried working in a computer firm until he found something really up his street. This came his way when he joined the Malaysian Airline System (MAS) in the engineering projects department. He later joined General Electric and is now at Maxis.

Working at Home and Not Migrating

We were grateful that our sons came back to build their careers at home and not abroad. There are too many of our students who start working abroad soon after their education and then stay there and ultimately settle down abroad.

I appreciate that the U.S., the U.K. and Australia *inter alia*, provide higher incomes and maybe even a higher quality of life. But to me, home is home. Be it ever so humble, there is no place like home. "Home", is where God in his great wisdom placed us at birth. We must have been born in a particular country for a special reason. It is our duty therefore to prepare ourselves to live and work and to contribute to the enhancement of the quality of life in the country of our birth. For me, it is Malaysia.

There are handicaps and inequalities in different countries and Malaysia is no exception. The challenge in life is to work hard to overcome the obstacles and to help build a better and more meaningful life for our community, our people and our country as our first University of Malaya Welfare Week motto proclaimed: "Help Us to Help Our People". Thus those of us who have been blessed with a good education, should take the lead to serve our people in the many ways that are available here. There are always those who are less fortunate than we are and so we owe it to them to help enhance their lives too.

If we believe that we are not treated equally or that we ourselves should have had a more equitable and fairer deal, then there are others who are less equipped who would feel an even greater sense of alienation. It is these marginalised groups, regardless of race, that those of us who are better off should help.

But if we feel that we are not treated fairly and therefore choose to opt out and become selfish and uncaring for others, then that would be unfortunate as well as unfair in itself. Worse still, if we choose to avoid the problems and escape from the issues via migration, then it would more regrettable.

I believe that God placed us where we are born, and it is our duty to give our best to serve the country of our birth.

Secretary-General of the Ministry of Transport

I continued to serve in the government. I took over from Tan Sri Ishak Tadin as Secretary-General of the Ministry of Transport in 1987. Dr (now Tun) Ling Liong Sik (as he told me much earlier) had asked for me to become his Secretary-General in his Ministry. The Deputy Minister was Datin Zaleha, my former university mate and a good friend. I had as my first two Deputy Secretaries-General, Tuan Haji Hamzah and Cik Norminshah Sabrin. Later Tuan Haji Othman Rizal (now Tan Sri) and Samsuddin Osman (now Tan Sri) took over and then became Secretary to the Treasury and Chief Secretary to the Government respectively. Dato' Ong Kah Ting was political secretary then! It was gratifying to me that those who worked with me did so well!

Norminshah was about the most senior lady in the whole civil service and she felt a sense of grievance at not being given her fair due because she was not a male. That made it difficult for some of her colleagues to work with her. I called them together and explained that we had all to work as a team. The situation improved but before long Norminshah got transferred to the Ministry of Works while Hamzah became the Director General of the Road Transport Department. Those moves solved the problems and both officers were happy.

Othman Rizal and Samsuddin Osman made a good team with me. Othman has a strong personality and we took a little while to adjust to each other. But once he realised that we could learn from each other and that I was trying to be a firm yet fair boss, Othman turned out to be loyal and committed.

Samsuddin was from the Military College. He was a gentleman and a soldier. He would rationalise and sometimes differ, but once I made a decision he would back me to the hilt in the true tradition of a fine civil servant.

Minister of Transport Dr Ling Liong Sik further strengthened our strong fraternal and professional spirit. He had also been trained in the Military College and had all the good qualities of an able leader, besides having a sharp analytical mind as well as being a medical doctor. We were grateful that Dr Ling actually empowered us to initiate transport policies and to take our own initiatives to implement the Ministry's policies, programmes and projects.

All we had to ensure was that we undertook our work in good faith and that we kept Dr Ling fully informed and appraised of developments. Dr Ling believed in consultation and consensus building. If we observed these basic rules, then we were on the right track. We liked his style in leading and running this large and vital Ministry. All the airports, shipping ports, Malayan Railways, the Road Transport Department and international aviation traffic rights came under the purview of the Ministry of Transport.

Quality of Governance in Government

For the first time in my career, I felt that I was alone in the leadership and management of my official responsibilities at the Ministry of Transport. I was the most senior official in the whole Ministry. The Minister of Transport, as my political boss, was always answerable to the politicians and the public. But we had to provide him with the answers. We would have to recommend the policies, present them to the minister and implement the decisions of the government.

In our system of government, the civil service plays a vital role. No minister would survive for long or be really effective unless he has a good team of highly qualified and dedicated civil servants to back him up. I think the book *Yes, Minister* gives a fine flavour of how the civil service could rule the roost, unless there is a strong government and able ministers.

In Malaysia, we do have a very strong government with a two-thirds majority in Parliament. I believe that if this majority was far less, then the civil service would have stronger powers and greater influence in the government. But a small majority in Parliament would have weakened the political capacity and the will of the government to govern effectively.

I am not sure whether it would have been better for the country to have a stronger civil service. Since the civil service is predominantly Malay, it naturally has a built-in bias to formulate and implement socio-economic policies from a different angle. The civil service cannot possibly feel and have adequate empathy for all the ethnic groups in this diversified multiracial society if it is dominated by one racial group.

Even now, after more than 45 years of Independence, there are many who believe that the civil service still shows considerable bias in the formulation and implementation of government policies. There is this perception that the government looks after the *bumiputeras*, and especially some sectors of the *bumiputera* community first and then the other communities. Here again some think that those *bumiputeras* who are favoured by the government get preferential treatment over other *bumiputeras*. So not all *bumiputeras* gain, as is often thought to be the case.

However, if the civil service was more multiracial, there would be a greater chance and opportunity for the civil service to become more neutral and objective in providing more professional, holistic and wholesome advice to the government. It is understandable however that in a multiracial society, the dominant ethnic group in the civil service will want to concentrate its interests and focus its attention on the ethnic group it comes from and from which it draws its natural inspiration. Nevertheless the civil service must be apolitical and neutral.

This is why I have always asserted that in a multiracial society like in Malaysia, the civil service has to be more multiracial and more closely reflective of the ethnic composition of the Malaysian society, if it is to be more empathetic and be of greater service to the country as a whole.

In fact, several years ago, when I took part in a seminar at the government Training Institute (Intan) in Kuala Lumpur, I made the point that "there is a perception in the civil service that non-Malays feel a sense of alienation in the civil service". Although it was a seminar behind closed doors, *The Star* got wind of it and played it up on its front page. The reaction from my Malay colleagues was invariably unfavourable. However, many non-Malay colleagues congratulated me for reflecting and revealing their silent sentiments openly.

Some of my bosses in the civil service however thought differently. They did not like my honest assessment and outspoken views. They did not show their reaction openly but in a somewhat characteristic style of theirs, some of them quietly schemed against me. When I thought that this resentment against me had died down, I got a bolt from the blues several months later in the form of a stern letter form the Public Service Department (PSD).

The letter asked me to explain why I had made that statement to the press. I replied that my statement was made in good faith and as frankly as possible, as requested by the organisers at the seminar, behind closed doors. Furthermore, I stressed that I had not given my statement to the press and was not aware of how they got hold of it. I was advised in the letter not to make similar statements again. My reply put the matter to rest, but I have no doubt that there were many colleagues who were disappointed that I was not severely dealt with.

I believe that my interpretation that non-Malays in the civil service generally feel a sense of alienation is correct. It is unfortunate. If some staff of any organisation, regardless of whether it is in the public or private sector, feel a sense of alienation, then we will not be able to get the best of their potential. To that extent the organisation will lose out. The productivity will undoubtedly suffer.

On the other hand, if some sections of the civil service or a business organisation feel "a sense of protection and patronage" then those in that category would feel comfortable. They could even run the risk of becoming complacent. After all one cannot deny them the choice to be relatively relaxed, since they do not have to feel the anxieties of insecurity or the cutting edge of severe competition for excellence, as felt by the non-*bumiputeras*.

In my career, however, I did not feel insecure. This was because I felt sufficiently confident in my work. I also was prepared to fight against any discrimination and to prove to myself that I would "do my best", regardless of the rewards. For me it was a matter of self-respect and self-worth that mattered most. I knew that if I got discouraged and faltered in my enthusiasm for my work, then I would become vulnerable. Then those who did not like me or who felt that I was a threat, would then have a good basis for putting me down. When that happened, I would surely go down, as I did not have a godfather as many of my Malay colleagues had. I had seen that kind of scenario unfold for some of my non-*bumiputera* colleagues and I was determined that I would try my best to ensure that it did not happen to me. My self-respect would not allow it to happen.

I decided that my moto would be: "To do my best, and to God I leave the rest."

30.
PRIVATISATION

AFTER INDEPENDENCE, the public services expanded rapidly. So the government decided to downsize the public service. There were already about 900,000 public servants and more than a thousand public enterprises in the government sector in the 1990s.

It was quite impossible to retire or phase out large numbers of the civil service or even close down the public enterprises without causing major socioeconomic or political problems. The issues and implications were far too sensitive. On the other hand, the federal and state government budgets were gradually getting more and more strained as a result of having to bear the burden of a large and sometimes bloated public service.

The trend in the U.K. under Prime Minister Margaret Thatcher was towards greater competition and liberalisation as well as privatisation. In the U.S. too, the philosophy of liberalism was sweeping the land under President Ronald Reagan. These trends were even called "Reaganism" and "Thatcherism" and were becoming universal. There was a growing reaction against state intervention, state management and too much government control in the economy.

The government therefore commissioned a merchant bank to study the prospects of introducing privatisation in Malaysia and to make recommendations for a fee of RM2.5 million. The ensuing report indicated the vast possibilities and the considerable potential for privatisation in Malaysia. When the government first announced the concept of privatisation, there was doubt and resistance. Many asked whether the government was abrogating its responsibility. It appeared as if the private sector was being unleashed to exploit and profit from the people. Some critics felt that there was going to be an "unholy alliance" between the politicians and the private sector to take the *rakyat* for a ride, under privatisation.

In the civil service too, there was considerable scepticism as to the sincerity, integrity and viability of privatisation. Would the profitable public enterprises be taken over by greedy businessmen and the non-viable "social" kind of state enterprises be left to languish in the public sector? Also, would the government and the people now blame the public servants for inefficiency and irresponsibility for not being able to generate profits? But how could profits be churned out from the government machinery that was hamstrung with so many rules and regulations that had also to stand up to the scrutiny of the government and opposition members of Parliament?

The government had therefore to prepare the ground carefully and well in advance to ensure wide public support for the concept of privatisation. The government recognised that they would not be able to push privatisation far if the public did not support it. So they worked hard to sell privatisation and we in the civil service played our own role to promote the privatisation policy among our staff.

Where the public and the *rakyat* were concerned, what mattered was not the ideology of whether it was government or business that provided the service, but whether the service to the public would be more efficient and more reasonably priced. They wanted access to good quality service at low and affordable prices. They had got tired of many of the inefficiencies and inconveniences in the government machinery and its services to the public.

The road system, for instance, was becoming increasingly inadequate as the economy expanded rapidly. Similarly, the shipping ports were getting congested. The railways, once the backbone and the mainstay of public transport all over the country, were becoming inefficient and cumbersome.

The bus and the taxi services within the major cities were in the hands of private operators but were quite inefficient due to over competition and undercutting. Too many licences had been given (and some on the basis of political patronage), not only to run small bus companies but also to operate individual taxis and little taxi companies.

There were a whole host of services in the public sector that had reached their optimum performance. They could not cope with the rising demand for more and better services as the incomes of the people rose rapidly. The middle income groups were no longer content to send their children to government schools that could not offer more modern equipment and facilities to advance their children's education.

Similarly, in the field of health services, the government found it impossible to keep up with the increasing demand for better facilities. Whereas in the past, the rural and lower income urban folks would generally seek traditional medicine, now more would go for modern western medicines and medical treatment.

So the government took the line that it could not afford to provide all these services at such a rapid pace of expansion, without running into serious budgetary difficulties. Furthermore, the government made the whole privatisation exercise attractive to the *bumiputeras* by stating that it would provide opportunities for them to buy over these large enterprises at reasonable prices and create *bumiputera* employment in the private sector. In any case, they would also be able to raise finances quite easily. The government would encourage the larger banks, to lend money out to *bumiputeras* on fair terms.

The labour unions, however, were more difficult to handle. They believed that the welfare of the workers would be sacrificed if big business took over the ownership and management of these former government enterprises. The government was empathetic here. The unions and the Labour Movement in general were assured that there would be better terms and conditions of service and that workers would also be able to earn more by opting to work in the privatised entities. They were also assured that they would not be relieved of their jobs for at least 5 years after privatisation. After that they could keep their jobs if they wanted, but of course they had to be more productive. In any case, there were legal recourses for redress, if the new employers were unfair and if they broke the terms and conditions of their contracts.

When all sections of the public were persuaded that privatisation was good, the government took the bold step to announce privatisation of some of the major government enterprises.

Many of these enterprises, however, went through the process of corporatisation before graduating to privatisation. This was an ingenious way of providing a smoother transition from a government department to a privately run business enterprise. It also enabled the government to own and control strategic enterprises in the public interest.

Thus the National Electric Board was given more autonomy to run its operations on a more business-like basis. The Telecommunications Department was corporatised and so were many of the shipping ports, the railways, the airports and many other government agencies.

Many of the huge new development projects however were privatised outright. The best example is the case of the North-South Highway. The Public Works Department had always been responsible for building the roads in the country. They had done well. But times had changed. As the economy expanded rapidly, the demand for more and better highways, increased by leaps and bounds. The Public Works

Department (PWD), could not keep pace because of the lack of budgetary allocations. The high turnover of professional staff and the inability to recruit sufficient staff because of the unattractive government salary structure, aggravated the difficult situation.

The obvious and rational answer to these problems was to privatise the whole massive highway project. This way, the detailed government regulations that cover tendering and the problems of bureaucracy could be overcome. From Bukit Kayu Hitam, the northern most town in Peninsular Malaysia, right down to Johor Bahru, the old roads were adequate in the earlier days. But their usefulness had been overtaken by the explosion in the volume of traffic, freight and the movement of millions of people.

But this massive North-South Highway project had to be financed with huge funds. Thus tolls were introduced widely in Malaysia for the first time. In retrospect, it is surprising how readily the people accepted this concept of toll collection and the higher costs of road travel. They realised that in fact the real costs were less if we take into account the considerable amount of time saved, the reduced wear and tear of vehicles and the greater comfort and safety of the new superhighways. Indeed, the new roads were comparable to the best in the world. It would have been difficult to build the modern North-South Highway without privatisation.

Protecting Privatisation

The privatisation policy had proved successful. However, this success has to be protected and preserved if the *rakyat* are to continue to support the government in its quest to undertake even more privatisation.

There are some areas that may not be suitable for privatisation as had been proven in many other countries. In fact there are some real limits to privatisation. Indeed even within the context of privatised projects, there are constraints.

For instance, there are already growing concerns that the privatised entities are not as efficient as they claimed, when the government and business were pushing for privatisation. In many instances, the quality of service to the public has deteriorated. On the other hand, the rates and charges have increased significantly. For example, the toll rates have been increasing frequently, contrary to earlier expectations. Telecommunication and telephone charges have also gone up after privatisation or corporatisation, but efficiency may not have gone up that much.

I have found that some public services are as bad or even worse than before when the service was under the government. At least at that time questions pertaining to the poor quality service could be raised in Parliament and ministers concerned had to give a full explanation as to why the service was poor. They also had to take quick remedial action, as otherwise they could be embarrassed repeatedly by the Parliamentary Opposition. After privatisation however, the ministers concerned need only reply to important policy issues and conveniently advise that minor matters like the quality of services (such as poor garbage collection and dirty drinking water) should be taken up with the privatised public utility companies.

I believe that privatisation will continue to have some serious negative features as long as there are "privatised monopolies". There is no use creating large monopolies and in the process destroying competition. Then the whole rationale for privatisation will be eroded. The *rakyat* will be paying more for less quality. The owners and shareholders of the privatised utilities would then be making much more profits and enjoying unduly higher dividends—at the expense of the poor *rakyat* and the unfortunate man in the street. I am sure this is not what the government wants nor is it in the government's best long-term interests to allow these unhealthy and undesirable trends to continue.

Already there are cynical remarks being made about privatisation. People complain about these monopolistic rights being given relatively inexpensively to the "chosen few" who cream off high profits at the expense of the lower-income groups.

Worse still, I have heard some more critical types describing privatisation as "piratisation", "personalisation", "profiteering" and even "polarisation". It is also more colourfully described as crony capitalism.

This is unhealthy. Even if this criticism is exaggerated, it must be addressed expeditiously and effectively. It is not difficult to do so if there is the political will to do so. There are many ways of eliminating the abuses and preventing the usual excesses of monopolies and the weaknesses of unregulated market forces. I will try to offer some solutions, although there are undoubtedly many more.

Improving Privatisation

First, some of the huge privatised entities should be broken up through suitable antitrust legislation. Competition has to be increased to bring about more efficiency and more competitive pricing, especially for the poorer sections of the populace.

Second, there could be an independent 'Privatisation Commission' that could ensure that the terms and conditions of privatisation are fair and reasonable and in the interests of the public. It could thus ensure that there is more consistency in the award of privatised contracts under the jurisdiction of different ministries, covering different economic sectors. Thus privatisation in the field of energy, telecommunications and water resources, for instance, can have terms that are generally comparable in terms of returns to investment and profits.

Third, quality standards can be agreed upon among all the parties concerned and voluntarily followed and enforced by law in necessary. This way there will be less misunderstanding and dissatisfaction on what can reasonably be regarded as acceptable standards of service to the *rakyat*.

Fourth, the prices and the charges of the privatised entities have to be carefully monitored on a continuous basis. Any request to raise fees and charges would need to be reviewed objectively by the Privatisation Commission to ensure that neither consumers nor investors are penalised.

Fifth, the Commission could ensure that only the most able consortia are given these privatisation contracts. This is essential if we are to protect the interests of the *rakyat*, the longer-term integrity of privatisation and the public support for privatisation.

At the Ministry of Transport, I was exposed to a great deal of thinking and planing for privatisation. In fact, most of the attractive possibilities and prospects for privatisation were in large and lucrative infrastructure projects under the purview of the Ministry of Transport.

31.
MY ROLE IN THE
MINISTRY OF TRANSPORT

I HAVE mentioned the circumstances under which I left the Treasury and got transferred to the Ministry of Transport and promoted as its Secretary-General and chief executive officer.

Due to the fact that Dr Ling Liong Sik had specifically asked for me, I enjoyed his confidence, trust and strong support. This was important because otherwise it would be known that I did not have the Minister's backing and my authority would be undermined and polarisation would have set in at the ministry.

It has to be remembered that under our Whitehall-type of administration, it is the Secretary-General who writes the confidential reports for the senior civil servants under him. The junior officers have theirs written by the senior officers serving under the Secretary-General, who also supervises the writing of all these confidential reports.

Thus the Secretary-General has a big say in the assessment of the performance of all the staff in his ministry—either directly or indirectly. The Minister himself has in theory no say in reporting on the performance and recommending the increments and promotions of civil servants in his ministry. In practice however, the Minister can, of course, influence the Secretary-General.

Dr Ling encouraged me to innovate. Since I was an economist by training, I tended to regard the Ministry of Transport as an economic agency that needed tighter economic management. Dr Ling liked that kind of macro approach too. The Transport Ministry had been traditionally run as an administrative agency. In fact, the transport sector is an integral part of overall economic development. I believed that the Ministry of Transport should therefore be run as an agency to promote socioeconomic growth.

The highest priority was therefore given to drawing up a longer-term Transport Economic Plan. We obtained assistance from the World Bank and established a planning unit within the Ministry to draw up this "Multi-modular" Transport Plan. Data was collected and collated for all the major transport systems such as roads, railways, air traffic, and shipping and in the case of Sabah and Sarawak, riverine transport. We soon obtained a far better picture of the overall transport system in the country.

We then began to plan in earnest, to coordinate the development and the future expansion of the different transport systems on a more integrated basis. We worked even more closely with my former colleagues in the Treasury to determine the allocation of development funds for the different forms of transport, on a more systematic and efficient basis. From all these studies, a more refined transport policy and plan emerged.

I found that our shipping ports were each going their own way with little coordination and the sharing of know-how. This was a pity because we were not able to enjoy the economies of scale that better cooperation and integration would have given us. In fact, often our Malaysian ports were undercutting each other. The result was that some service industries did not improve fast enough. What was even more regrettable was that Malaysian exporters and shippers were losing out by having to send so much of Malaysia's merchandise through the port of Singapore! That entreport city state was gaining at Malaysia's expense because our ports were not working closely enough. Our ports then were also not as competitive as that of the Singapore Port.

With the Minister's blessings therefore, I took the initiative to form the National Ports Consultative Council, which was made up of all the CEOs of all the ports in the country. We met at Port Klang initially but later we held the meetings by rotation at the major ports all over the country. We met about three times a year with the "host port" providing the secretariat facilities. Thus the burden of servicing these meetings was shared and distributed.

This innovation had a salutary effect on the overall morale and motivation of the port management. Sometimes we invited the Minister to open these meetings. He would have dialogues with all these senior port officials. This contributed to greater cooperation among the different ports. The problems faced by the ports were also discussed openly. The discussions often led to solutions, which could be shared with the other ports.

Later, I requested several of the bigger ports to do some research and to present their findings to the whole meeting. Thus these meetings became increasingly substantive and meaningful. The *esprit de corps* also increased as we introduced competitive sporting events among the ports.

I believe that the National Ports Consultative Council contributed to the enhancement of quality and productivity among all our Malaysian ports.

Malaysian Airline System (MAS)

The Malaysian Airline System (MAS) came under the purview of the Ministry of Transport. I had represented the Treasury on its board of directors from 1974, after returning from the World Bank. But when I was transferred to the Ministry of Transport as its Secretary-

General, I was also appointed as the representative of the Ministry of Transport.

Hence I served on the Board of Directors of the Malaysian Airline System for about 15 years. This was quite a record. My former boss in the Treasury, Tun Raja Mohar Badiozaman, had retired and had become the chairman of the national airline. He was an inspiring leader with an able board and first-rate staff. Justice Dato' Shanker and Dato' Yap Lim Seng were some of the luminaries on the Board.

Tan Sri Rama Iyer, Tan Sri Saw Huat Lye and Tan Sri Aziz Rahman were all past CEOs of MAS. They were all outstanding civil servants who proved to be fine leaders in the development and expansion of MAS. They were also the pioneer Malaysian civil servants who debunked the theory that civil servants cannot run business enterprises successfully. In fact, they started the airline from scratch and built it up into a premier world-class airline.

MAS was born after Malaysia and Singapore separated in 1965. It was difficult to hold both airlines together. Unfortunately, MAS lost out considerably in the terms and conditions under which both airlines split. Consequently, MAS had to fight an uphill battle to soar to its present success. Singapore is so small that commercial aircraft would be flying out of its airspace before they even gained cruising speed and height. Thus Singapore was not interested in domestic flights. On the other hand, Malaysia was comparatively a big country with a vast hinterland, with Sabah and Sarawak separated by about 1,000 miles of the South China Sea.

Malaysia therefore had very different policy priorities. The first priority was to provide good airlinks to Sabah and Sarawak and the wide hinterland in Peninsular Malaysia. This meant that MAS had to give preference to the allocation of our resources in aircraft, airports and its technical aspects including the personnel, to the large rural network of airports. The national airline's policy was to promote better domestic air communications for the building of stronger national unity. This was in direct contradiction and conflict with the Singapore International Airlines (SIA) which had to be international since it had no domestic destinations. SIA had to expand abroad whereas MAS had to do both—to expand the domestic as well as the international air routes. Thus the intrinsic conflict of interests, priorities and policies led to the almost inevitable split.

MAS lost out on several counts arising from this split. First, Singapore benefited enormously from the heavy investment in the infrastructural development of the airport in Singapore.

Second, Singapore took over more of the bigger aircrafts for its international flights.

Third, and most importantly, a lot of the traffic rights went to Singapore. We had not expanded international traffic rights for Peninsular Malaysia separately because we were supposedly to have one airline for both territories. So we in Malaysia had to start all over again to negotiate all over the world to have our own international traffic rights. This became extremely difficult as the international airlines were well established with their airlinks to this part of the world to and through Singapore. Furthermore, they argued that they need not land in Kuala Lumpur as the passenger load in Singapore was much heavier, with passengers coming to Singapore as a hub from all over the world. Foreign airlines also knew that many Malaysians were travelling the short one-hour flight from Kuala Lumpur to Singapore to catch international flights from Singapore through SIA or any of the many international airlines operating from Singapore.

I know how difficult these international airline negotiations are, as I was fully involved in all the air negotiations as the Secretary-General of the Ministry of Transport. I headed these negotiations with representatives from MAS and my own ministry officials. We had a competent and experienced team that took part in all the negotiations. We therefore developed good rapport and understanding among ourselves. From the Ministry's side, we always took Puan Zaharah Shaari, who later became the Secretary-General of Transport. From MAS, we invariably had Bernard Thomasio and Dato' Bashir Ahmad Abdul Majid, now CEO of KLIA. Both were seasoned negotiators on airline matters.

Sometimes the Minister himself would lead the delegation although he would not take part in the negotiations, which would be conducted by officials on both sides. But the Minister's presence was always useful as we could then readily consult him on the finer points of the negotiations and have his blessings as to whether to be tough or soft. These guidelines were most helpful as these negotiations were often rough and sensitive and could lead to misunderstandings and even friction between countries.

Losing my Pants in India!

Airline negotiations can be some of the most acrimonious international negotiations. This is because not only governments are involved with all the attendant political considerations, but also because the negotiations become bitter since sizeable profits are derived by the national and commercial airlines from the establishment or withdrawal of traffic rights. One could lose one's pants, speaking figuratively. But I myself literally lost mine at one of the many negotiations that I handled.

It happened in India. Dr Ling Liong Sik led the delegation. His wife Datin Seri Ena Ling and their two adventurous sons, Ah Leong and Ah Kiat, accompanied the Minister on a holiday to India during their school break.

The Indians were tough negotiators. They did not want to give us any more traffic rights into India, as they feared competition from our more popular national airline. Air India, in particular, was resistant to changes in the existing arrangements, which we felt were in India's favour. We wanted to expand our air traffic, but the Indians were quite protective of their national airline.

The negotiations carried on late on the last night of our stay in Delhi. They hosted the farewell dinner and we really did not have much to show for our hard negotiations. The Minister was also not happy as he found it difficult to return home without achieving much. So he had a good private discussion with the Indian Minister of Civil Aviation during dinner. Then towards the end of dinner, Dr Ling called me aside and mentioned that the Indian Minister had agreed that we could carry on the discussions after dinner to cover some new ground where they were prepared to concede more.

We were happy to continue the discussions immediately as it was already near midnight. So we got down to work in earnest. After putting in our best efforts, we managed to initial the Memorandum of Understanding (MOU) at about 2am the next day! We had planned for our packed bags to be ready for collection from our hotel rooms at 5am for dispatch to the airport as we had to board the plane at 7am.

I was very tired, if not somewhat exhausted from jetlag, the tough negotiations and the late nights of hard work. On getting to my hotel room, I quickly packed my bag and placed it near the door ready for collection by the hotel porter. Then I got into my *sarong* and jumped into bed for a well-deserved rest. At about 5am, I was awoken by the porter for my bags. I just got up sleepily, opened the door and shoved my bag to the porter. After that I closed the door and went back to sleep.

At about 6am, I got my wake-up call. I rushed to have my bath and came out to change. I looked around for my pants but it was nowhere to be found! I panicked when I realised that I had mistakenly put my pants in my bag without thinking, and now it had been taken to the airport! I was desperate. How could I travel on the flight with the Minister with only my *sarong* on. I might have done so if it was not an official delegation or even if the Minister was not around.

In desperation, I rang the hotel laundry and appealed to the man on duty to sell me a pair of pants from the many that he would have with him. The chap thought that I was crazy to ring him up so early in the morning and to tell him that I had no pants. He turned me down!

Then I rang Puan Zaharah, my colleague, to explain my predicament. I asked her to tell the Minister that I would take a later flight. She was sympathetic. But in her enthusiasm to help me out, she rang Dr Ling's wife and asked her if she could get one of her son's pants for me to use!

Being a kind person, Datin Ena wanted to help, too. Since she thought neither of her sons' pants would fit me, she woke up Dr Ling and asked whether he could lend me his pants!

Dr Ling was half-asleep and when he heard his good wife's request, he was naturally annoyed! Obviously, his pants could not fit me, as he is much bigger than I am. In the meantime, I rang our Malaysian Embassy councillor, Thanarajahsingam who was about my size, for his help. He came over soon after and I found that I could get into his pair of light brown pants—much to my relief. I then went down to the dimly-lit lounge to join the delegation and wait for the Minister to come down before we all went to the airport together.

The Minister of course had been told that I could not make it as I had lost my pants. So he did not expect to see me at the lobby. When he came down and saw me in the dim light with my brown skin-coloured pants, he momentarily thought that I was there without my pants and exclaimed surprise at seeing me!

Right through that trip back home, I was the butt of the delegation's jokes. I promised myself that I would never part with my pants again! It was the most uncomfortable flight I ever took.

32.
NEGOTIATIONS WITH
THE BRITISH

AIR NEGOTIATIONS with the British in 1987 were a different cup of tea altogether. I felt a great sense of satisfaction that I was leading a Malaysian delegation from an independent Malaysia to London for the airline negotiations with our erstwhile colonial masters. I was sure that they had not envisaged that in just about 30 years after independence, we would have a national airline of international class and would want to negotiate with them about reciprocal air traffic rights!

But that is the way of the world. I am sure that as I felt elated at being able to negotiate with the British civil servants, with dignity and on equal terms, they on their part must have felt privately, that talking to us, was perhaps below their dignity. I say this because the negotiations that followed showed their condescension. On our part, we were determined to show them that we were not only able to stand up to them, but could be better than them! I soon found that we could match them!

The team comprised the usual foursome, i.e., Zaharah, Bernard and Bashir and the representative from the Malaysian High Commission in London. We held our negotiations at the Ministry of Transport at the Whitehall Buildings by the River Thames and near the famous Big Ben and the British Parliament. The environment inspired me. I naturally felt a sense of history pervade the whole atmosphere of the negotiations that ensued.

The negotiations started pretty well, with both sides presenting their compliments and submitting their respective cases. We had assigned a Thursday and Friday for the talks, and had planned to return home over the weekend. The first day was spent going over the traffic data, the passenger load factors and the projections made by both sides of the future passenger traffic.

My experience had shown that when both sides wanted to enhance cooperation, the differences in the data and traffic projections could be easily narrowed and resolved. However, if either party was not keen to cooperate, then there would be endless and often acrimonious arguments over the veracity of the figures. This would usually take place in order to undermine the case for settling the issues and finalising the negotiations successfully. In such a case there would be a stalemate and both sides would have to agree to postpone the negotiations, until the passenger traffic improved and justified a new traffic agreement. The parties concerned sometimes agreed to have the negotiations, just to satisfy governmental pressures to have more "air talks".

This was the situation with the British. They wanted to finalise the negotiations with as little to give as possible. This was the time just after the cooling-off period in Malaysian diplomatic relations with the British under Prime Minister Margaret Thatcher. Our negotiations were held after the "Buy British Last" episode when Malaysia retaliated against British ill-will to us. Malaysia had adopted the policy of buying British goods and services as a last resort, to teach them a lesson. We understood that as a consequence, Prime Minister Thatcher wanted to make amends. She expected her officials and the British Airways (BOAC) to work out a fair agreement with Malaysia. But the BOAC and the British Ministry of Transport officials were resistant to giving us the traffic rights that we thought were fair and reasonable.

The British strategy was to get us to agree to a minimal agreement whereas we wanted to get a major change in the existing air agreement. I felt that the British team wanted to get the negotiations over with as soon as possible so that they could tell their prime minister that an agreement had been signed. But we were not prepared to sign any agreement that did not meet our government's expectations and our mandate. Herein lay the crux of the problem and the source of the conflict.

Thursday, the first day of the negotiations, was soon over and then we settled down to the second and final day of negotiations. Friday morning went slowly by and we did not make much progress. So we decided to have only some tea and sandwiches for lunch and carried on with the negotiations. It became clear to us however by 7pm that evening that we were not going to finalise the agreement; and so Bernard and Bashir cancelled their flight back to Kuala Lumpur that night. We were quite upset that the British were dragging their feet and trying to twist our arms into submission — knowing fully well that we had planned to leave on Friday night for home. Since we had decided to stay on and fight at the negotiation table, we could now take it easier in terms of time. However, we were very tired.

Realising that my team was jetlagged, hungry and getting frustrated, I asked for a break. The British leader demurred. He felt we should carry on. I felt that they were trying to take advantage of our tiredness to push us against the wall. I insisted that we needed to have a

decent meal to carry on with our negotiations. The British leader relented and suggested that we could have a substantial meal at McDonald's down the street! We nodded our heads but we had other plans.
My delegation wanted a hot Malaysian meal at Bayswater where there
was good Malaysian *satay* and spicy *rendang*. The High Commission
cars were at our disposal so we dashed off to the Malaysian restaurant.
We had a great time and brought some *satay* back for our British
friends, some of whom were pretty decent fellows.

When we got back, the British delegation was waiting for us. They
thought that we would just nip across the street to McDonald's in the
nippy London weather. We gave the *satay* to the British delegates who
relished it since they had only taken cheese and wine. They appreciated our gesture of goodwill. But when their leader saw them enjoy our
satay, he was furious and ordered them back to the conference room.
We were now ready.

I apologised for taking longer than expected but the British leader
was unforgiving and recalcitrant. We carried on with the negotiations.
At about 11pm, the phone rang and the British delegation leader was
summoned. We heard him say apologetically that the talks were still going on. He returned to the table quite upset. I quickly deduced that he
had been reprimanded by Whitehall for not having finalised the negotiations. I think I was right for he demanded that we end the negotiations and sign on what we had already agreed to. I refused on the
grounds that we could carry on the negotiations the next day which
was a Saturday. He got more upset at my suggestion and shouted to me
that his staff needed their rest and had weekend holiday plans!

I told the British leader in no uncertain terms that I was extremely
disappointed with his attitude. I added that if he took that indifferent
line, then I would break off the negotiations and report to my minister
in Kuala Lumpur and ask for fresh instructions. I said that I would
place the whole responsibility of the breakdown of these important negotiations on his reluctance to extend the negotiations, because he took
his weekend holiday more seriously than the successful conclusion of
the negotiations! I elaborated that we Malaysians were always prepared to put our duty to country first before our holidays and that we
were disappointed that the British civil servants in Malaya, from
whom we had learnt so much, had indeed changed!

That did the trick. The British were badly embarrassed. His delegation was in disarray. We could see that they had not anticipated this

turn of events. They obviously realised that their leader had put his foot in his mouth and that he had unwittingly shot himself in his foot. There was a deadly silence. I broke the silence by strategically asking for a recess. Then our delegation walked out of the room with a sense of drama!

We went over to the reception room and had our own consultations. Our Malaysian High Commission representative thought I was a bit too hard on the British delegation leader. But my delegation felt that he deserved it. Personally I felt that I was rough and tough but that it was the right strategy to use under the circumstances. I was confident that my strategy would work. If it did not, I was prepared to call our minister Dr Ling for instructions on whether to break off the negotiations or accept what was already agreed upon thus far and return home.

After about ten minutes, the British leader came up to me and asked for a private meeting with me. He regretted his outburst and asked for a continuation of the negotiations. I told him that I was planning to ring Dr Ling and advise breaking off the negotiations—unless the British were prepared to concede to more of our requests. He hesitated and then I suggested that we should call off the discussions. It was already approaching midnight. I was certain in my mind that the British wanted to complete the negotiations and I was prepared to go for the *coup de grace*!

My judgement proved right. He capitulated. Soon after Big Ben struck twelve on Friday midnight (7am on Saturday at home in Kuala Lumpur), the British leader agreed to my terms for the signing of the agreement. We had won! We were all jubilant on the Malaysian side. The British were weary and dejected but proper. We signed the agreement for the additional landing rights and several other landing points and parted in a formal fashion for a well-earned rest.

Dr Mahathir was arriving in London on Saturday, but I left that evening for home to report to my minister. I left it to our Malaysian High Commission officials to brief him. No doubt the imminent arrival of our Prime Minister in London had put pressure on the British officials to relent in the end. I had guessed it and as a negotiator, I seized the opportunity and struck while the iron was hot.

What I learnt was that, when the British and other Westerners are tough, we have to be as tough or even tougher still. Otherwise their perceived sense of superiority is involuntarily reinforced in their psyche and they will believe that the best way to handle us is to bully or browbeat us. As Dr Mahathir recently said, "We in Asia and the developing world got to speak up or be bashed down." The Westerners invariably have problems of arrogance, a false perception of superiority and misplaced pride. So, when they meet their match, they do not know how to handle the situation. They get bewildered, confused and lost. That's the time to go for the kill in negotiations with them — and we did!

Negotiations With the Dutch

A similar scenario took place in our negotiations with the Dutch later on. This was a particularly difficult negotiation for me personally.

Our son, Dharm had had a very bad accident in Australia on his way back to Melbourne after a hockey match in Adelaide. A huge trailer had sideswiped an oncoming car onto Dharm's car and caused it to crash. It was a tragedy as a few young people died on impact. Miraculously, Dharm escaped — but with serious internal injuries. We rushed down to Australia as soon as we heard the dreadful news. My cousin David Selvaratnam was kind to meet us at the Melbourne Airport and to drive us straight to the hospital in the small town of Horsham, where Dharm was admitted for surgery. He was all bandaged up like a mummy when we saw him. But his spirits were high and he managed to pull through and recovered pretty fast with God's help.

When we felt confident that he was out of danger and just needed to rest after the surgery, I left Samala and flew straight back to join my delegation in The Hague, Holland.

We started the negotiations for additional air traffic rights the day after I arrived. The Dutch were more relaxed than the British in their conduct but definitely more rigid in their negotiation style. They took much longer to understand our views and to respond on the same wavelength. I think that it was partly because we had both a different way of expressing our thoughts in English. We were obviously better in articulation whereas they found some difficulty in negotiating clearly in the international language. The point is that not every one speaks English as well as the British do. We were however quite similar to the British in our style and usage of the English language.

After nearly two full days of discussions, we were ready to put down all our points of agreement in writing. Officials from both sides sat down to work out a common document, but they were unable to agree to what we thought we had agreed on earlier. So we decided to work out separate drafts and then to try to consolidate the draft agreements.

We had dinner that night hosted by the Dutch. They took us to a nice cosy traditional Dutch restaurant at the base of a huge windmill that had been cleverly converted into a fine tourist attraction. The interior was fitted with 16th-century period furniture. The tables were laid out elegantly and the lovely ambience brought to mind the great wealth and grandeur of the Dutch Empire in the heyday of their colonial era in the East Indies.

After a sumptuous meal, we were ready to consider the final draft, which the Dutch had offered to consolidate. I received the draft agreement and gave it to my officials to carefully consider while the Dutch leader and I enjoyed our coffee.

Ten minutes later, Zaharah came up to me and told me in Malay that the draft agreement was quite different from the understanding we thought we had reached! I politely excused myself and went over to my delegation to consult with them. I could clearly see that the Dutch had prepared a one-sided agreement. So we marked the parts of the agreement where we differed and made our amendments. Then we submitted the amended draft to the Dutch officials and I returned to join the leader of the Dutch delegation. Shortly afterwards, his officials came over to advise him that there were major differences of view in the interpretation of our respective positions.

The Dutch leader turned to me and suggested that he was not happy with our position and insisted that I instruct my delegation to accept his delegation's stand. I could not believe that he was insisting that I change our stand just to suit his position. Naturally I refused. I added that if we could not iron out our differences, we would have to leave these differences to be settled by our respective ministers who were meeting the next day. In fact, our Minister of Transport, Dr Ling Liong Sik was already flying from Kuala Lumpur that night to sign the agreement that we thought would be ready by the time he arrived the next morning.

My response made the Dutch leader angry. He lost his cool, banged his fist on the table until the lovely crystal glasses shook. He shouted at me rudely: "Who do you think you are to disagree with what we have agreed!"

That was enough for our delegation. I was taken aback and was on the verge of shouting back — but thank goodness I got hold of myself and kept my cool. I realised that I was the leader of my delegation and I had to maintain the dignity of Malaysia. So I signalled to my delegation that I was prepared to leave. I thanked our host for the dinner, before leaving for our hotel amid much confusion and apologies from the Dutch foreign office officials, who were also present at the dinner.

I sensed that we had won the negotiations for I was prepared to capitalise on the Dutch leader's indiscretion! I had a good rest but I was awakened early the next morning by a phone call. It was from the Dutch Foreign Ministry official. He apologised for disturbing me and for the previous night's episode. He asked what I intended to do about it. I said that I felt that as a Malaysian official, my delegation and I had been insulted. I would have to report to my Minister and that, unless I received an apology from the Dutch leader, I would urge my authorities to lodge a diplomatic protest. The Dutch official was rattled and appealed to me to accept his apology and to let the matter rest. I said I would do my best but that it depended on my minister.

We went to the airport to receive Dr Ling. The Dutch minister, a distinguished-looking lady, was there too. I was introduced to her and she kindly enquired about my son Dharm's recovery from the nasty car accident. Just then, the MAS aircraft landed and we went forward to meet Dr Ling. However, before he came out, I went into the aircraft, warmly greeted him and briefed him of the progress in the negotiations and the previous night's incident.

As Dr Ling emerged from the plane, the Dutch minister went up to greet him. He presented her with a bouquet of fresh Malaysian orchids. She was delighted. Then, she apologised for the bad conduct of their leader of the Dutch delegation. She said that she was replacing him with a more seasoned official. We were satisfied. The negotiations that carried on at official level, were held under much more civil conditions. The differences that we had earlier were nicely resolved, and the new air traffic agreement was signed in the presence of both ministers.

Like the British, the Dutch too had taken us for granted. They thought that we could be taken for a ride easily. They had not realised that here was a new breed of Malaysians, quite unlike those of a bygone colonial era. It proved to me again that we had to fight harder and at every stage before we could remove the inherent prejudices that many of our Western counterparts had, unfortunately, built into their psyche. It turned out to be to their great disadvantage which earned us victory in these negotiations!

Subsequently, I led negotiations with several developing and non-Western countries but the tone and attitudes were much more friendly, fraternal and fairer. We had negotiations with China, Egypt, Russia and East Germany on new air as well as maritime agreements and they were always much more pleasant and productive.

Negotiations with the Chinese

We next had negotiations with the Chinese authorities in Beijing for a new air agreement. The Chinese were proper and polite. The Chinese officials were humble and gracious. They were kind, hospitable and had great pride in their history. They proudly showed us their great monuments, such as the Great Wall of China, Tiananmen Square and the palaces and tombs of Emperors.

We had smooth discussions. When I finally suggested that we should sign a Memorandum of Understanding, the Chinese leader, in perfect English, gently declined. I explained that it was a standard practice in all our other negotiations to sign MOUs, but he replied as follows: "We Chinese have a long sense of history. We do not like to rush into agreements with new friends. We want to know you better. We would like you to know us better. We believe that when we become close friends then we will both be more comfortable with each other. When the time is ripe, agreement will come to both of us quite naturally. These agreements will be lasting testimonies to our close friendship and fraternity."

"Agreements made in haste run the real risk of fading away soon. But agreements that are negotiated carefully and between close friends, will surely stand up to the test of time. Why not postpone the signing of the agreement for a little longer. For what does it matter to lose a little time as the agreements we sign later are bound to last longer!"

What could I say to this wisdom from the ages? I agreed and suggested that we then keep some record of the discussions for the sake of continuity. He nodded his head with a satisfied smile and bowed slightly. We then settled down to another small cup of good Chinese tea. This was a wise move as we were able to sign the agreement the next time we met — several months later!

Russian Roulette

The Malaysian government had longstanding invitations to negotiate with the Russians on shipping agreements. It was thus time to open
these negotiations.

I had no idea of Russian shipping policy nor how to deal with them.
Datin Ranita from the Attorney-General's chambers joined us. She
was bright and diligent and had worked out a draft agreement, which
we examined from our transport and marine policy points of view. But
we needed to appreciate the environment and the thinking of the Russian mind, for which we had little experience. So I checked around the
Malaysian shipping industry and found that there was a Malaysian
who had strong ties with the merchant shipping agents in Russia. He
was Teo Seng Lee from Penang.

I got Dr Ling Liong Sik's permission to include him in the official
delegation in order to provide us with the market intelligence for the
negotiations. We did not pay for his expenses. However, he gained the
privilege, prestige and goodwill from both sides in being included as a
member of the Malaysian delegation. This was quite unprecedented at
that time when the concept of "Malaysia Incorporated" was not so well
developed. But it was mutually beneficial for us to have Seng Lee with
us. He had been making frequent trips to Moscow and was an asset to
us as he understood the Russian language and Russian maritime practices.

We found the Russians warm, accommodating and hospitable.
They enjoyed their vodka and caviar and were always ready to offer us
lunch and dinner. I found out why they appreciated the meals and liquor much more than we did. Meals were financed by the government
at expensive restaurants. They would prolong the dinners with good
humour and some fine jokes—mostly about their own wives and
women, while they drank heartily. I tried to keep up with them but I
had a low tolerance level. They would laugh good-humouredly at my
inability to drink "good Russian vodka"! Because of these friendly social exchanges, we built up some "comraderie", which stood us in good
stead at the meetings.

The Russians are very proud of their country and persuaded us to
visit Leningrad or St Petersburg. We were struck by the great beauty
of that famous city of the Czars, the rich cultural heritage and the great
works of art at the famous art museum called the Hermitage. Rich
paintings, wonderfully woven heirlooms and tapestries adorned the

walls. The sculptures were exquisite while the indescribably intricate jewellery worn by kings and queens, the czars and czarinas (during their golden age) were there in all their splendour for all to see. The Hermitage must easily be one of the richest and most beautiful museums anywhere in the world.

We were in Russia during winter. It was so cold that my ears hurt and I felt numb in parts of my body, with temperatures down to -40°C. I remember walking along the long railway platform in the freezing cold to our coach with sleeping berths in small compartments for two. I got into my warm compartment with much relief, only to be disturbed by a furore outside. Our lady legal adviser Ranita was told by a husky-looking female Russian railway guard that she would have to share her apartment with one of our male officials. The guard pointed out that she could not find a lady passenger to share the room with her and so there was no other alternative! We asked our embassy official who spoke some Russian to help out but he too initially, faced a brick wall. According to him, the Russian railway guard could not understand why we were making a fuss. She claimed that in Russia there was no problem for male and female strangers to share a common room as morals were high in Russia! She wondered what was wrong with us. We appealed to her that our customs would not allow this arrangement, but she insisted that in Russia we should follow Russian customs!

We were at a loss. We were getting annoyed with what we regarded as the Russian guard's negative attitude. Then we saw our Embassy colleague move away with the Russian guard to the far end of the train. Soon he came back happily to tell us that he had finally persuaded the guard that Ranita could have the double room all to herself! We asked him how he managed it and he replied with a smile that a few packets of foreign cigarettes had settled the big debate about the high standards of Russian morality!

The negotiations were held in a relaxed manner. We spent much time waiting for the Russian interpreter each time the Russian leader or I spoke. But on the other hand, this process gave me time to think of my next move and even to consult with my delegation, without the pressure of having to reply almost immediately, as we were required to do when the negotiations were undertaken in English.

The Russians did not seem to have a definite line of argument. They would try one line of logic after another and sometimes these lines would get knotted up, causing confusion. Fortunately, we did not despair or give up. Finally, they realised that we were able to stick to our guns despite the confusion they thought they were causing us. We had set a definite time frame for our negotiations and were prepared to break off and return home if we were not going to gain ground. The Russians realised that we meant business and that we did not have to wait for instructions from home each step of the way. They also realised that I could make some serious decisions on the spot, like terminating the negotiations, if my delegation so decided. They also were aware that time was also running out as we began to make plans to depart. So they started to focus on the issues more closely. We had called off their attempts at playing Russian roulette by trying their luck with us. The negotiations then went on more smoothly. Both sides parted happily and we felt that we had achieved a win-win outcome.

Arguing With the Australians

I found that even the Australians were far better disposed to us than the other Westerners. But that was because the Australians are physically far away from the West and closer to Asia. I remember one official visit to Australia with Dr Ling in 1989, when the Hon. Gareth Evans was the Minister of Transport. He was gracious and spent a lot of his hard pressed time showing us around the new Parliament in Canberra that had not yet been officially opened. At the end of the tour we adjourned to his room where he pulled out a good bottle of whiskey!

Though the Australians were tough negotiators, I found them civil, professional and polite at all times. They were never condescending like ex-colonials are prone to be. That way, it was easier to negotiate and we invariably worked out "fair dinkum" and mutually beneficial agreements that speak well of the "Asianess" among most Australians!

33.
MALAYAN RAILWAYS

AS SECRETARY-GENERAL of the Ministry of Transport, I also had overall responsibility for the Railways. Dato' Badri Basir was the chairman and Dato' Rahim was his deputy general manager.

Keretapi Tanah Melayu (KTM) was always an independent kind of organisation. It had a culture of its own with a great sense of *esprit de corps* and pride. After all, it is one of the oldest institutions in Malaysia, dating back to the earliest colonial days.

Thus we in the Ministry left the Railways very much to themselves and got involved with them only on policy matters. I was on their board of directors but I often sent my Ministry representative since it was a bit odd for the Secretary-General of the Ministry to sit on the same board with the General Manager as an equal member of the Board. I would be embarrassing the General Manager of the railways if I demurred with any of his views as he had to report to me and the Minister. But we had a good working relationship.

I shared some of the fascination that the railwaymen and most people have with railways. I used to enjoy visiting the Kuala Lumpur Railway Station to see the many changes that were made from time to time to improve the services to the public. One day, I decided to take a long train ride south. It was like an inspection by the Secretary-General of the Ministry of Transport.

I boarded the train at the Kuala Lumpur Railway Station with some of my Ministry and Railway officials and travelled down to Singapore. We got down at every station that the train stopped at, to talk to the stationmaster. I asked each of them their problems, their ideas on how to improve the railways further and what I could do for them in the short term. We received many constructive suggestions, which we took back to the Railway Board and the Ministry for follow-up action.

I was getting pretty bored sitting in the first class compartment and felt that I needed to get a better feel for the railways and the people working in the railways. After all that was the purpose of my inspection. So at one of the stations, after we had a chat with the stationmaster, I asked for permission to board the railway engine that was pulling the long train. The railway officials were quite uneasy as it was against all protocol. For instance, I was not covered by any insurance for travelling in the railway engine. But I explained that I would bear my own risk and not hold anyone liable for any untoward incident. And so I boarded the railway engine and we set off to the sound of the railway engine whistle, a mighty toot and a heavy chug!

I could understand the reluctance of the railway officials to let me get into the engine driver's room. It was hot, greasy and there was no passenger's seat. We had to stand, but they offered me the assistant engine driver's seat. It was real fun and a great experience while it lasted. It was there that I offered one of many suggestions for improvement.

Caring for the Staff

I found that the poor engine driver had to use a seat that was unacceptable to me. Originally it must have had a comfortable cushion on the steel stand that was to be his driver's seat. But over time, the cushion had worn out completely and the poor driver was actually sitting on a solid steel stool that had no cushion. Imagine travelling for hours on end, sitting on that kind of hard seat. I bet he would have developed an "iron bum" or worse still some bloody piles. I felt sorry for the driver and was upset at how uncaring some senior officials could be for the welfare of the lower-income employees even over simple matters like the need for a comfortable seat.

I therefore instructed that the cushion seats should be provided as soon as possible. The driver just smiled in appreciation but I could see that he still had his doubts. So I decided to follow up myself on my return to the Ministry. I am sure that at least the engine drivers were grateful although there were many high railway officials who were embarrassed and may not have liked my "interference" in the independent running of the railways!

A similar story unfolded during the height of the Malaysian Airline System (MAS) industrial unrest crisis in the early 1970s. The airline employees were dissatisfied with the management and wanted to go on strike. The government would not allow this to happen as the national airline is a strategic and essential service.

As a MAS Director, I tried to find out what made the many junior employees so bitter against the management. We had sensed that there were different views that we had been hearing from the top management and some of the staff whom we met casually on our MAS flights.

The deputy chairman, Dato' Sulaiman Sujak, and I decided to visit the airport during the tense negotiations that were going on between the management and the MAS unions. The government of course was anxious for both sides to get together and work out an early agreement. As we walked around the airport we observed that we were being watched closely by a large number of angry and tense looking ground staff. Then one of their leaders came up to Dato' Sulaiman and asked why he was at the airport. Dato' Sulaiman and I explained frankly that we were trying to find out why there was so much hostility from the MAS staff whom we regarded as generally pleasant and polite. The union leader was taken aback at what he must have regarded as our naïvete and agreed to our suggestion that we could have a chat over a cup of coffee.

Instead of going to the restaurant, we asked to join his colleagues in their own rest-room. He was surprised, but we could see that he was glad to oblige. What we saw in their rest-room shocked both of us. It was a little room with several broken seats and badly maintained long benches. The cold water fountain was not working. The curtains were in tatters and the floor was dirty. Worse still, the toilet was in bad shape and the rest-room itself had a faulty faucet running down from the ceiling that caused a bad odour. It was altogether most unsuitable as a rest-room! When we raised this matter at the board meeting, a personnel officer explained that they had already repaired the rest-room several times and suggested that "management had given up."

"What kind of attitude," some of us mumbled at the board meeting. No wonder the staff felt so neglected, alienated and resentful to the management. The board ordered that matter to be put right—but it was a pity that this issue had to be settled only after it was brought up at the board meeting. There had to be a change of attitude. When this and other issues were settled, the industrial relations improved considerably.

Similarly, early in my assignment at the Ministry of Transport, when I was making my familiarisation visits to the different departments, I noticed a young pregnant mother sitting most uncomfortably on her chair. On closer examination, I found, to my horror, that she was sitting on a hard plank that had been placed on the chair. When I asked her why, she shyly showed me the hole in the rattan seat. The chair itself was shaky. I thought to myself how I would feel if my pregnant wife or sister had to sit on that chair in their fragile state. As the boss, I had some authority and I used it to ensure that the lady was soon given a comfortable chair, regardless of whether the indifferent chief clerk there had to beg, borrow or even give up his own chair!

The trouble is that not many cared. If the most senior officers did not do anything about it because they were not aware, I can understand. But how does one condone this kind of situation when one is the immediate senior officer who should look after the interests of his own subordinates? After voicing my feelings, the next time I went around in my usual style of "management by walking around", I did not find any more broken chairs or tables around—and I was greeted with smiles all round.

Moral to the "Caring" Stories

The moral to the stories is that a little care and kindness goes a long way. Also, managers must show that they care for the welfare of their staff. Otherwise, the staff will not care for the boss nor share in his ideals to achieve goals and high standards of quality and efficiency.

These stories have another moral to them. I have found that people in senior positions often do not go down to the grassroots to see and understand the work, the feelings, fears and aspirations of the less fortunate in our society. This negligence of the interests of the ordinary man in the street is not peculiar to many corporate managers alone, but is pretty widespread at many levels of society anywhere in the world. If we do not show more fairness and compassion in our management policies at the national and company levels, there would be resentment and social unrest.

Thus it is important for the government to ensure that the mass of the people, the *rakyat*, are not neglected in our big rush toward rapid economic growth and the accelerated pace of modernisation through unprecedented technological changes. This is why we talk about balanced growth, equitable development, and the provision of the basic needs of life. That is why we want a reasonable standard of living and a good quality of life for all our citizens — not only the privileged minority. This is all about our human rights!

But are we doing enough? Are we fulfilling the high ideals and noble aspirations of our Vision 2020, at an acceptable pace? At the rate we are going, will we be able to reach our targets — not only in the field of economics but in all the other goals that make the sum total of the essence of Vision 2020?

At this stage of our development, I am sceptical of our prospects of achieving all our nine goals simultaneously. It is possible that we could reach our economic targets. But that achievement in itself could militate against the achievement of the other goals. This is because we could be giving more priority, in our resources and efforts, to economic, legal and technological issues at the expense of our social goals.

Road Transport Department (RTD)

As Secretary-General of the Ministry of Transport, the RTD came under my purview. Somehow or other, there are many members of the public who think that the (RTD) and the Ministry of Transport are one and the same! The reasons for this misconception could be because most people know the RTD because most of them drive cars! The Minister of Transport also makes the most number of statements connected with road transport as there are always road accidents, problems with school busses and at one time, mini-buses.

The Road Transport Department is one of the largest revenue earning departments of the government. Unfortunately, however, the Financial Procedure Act does not allow the department to keep all its revenues to itself. Instead, all its earnings are credited to the Government's Consolidated Fund. Expenditure allocations are then provided to the Road Transport Department. Hence the main grouse of the department is that it gets back much less than what it earns. Thus it is not able to get enough funds to provide better services to the public.

Corruption

But the greatest criticism of the RTD was for the alleged petty corruption is present on a pretty large scale. But we found it difficult to find real evidence that we could use in the courts. How could we get evidence when there are, most times, a willing giver and a willing taker of bribes?

As they say, you need two hands to clap. But on the other hand, I am told that it is difficult to resist offering a bribe when a businessman wants something from the authorities. He finds that he cannot get his license or permit quickly enough until and unless he offers a bribe to the officials concerned. Of course, it can be argued that the businessman must stand for principles and good business ethics and not tempt the poor official with a bribe. But how often do we have businessmen who are so principled or even so ethnical?

Businessmen are pragmatic and profit-orientated. Most of them will do almost anything to attain their objectives. They will do their best to remove any obstacles, even legitimate ones, in order to get a higher share of the market to maximise their profits. In most places, that is the way of business. So what is the way out?

How do we reduce corruption?

Firstly, we have to remove the perception that most leaders are corrupt. There is this perception among most Malaysians that many of our rich and wealthy leaders became rich because of their corrupt practices or through questionable methods. This notion gets more currency when they find relatively young people becoming so rich so fast, while others have taken perhaps generations and through the sweat of their brow, to accumulate and preserve that wealth.

We can remove this impression only if we are able to get almost, if not all our leaders to set good examples of high ideals and scrupulous integrity. It would be ideal if the top leaders could have their assets and liabilities made public. But it has been argued that this would be an unfair imposition, since it would expose the declarant to the risk of extortion. In that case then, the government could have all members of parliament declare their assets and liabilities to a 'Special Integrity Panel' of Supreme Court judges and elder statesmen, in strict confidence. The special panel would also be able to ask for any explanation for any undue changes in the wealth of the members of parliament and then take appropriate action if necessary.

As the Chinese say, a fish begins to rot at the head! So if we keep a tab on top management, then it is likely that they in turn would ensure that those below them would not unfairly benefit from the sound leadership that they work so hard to provide at the top.

Secondly, the paperless electronic government should be introduced more speedily. Additionally, when more computerisation is introduced we have to take tough measures to ensure that the staff who would be denied opportunities for corrupt practices do not sabotage the sophisticated computer systems. Those found guilty should be severely punished. This has happened in some places when they introduced brand-new Electronic Data Systems (EDS).

Thirdly, the evils of corruption should be taught in schools. Children must be taught to despise corrupt practices so that they themselves do not accept it as a way of life when they grow up.

Finally, corruption will not thrive when there is efficiency and transparency. Rules and regulations should be reduced. When they are required, then they should be transparent and made known widely. Discretion in the interpretation of rules should only be made at high levels of government and corporate management, and not at the whims and fancies of minor officials and politicians.

We will have to address these serious problems of corruption, patronage, nepotism and cronyism, if we are to continue to prosper and progress as a nation. Otherwise we will be undermined and even destroyed as a successful nation, if we do not take effective action as a matter of urgency. At present, there is a general perception, especially abroad, that we are not serious enough about or that we are not giving sufficient priority to stamping out corruption and cronyism.

We must take priority action or suffer the consequences. The lower income groups and the mass of the people will suffer most. The *rakyat* will not take the deterioration lying down when their rice bowls get broken.

We have to battle corruption, as if it is a war. Otherwise, all that we have so strenuously built up will be lost. It is therefore worth giving of our best to fight this curse of corruption. Only the leaders can make the decision to go to war against corruption. The masses will no doubt follow willingly for their own benefit and survival. But we should go for the 'big fish' as well, otherwise all worthy efforts to combat corruption will lose their credibility and become wasted.

There is a story about the 'big fish' and the 'small fish'. A mother kept feeding her child even when he was full. One day, the child asked the mother why she made him eat so much. The mother replied, "Son, when you grow up you'll be grateful to me. In life, it is only the 'small fish' that will get caught while the 'big fish' will get away!" I hope that is not true in our society!

Transport Planning

All these large transport sectors (such as road transport, railways, airlines and shipping) had to be well coordinated so that an integrated transport policy and network is in place. Otherwise, there would be wasteful duplication and unnecessary undercutting in the transport sector. We could do this only at the federal government level. For instance, the transport system within the local authorities were outside our purview. Perhaps that's why the traffic conditions in Kuala Lumpur have been under severe strain for such a long time!

However, the transport system for the country as a whole also left much to be desired. This is mainly because of the lack of priority placed on proper planning, especially in the allocation of funds. It was also quite impossible to imagine that the traffic demand would expand at such a fast and unprecedented pace.

Realising the problems that could arise from inadequate transport planning, we took the initiative to consult with the World Bank to organise a group of consultants to draw up an integrated Multi-Modal Transport Plan. We had our ministry officials work with these foreign consultants and also engaged local consultants for this massive project.

We made good progress and the draft long-term transport plans were finalised. However they had to be cleared with the other relevant government agencies like the Treasury and the EPU. All this took time. Furthermore, this was in 1988, when the government had other priorities after the severe recession. Thus the transport bottlenecks became worse and we found ourselves always falling short of satisfying the rising demand for better transport services.

The lessons to be learnt are that we should constantly keep updating the statistics and keep reviewing the transport master plan (or any other plans for that matter). We also have to provide transport infrastructure well ahead of the demand for transport services, even if it means that we may not be able to fully utilise the infrastructure soon after the completion of a project.

We must place more emphasis on the planning capacity in the ministry as well as all the transport agencies, instead of centralising transport planning mainly in the EPU. No agency of government will know more than the Ministry of Transport or its agencies regarding transport planning and implementation. This principle must be recognised and accepted by the government (not only for the Ministry of Transport but for all other sectoral planning as well) if we are to have proper and professional sectoral planning in the future.

Some people think that the Ministry of Transport did not plan and has no 'Transport Plan'. This is not true. There has been a lot of planning that has been going on quietly in the Ministry of Transport, but this has not been trumpeted. It has not been adopted as a 'National Transport Policy', like the National Agriculture Policy. This is largely because the transport sector has been so dynamic that it becomes outdated so fast. Thus the reluctance to come out with a firm plan which we know cannot adequately reflect the real situation on a current basis. But maybe now that the transport situation has been largely stabilised, it is appropriate to adopt and launch a new 'National Transport Plan' which needs to be constantly reviewed and revised.

Asean COTAC

COTAC stood for the Committee of Transport and Communications. It was an Asean standing committee that I chaired during my tenure as the Secretary-General of the Ministry of Transport.

COTAC was charged with the responsibility to coordinate the transport systems of the Asean member countries. It was not an easy task as these countries had different systems and priorities in the development of the transport system. This is understandable as we were under different colonial powers. We were also of different sizes, from small states (like Brunei and Singapore) to the vast archipelago of Indonesia. But there was plenty of scope to rationalise and link up our diverse transport systems in order to further facilitate the smooth flow of trade, investment and tourism.

Asean transport officials used to meet at least once a year in each of our countries to learn from each other on how to improve and coordinate the development of our varied transport systems.

At one COTAC meeting I opened, I came up with the idea that all the Asean countries should strive to link up their varied transport systems. I proposed that we could have an 'Asean airline' that could combine forces in our flight operations among Asean countries and outside the Asean region. The railway could be linked even over land that was separated by sea via ferry and even bridges where possible, as in the case of Malaysia and Singapore. We could also have an Asean Shipping Line. All we needed was to get help from the World Bank and the Asian Development Bank that would finance these regional transport projects. Foreign direct investment would also be forthcoming.

I had made this statement at a COTAC meeting without consulting my minister, Dr Ling Liong Sik. So when it was reported in the press, some countries thought that it was the official proposal of the Malaysian government and asked for clarification! I was called up by the Minister of Transport for an explanation. But he was understanding and advised me to be cautious in making public statements that involved other countries.

However, I am happy to the say that Asean has now decided to construct a railway that would link the Asean countries and move even farther to link up with China. I believe that in the years ahead we will establish stronger links with Asean airlines, shipping and land transport. Asean will then be able to achieve economies of scale and prosper further. It is hoped that the dreams we had many years ago at our COTAC meetings will be fulfilled in the not-too-distant future when we could have great land, sea and air 'Asian Euro Bridges'!

34.
RETIREMENT FROM THE GOVERNMENT
(1989)

I CELEBRATED my 54th birthday on the January 6, 1989. It was therefore about 30 years since I joined the Malaysian Civil Service (MCS). When I left the Treasury on transfer to the Ministry of Transport I had informed my minister, Tun Daim Zainuddin, that I would like to continue to serve the government in any capacity that he thought would be appropriate. Tun Daim had said that he was reluctant to let me go from the Treasury. However, he would bear me in mind, should any opportunity arose for me to serve the government after I retired.

Before I left for London to negotiate the Air Agreement with the British, I went over to the Treasury to get Tun Daim's advice on how to handle the negotiation. As I left his room I reminded him that I would be retiring in about six months from the time of our meeting. He smiled and promised to remember my interest in continuing to work, especially for the government.

Sometime in mid-1989, at an investiture function in Istana Negara, I happened to sit next to the then governor of the Bank Negara, the late Tan Sri Jaafar Hussein. He leaned over and asked me if I would like to work in a bank as the CEO. I readily responded that I would if he thought I could handle the job — not having been a banker before. He nodded his head and I let the matter rest. About a week later I received a call from Dato' Ahmad Basir (now Tan Sri) of Bank Negara telling me that I was now formally invited to take over as CEO from Dr R. Thillainathan, who was leaving Bank Buruh to join the Genting Group in July 1989. I had just a month to get ready, if I decided to take the job. Dato' Ahmad said that they had spoken to the head of the Public Service Department, my old friend Tan Sri Alwi Jantan. He had agreed to expedite my premature retirement by about 6 months since I would reach the retirement age of 55 on January 6, 1990.

I was grateful and greatly relieved that I was given the opportunity to carry on working by Tun Daim. He was a man of his word. Unlike some politicians and others in high places who say 'yes' for the sake of it, he really meant what he said. I was relieved because I had the desire to carry on being useful to society, to my family and to myself. My nature is such that I would be frustrated if I did not continue to be purposefully occupied after retirement from government service. After reaching the upper echelons of the MCS, I had to feel that I was sufficiently equipped and experienced to work in a senior capacity in the corporate world.

I think that it is indeed a pity that we have to retire at the age of 56 in the public service. We must be the only country in the Asean region or even in the world to have to retire from the public service at that early age. Most of my colleagues and peers in other countries retire at 58, 60 or 65. I think it is a waste of talent and scarce human resources to retire the most experienced officials at their prime considering their knowledge and capacity to contribute to nation building.

Apparently some of our leaders have consistently not been in favour of raising the retirement age, except on a restricted basis, such as in the case of our ambassadors and a few individuals at the highest levels of the civil service. Why this is so is not clear. Some political leaders have said that it is because they want to give younger officers a chance to get their promotions. But this argument does not hold water because the younger officials will still have their chances since the older ones are not going to stay on forever in their posts. Yet the politicians do not have a retirement age for themselves! Perhaps it is felt that the politicians find it hard to influence the older civil servants?

In any case, I was happy to be asked to continue to serve. Many of my colleagues have retired and, like old generals, they have just faded away. They have taken seriously to golf or to looking after their grandchildren. In response to questions as to how they are spending their time, they would reply, "*Main golf dan jaga cucu*" ("Play golf and look after the grandchildren"). Good luck to them, but I could not live that kind of life happily. I believe that there is so much in life to learn from and a lot more to give to society to which we owe so much.

My Tan Sri Award

As I approached retirement, the government was gracious to me. In June 1989 I was awarded the title of 'Tan Sri' by the Yang di-Pertuan Agong, the Malaysian King. I received this title in recognition of my long and dedicated service to the country. Under the able leadership of Dato' Seri Dr Ling Liong Sik (now Tun), we were blessed with the devotion to duty shown by all the officials and staff at the Ministry of Transport and the many professional departments and agencies under the ministry.

I know that Dr Ling was keen that I should be rewarded for the efforts I had made under his guidance to wield the large Ministry into a united family, to move as one wholesome team in one dedicated direction to achieve our mission. It was by no means automatic for the Secretary-General of the Ministry to be awarded the high honour of 'Tan Sri', which in Britain is equivalent to a knighthood ('Sir'). There have been those before me and even after me who have been Secretaries-General of the Ministry but have not been bestowed with this distinctive honour.

I believe that it was the strong support that I had received from my own Minister, Dr Ling Liong Sik, and that the Prime Minister, Dr Mahathir Mohamad (now Tun), and of course my official boss, the Chief Secretary to the Government, Tan Sri Sallehuddin Mohammed, that made this possible. When one considers that I am not even a Malaysian Indian (but of the small Ceylonese minority), it will be appreciated that it must have taken some effort to agree to award me with this distinguished title. I gratefully accepted the award on behalf of all the sacrifices of the public servants whom I was privileged to serve and lead.

I have a feeling that unlike many others I am not a wealthy Tan Sri. But I consider my dear family and myself blessed in so many ways. We are comfortable but not rich. Thank God, Samala, my good wife, and I have never yearned for or sought wealth. But Tan Sri's are thought to be rich. This is because increasingly it is the rich businessmen and political leaders who are getting the title of 'Tan Sri' these days. They may have contributed much to the government and the society, but not without consideration of profit to themselves too. The new title of 'Dato' that is now given as a federal government title seems to be increasingly given to top civil servants as a substitute for Tan Sri.

But I must say that I do enjoy the title of Tan Sri and I am grateful to the King and the government for having given me this high honour, which I accepted with humility and an obligation to serve society even more faithfully. I only hope that with God's help, I will live up to public expectations and be worthy of the title.

35.
BANK BURUH:
REORGANISING THE WORKERS' BANK

DR R. Thillainathan, the CEO of Bank Buruh, was waiting for me to take over as he was urgently required by the Genting Group of Companies.

On a Saturday morning in July 1989, I was given a *kompang* send off by the Ministry of Transport officials and staff at the entrance to the Ministry's headquarters at Wisma Perdana at Jalan Semantan in Damansara. It was sad for me as I punched out my attendance card for the last time in my long government service. I had enjoyed my career in the government. The continuation of the tradition of my father and my grandfather before him in the service of God, king and country had appealed to me. I felt that I was fulfilling a mission of service to society. I felt humbled by the satisfaction and the honour to be able to serve my country and my people, with dedication and commitment, and without much remuneration compared to the private sector. But now I was leaving the government to join the private sector. I would have liked to continue working for the government if I could.

I felt nostalgic as my faithful government driver Shamsuddin (or Din for short), drove me for the last time in my Mercedes 200 which I had bought from the government at a nominal price.

It did not take me long to get to Bank Buruh, which was then situated at the EPF Headquarters Building at Jalan Raja Laut, opposite the City Hall. The secretary of the bank, Albert, met me at the entrance and escorted me straight into the conference room. There I was introduced to about 15 of the senior officials of the bank.

In my first address to my new staff, I thanked them for their warm welcome and mentioned that I hoped that we would be able to carry on and build upon the good work of my able predecessor, Dr Thillainathan. I said that we should work closely as a committed team and as a family, and that we should do our best to serve God, King and Country! I thought that I was making a good impromptu speech until I found some of the bank officials feeling uneasy and even smiling and whispering to each other! I did not know why at that time, but I got to learn later why I had not struck the right note in my first speech to my new staff in the private sector.

When I asked some of the staff afterwards, they explained that they had asked themselves in response to my call to serve God, King and Country—"Why King? What God? How Country?" They indicated that they were only interested in 'money'! So that was a rude awakening for me in the private sector.

I realised from then the great importance that 'more money' played in the role of motivating and driving the private sector forward. It was not the question of serving the country, but how much money one can make and how fast one could make money! It was sad for me but alas that was the hard reality I had to face in the business world. That is what made the business world turn around and move so fast. It was not ideals but the sheer acquisition of money and wealth that motivated people. I think it is greed!

The shareholders of the bank were however not businessmen and were not interested in pursuing profits *per se* but were keen to help the workers to have easier access to the banking system. Therein lay the conflict in managing the bank, that I was to be the CEO.

The Bank Board
Fortunately, I had a good board of directors under the chairmanship of my old friend and senior colleague Tan Sri Rozhan Kuntum. We also had Tan Sri John Daniel as deputy chairman and my former college mate, R. Balakrishnan. The late Dr P.P. Narayanan, whom I had met as a student when I was doing my thesis for my honours degree in Economics, was also on the board. This was the only bank in the country that had a strong ownership by a union of workers—the Transport Union Workers.

Most of the board members were well recognised as leading former civil servants, with high standards of ethics and integrity. But the previous board members were mostly union leaders who were not necessarily well equipped in the art of management. Thus they had recruited many trade union types and the sons and daughters of union leaders, who often were not qualified for a career in banking.

Poor Working Culture
We had therefore inherited staff who did not have a good work culture or strong work ethics. Many were more interested in their rights and privileges, rather than their responsibilities to give of their best to enhance the competitive position of the bank. The staff at the lower lev-

els had in general a laidback disposition. The slightest reprimand would soon be referred to the Union, which was not only strong but quite assertive.

I had been alerted and cautioned that Bank Buruh had the most unionised staff in the whole banking industry, so I decided to start on a good footing with the President of NUBE, Mr Shanmugam. I rang him up, introduced myself and invited him for lunch. He was obviously glad that I had rung him up. He sent a bouquet of flowers to my office the next morning as a gesture of welcome! It was a good start that helped me later.

Within a week after I had joined the bank as the CEO however, the vice-president of NUBE confronted me. What happened was that I had called for a meeting with all the junior staff to get to know them. I also wanted to find out what I could do for them to make them happier in their workplace. I had thought that as in the case of the government, the occasion would be treated as a family gathering and a get-to-know-you session. But it turned out that the union leaders had other ideas. They apparently had planned to make the meeting confrontational and to embarrass me, and 'to flex their muscles' in front of their new CEO. During the discussion there was a union leader who was repeatedly provoking me with questions that raised issues of management's effectiveness. I answered him but he kept repeating the same questions. He raised what I thought were unfair and unreasonable proposals. When he was getting out of hand, I told him off. That was it! The unionised staff reacted strongly to my remarks. I adjourned the meeting with thanks for some of the good ideas that they had given and promised to study them carefully.

But the next thing I knew was that the union headquarters had been informed of the incident and that their leaders wanted to see me. I agreed to meet them on a Saturday morning and would not apologise for no good reason! The leader asked me to apologise. I explained that I did not mean any offence. The union leader did not accept my explanation and said that he would call for 'non-cooperation' of the bank staff if I did not apologise.

It was just a few weeks since I had joined the bank and I did not want a problem with my staff so soon after I had taken over the reins of the bank. I was told that one form of non-cooperation was for the staff to wear big badges with large inscriptions such as 'this bank is not good for you and for us'. Imagine the adverse psychological effects it would have on our customers.

On the following Monday morning therefore I went to my office with some apprehension. I looked out for evidence of any non-cooperation, but there was none. Then I was told that the protest badges could be worn anytime. My waiting for the reaction from the union members was stressful. The whole atmosphere in the bank was tense and strained. I had to do something about the situation or else the productivity of the staff would be adversely affected.

So I decided to ring up my friend, the NUBE leader Shanmugam to find out what was happening. I found out that he was fully briefed and that he was waiting for my call. I explained my side of the story and he was receptive. It transpired that some of the leaders at the headquarters of the NUBE itself had found that the Bank Buruh staff were difficult. The Bank Buruh branch staff had a reputation for being belligerent and had consistently demanded that the headquarters should be more militant against the management of Bank Buruh.

Some of the younger union leaders did not like my style of dealing with the employees direct, without going through the bank's union leaders. They felt that my style of management would undermine their popularity and their strong leadership position.

I was advised to introduce my changes more gradually and in the meantime to let my personnel manager deal directly with the union members. But I had a real problem because the head of the Personnel Department was about 65 years old and was quite ineffective in his role. In fact, most of the staff problems were due to his bad handling of the junior staff.

I remember that a young girl responded to my request for any staff to see me if they had a problem. So this girl came to see me. But when I asked the head of personnel to help her out, he quietly took it out on her. She came to me crying, saying that the head of the personnel department had scolded her severely and that the union leaders too had pulled her up for not taking her grievances to them. She was caught in between and felt a sense of persecution. I promised to help her out but she could not stand the strain of the cold treatment that she received from many of her colleagues and some unsympathetic bosses. So she decided to resign.

That was the state of the poor personnel management in the bank. I then decided to give high priority to improving staff relations. I introduced what I learnt from the government, that is, 'The Family Concept'. By this I meant that we should all work like members of a family. We should help each other like brothers and sisters. We should care for each other, both management and staff. This concept was again resisted by some union leaders as they felt that only the union could and should look after the interests of the staff as a family!

I got rid of the head of the Personnel Department and replaced him with a younger and much more empathetic person called Samarason (Sam). It turned out to be a boon. With his assistance I discovered that the Union leaders had quietly built up a kind of 'cell' within the bank. This was made up of the main union leaders that were clustered together in one area in the bank where they operated as an 'office within the office'. This was most unhealthy, as they were spending more time plotting and planning their union activities rather than doing their official work seriously. So we broke up the group. There was resistance to our move but it had a salutary effect on the whole morale of the bank staff, most of whom wanted to do an honest day's work without the hassle of having to confront management—and sometimes over nothing!

Audit Department

The next area that I felt had to be put right was the Bank's audit department. The attitude in the bank towards the auditor and the audit department was simply bad. At meetings of the senior staff I found that the auditor was treated with disrespect and almost frivolously. The staff did not respond to his queries seriously nor promptly. They almost treated the auditor as if he was a nuisance.

I was upset and warned the senior officers that I would penalise anyone who treated the audit queries lightly. I requested the auditor to refer all the unanswered audit queries to me for my personal attention. I told them that when I was in the government, I treated the auditor as my best friend and not as a pain in the neck. He was the one whom I could count on to advise me on any financial irregularities and even possible abuse, even before it happened.

That changed the whole audit environment. The auditor himself was expected to be more diligent. However, he could not cope with his new role, especially when he had been quite relaxed earlier. He resigned and I promoted his able assistant Prabakaran to his position. The situation improved greatly after this move!

Loan Recovery

Loan recovery in the bank was badly neglected, too. Most of the borrowers were from the low-income groups. Many of them were also former union leaders and union members. The collection of loan repayments was therefore subject to a lot of tardiness and delay. The debtors would often plead for more time and they would often be given approval to delay their repayments. There was not much will to enforce the conditions of the loan repayments. The person in charge of the Loan Recovery Department was an elderly person. I did not think that he had the commitment as he was also employed on an annual contract.

One day, I called his deputy, a young and energetic officer, who seemed to be doing all the work. His chief came to work for only about 4 days a week according to his contract. For this reason alone, I did not think that he could have been very effective. So, I asked Moorthy the deputy to compile a full schedule of the outstanding loans and monitor the repayments on a weekly basis. I told him to have an Operations Room similar to those in government departments. I advised him to organise different teams within his department to compete, to see which team could recover the most loans and to reward them for their success. That idea worked well, so I soon made Moorthy the new head of the Loan Recovery Department.

Credit

The Credit Department, which brought in the business, was strengthened with better staff. The lending guidelines were made stricter and clear. Thus it was easier to approve loan applications as they were considered on a more uniform basis. We made sure that all loan applications were thoroughly scrutinised. If there was no unanimity at the Loans Committee, then as chairman of the committee, I would postpone consideration of the loan application until new facts were brought to light. Since the credit processes were streamlined, the Loan Committee was able to clear loan applications at a faster pace. This helped to increase the satisfaction of the customers who wanted quick decisions as time meant money and profits to the business borrowers.

Members of the board felt that since we were a 'workers' bank', we should provide more lending to the small businessmen. That made it easier for me to also advance my own inclination to help the small businessmen whom the banks generally avoided. They found that they had to work as hard in processing the loan applications and then lend out relatively small loans. On the other hand, the banks made much more profits by lending larger amounts to the big corporates for about the same amount of effort. We therefore decided to work closely with the government-sponsored Credit Guarantee Scheme, which encouraged banks to lend to the small and medium business enterprises.

The small *bumiputera* businessmen had a wider range of opportunities and access to bank lending. So we felt we would focus our lending efforts on the small Chinese and Indian businessmen. We called a meeting of small businessmen from Salak South and talked to them in Malay and Chinese about the principles of the Grameen Lending Programme in Bangladesh. We thought we would safeguard the bank's interest by getting the members of the group from Salak South to provide group guarantees for each other on an informal basis.

Thus if a few of them borrowed, then the others in the group would vouch for the borrowers repaying the loans. It was encouraging to note how well this Grameen-type scheme really worked. There was no default on their repayments. If one of the borrowers began to have a business problem, the others in the scheme went out to assist him in his business. If one of them tried to escape repayments, the others would apply peer pressure on him to pay up in time. We had even heard of one borrower who was threatened with bodily harm by his peers if he didn't pay up on time. The group took this tough line of self-regulation as a matter of honour because they had wanted to protect their own credibility in order to be able to continue to borrow from our bank. After all they were charged normal banking rates of interest of around 10 per cent per annum in about 1988, whereas they were used to paying the 'loan sharks' as much as 120 per cent per annum or about 10 per cent per month!

I tried something similar for the Indians. We had a meeting with the leaders of the Indian Chamber of Commerce at their premises at Jalan Tuanku Abdul Rahman. They assembled a good number of small Indian businessmen who showed interest, but somehow few took advantage of our offer. We had asked the Indian Chamber to help the Indian businessmen to apply for loans on the simple standard forms that we provided them, but nothing much was done. Somehow there was a feeling that if we wanted to help we should give them interest-free loans. Otherwise they seemed to prefer not to borrow to expand their business. Alternatively, they preferred to continue to deal with the *chettiar* moneylenders, who were often as bad as 'loan sharks'. So I too, despite my earlier enthusiasm, lost interest in wanting to assist the small Indian businessmen. Some that we managed to persuade to borrow also let us down by defaulting on their loan payments. I suppose there must be willingness for them to help themselves first.

Money Letter

Bank Buruh had a monthly newsletter called the *Money Letter* before I took over the management of the bank. It gave some basic economic and monetary data and was sold to the corporate clients of the bank as well as some closely-related banks. I had been writing the monthly report 'Economic Trends' that was sent to the Cabinet when I was in the Treasury. So I liked the idea of developing the bank's *Money Letter* along the lines of the Treasury's *Economic Trends*. Thus, I quickly transformed the banks *Money Letter* into a policy-orientated monthly publication.

We gathered the latest economic and financial data from the publications of the Statistics Department and Bank Negara and I personally wrote the public policy analysis. The Statistics Department merely presented the facts and just described the changes in the data, but never attempted to interpret the trends nor make economic forecasts. I looked at the economic and financial trends independently of the government ministries and Bank Negara. This initiative made the *Money Letter* more interesting. Sensing its popularity, I used to hold monthly luncheon press conferences for the release of the *Money Letter*. We used to invite 10 to 15 journalists from all the major newspapers to attend our press briefings. The sale of the *Money Letter* soared.

I realised that the *Money Letter* was causing some concern with Bank Negara as well as some of my former treasury colleagues. I felt that some of them even showed some reluctance to be seen talking at length with me at formal functions. However, the press always covered the *Money Letter* well. We provided an independent and objective view that was professional and fair. Unlike the government pronouncements, we were prepared to be more open and critical. I was quoted quite widely in the local and foreign press too.

I do not think my friends at Bank Negara in particular took too kindly to me. In fact, I received some signals and messages that I was being too critical. Some even tried to downgrade my comments as a lack of understanding of the real situation. It was true that I was no longer in the corridors of power, but that did not mean I did not know or did not understand how the Governor and Bank Negara officials thought. After all, I had been a senior government official for 30 years!

I did not bother too much how some officials felt. I believed that I was fulfilling a public need and that the government actually encouraged healthy and constructive criticism that was sincere and not politically motivated. So I just carried on and enjoyed my role.

My Relations with Bank Negara

Some friends who considered themselves close to Bank Negara's senior officials cautioned me to go slow because I was upsetting some officials. After all, I believed that I was well motivated. I believe in open and honest debate and discussion, so why should I be concerned with a few officials who did not like my constructive public criticism in the *Money Letter* and the press?

But the problem persisted. There was hardly any tradition of public debate on economic and monetary issues. Anyone who criticised Bank Negara felt that he would suffer in one way or another, especially if he is a banker or a borrower. Unfortunately, too, most of the businessmen are borrowers. So that is why we rarely find businessmen openly criticising economic and monetary policies.

It is a pity because I believe that the government actually does not mind constructive criticism, even publicly, as long as there is no ill intention or political motive. As they say the *niat* (intention) has to be noble.

For instance, at Bank Negara's Annual Consultations with the Association of Bankers, it was quite difficult to get the bankers to talk freely with the governor and the deputy governor, at least in the past. During the late Tun Ismail's stewardship of Bank Negara, the meetings with the bankers were usually quite tense. It used to be almost a monologue. He would rarely shake hands with the bankers or smile at them, unless they were very close to him. However he enjoyed great respect for his ability and integrity and was regarded with some trepidation. With that kind of relationship with the governor, it was no wonder that the tradition was set from the early days of the establishment of Bank Negara, that it was best for bankers to be seen and not heard.

Even when the late Tan Sri Jaafar was the governor, the tradition was still prevalent, except that the atmosphere was more relaxed. Actually, when Tan Sri Jaafar found the annual consultations slow and uneasy, he would crack a joke and prompt the bankers to ask questions or to comment on the excellent economic briefings that he and his able deputy, Tan Sri Dr Lin See Yan, would always give at the annual meetings with bankers. Often enough, the governor would invite me to comment. So I sensed he did not mind my open criticism in the *Money Letter*. But some of his subordinates were quite negative and not very warm.

Bank Negara's surveillance and supervision were stern and severe. Whereas the policy from the top was clear and acceptable, the actual administration and implementation of these policies were often quite rigid. For instance, the Minister of Finance, Dato' Seri Anwar Ibrahim, and the Governor, Tan Sri Mohamad Ahmad Don, would urge the bankers to be liberal and to provide loans on the basis of character and not mainly on the basis of collateral. But some of Bank Negara's supervisory staff, most of whom were relatively young, would invariably go strictly by the letter of the word and not by it's spirit. They would be happy to throw the book even at the more experienced but liberal bankers.

We often wondered how banking could become innovative and imaginative if we had to operate under such conservative constraints. We found serious conflicts between what we were urged publicly to do and what we were privately expected to practise. That is why lending to the small businessmen by banks and the venture capital funds have been so low for so long.

The relations between Bank Negara and the banking community however gradually became much more cordial and comfortable. Both the governor Tan Sri Ahmad Don and the astute and affable deputy governor Dato' Fong Weng Pak were both professionals with commercial banking experience. They had a good sense of empathy for the bankers in the private sector.

Obviously much more could be done to further strengthen the cooperation and consultations in the larger financial community. And the institution that can bring about greater improvement in these relations is undoubtedly Bank Negara. It has to move more deliberately from the stern and stiff traditions of the past, if the financial sector of the economy is to innovate and compete more effectively in the 21st century. This is now highly probable with the affable disposition of the first lady Governor, Tan Sri Dr Zeti Akhtar Aziz.

I enjoyed banking. Bank Negara asked me whether I would work for another term of two years and I happily agreed. There was already talk that the Post Office Savings Bank (Bank Simpanan Nasional) would be taking over Bank Buruh. I knew that I would have to hold the fort and strengthen the bank for the takeover by Bank Simpanan Nasional soon.

Worker's Institute of Technology (WIT)

Our loan recovery plans were bearing fruit. As the bank became better established, our borrowers realised that we had the ability to act tough and to follow up with a lot more serious litigation against defaulters. We recovered a large number of loans that had gone sour. In the process some of us became quite unpopular. But we had a job to do and we did it to the best of our ability, without fear or favour.

But one of my happy achievements was to help to save the Workers' Institute of Technology (WIT) from liquidation. WIT was founded by the Transport Workers Union and mainly initiated by early trade union leaders like Dr V. David and Zainal Rampak. It was strongly supported by the Malaysian Trades Union Congress (MTUC). The children of trade unionists were given priority for admission into its large campus at Pandamaram near Klang. There were therefore strong emotional ties between the Malaysian labour movement and the WIT.

WIT had borrowed a large loan from Bank Buruh. The problem was that WIT, as an educational institution, faced considerable financial difficulties and found problems in settling its loan repayments. Since Bank Buruh's board of directors had several labour leaders, the previous board was very considerate with WIT. Thus the bank officials were not able to be strict with the loan repayments. The interest on the loans accumulated and WIT was becoming insolvent. With changes in the board membership and me as CEO, we were able to apply more pressure on the WIT to pay up their loans or to sell their interests to some other party.

After prolonged negotiations with WIT, the Bank's directors decided that the only way to redeem the loan was to foreclose our loans and to auction the whole WIT campus. The unions appealed but we could not do anything about it because the bank was losing money from this sour loan.

On the appointed Saturday morning that WIT was to be auctioned, Zainal Rampak, V. David and businessman Kamal came to see me early in the morning to persuade me to further postpone the auction. I refused to move on the grounds that I had no mandate to do so, unless there was new evidence for repayment of the loans that I could present to the board. However, I must admit that I was sympathetic to their case, because I believed they were genuine in their efforts to save WIT. They had no business interest in it. They were just committed to helping their members' children to get a technical education at a lower cost.

In trying to help them I tried different solutions. We then hit upon the idea of Kamal giving Bank Buruh a sum of money as part of the settlement of the outstanding loan on the understanding that he would buy over a major share of WIT. This formula was acceptable to the union leaders. However, I had no mandate to agree to call off the auction that was due in half an hour's time. I tried desperately to get the chairman of the bank on the phone but Tan Sri Rozhan Kuntum was not available.

So in good faith I asked my staff to ring the court officials to call off the auction. The minutes were ticking away towards the time of the auction which was at 10.30am. I then got a word from Nadarajah my senior manager and Moorthy who was in charge of this case that the court officials, like me, did not have the mandate to postpone the auction. The tension in my office was building up and I could see that V. David was distraught. All his valiant efforts to establish WIT and to save it from liquidation were now coming to a sad end.

Suddenly a brainwave hit me and I rang up the Secretary-General of the Ministry of Justice (who was my former colleague) for help. She was understanding and gracious and agreed to instruct the officer concerned to postpone the auction! WIT was thus saved in the nick of time. The union leaders were overjoyed and grateful.

Although I was glad to be able to help the union leaders, I realised that I had to face the music for acting beyond my mandate. In fact, it was against the instruction of the board members to finally auction WIT, because of the several earlier postponements and firm promises to repay the long outstanding loan. But I also knew that my board of directors was generally quite sympathetic to the cause of the union leaders. Thus when I reported to Tan Sri Rozhan on the following Monday, he was surprised that I had gone against the board's instructions but he understood and respected my discretion and judgement. Fortunately, the board subsequently endorsed my decision to postpone the auction.

When one has a fair-minded board of directors, which also has confidence in its CEO, then there is plenty of scope for innovation and enterprise. This is more easily done in the private sector. I'm sure it would have been more difficult or well nigh impossible to do the same thing if I were in the government.

Bank Buruh's Open House

Bank Buruh did not enjoy a good public image earlier. Labour unions had owned and managed it. This fact did not go down well with the large corporations. They therefore did not choose to do much business with the bank. Furthermore, there had been some cases of financial mismanagement in the past. Some of the bank officials had actually gone to jail for it. The bank was also regarded as a "poor man's bank". This meant that it was difficult to mobilise enough deposits, thus leading to the constraints on the capacity to lend more to expand the bank's business. Unfortunately, the bank also had an uninspiring name which also sounded like *Bank Buruk* with the emphasis on the letter 'k'. In Malay the word *buruk* has a bad connotation. So one could understand why Bank Buruh had such a poor corporate image.

I was determined to improve this poor image of our bank. The new format of the *Money Letter* and the press briefings had done much to improve the image of the bank. But we obviously needed to do a great deal more. A bigger bank would have hired a consultant to plan and execute a public relations programme to improve its image. But we were constrained by inadequate funds for this purpose. So I thought that we would do what other banks were not doing and thus get more exposure and a higher profile. I introduced the idea of having an open house on Hari Raya, Chinese New Year and Deepavali—to cover all the major ethnic festivals in the country. I invited the senior ministers to officiate at these functions at our bank premises at the EPF headquarters' building in Jalan Rajah Laut. We had cultural dances and lunch and speeches. The press was invited and they interviewed the ministers who graced the functions.

We had as our guests of honour Dato' Seri Dr Ling Liong Sik, Dato' Seri S. Samy Vellu, Dato' Seri Lim Keng Aik and Dato' Napsiah. For each festival we decorated our premises in the style of that particular festival. For Hari Raya we had *bunga mangga* and *ketupat* decoration together with *kompang* music. For Chinese New Year we had dragon dances with *angpows* (red packets) containing new currency notes. For Deepavali we had the *kolam* with its brightly coloured rice designs. The bank staff did all these decorations with the help from the 'experts' like those from the Temple of Fine Arts. We thus earned a great deal of good will from both the public and the political leaders. Bank Buruh's public image kept improving!

Administration and Finance

The bank's business was expanding rapidly. We took additional floor space in the EPF headquarters building and then later moved to larger premises at the Mall opposite the Putra World Trade Centre. This bigger space gave the bank staff a greater sense of pride in their place of work. The customers were given more facilities. The banking counters were made more customer-friendly, and business boomed.

I then found it necessary to further strengthen the financial controls. More staff was made available to enable the faster processing of the business accounts. This way we were able to better monitor the financial performance. We were also more able to assess the cost and profit centres of the individual departments, as well as the individual performance of the bank staff. I promoted a good young accountant, Sathianathan, who was enthusiastic to prove his abilities to head the administration.

With the better data now available we were able to make rapid adjustments for our policies and practices. We could also introduce more competition among the staff and the various departments on a continuous basis. The budget targets were broken down to quarters, months and weeks. The heads of departments were asked to put these targets on graphs and to show actual achievements. Thus the staff were fully aware of their progress or failure in meeting their targets.

I would myself visit these departments and go straight to the wall charts to see how a particular department or staff was performing. Thus the pressure was always on. Because of me, the pressure was even stronger from the senior officers, who were answerable to me as their CEO for any shortfalls in the targets. Of course, I would praise them and spur them on when I saw that their performance was good.

My Secretaries

I had to have a strong back-up staff in order to perform effectively. I used a flat system of management as I realised that some of my senior officers were just passing down my messages without doing much themselves. So I got the secretary of the bank to act as my personal assistant. I called him to my room every morning to give him instructions for the different departments. This way he would record the instructions and then follow up on the progress made by the officers and then brief me.

I had tried this technique with my private secretaries but it did not work so well. The secretaries were not familiar with the technicalities of the bank business and would often give the wrong instructions. Furthermore, I noticed that the senior officers did not take the secretaries seriously enough and would also blame the secretaries for not giving the right messages. But they could not fool Albert who was the secretary of the bank since its inception. He knew how to handle the staff. I was thus able to keep a tighter rein on the developments in the bank and make sure that my instructions were followed up efficiently.

I had got this idea of close monitoring from the post-cabinet meetings that we had in the government. The 'morning prayers' were held in the Ministry of Foreign Affairs or Wisma Putra and the government's Operations Room technique that was monitored by the Implementation Coordination Unit of the Prime Minister's Department, were good models to follow.

I realised that there were a lot of ideas and techniques of management in the government that could be adapted to advantage in the private sector. Unfortunately, it is not realised in business circles that there is indeed much that can be learnt from the government sector in terms of discipline and careful analysis (not just rough calculations made on the back of an envelope). There were always full consultations with all the relevant agencies to ensure that the best interest of the public and the nation were considered.

However, the problem with the government is the poor image it gives to the public through indifferent quality of services provided by its staff at the level of counter services. These staff are relatively poorly qualified and are not well trained or motivated. In the private sector, however, the lower staff are better paid, and so they are better motivated. They are also sent for much more training and given bigger bonuses for higher productivity. They accept that they generally have to work harder if they are to benefit from higher bonuses and rewards.

I had problems with my own secretaries. I had Mariam Lisut as my secretary for 17 years in the Treasury and then she followed me to the Ministry of Transport. She was able, reliable and efficient.

But in the bank it was not easy to find someone who could perform like her. I was expecting high standards, but could not get it from many of the secretaries that I hired. Then in desperation I asked Samarason, the Director of Personnel, to get someone who was new but could be trained to be a better secretary. I was tired of getting experienced secretaries who had been trained the wrong way.

After several recruitment exercises to get good staff for the expanding bank operations, he sent me a new recruit who had obtained a certificate in secretarial work. Her name was Haema Latha. She was good in English, and keen to learn, willing to take constructive criticism, presentable and keen to improve. She slowly picked up and learnt my working methods. I found her suitable as she gained experience. Despite the politicking among the unionised staff, she was loyal to me. She then followed me when I left Bank Buruh and has been my loyal secretary at Sunway.

Farewell, Bank Buruh

After nearly 5 years as Chief Executive Officer of Bank Buruh, I retired from banking. I had anticipated only completing my 3-year contract when I would have reached the age of 58. But banking is very responsible and stressful work, especially if one has not been in it before—and I was ready to leave it!

Furthermore, in my case I was the only Malaysian Indian (Sri Lankan) CEO of a bank in the country and I was aware that there were many who were watching to see how an Indian CEO of a bank would perform. The only previous CEO of a commercial bank was Mr Murthy who was an expatriate from India who had been a CEO of the United Asian Bank. It was an amalgamation of three Indian banks and had a substantial foreign Indian equity in its capital structure.

When I joined the bank the profits were just around a million ringgit per annum. Earlier, the performance was even worse than that. But Dr Thillainathan did a lot to put the bank on a stronger footing. The profits grew slowly under my stewardship with the hard work of the majority of my staff. There was much reorganisation and displacement of weak staff and a radical change in the culture that had to be imposed. However, I am grateful that when I left the bank, we had made almost RM25 million in just one year, i.e., my last year! This was very gratifying to me and the board of directors, as well as those who meant well for me.

In the end, since the bank was now well established and had great potential, Bank Simpanan took over with its purchase of the majority share in Bank Buruh. The transfer of ownership and management was very graciously done by the leadership and management of Bank Simpanan. For this I am indebted to Dato' Zahid, the chairman of Bank Simpanan Nasional, Tan Sri Rozhan Kuntum, Tan Sri John Daniel and my board of directors.

I was given a good gratuity and allowed to buy my Mercedes 220 at a fair price. I think the majority of the staff of Bank Buruh did appreciate what I had done to improve the image and profitability of the bank. At a grand farewell dinner they presented me with a beautiful brass plaque with the following tribute, which I have appreciated. The tribute, which was composed by Prem Subramaniam, reads as follows:

ADIEU CAPTAIN
Tan Sri, Tan Sri, Puan Sri, Puan Sri
Dato' Dato', Datin Datin, Ladies and Gentlemen.
An unforgettable story you're going to hear
Of a ship, her voyages and her adventures
Of her captain, officers and sailors.

The 16th of July 1975 saw the brave
Launching of the ship christened Bank Buruh Berhad.
Amid great pomp and splendor
With great promise and expectations
The voyage commenced, with tremendous ardor
Alas! The ship ran into foul weather
Often tossed about by the merciless waves.
When in calm waters she was content to be
Merely afloat, or to drift aimlessly.
Such was the disappointment
Both to the owners and the users
That they wondered whether the ship
Was seaworthy any longer, when suddenly

In 1984, like a knight in
Shining armour, came a captain.
A man of valuable experience and proven skills
The ship gained buoyancy, maintaining its course
Owners and users now had a glimmer of hope.

Alas! that captain was soon to be no more.
The fate of the ship was again questioned
When lo and behold, almost divinely
There was a lucky streak
The ship came to port
A new captain took over the helm.
It was we cannot forget.
It was on the first day of July 1989,
Our captain was Tan Sri Ramon Navaratnam
From the word 'go' he set out
To refurbish the ship and to give her
A new identity, a new direction
A new hope and above all
An unfailing inspiration to
The officers and the crew.

Since then, there has been no turning back.
No sluggishness, no despondency.
Owners and users were equally thrilled
For their fortunes had improved,
In tandem with the fortunes of the ship

We the officers, the Heads of departments
Salute you, Sir, Tan Sri Ramon Navaratnam
For the opportunity bestowed on us
To be under your able captaincy
Seamanship and stewardship
In steering this vessel
Through stormy weathers
And will always remember
With pride, gratitude and warmth
Your guidance, understanding, and compassion.

Captain sir, you have brought us to port
Safely and securely, our beloved ship
Bank Buruh Berhad, looking so resplendent
In all her glory, with the comforting thought
That she has been conditioned
To weather all storms, however severe
One to hold her own among the other ships
In the care of her new master.

Our respected and beloved Tan Sri
We the Heads of Departments wish 'Bon Voyage'
And to Puan Sri and your family
Our best wishes always.

From all the Heads of Department
of Bank Buruh (1994)

I was touched by this tribute that was presented to me at the farewell dinner. I left the bank in 1994 and immediately joined the Sunway Group as their Corporate Adviser.

36.
INDRAN MARRIES PREMALA

INDRAN, our second son was staying at home with Ravi and Dharm. We were grateful that they all chose to stay at home although they were all working and could easily afford to stay on their own. I think this is mainly because all our three sons knew that Samala and I have a very strong preference for our sons to stay with us at least as long as they are bachelors.

We soon realised that although our sons stayed at home we had to give them more space. We do not have a big house, but it's comfortable enough. They had to feel that they had their privacy and independence. Each one had their own house keys and could therefore come in and go out without having to disturb the others.

We speak to them about anything that would interest them. However, I believe they tell us only what they want to. They would bring their friends home and we would greet them and chat before leaving them to themselves. We allow them to "do their own thing" and try as much as possible not to be obtrusive. We therefore have a good relationship.

One Sunday morning, when we were all at home, Indran came down to the breakfast table and said that he wanted to talk to both Samala and me. So we sat down at the breakfast table and he announced to us that he planned to get married to Premala Pathmanathan! Samala and I took this news happily. While we were talking, Ravi and Dharm came down the staircase. They had positioned themselves there to watch our reaction and response. I think they were pleasantly surprised that we did not ask Indran why we had not been told earlier.

They know that we had a preference for our sons to marry Tamil girls from good homes. Perhaps this is a universal aspiration for well-meaning parents, to hope and pray that their children will marry 'their own kind'. Some would regard this hope as being parochial but I do not agree. I believe that the basis for this aspiration is that we believe that marrying your own kind would increase the marriage compatibility and provide a stronger foundation for a happy and lifelong partnership.

We were happy to welcome Prem to the family. Our origins were similar. Our ancestors hailed from Jaffna in Sri Lanka and she came from a good family. Prem's mother visited us with Prem and we took an immediate liking to her sweet and gentle manner. Her father had passed away when she was very young and her mother Mrs Ambigai Pathmanathan, like a typical Jaffna lady, had worked hard as a teacher, saved and sent all her three children abroad for higher education. Prem, who is the eldest, read law, Ravi did medicine and Sheila studied accountancy.

I have described Mrs Ambi as a typical Jaffna lady as most Malaysians of Sri Lankan origin would go to great lengths to sacrifice to send their children for the best education possible. That is why this community, although one of the smallest in Malaysia, has done well even without direct government aid.

Indran and Prem did most of the arrangements for the wedding, which they wanted to be small and meaningful. So they drew up the wedding invitation list. We had about a hundred of our relatives, a hundred of Prem's relatives and about a hundred friends from both sides. That was a small crowd by the standards of weddings of most of our friends. But both Indran and Prem sensibly insisted that they wanted to have only friends they knew and not necessarily those that we knew!

Most of our peers have had large weddings. They had them in big hotels, but Indran and Prem chose the Hyatt Saujana in Subang.

Indran and Prem had a pretty wedding. They were married at the Wesley Church in Kuala Lumpur. He looked dashing and Prem made a lovely radiant bride. Samala sang a solo in church as Indran had requested. Her voice came out beautifully as she reflected her joy over the wedding.

The reception went off well. Indran's friends made all the toasts. He said he did not want any elder to give a long speech. Leonard Arif, Paul Subramaniam and Kevin Tan ribbed him almost to the point of embarrassment and the assembly of close friends and relatives enjoyed the blessed marriage and relaxed evening.

Member of the Securities Commission (1989)

In my last year at Bank Buruh I was appointed by the Minister of Finance, Dato' Seri Anwar Ibrahim, to serve as a member of the newly established Securities Commission with Dato' Dr Munir Majid as its first chairman. I considered this appointment an honour since we had some distinguished members on the commission who were my former colleagues and old friends: Tan Sri Clifford Herbert and Tan Sri Aris Osman, the Secretaries-General of the Treasury; Tan Sri Ali Abul Hassan, the head of the Economic Planning Unit; Tan Sri Othman Yeop, the Secretary-General of the Ministry of Primary Industries; and distinguished lawyers like Azat Kamaluddin and Kadir Kassim.

The work on the commission was heavy and quite demanding. It was however challenging and stimulating as we considered the excellent reports prepared by the very professional staff of the commission. Munir was a very able chairman who demanded and got high standards from his staff. It was a pleasure to read their reports. I believe that the high standards they had were second to none. I wish that the same high standards were prevalent in many more places, both in the government and the private sector as well.

There was much to read and I was finding it difficult to give much time to my work in the Commission. Furthermore, I was getting wary of the heavy responsibility of keeping the secrets of the deliberations of the Commission. I had enough of that kind of strain when I was in the Treasury. There I had to shred all my secret papers and avoid the company of my friends, in case it was thought that I was sharing some of the budget secrets with them. But the budget came out only once a year whereas the public followed the stock exchange on a daily basis. Some people gambled on the stock exchange so that they ate and slept over the stock exchange. This meant that some of them would do anything to get any information they wanted. I used to even be asked whether a certain counter would be on the agenda of a meeting of the Securities Commission. I suppose even that piece of news helped them gamble. Of course, I refused to give them any information. But I was getting peeved. So when I had finished my term of two years on the Securities Commission, I declined to a further extension on the grounds that I was then working for a public listed company. They pointed out that I could 'declare my interest' when something came out about the Sunway Group of companies. But I politely declined their kind invitation to continue to serve for another term. I had done enough of 'National Service'!

Joining the Sungei Way Group (1994)

After I left Bank Buruh, Tan Sri Jeffrey Cheah asked to meet me at his lovely house in Bangsar one Sunday for lunch. I thought that it would be a private lunch but when I went there I found that Puan Sri Susan Cheah, Dato' Chew Chee Kin, Dato' K.L. Tan, Yeow Thit Siang, Henry Yuen and Yau Kok Seng had been invited too. The lunch turned out to be a subtle interview. They asked me about my work and experience and my views on a wide range of subjects. It was altogether a pleasant ocassion. The food was good, the ambience at Tan Sri Jeffrey Cheah's house was conducive and the company and conversation were invigorating. I felt enthused by the occasion, thanked Tan Sri Cheah for the fine lunch and left on an upbeat note, without really knowing why I felt so.

The following morning I saw the President of the Sunway Group, Tan Sri Jeffrey Cheah, at his office. He offered me terms that were as good as and in some ways better than what I had been earning as CEO of Bank Buruh. I was appointed Corporate Adviser to the Sunway Group and Executive Director of the Asian Strategy Leadership Institute (ASLI). I was also later appointed Executive Director of Sunway College, which is part of Sunway Group.

I was given a comfortable room on the 18th floor of Menara Sunway. Dato' Chiew Chee Kin, the Managing Director, was on the same floor. He and Henry Yuen, the special assistant to Tan Sri Jeffrey Cheah, as well as Puan Sri Susan Cheah, were most helpful in getting me to adjust to the new environment. I was just getting to know the senior staff in the company and in ASLI and was getting to enjoy their fellowship and the work, when I had to stop work for over a month, due to a medical problem which I will elaborate upon next.

37.
MY HEART BYPASS

I HAD taken my periodic medical examination under my good old friend Dr Joe Irrawally. The stress test was difficult but I had done well. The doctor advised me to do more exercise and to keep fit to retain my clean bill of health. So when I was invited to attend the 'Langkawi Camp' by the Prime Minister's Department, I gladly accepted. I felt that going to the Langkawi camp would give me the opportunity to have a break, to take part in the socioeconomic, political, and spiritual discussions that I enjoy. I would also be able to take part in the semimilitary exercises to continue to keep fit and to maintain my clean bill of health!

The experience itself was enjoyable. Dr Mahathir and his deputy, Dato' Seri Anwar Ibrahim, were there with several other ministers and political leaders as well as leaders in the civil service and business community. We had discussions late into the night and dialogues with the Prime Minister and the Deputy Prime Minister on the state of the political and socioeconomic development in the country.

At the end of the week-long camp, we were taken on a jungle hike. We climbed up and down the hills and valleys through some thick jungle. We had to ford rivers and cross precarious bridges. Some of this was quite nerve-racking. In the end of it all, I was very tired and almost exhausted. When the team had to choose an imaginary 'casualty', they readily selected me. In retrospect, I thank God that nothing really happened to me during the jungle trek as I would then have been a real casualty!

After the camp, I returned to work, happy with the thought that I had 'passed the test' and that I had made the tough physical course without incident. However, I noticed that I was out of breath when I climbed steps or exerted myself. I thought that I was not exercising enough as the doctor had told me to do. So I resumed my morning walks which I had done for many years. This time I walked more regularly and for longer distances. However, my shortness of breath did recur from time to time.

When Samala and I visited Dato' Dr Sarvananthan to see his kind wife Dr Ratna who had been ill, he asked me about my health. I told him that I was happy that I had gone through the rough jungle-trekking in Langkawi, but I felt short of breath sometimes. He immediately reacted that I should see him for a check-up. I just laughed his suggestion off and told him that I had had a stress test just two months earlier and that I had done well. But I added that I felt that I was not physically fit and that I should be doing more exercises. Nevertheless, Dr Sarva insisted that I should see him and Dato' Dr Robaayah of the National Heart Institute for a second opinion and another check-up. I still felt that it was not necessary and let the matter rest.

One early Friday morning a fortnight later, Dr Sarva rang me up at home and said that he had arranged for me to see Dr Robaayah at 12 noon that day. I was a bit concerned that he should fix an appointment for me, not knowing whether I was free or not. Nevertheless I agreed, partly to get the matter over with and also because I felt it was the least I could do to respond to his sincere concern for me. So I went to see Dr Sarva. He gave me a general check-up and an ECG, and then we went to the Heart Institute and waited to be called by Dr Robaayah.

Incidentally, the late Dr Joe Verghese was also waiting to see Dr Robaayah, so all the three of us had a long chat. When we found out that Dr Robaayah was delayed with an emergency case, I rang my secretary Haema to say that I was delayed and that I would return to the office in the afternoon after my medical test. Dr Sarva took me for a light sandwich and we returned to see Dr Robaayah. I felt that we could postpone the appointment but Dr Sarva insisted again that I stay for the stress test, so I relented and I thank God for it!

Dr Robaayah examined me and then took me with Dr Sarva for my stress test. I started walking on the treadmill. But after my first stage of just three minutes, I began to feel tight in the chest and I could sense the concern of the doctors and the medical staff as they monitored the recordings on the machine. I began to get seriously out of breath as I was struggling to keep pace with the speed of the treadmill. At that point, the doctor-in-charge shouted that the machine should be stopped!

Then they suddenly rushed around and got me to place a pill under my tongue. They carried me on a stretcher and gave me oxygen as they wheeled me quickly to the Intensive Care Unit! Apparently, if I had carried on with the stress test, I would have had a heart attack! Thank God that Dr Sarva had insisted that I go for that stress test. I had got heart pains but not a heart attack. It happened at the best place possible, at the National Heart Institute. I then knew and felt that God was with me.

Dr Sarva rang Samala and she came immediately. I was in the state of near-shock as it was the last thing I had expected. I always thought that I was very well with all those medical tests just two months before and with all the annual checkups that I had been regularly going for. In fact, I had never had any problems with my cholesterol, blood pressure diabetes or obesity. I never smoked and had never had any serious illnesses in my life. The only time I had been in the hospital for an operation or any serious treatment was when I had my tonsils out and when Dr T.V. Nesaratnam had arranged to remove the painful boil I had in my groin.

(But previously I had also been admitted to Universiti Hospital on suspicions of a heart attack in 1982, but it had turned out to be a false alarm! I had just returned from an official meeting in Japan with Tengku Razaleigh and went to the Treasury the following day for a *gotong-royong* (cooperative cleaning up) function. I had helped to clear out a blockage in a deep drain. I then returned to my mum's house to fetch Samala. I had a drink and some lunch, and then I suddenly felt weak. I went to lay down, thinking that I was tired with jetlag and after the hard work at the clean-up. I begun to sweat lightly too, so I called my good friend, Dr Iyengeran, who lived nearby. He insisted that I go immediately with my brother-in-law Soren Beck to Universiti Hospital. They observed me for a week but could not find any signs of abnormality. So I was discharged with a clean bill of health.)

I had to go for an 'angiogram' at the Heart Institute the following Monday to find out the severity of the narrowing in my arteries. But I had been asked to lunch with Dr Mahathir and a visiting professor the next day. So I asked Dr Sarva if I could attend the lunch and then come back for my ECG on Monday. I still believed that I was well and that I just had 'an episode' due to tiredness. Dr Sarva promised to let me know early on Saturday morning to give me time to go home and change. But that Friday night I had a restless night and some chest discomfort. When Dr Sarva visited me at 7am on Saturday he and Samala persuaded me to cancel the luncheon appointment with the Prime Minister as my health was more important. For the first time I felt that I might have been wrong in assuming that I was all right. Now only the angiogram (or 'The Gold Standard') could tell the truth about the real state of my health.

Sunday was a quiet day at the hospital. Samala and the boys, my mother, Tina and Kamal came to visit me. They all looked quite solemn and that concerned me. This is why I still feel reluctant to visit friends in hospitals. We could be causing anxiety inadvertently instead of providing comfort and cheer. But of course it is quite a difficult role for any hospital visitor.

Dato' Dr Yahya Tun Awang (now Tan Sri), the head and chief surgeon at the National Heart Institute, visited me. He was extremely kind and reassuring. He explained to Samala and me about the angiogram procedures and advised me not to be anxious, as he was confident that all would go well. He talked to me about my lifestyle and expressed surprise that I had shown no symptoms of any cardiac problem. Nor did I exhibit any of the usual 'risk factors'! But he said we would just have to wait and see what the angiogram had to show.

I had to have a complete shave for the angiogram as my groins had to be very clean since the thin catheter had to be sent up to the heart through the artery in the groin. The shaver told me with some exasperation that he had not seen a more hairy pair of legs!

I had a restless night as I waited for the angiogram the next morning. Although it was now a routine procedure, it was still a serious matter as the dye that was to be sent up through the blood vessels could sometimes cause a reaction. Some people had even collapsed on the operation table although it was quite rare. Only 0.5 per cent of those who go for the angiogram have problems.

Early on Monday morning, I was wheeled to the operation theatre for the angiogram. I was nervous and prayed earnestly for God's blessings. They cleaned me and a sterilised plastic sheet was put over my stomach and legs. Dr Robaayah then came in and in a very gentle way explained to me what I would be going through. She said that I would be given local anesthetic, which meant that I would be fully conscious right through the angiogram. I could even watch on a TV screen (if I wanted to) the catheter being pushed up to my heart.

I thanked her for her explanation and they gave me a jab for the an-esthetic. She explained that she had inserted the catheter and that I could now watch it moving slowly up the artery, from my groins up to my heart! I watched the whole scene on television with awe. There was no pain at all. I just 'felt' something moving within me. Then Dr Ro-baayah alerted me that she would be releasing the dye and that it would cause 'a hot sensation'. It was good that she warned me. I then braced myself for this warm feeling that went through my whole body. It was as if I was having a hot shiver that went up from my hips to my head. But it was over in a few seconds and I felt normal again. They took a few x-rays and then it was all over as Dr Robaayah slowly with-drew the catheter.

They wheeled me out and allowed me to rest as the anesthesia wore off. After some time Dr Robaayah came out of the operation thea-tre to see me. She was warm and comforting as she told me that the angiogram had been successful. She then gave the verdict. She could see that I had three serious narrowings. If it were just one or two slight narrowings, she would have recommended angioplasty. This meant in-serting an instrument into the narrow arteries to widen them. But in my case, she would recommend to the surgeon, Dr Yahya, open-heart surgery!

I was disturbed and distressed by the prospect of surgery. I had not expected such a serious outcome, particularly since I did not have any of the usual risk factors. No doctor had even warned me of the possibil-ity of arterial disease in spite of my regular check-ups. There is a moral to this story. Only God knows what's inside us. We get to know about our poor health only when it is often too late. So all those who think they are all right should always think again. Only God knows! That's the message I have for all my friends who care to listen.

Dr Yahya came to see me in my ward. He sensed my anxiety and comforted me. Samala was always courageous beside me. She was a real pillar of strength and I thank God for her. Dr Yahya once again said that I was an unusual case, as I did not have the usual risk factors. For this reason alone he felt very confident that the surgery would be successful. He said that the only reasons for my problem could be due to hereditary factors or accumulated stress. Whatever it was, he thought that since the arterial narrowing was quite severe, he advised that I should have surgery as soon as possible. If I chose not to be oper-ated on, I could be discharged and lead a normal life as I had been used to, but he could not guarantee when I could be faced with a heart attack! I took his advice and agreed to have the surgery.

Dr Yahya then told me that he had a slot for surgery the following Wednesday—just two days from that Monday—the day of my angioplasty. It was all so bewildering; I said I would leave the decision of timing to him and then he asked me with his characteristic humility whether I would want him or someone else to do the surgery. I exclaimed, "You, of course, Dr Yahya. Who else do you think I would want!" He just smiled and made the necessary arrangements right away. After all, he had operated on Dr Mahathir as well. I could not have had a better cardiac surgeon than him.

It was a time of great concern. It was a time of waiting and of hope and prayer. My relatives came to see me and so did many good friends from the office, including Tan Sri Jeffrey Cheah and Puan Sri Susan Cheah who offered to pay my operation bill. But I was a retired government official. The government would pay for everything except for a very nominal fee.

The Tuesday before the operation was quite traumatic for me. As the relatives visited and prayed for the success of my operation, I sometimes felt that I would not see them again. That night before my operation my elderly mother prayed for me with my own immediate family and other close relatives around me. As my loving mother prayed, I broke down and cried, for I felt that if God called me home at the operation theatre the next morning, this would be the last prayer from my mother for me. Samala came to me and wiped my tears and they all realised that it was time for them to leave me to rest—and pray.

My family were the last to leave me for that long night that I had to go through alone before my bypass operation early the next morning. While they put on a brave front, my eyes were wet as I wished them goodnight. They left me with a word of prayer that God would bless me with a good night's sleep and a successful operation the next day. Then they reluctantly left me to myself. I suddenly felt all alone.

The nurse came in soon after at about 9pm to give me my medication and sleeping pill to ensure that I would be able to sleep. The lights were put off except for the reading light. I read the Bible for comfort and assurance. The scriptures calmed me. I prayed for grace to survive the operation and to be well again. But I also prayed that, if God wanted to take me, then I asked God to take me straight to Him. I was now resigned. I said repeatedly, "Lord, Thy will be done. I surrender myself completely to Thee."

Despite the sleeping tablets, I had a restless night. I would get up at odd times in the night to recall my past life. I asked God for forgiveness for the many misdeeds in my life and I prepared myself for any eventuality and to meet my Maker. I wondered if my feelings were similar to those of condemned prisoners on death row, on the eve of their execution. Perhaps their feelings might be far worse. But every time I prayed I felt a sense of peace that passes all understanding!

Early the next day I got up and prayed at about 6am. Then the nurse came in to see if all was well. Soon Samala, Ravi, Indran and Prem came in, and I was reassured to see them. I wanted to have a bath as I was told that I would not be able to do so for a few days after the operation. Furthermore, I thought to myself that if God were to take me, then I better go to Him clean! It's awesome how the imminence of death is always present at that time before a bypass operation or any other major operation. Or was it just me who felt like that, I do not know.

Ravi kindly came into the bathroom with me to help me bathe. I dried myself and slipped into the gown that they gave me to go into the operation theatre. I thought quietly to myself that it looked like a shroud! We prayed and the nurse then put me on a narrow stretcher on wheels and gave me an anesthetic jab. That was it. I was now slowly wheeled away to the operation theatre. Samala kissed me and my loving family held my hands as they all committed me to the Lord's protection. The nurses good humouredly told me that they would keep my lunch for me as they wheeled me to the operation theatre.

I prayed as I moved closer to surgery. I was at peace and a calm feeling descended upon me. I could feel the anesthetic slowly taking affect on me. When I reached the operation theatre, there was Dr Yahya with his reassuring smile to welcome me. I recall that he said "Don't worry, you'll be alright". I remember replying, "I leave myself in God's hands and through Him, in yours!" he smiled again. He gave me another jab and I soon faded gradually into oblivion and God's keeping.

The next thing I knew was that I was in the Coronary Care Unit (CCU). I came around and slowly opened my eyes and saw Samala's compassionate face and heard her ask, "How do you feel, Ray?" I acknowledged her presence through my eyes and a smile, as I was all wired up and immobile and exhausted. The next 24 hours were critical.

If I pulled through, it would show that I had no complications and that I would recover. I needed full rest. Samala and the good doctors and staff ensured that I got as much rest as possible. Many loved ones and visitors were politely requested to let me rest.

I was soon moved back to my ward and I began to heal. It was now up to me to do my best to return to normal life. I was determined to do so, with God's help. The real problem was to get rid of the phlegm that had accumulated in my lungs as a result of the operation. I was advised to keep a pillow close to my chest to help me reduce the pressure on my ribcage as I coughed out the phlegm. My ribcage had been literally sawn open for the operation. That is why the operation is called 'Open-Heart Surgery'. Thus each time I coughed, the pain was severe as the wired ribcage strained. I would hurt under the pressure of the act of coughing. Thank God, my coughing bouts were not intense. I had seen some other patients go through excruciating pain. Not being a smoker helped tremendously.

I began to walk slowly after about three days, although unsteadily and with help, in case I lost my balance. That would have been bad, so I was encouraged to take a step at a time. I felt that I was returning to childhood. It was psychologically distressing, as we will see later on. It was a time of prayer, reading, resting and receiving a limited number of visitors. I used to get depressed and tried hard to fight back the post-operation blues. In about three weeks I was back home and feeling better.

Institut Jantung Negara (IJN)

I have to say that the doctors and staff at the Institut Jantung Negara (IJN) were marvelous to their patients and to me. I always felt that there was help at hand anytime I needed it. Dr Yahya would see me at least once a day and encourage my recovery with warm assurances. My anesthetist, the quiet and unassuming Dr Karthigason and the other doctors in the operation team, would drop by on their rounds to say hello and keep track of my progress. The facilities at the IJN were excellent and the services were efficient. The nurses were polite and I felt well treated.

The overall standards were high and I often wondered why the same level of dedication and commitment could not be shown in the other parts of the government machinery, particularly at the middle and lower levels of the public service.

My cousin Dato' Dr Sam Abraham visited me often. So did my nephew Dr Anand Bhupalan. Dr Devan Pillay and Dr Sunita Bavanandan (whom I had known as children). They would stop by and enquire about my well-being. Sunita used to come in to check on my condition and wish me goodnight before going home. I felt good that they showed so much concern.

Once I went home it was obviously more comfortable, more re-laxed and just more normal than being in the hospital surrounded all the time by doctors, nurses, patients, suffering and even death. The at-mosphere at home was obviously more cheerful. I would spend the quiet hours reading on the verandah by the garden. It was also easier to receive more visitors, who broke the monotony and helped me get my mind off the operation and it's consequences. Most of all, it was good to be home with the family and to eat Samala's carefully prepared food, with no oil, no fries and no fats. Nevertheless she made the food appe-tising.

But I soon realised that my real problem was psychological. I would feel depressed and wonder if I would ever get back to my active self. Would I be treated as an invalid. Getting up in the morning, I would have the blues heavily upon me. I would just feel depressed, without knowing why. I tried to probe into the source of my depression and then slowly began to realise that it was perhaps my sense of my personal worth that I now doubted. I wondered how long it would take me to become as self-confident as I had been. There were sometimes excruciating thoughts, especially when some well-meaning but thoughtless person would ask whether I could eat this or that or do this or that or even suggest that I should stop working and retire for good. Where was my life heading? I kept on asking myself. Only I, however, could provide the right answers with God's help. So I decided to fight back and counter the negative thoughts that were haunting me.

I consulted Dr Sarvananthan and when he agreed that I could go back to work for a few hours a day, I jumped at the idea. I returned to work, thankfully, in about four weeks after my operation!

Then Tan Sri Azman Hashim rang me up to enquire about my health. When I assured him that I was looking forward to getting back into mainstream activity, he asked me if I felt well enough to appear on his television programme to discuss the 1994 Budget on the night of Budget Day. I readily agreed without thinking about whether I could actually handle the situation. I had to read the budget documents, prepare some notes and get ready for the TV programme in just two hours, after the budget speech was delivered at 5pm that evening. But I was surprised that I looked forward to this TV opportunity. Inside me I realised that I wanted to prove to myself that I could handle the challenge.

I appeared on TV and performed pretty well. Many people who saw me on TV said that I looked very tired and thin and told me that I should not have subjected myself to that kind of pressure, so soon after a major operation. But I was proud of myself that I did it. I felt that I had proved to myself that I could now return to the mainstream of an active life and wondered what God had in store for me in the years ahead.

I have discussed at length the circumstances leading to my heart bypass, the operation itself and the trauma of my post-operation days, only to provide those who may have to go through similar circumstances, the opportunity to appreciate and understand what they can expect.

To those who, fortunately, will not have to go through this kind of trying experience, it is well worth their time to try to avoid it—if they can. Thus the moral of my story is that 'only God knows what is in us and what is in store for us'. So please let us not be arrogant to think that we are in full control of our health and our lives. There is a God above who knows and does what is best for us.

38.
THE SUNWAY GROUP

I WAS GRATEFUL and happy to be back at work. My duties as Corporate Adviser to the Sunway Group of companies meant that I provide my views and comments on any issue referred to me and to provide advice at meetings especially at the Executive Committee that met at least twice a month. From time to time I was asked to sort out problems with government agencies. I also did a lot of representational work such as representing Tan Sri Jeffrey Cheah on several governmental and non-governmental committees as well as in my own capacity. My representational role enabled me to project the Sunway Group in both the government and private sector circles.

At ASLI, I worked with Mirzan Mahathir who is the president and also with Dato' Michael Yeoh, the executive director of ASLI. I enjoyed the work at ASLI since it was very much up my street. For instance, I was made chairman of the Strategic Issues Forum of ASLI. This forum was composed of about thirty CEOs from major corporations who interacted with top officials, experts, ministers and ambassadors who addressed us about once in two months. I took part in the discussions and helped to stimulate brainstorming among the group.

At its early stage I found the ASLI staff were young and inexperienced. This contrasted significantly with the better and more experienced officers I had been dealing with at the senior levels of the civil service. Thus I had some problems in communicating with them on the same wavelength. I was careful about maintaining high standards but it was with some difficulty that we were able to maintain acceptable levels of performance. As time went on of course, the quality and standards that Mirzan, Michael and I wanted were achieved.

Furthermore, there was always the concern that we were a bit "top heavy". Thus there was some reorganisation and I became the director of ASLI and thus gratefully shed my 'executive responsibilities'. Thus I was spared having to do the day-to-day operational work.

I was happy to take a more detached view and yet be involved in chairing some of the many ASLI conference sessions and also taking part as a panelist in several of their forums. I enjoyed this new arrangement even more.

I am glad to be associated with ASLI as it gives me the opportunity to share my experiences with the government and private-sector participants at conferences. Here I could also keep learning from the foreign gurus and others on the latest developments in management technology all over the world. It is also good to be associated with ASLI, which is about the biggest and the most successful conference organiser in the country. It is especially gratifying that ASLI is established on a 'not for profit' basis. This means that it is able to get the moral support from the top government leaders, the intellectual cooperation from academe and, just as importantly, the financial backing from leaders in the business sector.

I have no doubt that under the strong leadership and with the ability and influence of Mirzan Mahathir, and the enterprise and experience of Dato' Michael Yeoh, ASLI will do even better in the years ahead.

The lesson to be drawn here is that an organisation that is well led and managed can progress rapidly, when its motives are not merely to make money, but to promote national aspirations and to operate on sound business principles, such as ASLI.

Sunway College (1996)

About this time in 1996, Sunway College was without a principal. The college had had many principals in eight years of its existence! This fact alone would tell any management consultant or even a good observer that something must be wrong!

Michael Yeoh had spent half his time at ASLI and the other half as principal of Sunway College. Given the heavy work and the management problems at the Sunway College, it was not the best of arrangement. It was necessary to get a full-time principal but if it was not possible, then it was necessary to get someone who could spend more time at the college as its principal. But ASLI too needed some streamlining and consolidation in its management, so it was decided that Michael Yeoh should spend all his time at ASLI and that at least in the interim, I should take over as principal of Sunway College!

That was a surprise to me. And I am sure it was a bigger surprise to those of my university mates who would never have thought that their playful colleague at university would one day become the head of a large private college of about 5,000 students.

Dato' Chew Chee Kin had previously been keeping an eye on the college among his many duties. He was the able and enterprising managing director of the Sunway Group of companies. Together with the founder Tan Sri Jeffrey Cheah, they had built the company to become a huge conglomerate in just about ten years. He had from time to time got himself more involved in managing the college. It overcame its problems and built a good external image. But as managing director of the group, he had to focus on other priorities.

When I took over, I was given the mandate to improve the administration and standards of the college. I had a series of discussions with the academic and administrative staff. I could see that morale was not high and discipline was not good either. Some heads of departments had been comfortably placed for too long. As the principals changed so frequently, the heads of the academic departments became more entrenched. They created their own little "empires" and had their own little camps.

The staff association was pretty strong for the wrong reasons. For instance, they had called for an Extraordinary General Meeting to discuss the supply of milk powder before I took over! This was because the administration had changed the type of milk for their morning coffee, which in any case was provided free! When I heard about this, my general impression of the lecturers suffered. I wondered what could be the reason for this kind of mentality of these lecturers of higher learning! I had never come across this kind of attitude in all my years of management.

I tried to get the lecturers involved in the overall management issues of the college. I thought that since they lectured on marketing, management, public relations, accounting and academic analysis, they would be able to contribute to good governance of an academic institution. I thought that since they were so ready with their criticism, they would want to get more involved in the actual and practical problems of management in the real world.

But I was disappointed. Many lecturers rallied positively and even enthusiastically to contribute towards improving the college. However, there were also some lecturers who felt that their job was to just teach and do nothing else. Some were reluctant to come for extracurricular activities, while others were not even keen to come for academic and career guidance programmes for potential new pupils and their parents.

I felt that the college would improve only if I had the academic heads of departments and leaders committed to quality and the active promotion of the college. If the academic leaders were sufficiently dedicated to the cause of providing good education, then I thought that the lecturers under them would also respond favourably. But I soon found out that good leadership was lacking in some areas at the more senior academic levels.

Many of these senior staff had become jaded. I tried to motivate them but they were really far gone. They thought that as senior lecturers they knew a great deal more than anyone else. They had been teaching young students just out of school for so long that many of them genuinely felt that they could not learn anymore. Worse still, some of them believed that they could not be told anything by anyone. I had checked around with some of the other principals of colleges and some university vice-chancellors and administrators and they confirmed my suspicions that many lecturers fancied themselves as 'prima donnas'!

The culture was such that it was difficult to change. Many of them asked why they were not paid as well as their peers in the management and professional classes who earned much more than lecturers!

I decided with Dato' Chew that we could not go on like this and that we needed to change the culture to improve the college. There was no other way. Many attempts had been made before to change and improve them, but they were all shortlived and inconsequential. But we needed a structural change. I believe that if you want major change rapidly, then you have to be radical and strategic in your management approach. Previous measures were soft and not sustained. The opponents to change were tough and wanted to maintain the *status quo*.

I encouraged the heads of programmes to take their own initiatives to improve their departments, their academic results and their overall performance. But they would invariably come out with some excuse or other to justify their old easygoing styles of management. No one wanted to rock the boat. Some of the college leaders were even populous in their approach with their staff. "You scratch my back and I'll scratch yours" was the unwritten code of conduct for many of them. But the bottom line had to be good academic performance and profits. Just because the owner Tan Sri Jeffrey Cheah did not insist on profits, it did not mean that the others should take advantage and do the minimum.

I gave the senior staff more time to reorganise and to show more commitment and better performance. But I could see little response. So I decided that the best way would be to put the pressure on, to get better performance and better results. I developed a whole new series of performance criteria, like punctuality, preparation of work, the teaching load targets, monitoring of teaching standards and academic results, meeting deadlines and the ability to cut costs and generate revenue. Many heads of programmes demurred and resisted being assessed. I persisted and did not give in unless they had good reasons for their resistance.

The pressure was on them like never before. Many of them went behind my back to complain. My most senior lieutenants also requested me to go slow. But I felt that one had to proceed purposefully. Otherwise the whole purpose of the exercise, which was to change direction and to move forward, would be defeated—as in the past. That's what the staff wanted to happen and that is exactly what I refused to give in to.

At this time, the market for lecturers was tight. Many new colleges were outbidding each other to get more staff to manage the growing demand for college education. There were therefore many pull factors operating in the market for college teachers. I was also providing many of the push factors. Hence the results were quite easy to anticipate. Those who could not take the new pace and pressure to deliver properly and on time felt the squeeze more severely. When they found that their appeals to the higher authorities were not gaining sufficient support, they began to quit. I realised that my pressure for quality and better academic results would cause some of the poor performers to leave. I was prepared for the consequences. This is why the whole exercise worked this time, compared to the past. Then the changes that were introduced were *ad hoc* in nature, and not followed through in a sustained manner.

Within six months of my taking over the management of the college, about eight of the senior heads of programmes and administration left the college! I also changed some of the leaders, to ensure that those who succeeded them would promote higher academic and professional standards at Sunway College.

I fulfilled my mission. Now it would be easy to get the college moving up towards greater heights. Once the negative leaders were removed, the others would follow the new and better leadership that had been carefully handpicked from within and from other colleges.

I reviewed and discussed my views on the future direction of the college with Dato' Chew and Mr Henry Yuen, who is an experienced and mature person with sound judgement, and had served on the board of directors of the college. I explained to them and to Tan Sri Jeffrey Cheah that I did not enjoy day-to-day executive and administrative work at the college. I was asked to do a job and in the true tradition of my civil service background, I had done it and achieved the desired results.

But now I would rather leave that responsibility to someone else, while I could continue if necessary, to deal with only overall management and the external relations of the college, especially those pertaining to the Ministry of Education. What we needed now was to let the wounds heal and to allow the college staff to recover from the necessary shock treatment that I had administered.

This responsibility of doing the day-to-day administration therefore went on to an able young man, Mr Lee Weng Keng, who had a quiet but firm style of management. We believed that under the circumstances, where there was now hardly any resistance to positive change, his style would do. Tan Sri Jeffrey Cheah appointed Lee as director of the college, while I became Tan Sri Jeffrey Cheah's deputy chairman. The new arrangement worked well for all, especially for me.

After the necessary reorganisation, Sunway College today is a premier college in the country, ably led by its affable principal, Ms Elizabeth Lee.

39.
TRADE MISSION TO SOUTH AFRICA
(1996)

I CARRIED on as ASLI Director. ASLI had organised a South Africa-Malaysia Dialogue in South Africa in connection with Dr Mahathir Mohamad's official visit to that exciting, newly independent country.

Tan Sri Jeffrey Cheah and I went along on the PM's business delegation. The idea of the whole mission was to identify business opportunities in South Africa and to increase trade and investment there. Indeed this was Dr Mahathir's policy of expanding mutually beneficial trade relations on the basis of equality and equity or a 'Smart Partnership'. For this reason, Dr Mahathir has led many such delegations of Malaysian businessmen to so many countries that have been hitherto quite unfamiliar to Malaysian business.

We flew on a chartered MAS flight to Johannesburg. It was a long journey but the time passed by pleasantly since we were in good company. After the night flight we approached the sleeping giant of Africa. Over South Africa, the view from the air was awe-inspiring. The great green fertile lands and vineyards, the high, blue and purple mountains, and the vast dry brown deserts impressed upon me the grandeur of God's beautiful creation.

We had a fruitful conference in Johannesburg. The only problem was that the modern city was quite unsafe. We had to travel in groups or stay indoors. One of our delegates was actually mugged just outside our hotel. The blacks were never allowed much room in the city, under the Apartheid regime of the whites in the past. They had to go back to their shanty towns at night. Now they were allowed to live in and visit the city freely. Thus the unemployment rate has surged, as thousands who had never been to Johannesburg before now stream into the city for jobs they cannot get, and many turn to theft and robbery.

From Johannesburg we travelled by bus for about three hours to the hill resort called *Sun City*. It was beautiful up there. The buildings were like castles out of a fairy tale. It was picturesque and the whole ambience elates the spirit of all those who visit the resort.

From Johannesburg we flew to Capetown. The enchanting port was at the tip of the cape. The majestic Table Mountain and the craggy high mountains in the background, easily qualify Capetown as one of the most beautiful cities in the world. The Atlantic and the Indian oceans meet at a point just beyond the tip of the cape and adds a sense of mystique to this marvellous city.

From Capetown, we flew in a small light aircraft to Reebok that is situated in the high mountains in the desert. I thought that it would be hot in the desert but it was so cold in the mountains that we had to eat our lunch by a raging campfire that our hosts had made for us! Reebok is the town that makes the famous sports shoes, which bear its name. The purpose of our private visit was to see the mountain that is entirely formed of a green stone. Fancy driving up a jade mountain in a 4-wheel drive vehicle over some of the roughest terrain I have ever seen. Once up on the mountain, the view was fascinating. Walking on green jade-like rock made me feel very wealthy. Our purpose was to examine the feasibility and viability of mining that precious green rock. But it proved too costly a venture.

Briefing Dr Mahathir on the Plane

Back in Capetown, we prepared to leave for home. It was decided that since I was travelling back home on the plane with Dr Mahathir and his wife Datin Seri Dr Siti Hasmah Mohd Ali (now Tun), that I should try to get the opportunity to brief the Prime Minister on the SungeiWay business plans! Frankly, as a former civil servant I felt quite uncomfortable with this kind of assignment.

But I had to remind myself that I was now in the private sector. To the businessman what was important was to get the job done. It did not necessarily matter how it was done. The value system was different. To argue that it would be in bad taste to disturb the Prime Minister in the plane on a business matter, especially on an overnight flight, could be misconstrued as an excuse for not being 'enterprising or en-trepreneurial'.

I decided that I would find a compromise. I would only go up to the Prime Minister if the time and the circumstances were favourable. I decided that I would definitely not intrude on his privacy, unless I found him relaxed and in the mood to talk to me.

I explained to Dato' Ali, the Prime Minister's chief of security, that I wished to see the Prime Minister and he kindly agreed. I did not want to just go up and have the security guards shoo me off! At the right moment I got up from my seat and approached the Prime Minister who was seated at the aisle seat, with Datin Seri sitting at the window seat. I wished them both *'Selamat Pagi'* and immediately pulled out from my pocket the green jade stone and thin translucent slabs that I was carrying from Johannesburg. The green stone caught their attention, as it was truly beautiful. I held the thin slabs against the window light and they both admired the translucent and patterned fresh green colour of the natural stone.

I then showed them the plans to build the Sunway Lagoon Resort Hotel and the Pyramid Shopping Mall at SungeiWay's Sunway City. Dr Mahathir admired the colourful plans and drawings as I explained some of the significant features. I pointed out the large phoenix head at the entrance of the Pyramid shopping mall, and he quickly said that he thought that there would be some objections to it, since it depicted the pharaohs. I then indicated that we were prepared to accept modifications and any other image that he might want to suggest. I asked whether Dato' Jeffrey Cheah (who was not a Tan Sri at that time), could meet the Prime Minister to get his advice when we returned to Kuala Lumpur. Much to my relief, the Prime Minister agreed!

Malaysia, Inc in Action

Soon after our return we had a briefing with the Prime Minister in Kuala Lumpur. He very kindly agreed that we could go ahead with the building of the pyramid but that the face of the phoenix should be replaced with the head of a lion. Now the project would move. To me, it was a wonderful example of how the concept of 'Malaysia Incorporated' actually worked in practice. I believe that if not for the Prime Minister's advice and assistance, we would have had to wait much longer for the necessary approvals.

Today, the Sunway Lagoon Resort Hotel and the Pyramid shopping complex (one of the largest shopping malls in Asia) stand as testimonies to the concept of "smart partnership in action". The Resort Hotel also has the world's largest wave-making pool where you can actually surf. Tan Sri Jeffrey Cheah had brought back many ideas from Sun City in South Africa, and then improved on them with the help of Malaysian experts like architect Ray Cheah, engineer Yeoh Thit Sang and designer Nelson. Today, Sunway City has become world class, thanks to the vision of Tan Sri Jeffrey Cheah and the support of Dr Mahathir Mohamad, within the context of Malaysia Incorporated!

40.
MY NATIONAL SERVICE CONTINUED

ONCE a civil servant, always a civil servant, so they say. I must confess that deep in my bones and the recesses of my mind, I am still a civil servant in my values—and I am proud of it. Thus whenever I am asked to serve on some government committee, I have seized the opportunity to continue to serve the country. This time, however, it was not as a civil servant but as a member of the private sector and as a businessman!

Malaysian Business Council (MBC)
In 1994, I received an invitation from the Institute of Strategic and International Studies (ISIS) to serve on the newly formed Malaysian Business Council that was to be chaired by the Prime Minister, Dato' Seri Dr Mahathir Mohamad. I considered this invitation a great honour. At the first meeting, they elected four vice-chairmen from the private sector and I was one of them. The other four vice-chairmen were Cabinet ministers.

My responsibility was to chair the Committee on Science, Technology and Environment for Sustained Development. I chaired several preparatory meetings and presented briefings to the Council chaired by the prime minister in the first two years of the MBC. My term of appointment was for two years but it was extended by the prime minister for another term.

The MBC worked very well. It was the epitome of the concept of Malaysia Incorporated in action. The four ministers who are also chairmen of different committees met separately like those chaired by the four vice-chairmen from the private sector. Recommendations were made at the full MBC meetings in the presence of the prime minister and his deputy. Often enough these recommendations were referred to the Cabinet by the respective ministers concerned for decision. This is how interaction between the private sector and the government is strengthened and understanding between them is enhanced.

The MBC had great potential but I think that the big business representatives present could contribute much more if they participated more actively in the discussions. They seem to want to listen more than to give their views on the state of the economy or the business issues and prospects. I have never fully understood why they are relatively quiet especially when they have shown that they have the ability to create wealth. Is it their reluctance to run the risk of being thought to be critical? Is it because they are shy in front of the Prime Minister, ministers and other business leaders? Or is it simply selfishness that prevents them from sharing their views openly? Perhaps they would rather whisper in the Prime Minister's ear in private and thus steer clear of any problems that might arise, if they are more open in the large meetings that are held behind closed doors!

However, I have to admit that I have had no qualms about expressing my views openly and frankly at these MBC meetings. Sometimes I have been approached by other MBC members to express their views, which they themselves have been reluctant to articulate for one reason or another. When I have shared similar views, I have had no inhibitions expressing those views — to the appreciation of fellow members of the MBC. But sometimes some of my views have not been so well received by members of the government.

In my case, I have no vested interests. My interest is purely professional and nationalistic. I am neither rich nor obligated to political leaders. I do not seek favours for government contracts and concessions. I have no wealth to protect nor am I interested in hiding any skeletons in the form of unfair business practices or for not paying my taxes in full. Thus I suppose, I can say what I want, and when I want, provided of course I observe my own, self-imposed standards of saying whatever I have to say, however sensitive, frankly and freely, in a polite and respectable way.

I believe that if my criticisms are well-meaning and sincerely motivated, then I should say what I want to, as long as it is in the public interest. That is the way I was brought up and that has been my training and the traditions of the Malaysian Civil Service, to which I have been always proud to belong! I can only hope that this tradition of free and open debate is still being carried on in the civil service. But I have now some doubts as to whether this tradition has been observed as widely as before!

The business community has a much longer way to go in this regard. They tend to be more opportunistic and try to avoid the differences of view and argument, even on an intellectual basis. That is to me most unfortunate. The government will not be able to get the real truth and effective feedback, if the business sector is not articulate or intellectually honest enough. They should think of public and national interests instead of being overly concerned only with their bottom lines and of protecting their rear!

There is this feeling too that the civil service is not proactive enough in promoting the interests of the businessmen. This was one of the themes raised at the Southern African Dialogue held in Botswana in May 1997. However, it was pointed out that the private sector should not expect to get full support for any proposal that they make, as some of their proposals were often purely profit motivated without any care for public interest. How could, for instance, a dedicated civil servant approve a proposal that goes against the environment or which is exploitative of poor farmers, just for the sake of enriching wealthy businessmen and even powerful politicians?

Does it mean that the civil service is negative and obstructive, if it faithfully enforces law and order, rules and regulations and government policies that are designed for the benefit of the people? Our criticisms of globalisation and multinationals can also apply to our large domestic companies! We must practise what we preach too!

Matrade Director

As part of my national service, I was also appointed to the board of directors of the Malaysian Export Council called 'Malaysia Trade' (Matrade) in 1995 by the Minister of International Trade and Industry, Dato' Seri Rafidah Aziz.

The board was chaired by Tunku Ahmad Yahaya, chairman of Sime Darby, a fine gentleman from the royal household of Kedah and a very distinguished and able corporate personality. He was determined to make Matrade more business-like.

I was enthused by his leadership and was committed to support his initiatives to make Matrade more enterprising and aggressive in its export drive. He tried hard but I could see that he was up against the wall in trying to change the bureaucratic systems of the government. Since Matrade was financed wholly by the government, the policies, rules and regulations of the civil service had to be complied with. For instance, the salaries of the employees had to be aligned to that of the civil service. This was the surest way to inhibit the dynamism of Matrade officials. How could we have good export promotion if our Matrade officials were not sufficiently motivated due to relatively poor salaries, particularly since they operated in the business sector?

Because of the increasingly widening gap between the salaries of the civil servants and the businessmen, dissatisfaction and frustration tend to grow. Even when salary adjustments are made, they are usually quite inadequate. The moral of the story is that in the future we will have to ensure, as far as possible, that only those highly committed to serving the nation, should join the civil service. The civil service should in time become more of a calling. The government also should be more selective and pay civil servants much more if it wants a strong civil service.

The corporatised entities should also be able to operate like business organisations, rather than government departments. There is little flexibility or discretionary authority that can be exercised in Matrade. Mediocrity is thus encouraged as initiative and aggressiveness are constrained. This kind of atmosphere cannot promote the spirit of risk and enterprise. But these are the qualities that contribute towards a rapid expansion of trade and investment. Tunku Ahmad therefore had only limited success in Matrade, before his contract expired.

We were without a chairman for many months. It was difficult to get a dynamic businessman who was an active exporter and who would be daring enough to take new initiatives. After some time, the Minister of Trade Dato' Rafidah Aziz managed to persuade Tan Sri Kishu Tirathrai, the owner of Globe Silk Store, to take over the reins of Matrade. Kishu had the right credentials. He is a successful exporter, a wealthy businessman who would not stint on travelling and entertaining, although much of this would be borne by Matrade. He knows the techniques of trade promotions and marketing.

Being polite and cautious, Kishu was shy to take initiatives that might upset anyone. He tried to introduce new ideas and some initiatives. Before making any move, he always tests the water to get a feel of the situation. Before long he too was absorbed by the system.

The other alternative is for Matrade to become incorporated as a company. This would mean that Matrade would have to be 'privatised' in the full meaning of the word. Then the chairman and the CEO could hire and fire staff, pay better salaries, and impose a stronger sense of discipline and diligence. Most importantly, performance could be made the major consideration for reward. This approach would be much more market orientated and would motivate Matrade staff to really take off and contribute substantially to the rapid promotion of trade and investment.

The problems that I have outlined for Matrade are not peculiar to Matrade alone. These problems are almost typical of all corporatised entities. This is because they are neither fish nor fowl. They are neither government departments nor real business entities. They are caught in between and therefore experience the 'worst' of both worlds! The Malaysian government should therefore move faster to convert Matrade and other similar 'corporations' to full independent entities to operate along actual corporate lines. Unless this is done early enough, the government will have to face the consequences of these corporations becoming inefficient. Instead of being assets to the government and adding to wealth creation, they would become large liabilities that will weigh down the progress and slow down socioeconomic and intellectual development in Malaysia.

Member of the Education Committee

In 1997, I was appointed by the Minister of Education Dato' Sri Najib Razak to serve on the Ministry of Education Committee to review the terms and conditions of the teaching profession in the government.

Tan Sri Rahman Arshad was the chairman while several former heads of schools, academics and leaders in the education profession were appointed members. I was the only non-educationist on the committee. Maybe I was appointed because I was the executive director of the Sunway College or because I was a retired former Treasury officer.

However, what concerned me as I served on this committee was the disturbing decline in morale and commitment that I perceived during the meetings among the teaching profession. We met among ourselves as well as with a wide range of teachers, leaders of teachers' unions and Ministry of Education officials. Almost without exception I sensed or was told about the frustration of primary and secondary school teachers from all over the country. Many of the members of the committee also visited schools of different language streams and in different parts of the country.

There has obviously been a great deal of progress made that even the most remote areas in the country have some kind of school facility. This was in stark contrast to what had been the dismal neglect and marginalisation in the old colonial days, just about forty-five years ago. But there was no doubt that there is still a great deal that needs to be done to upgrade some of these schools in the rural areas, especially those primary national-type Tamil schools (Chinese schools are well supported by the community). If we do not do more for these disadvantaged schools and for other neglected remote schools, the children would be marginalised and Malaysia's progress will be impaired.

41.
TAMIL SCHOOLS

THE EDUCATION Committee found Tamil schools to be in the worst state. Their physical structures were often dilapidated in the estate schools: roofs leaked and the walls were in a state of disrepair. When it rained, the poor pupils would get wet. Often, classes would have to be suspended when it rained heavily. The furniture was sparse and usually old and broken down.

There are about 500 Tamil schools in Malaysia, mainly in the rubber estates. The British colonial masters brought Indian indentured labour from India, used them badly and treated them and their educational needs indifferently. Their socioeconomic status increased slightly through the pressure from their trade unions led mainly by able trade unionists like Dr P.P. Narayanan. Sadly, however, their educational standards remained essentially weak even well after Malaysia's independence in 1957. Although many years have passed since then, it remains a sorry story that a lot of Tamil school students and their schools and teachers have not improved much.

Why it has not been possible to improve the welfare of these 'depressed' estate Tamil schools is somewhat a mystery. There is no question of the citizenship status of estate workers. They are invariably all Malaysian citizens. The minority who are not would under normal circumstances qualify to be citizens. But many were illiterate. They could not keep the necessary documents to register as citizens, nor were they helped much. In the end, they just forgot about it all and remained as permanent residents with 'red' identity cards. But there is no valid reason to treat these poor people indifferently.

The estate Tamil schools do receive small amounts of assistance from the government. But this has been well below what the fully aided government schools receive and is woefully inadequate. As a result, the teaching standards in Tamil schools leave much to be desired and the academic performance is below the average, especially in Bahasa Malaysia. The dropout rate is thus very high, largely because of the low pass rate in Bahasa Malaysia. It is poorly taught by under-qualified Tamil schoolteachers who are badly paid and a large number of them are untrained. They often do part-time jobs outside teaching. Many of them have been active politicians, usually activists in the MIC, and often beyond reproach.

However, the Tamil schoolteachers are not entirely to be blamed for the dismal performance of their students. The parents of these unfortunate and helpless children also bear the responsibility for their children's bad record at school and in later life. The upbringing that these poor Tamil schoolchildren receive at home is highly questionable. The parents in the estates are usually poorly educated. Their wages are low and they are exposed to living in what I would call 'the Green Ghetto'. They are surrounded by rubber or palm oil plantations and the depressing and deep green jungle. They have been entrapped for decades and quite isolated from mainstream development. Consequently, they have a kind of siege mentality and have generally lost hope and ambition. Only those with the will to break away from the shackles of bondage of their indentured labour history have made it in life, outside the estates.

It is particularly regrettable that those of us in the professional class in the Malaysian Indian community have not sufficiently risen to the occasion to help our own kind. It is true that there are among the Indian community, many professionals, rich businessmen and a wealthy middle class who have rallied to the cause of uplifting the poor lot of the Indian lower income groups. But the number of such individuals is pathetically small.

Most of the wealthy and successful Malaysian Indian and Ceylonese are unfortunately too selfish and self-centred. They do their best to advance themselves and their own children and are almost indifferent to the welfare and future of the poor in their own community. I do not understand why this is so. Is it because of the environment? Is it because of our own culture and religion or just simply our narrow sense of survival, selfishness and self-centredness.

On the other hand, the Chinese schools have much greater support and sustenance from the Chinese community. Perhaps it is because the Chinese in Malaysia are generally far better off than the average Malaysian Indian. But I am also aware that even the small private Chinese schools in the small towns and relatively remote areas of the country, are strongly supported financially by even the poor Chinese communities. Is it because even the humble stallholders, the taxi drivers and the rubber tappers among the Chinese feel a greater loyalty to the Chinese language and Chinese culture?

From the government's point of view, I suppose it need not have to do much to improve the lot of the Indian estate workers or the estate Tamil schools because they do not feel much pressure from the Malaysian Indian community. They have their own problems in trying to meet the high demands and rising expectations from the *bumiputeras*, many of whom take it for granted that they deserve more and more, simply for being born *bumiputeras* or 'sons of the soil'!

Hence most of the Tamil schools and the Tamil school students are left to their own devices — to sink or swim. Regrettably, most of them sink to low levels of academic performance and at the lower levels of employment and incomes. Their prospects in life are poor. Their fates are sealed as they are not equipped to face the challenges of life nor do many of them have the will to succeed. They will miss out on the new knowledge economy.

Our traditional language can be a vital factor in our trade, economic and diplomatic relations with our countries of origin — that is Indonesia, China, and India. We should be proud of being Malaysians first and foremost, but also draw inspiration and enrichment from our roots. We cannot and should not deny our roots. Our roots give us our sustenance and our self confidence and sense of identity. We will know where we come from, without which we will not have sufficient basis to know where we are going and how to go in our long journey in life — with self-respect and confidence.

Proposals to Improve Tamil Schools

I would urge the following alternatives for the Tamil schools. I believe that these proposals would help to raise their standards and the future prospects of the thousands of Tamil children still going to Tamil schools. The proposals are as follows:

First, the government could provide more funds to strengthen the majority of weak Tamil schools. The government could buy over the few acres of private land for each Tamil school in the estates from the estate owners at reasonably negotiated prices.

Second, the estate owners themselves can also be persuaded to donate these small pieces of land on which the Tamil schools are built. After all, these estates have benefited so much from the sweat, sickness, sacrifice and loyalty of thousands of Indian labourers for so many generations. A little charity and goodwill would not therefore be out of place, compared to the rich profits that they have made over a hundred years at the expense of the Indian workers. Formerly, the British colonialists owned the big estates. Now mostly *bumiputeras* and Chinese own these estates. Should they not be kinder to their fellow Malaysian Indian citizens?

Third, once the land belongs to the Tamil school, then it would be easier for the government and the Indian communities to raise funds to improve the physical facilities in these schools.

Fourth, if the question of taking over the school land is not possible, then the government must make sure that Malay is well taught as a major subject in the Tamil school curricula. The new policy to teach mathematics and science in English could also help.

Fifth, Tamil can even be made a compulsory subject to be taught in national schools for those who want to learn it to assuage the fears of the Indian community.

The MIC leaders will have to seriously review how they can improve the Tamil schools and the poor academic performance in the Tamil schools. The government too will need to consider the problems faced by these Tamil schools. This is important in order that the Tamil schoolchildren will be able to get into the mainstream of the National Education System, and to provide the manpower requirements to enhance their employment prospects for Vision 2020.

If the adverse situation is allowed to continue, then the future of Tamil schoolchildren will worsen. They will fill the least productive and worst-paid jobs in the employment market or become gangsters, as is already happening. They will also most probably feel the greatest sense of alienation among the Malaysian population. This will not augur well for building a stronger sense of national unity and national harmony and progress in Malaysia. A country, after all, is as strong as its weakest link, which presently is the Tamil estate workers and students whose prospects for progress are depressing.

The Malaysian Indians and Ceylonese

Today, the MIC under the strong leadership of Dato' Seri S. Samy Vellu, is well established. The former record of open fighting and unruly behaviour is history. Dato' Seri S. Samy Vellu has injected a much greater sense of discipline and dignity in the conduct of MIC meetings and in the MIC organisation itself. Because the Malaysian economy has achieved notable success, the unemployment rates have been low. As a result, the Indians have had opportunities to get jobs. Many have migrated to the urban areas from the rubber and oil palm estates. The general welfare of the average Indian has increased considerably in the last 15 years.

The great efforts exerted by the early MIC leaders like John Thivy, Devaser, Tun V.T. Sambanthan, and Dato' Manickavasagam provided a sound foundation for the further progress of the Indian community. It must have been very difficult to organise the majority of the Indians who, in earlier days were mainly rubber tappers and labourers. While it is true that there were many professionals in the fields of law, medicine and education, there were much larger numbers of school-leavers who were employees of the Public Works Department, the Telecommunications Department, the Postal Services and the Railways. Those of Ceylonese or Sri Lankan origin were generally better off. They were hardly in the estates. When they were, they were estate supervisors and managers, like my late uncle, Barr Kumarakulasinghe.

My late father, K.R. Navaratnam, and my grandfather Kunaratnam on my father's side, were typical of the majority of those who came from Ceylon who worked in the clerical and executive services of the then colonial government. The Malaysian Ceylonese, however, did not generally join the MIC. They were different and jealously guarded their identity. The prevailing party today is the Malaysian Ceylonese Congress, which was recently led by my childhood friend, the late Dato' Dr Arumugasamy, and now by my cousin, Dr M. Thuraiappa.

Therefore, the Malaysian Ceylonese continue to be separate and distinct from the Malaysian Indians.

The Malaysian Indian and Ceylonese communities have lost out in a relative sense. However, the Malays and Chinese appear to have gained much more from Malaysia's rapid socioeconomic progress since independence in 1957.

One major obstacle for the Indians has been the poor condition of the Tamil schools. I have to add that if the political leaders had been able to do much more to improve the poor standards of the Tamil schools (or if they had improved the educational opportunities of the large number of Tamil schoolchildren in the country), the Malaysian Indians would be in a far better socioeconomic position today. We have missed many opportunities to accelerate the standards of living of Malaysian Indians and thus forfeited their chances to develop to their full potential. In time the Indians will be left further behind by the Malays and the Chinese and even the other minority communities, if more is not done for them now — before it's too late!

The Education, Welfare and Research Foundation (EWRF)

Thus several professional leaders have taken their own initiatives to help raise the educational standards and welfare of the Indian community. If the political leaders are not doing enough, others have to fill the gap.

One of the earliest of the major professional groups is the Education, Welfare and Research Foundation (EWRF). Some of the more illustrious leaders of the organisation were the late Dr K.K. Nair, Professor Marimuthu, Dato' Sadasivam the former head of the Malaysian Industrial Development Authority, Dr Thillainathan the financial consultant of Genting Bhd, Dr Iyngkaran, formerly in the University of Malaya and the Pantai Medical Centre, and Dr Thomas Verghese, a private medical practitioner.

Here again the trait of not being able to cooperate more closely for a common good cause has eroded the unity in the organisation.

CHILD

Hence a new organisation, the Child Health Information Learning and Development (CHILD), was formed to meet the growing demand for the dire needs of especially poor Indian children. The first president was Dr K.K. Nair, who did a great deal to establish the new organisation from scratch. He was followed by Krishna Bavan who was about the most senior Indian official in the Ministry of Education. Then Dr Iynkaran took over with his characteristic zeal, with Dr Thillainathan as deputy president, Murugaya, a senior accountant, Arumugam, an engineer, and Mrs (Dr) Kunaletchumy Iyengeran, as the principal movers in this dynamic, smaller voluntary organisation.

However, I still maintained a good relationship with the EWRF as well as CHILD. After all, they were both committed to the same ideals of serving the cause of the Indian community. Our people somehow seem to find it difficult to disagree in an agreeable way! We are perhaps too individualistic.

Both the EWRF and CHILD continue to do their commendable voluntary work of organising preschool classes in estates, training the teachers on a part-time basis and coordinating tuition classes for the Tamil school pupils from poor homes. But much more needs to be done to improve the prospects of Tamil school students.

The Sri Muruga Centres

Another major voluntary organisation committed to uplifting the welfare and academic performance of the Tamil school students is the Sri Muruga Educational centres.

The leader of this highly disciplined group is Dr Thambirajah, who was a professor specialising in Russian history at the University of Malaya. He was at one time active in the EWRF but later formed his own voluntary organisation called the Sri Muruga Centres (SMCs).

The SMC has a wide network and is perhaps the best-organised voluntary education organisation in Malaysia. They are highly centralised in their operations where Dr Thambirajah plays a strong leadership role. His SMCs have delivered much more than most Indian-based organisations. Perhaps this is because his style of management is firm. I do not think Indians mind being authoritatively led, provided that the leaders are sincere and those who are being led feel that they are benefiting from strong leadership.

It was at one of these SMC meetings that I openly said in a speech that Tamil schools are necessary but if we cannot provide good facilities, then we better ask the government to teach Tamil as a compulsory subject for Tamil children in the government schools. A leading Tamil daily misquoted me and said that I had proposed that Tamil schools should be closed. For this the newspaper called me a "traitor". However, with Dato' Seri S. Samy Vellu's support, the newspaper printed my letter of protest. I could have sued, as advised by some lawyer friends, but I asked myself why should I stoop to that low a level.

It was, however, gratifying to attend the 20th anniversary of the SMC on February 11, 2002, with Dato' Seri S. Samy Vellu as the chief guest.

Malaysian Community Education Foundation

There are many who feel that we cannot expect much from the political leadership from any quarter to help those from the Malaysian Indian and Ceylonese communities. The Indians at least have a larger population and a stronger political organisation in the MIC to help the disadvantaged Indians in education and employment. But the Malaysian Ceylonese community have little help from anywhere. In short, we have had to pull ourselves by our own bootstraps or fade away. But the Ceylonese community in Malaysia in general came from the more educated society of Ceylon during the prewar years. They attached much greater importance to the education of their children and had a strong tradition of saving, striving and sacrificing to send their children for a good education.

The Malaysian Ceylonese students went for higher education and had a strong representation in the Raffles College and especially the Medical College in Singapore, which were the only seats of higher learning for Malaya and Singapore then. However, it became increasingly difficult for Malaysian Ceylonese students to go for higher education mainly because they were not able to get places in the local universities, where the fees are relatively low. The government's 'quota system' made it difficult for admission to several local universities because Malaysian Ceylonese were included under the category of 'Others'. This meant that they had to qualify for the few places kept for 'Others' at the local universities.

There had to be a way out. Thus a few leaders of the Ceylonese community got together to form the Malaysian Ceylonese Education Foundation. The late Tan Sri C. Selvarajah took the lead with several committed professionals like Ipoh's Anglo-Chinese School headmaster P.S. Maniam, lawyer N.T. Rajah, veterinary surgeons Dr Kanagasabai and Dr Ratnasingam. I was persuaded as a young Treasury officer to serve in the committee in the early 1970s.

The foundation did well. It raised money from many members but there was never enough to meet the rising demands for more funds, especially to study in the U.K., Australia, New Zealand and the U.S.

On one of my official travels, when I went to Mexico City with Tengku Razaleigh for the Interim Committee meeting of the International Monetary Fund, my schoolmate, Ananda Krishnan, joined the Tengku, who was his good friend. Ananda was doing exceptionally well even in those early days and I asked him to donate to the Foundation. He heard me out, asked me a few pointed questions and decided straight away that he would support the Foundation.

Later Tan Sri V. Jeyaratnam, the prominent Ipoh lawyer, became the leader of the Foundation. I insisted that since I was a government official, I should therefore not take up a senior position on the Executive Committee. So they let me remain as an ordinary committee member.

Tan Sri Jeyaratnam did a fine job in raising about RM170,000 for the Foundation in the early 1980s. But that was a one time effort which was difficult to sustain. More significantly, even this large sum did not last long with so many applications for loans streaming in. So I spoke to Ananda Krishnan once again. He studied the situation carefully and we both agreed that the best way out was to convert the Malaysian Ceylonese Education Foundation into the 'Malaysian Community Education Foundation'. Ananda promised to establish a fund that would ensure a steady flow of funds, to provide adequate loans to Malaysian Ceylonese and, more importantly, to provide much larger funds to also finance the education of bright and needy Malay, Chinese and Indian students. The foundation's name was thus changed to the Malaysian Community Education Fund.

After the change of name and its restructuring, Tunku Mahmood was made president with a distinguished membership. Some of them were Dato' Rajendra, the chairman of the Rating Agency of Malaysia (RAM), prominent businessmen and professionals such as Khoo Teng Bin, Ooi Boon Leong, Dato' Dr Arumugasamy, Dr M. Thuraiappa, Ralph Marshall, S.K. Singam, Ms Chan and lawyer Anathurai, Executive Director Ramanathan and myself.

In retrospect, I am gratified at the wonderful way this education foundation has developed, thanks largely to the founders and to the high commitment of the members of the committee over the many years of its existence. Singam takes a very active interest in the Committee and has established a professional accounting and monitoring system for the Foundation. Thus, when there are so many public complaints as to the propriety in the management of so many other scholarship funds, we are satisfied that our system has been efficient and the loan recovery rate has been outstanding. The annual loans amount to about a million ringgit and the scholarship lending programme is expanding steadily every year. This is one of several Malaysian Ceylonese programmes that have survived and succeeded, thanks mainly to tycoon Ananda Krishnan's generosity.

42.
OTHER COMMUNITY SERVICES

BESIDES the community service that I have mentioned, it would be useful to briefly cover some of my other activities in voluntary work.

I was the vice-chairman of the Harvard Club of Malaysia for several years. Tan Sri Ahmad Sarji and Tan Sri Dr Lin See Yan have been the presidents for sometime. Both of them have worked hard together with the keen secretary Yusof and the prudent treasurer Dato' Fong Weng Pak (and later Dato' Venugopal), to build an impressive record for the Harvard Club of Malaysia. Tan Sri Ahmad Sarji was able to persuade the Prime Minister to give annual lectures for several years. The varied activities of the club have helped us to raise substantial funds to promote studies at Harvard and to contribute to a 'Harvard Corner' at the National Library.

I was also the vice-president of the Malaysian Economic Association for many years, until my retirement. When I was in the Treasury I took an active interest in the economic association as it was a rewarding forum to interact with the academics from the universities and economists in the business world. We were able to get a better 'feel' of the economy and the business response and the reactions to the Treasury's fiscal and monetary policies. It was at a Malaysian Economic Association conventions in Penang that Tengku Razaleigh agreed to my proposal to formalise consultations with the universities and the business community. He had had an informal meeting with many of the conference participants. I recall that Dr Chandra Muzaffar, Annuar Faizal, Dr Jagjit Singh Sidhu, Dr K.J. Ratnam, Dato' Dr Kamal Salih and several others, had interesting discussions with Tengku Razaleigh after an MEA Convention in Penang. He was highly impressed and agreed to have the Annual Treasury Budget Dialogues.

I have been on the board of the Kidney Foundation, representing Tan Sri Jeffrey Cheah, who has helped significantly to raise funds for this good cause. The kidney patients are a particularly unfortunate group of people. The dialysis is costly and often well beyond the affordability of the poorer patients. If they cannot afford regular treatment, they run the risk of renal failure and early and untimely death.

It is satisfying to spend some time doing my little bit serving on the board of directors, especially since they have got a highly dedicated team of volunteers and professionals who contribute selflessly to the Kidney Foundation. Moreover some of my old friends are in positions of leadership in the organisation and so it is easier to work closely with them. The late Dato' K. Padmanaban was the able president while Dato' Dr Sreenivasan was the indefatigable chairman of the Executive Committee who has been succeeded by Dr Gill while Dr Rajkumar served as a committee member. Thus the Kidney Foundation has been able to provide great service to the poor patients with the generous grants from the government. I am the chairman of the Audit Committee and with the ready assistance and advice from the highly experienced former Deputy Auditor-General, Mr Lyn Kulasingam, I find my responsibilities relatively light.

The former Minister of Entrepreneurial Development, Dato' Mustapa Mohamed was my younger colleague in the Economic Division in the Treasury, when I was the head of division. We worked well together and that must have been one of the major considerations for him to invite me to serve on this governmental committee, to advise on how to develop more entrepreneurs especially *bumiputeras*.

I have to state that it is to the credit of Dato' Mustapa that he refereed to me as "my guru who had taught me so much when I worked under Tan Sri in the Treasury", at the first meeting of the Committee. Very few ministers would have the humility to talk like that. I myself felt shy as he made those remarks in the presence of many corporate leaders. But that is the measure of the man. At the rate he is progressing, Dato' Mustapa has the capacity to go very far indeed in the leadership of the country. Later he became the Second Finance Minister with Tun Daim Zainuddin the First Finance Minister, and is now the chief executive of the National Economic Action Council.

MIC'S 50th Anniversary

Over the years I had always made myself available for consultations and advice on the socioeconomic issues facing the Indian community. The MIC is a member of the Barisan government and so I had felt comfortable about giving freely of my economic advice. But after I was attacked by a Tamil newspaper for my honest comments on Tamil schools, I felt that there was a lack of tolerance for open intellectual debate. I understood more clearly why many Indian professionals and intelligentsia had shied away from the MIC and its leaders.

However, in 1996, I was invited to take part in the MIC's 50th anniversary celebrations. This was, to me, quite surprising and ironic. The MIC planned a grand dinner at the Putra World Trade Centre to celebrate its 50th anniversary. Dr Mahathir was invited and the MIC had planned to have a citation read to him in his honour. The question arose as to who should read the citation. A search was made to choose "the right candidate".

One day, at the launching of Dr Mahathir's collection of his early writings by Tun Daim Zainuddin, I met YB Dato' Palanivelu. He grabbed my hand and proclaimed loudly, as if he had discovered a precious stone: "You are the one!"

I was startled and confused. He then explained to me that the MIC was looking for a suitable person to read the citation to the PM. I quickly turned down the request politely. He insisted and finally, I told him to consult Dato' Seri S. Samy Vellu again, as I was sure that he would agree that I was not the right choice. On the contrary, Dato' Palanivelu was confident that Dato' Seri S. Samy Vellu would agree that I would be the right choice. Dato' Palanivelu also insisted that Dato' Seri S. Samy Vellu had a lot of goodwill towards me despite my views on Tamil schools!

We bade farewell and I hoped to hear no more of the proposal. However, Palanivelu rang me up a couple of days later to say that Dato' Seri S. Samy Vellu was keen that I should accept the invitation of the MIC. The matter had been discussed at the Central Working Committee (CWC) of the MIC and they had agreed to invite me to read the citation to the PM!

I recalled that I was at one time quite close to Dato' Seri S. Samy Vellu. When my late father passed away, Samy Vellu came on three separate occasions to pay his last respects. He came twice to my father's house, and also to the cemetery in Petaling Jaya. I could not forget it. So I accepted the MIC invitation!

On reflection I wondered why he chose me to do the honour of reading the citation to the PM on that auspicious MIC occasion. I think it was because I am non-political, acceptable to the PM, and a professional. I am also of Sri Lankan origin so that there would be no problem over having to choose someone of Indian origin without raising charges of favouritism.

The MIC's 50th anniversary dinner was held in great style. I read the citation in Malay and Dr Mahathir was then presented a keris of gold. Both Dr Mahathir and Dato' Seri S. Samy Vellu gave impressive speeches and the function turned out to be a great success. I felt good that I had played my role and fulfilled the high expectations of me. I had done my duty to the Indian community, the MIC and writing — as a professional and not a politician or a party member.

43.
UNITY IS STRENGTH

IT IS VITAL that the government does even more to fulfill our national aspiration 'Unity is Strength'. Many of us tend to lose sight of this important theme of our founding fathers. The underlying theme is that we should actively encourage and draw inspiration and strength from our national motto. Instead, we often find that in the administration and implementation of government policies, we seem to be embarrassed to accept that we should be proud to be a unique multiracial society. We can indeed find 'unity in diversity'. Diversity should be our proud asset, and not a lamentable liability.

Already there is a subtle, growing culture that insists that the leaders of organisations, whether governmental or non-governmental, should have *bumiputeras* as presidents or chairmen. The vice-president could be from any race. However, the secretary can be Indian while the treasurer is usually Chinese. You see this happening in parent-teachers' associations, sports organisations and a whole range of clubs and societies.

My question is, why should the heads of organisations be mainly Malays or *bumiputeras*? Is it because it is thought that Malays must always be on top and that others must be on tap? Or is it felt that a Malay president or chairman should be more acceptable to the predominantly Malay civil service and the government? Would access to the government become easier if we have Malays to deal with the Malays at the top? Is it a reflection of the need for Malay dominance?

National Unity and *Bangsa Malaysia*

In the field of culture, the main emphasis is given to the promotion of the Malay arts and crafts, dance, drama and literature. While Malay culture is largely financed and promoted by government agencies, the other major Chinese and Indian cultures are left to be mainly promoted by the respective communities on a voluntary basis, with their own funding.

When it comes to official functions, state banquets and ceremonial receptions for foreign dignitaries, cultural presentations are essentially Malay in character. It is as if we are shy to admit that we are a unique multiracial and multicultural country, which is something we actually should be proud of. We have come a long way from the days of the terrible riots in 1969, to realise that our multiracial composition can indeed be our strength. But we must keep managing our ethnic relations firmly and fairly. We need to create a genuine *"Bangsa Malaysia"* (or the Malaysian race), where gradually everyone is treated equally according to his needs and abilities.

It has been a difficult path and there is a long road ahead. But I believe that we are slowly and steadily getting there. In the meantime, we all have to constantly remind ourselves that we are living in one of the most complex, if not the most complicated multiracial, multicultural and multireligious society in the world!

We will continue to need and exercise great understanding, wisdom and patience if we are to keep moving towards our noble goal of achieving our motto of 'unity is strength' through 'unity in diversity'. I believe that in the years ahead, if we continue to have strong, wise and benevolent leadership (as we have been blessed all these years), we will succeed in establishing a *"Bangsa Malaysia"*.

If, however, our future leaders are parochial and too partial to the *bumiputeras*, then the ideal of building a united Malaysian nation or *"Bangsa Malaysia"* will be jeopardised.

Since we reject Western dominance in the global, political and now economic fields, we should also be faithful to our ideals and reform our own thinking and our policies, to ensure that no one race will unfairly dominate the united Malaysian nation that we are all striving to build and hold so dear to our hearts. We should reject the hegemony of globalisation abroad and at home as well!

Multimedia Super Corridor (MSC)

Malaysia's future success will be spurred by the Multimedia Super Corridor (MSC). The 15x50km Multimedia Super Corridor includes the new capital city of Putrajaya, the new Kuala Lumpur International Airport (KLIA) at Sepang (which is about the largest and most modern in Asia) and the Petronas Twin Towers in Kuala Lumpur (the current tallest building in the world at 88 storeys). The MSC is the first 'green field' multimedia site in the world. It is intended to make it an international free trade zone and tax haven where any *bona fide* investor from anywhere in the world can come and innovate in Information Technology, with full freedom.

New 'cyberlaws' have been passed by Parliament to ensure the safety and security of intellectual property in research and new IT products, and to safeguard the integrity of transactions in the use of information technology in domestic and international trade.

The advertisements of this great experiment in establishing the 'green field' concept in Information Technology all over the world describes our multiracial society in the most favourable terms. It mentions that our Malay population can relate to the 200 million people in Indonesia, the 1.2 billion people in China and the one billion people in India, not to mention the large number of the world's Muslim population of about half a billion.

It is interesting that the government has openly accepted our multiracial society as an asset to our society. There has often been the feeling of regret expressed that our diverse society has been our liability. Surely our multiracial society is an asset as it plays an important role in reaching out to the billions in Asia, more effectively than any other country.

I also find that the MSC could well be the torch that will light the way to a new era of more open competition and less protectionism in Malaysia. In the field of information technology, Malaysians can feel more equal and competitive with the West than in many other fields of human endeavour for the following reasons:

Competitive with the Industrial West

First, information technology is relatively new all over the world. It is not as old as the advanced technology such as in manufacturing aircraft and space equipment. We therefore do not have such a wide gap to overcome. Most people are on a relatively level technological field at least in terms of learning and applying IT.

Second, information technology is 'soft technology'. It does not need highly sophisticated science that is necessary to manufacture the actual computers. We just need the less rigorous technological knowledge to 'use' the high technology computers. We have the ingenuity and imagination for this.

Third, we have actually set a unique worldwide precedent in enacting 'cyber-laws' that no other country has done on such a comprehensive and holistic basis. In this field we are therefore not just equal but actually ahead of the West.

Fourth, just as Silicon Valley set the lead in information technology, we have set the lead as an IT hub of Asia. We could therefore establish our own credentials in our own right, on equal terms, if we persist.

Fifth, initially we have to depend a lot on the technologists of the West, but as time goes by we will be able to have our own Malaysian technologists to take over and excel. We need to interact more and keep learning.

Sixth, it is possible that the MSC project could develop as a country within a country, with so many 'freedoms'. These are free tax regimes, freedom from censorship, freedom from employment restrictions of 'knowledge' workers and so on.

Seventh, it is possible the MSC concept of "openness" could spread throughout the whole of Malaysia and this would mean that we would be a fully 'liberalised economy'. This would change the whole face of Malaysia. We would be a free, open and highly liberalised country with a greater capacity to compete internationally. We will then be 'globalised'.

Eighth, when we become fully open and competitive, the National Development Policy (NDP) will no longer be fully applicable in restructuring Malaysian society. All races in Malaysia will be able to compete equally and freely, without restrictions. This way we will tap the best resources of all our people to the maximum.

Ninth, the only provision in the NDP that should remain firm would be the need to protect the poor and underprivileged. The second prong of the former NEP, which aimed to remove identification of occupation with race, will in time fade away.

Tenth, the implications of the MSC are radical and far reaching and could accelerate Malaysia's economic progress towards an industrial country when the MSC objectives are fully realised, even before 2020?

My Escalator Theory

With more IT, Malaysia is evolving into a state of greater competition. But we will have to remove the constraints that are found in what I illustrate in my own Escalator Theory.

My personal experience and that of many of my colleagues and friends is reflected in my Escalator Theory. I suppose this theory reflects the situation faced by the privileged and the preferred groups in most societies all over the world.

Let me explain my Escalator Theory. Given our affirmative-action policies, I have often visualised two men at the bottom of an escalator, ready to go up to the top of the escalator. There a judge will decide which of the two men will be the first to reach the top floor. But as we all know, in any escalator system, one side goes up and the other comes down.

However, the whistle is blown, the two men set off from the base of the escalator to reach the top. One of them has the easy ride. He just stands still on the rising escalator and maybe takes a few steps up, and he moves easily up towards the top floor. The other person has a real problem. He has to run against the downward moving escalator fast enough, not only to counter the downward movement of the escalator, but he has to run fast enough to beat his competitor to the top floor! He obviously has a much tougher job than his competitor, who rides up with the upward moving escalator quite effortlessly.

But they both happen to reach the top at the same time. The judge is therefore faced with a 'dilemma'. Who does he give the prize to? He congratulates them both and confesses that he has a problem in choosing the winner.

Finally, he announces that the one with the easy ride is the winner. Why? Because the other person is panting and sweating for having had to run up the descending escalator while the other competitor had a cool ride up on the ascending escalator. Can you imagine the feelings of the one who had to struggle up?

That is the way many in Malaysia view with much frustration, their careers in school, at work and in business. The privileged and preferred get the easy ride up, whereas the majority of the others have to struggle to go up. Even then, they lose out despite their strenuous struggle.

Obviously, this differential treatment cannot increase our society's competitive edge nor help Malaysia forge ahead in harmony, peace and prosperity. We will, gradually, but without taking too long, have to adjust the speed of the escalators and then eliminate the difference, for Malaysia to sustain its success in the future with national unity.

I must stress that the classification along the lines of the privileged and preferred is not necessarily made along ethnic lines. There are underprivileged from all ethnic groups and from all walks of life. What we need to do is to reduce preferences so that we would in time be able to develop the best people and the best in them, according to each person's ability. We have to be more competitive!

Then Malaysia will truly be great. I have no doubt that we are slowly but surely moving in that direction. But we have to make more reforms soon, before we lose out even more under globalisation!

The MCS in Retrospect

Meritocracy in the MCS is a case in point. The MCS is not sufficiently meritocratic or competitive. Having spent the best part of my life and career in the Malaysian Civil Service or what is now called *'Pegawai Tadbir dan Diplomatik'*, I naturally feel sentimental and nostalgic about the civil service to which I also owe so much.

I enjoyed serving in the government. I grew up and developed my life in the civil service. I continue to have considerable pride in the civil service. I am concerned therefore that the civil service should stay strong and professional as we used to know it.

But I have reluctantly come around to accepting the fact that the civil service has been losing some of its shine over the years. My reasons are as follows:

First, the civil service does not attract the best graduates in the market any more. The salaries have become even less attractive over the years. Consequently, we are getting some lower quality recruits.

Second, the promotion prospects have deteriorated. When we joined the civil service it took us only about 5 years before we rose up to superscale grades with much higher salaries and more perquisites than time scale officers. Today, these officers have to wait about 15 years before they can get to the superscale grade. Hence many promising officers get frustrated and leave for greener pastures in the private sector. Those who remain behind become demoralised and lose morale and productivity.

Third, the top civil servants suffer from a lack of relative continuity in service, as compared to the ministers and deputy ministers, who tend to serve for longer periods in one ministry, than their senior officials. Hence, the new Secretary-General knows less than his minister about the detailed policies of the ministry. Once he gets a good grasp of the ministry, he is transferred or, he retires at the age of 55. Most Secretaries-General assume that high office just a few years before they retire. The more cynical may wonder whether it is government policy to have the political leaders know more than the top civil servants. Nowadays, the ministers are usually more "permanent" than the secretaries-general, who were previously called "permanent secretaries"!

Fourth, it would appear that the concept of 'Malaysia Incorporated', has weakened the authority of the civil service. Big and small businessmen used to wait to see government officials for advice and approvals. Now they rather see the politicians and ministers. Once the minister concerned gives his approval in principle, it is difficult for civil servants to resist a business proposal, however undesirable it might be from a public interest point of view.

Fifth, because civil servants are not paid as well as their peers in the private sector, there is a loss of 'respect' for them. The civil servants feel a sense of loss of self-worth and self-esteem. The general feeling is that — "if the political leaders want to give the impressions that they are the only ones that matter, then let them take the responsibility to decide. We will only do what we are told. We will only implement and not take the trouble to advise, since many political leaders do not like to be advised against their wishes and pet ideas. They think they know everything." So let it be!

Unfortunately, many political leaders are thus not benefiting from the independent and professional advice of their experienced top civil servants as much as before. Consequently, the country and people will be the losers, especially with increasing technology and globalisation.

44.
MALAYSIAN INDUSTRY AND GOVERNMENT
FOR HIGH TECHNOLOGY

ANOTHER government-sponsored organisation that I have been closely associated with is the Malaysian Industry and Government for High Technology (MIGHT).

In 1994, MIGHT was formed (with Prime Minister Dr Mahathir Mohamad as patron and adviser) to persuade the public and private sectors to cooperate in prospecting for technology-based business opportunities. The initiative was largely taken by the Science Adviser to the Prime Minister Professor Tan Sri Dr Omar Rahman and Dato' Dr Michaela Smith of the Commonwealth Office in London. Between them and a few of us, we brainstormed the idea which was raised by our Prime Minister at the Commonwealth Heads of Government Meeting (CHOGM) in Langkawi in 1990.

I attended a meeting in London with this group where I presented a paper on how to encourage more cooperation between the government and the business sector. I was already in the private sector and I argued that the businessmen would support any proposal as long as it brought them profits. Thus, any kind of cooperation between the government and businessmen that resulted in business deals would be most welcome to businessmen. Of course most businessmen would like to jump at any business deal without having to bear any cost, if they could. But then it's up to the promoters, in this case MIGHT or the Commonwealth Partnership for Technology Management (CPTM) to be businesslike and to ask for some kind of fee from those who will benefit from technological cooperation with the government.

MIGHT has been doing a wonderful job at promoting collaboration in science and technology between the government and the private sector. This has been achieved at home in Malaysia and even overseas, particularly in Southern Africa.

In Malaysia, MIGHT has established a number of 'MIGHT Industry Groups' or 'MIGs'. The leaders from the private sector in different strategic industries chair these MIGs. For instance, there are MIGs in telecommunications, avionics, pharmaceuticals, freight, ceramics, composites, and the construction industry. These MIGs brainstorm on how the businessmen can work together with the government to improve the environment for greater efficiency and competitiveness through the use of higher technology.

Tan Sri Tajuddin Ramli, the former chairman of Malaysia Airlines (MAS), was the first joint chairman with Tan Sri Omar of MIGHT.

As part of the overall efforts to promote science and technology, I am also a trustee with Professor Ungku A. Aziz and lawyer Kandan for the Malaysian Inventors and Designers Society (MINDS). MINDS, under the enlightened leadership of Professor Dr Augustine Ong, has enabled Malaysian inventors to win many international awards.

Langkawi International Dialogue (LID)

The Langkawi International Dialogue had its first meeting in Langkawi in 1994. Prime Minister Dr Mahathir introduced the concept of promoting collaboration between the government and the private sector for mutual benefits. He talked about the need to promote 'prosper-thy-neighbour' policies rather than 'beggar-thy-neighbour' policies.

MIGHT organised this dialogue and out of the discussion, the philosophy of 'Smart Partnership' emerged. I was one of those who did not think much of this slogan. It sounded too simplistic and a bit of a 'clever by half' kind of definition. There were several applications of terms like 'Smart Cards', 'Smart Alecs', 'Smart Kids' and so on. But because it was a catchy call, it was adopted as the slogan for the Langkawi Dialogues and it has stuck. Now with the Multimedia Super Corridor and Information Technology and the Electronic Age, everything is going to go 'Smart'! So it was just as well that we have 'smart partnership' too.

But I was again one of the many locals as well as foreign participants who asked, *"What is so special and different about 'smart partnership'?"* We asked whether it was not the same as the well-established management concepts of 'joint enterprises', 'strategic alliances' and just plain simple business cooperative ventures, that take place by the thousands all over the world?

For raising these kind of questions in an academic kind of debate, I ran the risk of being misunderstood. Indeed some establishment types could make it appear as if we were not supportive of the concept of 'smart partnership'. But we were merely trying hard to probe our own thinking to see if we were promoting a genuinely new management concept or were we actually 'putting new wine into old leather bottles'?

It was just as well that we did not take all this 'smart partnership' presentations unquestioningly. For out of all this difficult debate emerged new thinking and insights that made us all realise that we could indeed promote a new philosophy in business relations between and among countries, between companies and between management and labour, and governments, through 'competitive cooperation' rather than the traditional Western model of confrontation and conflict.

"Smart Partnership" is actually about cooperation at all levels in a positive, non-exploitative way, where the partners work with each other for mutual and long-term gain, on a sustained basis, with "win-win" results for all sides. This policy is now well established and is getting more international support, especially in Africa, the Caribbean and now in the Middle East.

Smart Partnership

It is easier to grasp the essence of smart partnership by looking at the other side of the coin. Smart Partnership is, for instance, the antithesis of colonialism (and now imperialism in the political and economic sense). It is the response to the so-called 'new world order' under the World Trade Organisation (WTO). Free and unfettered trade sounds good but begs the question, "Good for whom?" Is it for the rich and powerful industrial countries to exploit the emerging countries in the South? Is it for the benefit of the rich and powerful countries and companies of the North that will use their superiority in capital resources, high technology and global military and diplomatic power, to continue to dominate the poorer countries in the South? Is the "new world order" meant to perpetuate "U.S. hegemony"?

In the business world, Smart Partnership is what we may call 'fair trade' without the precept or the practice of pursuing the profit motive *per se*, even to the extent of putting down the other partner. Smart partnership would also aim at fair prices for the consumer, reliable quality goods and services, and honest dealings that would last. It is good governance!

The first LID meeting at Langkawi turned out to be a major success. It was decided to follow up with other LID meetings. Several heads of government and heads of state had attended the first LID meeting. They were impressed with Dr Mahathir's presentations on the philosophy of the Langkawi Dialogue and the thinking behind 'Smart Partnership'. Tan Sri Noordin Sopiee also gave an analysis of

the underlying issues relating to 'smart partnership'. The LID meeting
with its special emphasis on 'Informal Dialogue' had set the foundation
and created the desire for more dialogues on this concept of 'prosper-
ing thy neighbour'.

The first LID was also genuinely 'international' in nature. About
half the delegates came from foreign countries and the other half were
Malaysians. The delegates included top national leaders, the CEOs of
multinationals and Malaysian corporates as well as senior government
officers. It was gratifying the way all these leaders from different fields
intermingled and interacted so warmly and informally. That was the
uniqueness of the LID meetings—the structure of the meetings provided the ambience for delegates to mix freely, to speak frankly, and
most importantly, to interact and learn from each other.

The heads of state and government, as well as other participants
sat at the same round tables of about ten each, in the same large hall
with about 25 tables all round. The businessmen were thus able to rub
shoulders with and even get advice from the political leaders on their
business proposals. Ordinarily it would be difficult for a foreign investor to meet or talk to a President or a Prime Minister or even a Minister. But at Langkawi it became quite easy for the businessmen to communicate with top government leaders. Many of them took full advantage of this rare opportunity to talk with the Ministers and senior officials casually over tea, lunch or dinner or at the numerous 'Interactive
Sessions' during the meeting over three days.

The second LID meeting was also held in Langkawi. Soon, the success of the Langkawi Dialogue was repeated at the Bahamas International Dialogue and the Southern African International Dialogue
(SAID) in Casane, Botswana.

45.
SOUTHERN AFRICAN
INTERNATIONAL DIALOGUE

THE SOUTHERN African International Dialogue (SAID) was held
in May 1997, in Casane, the beautiful holiday resort in Botswana.
About 12 Southern African countries were represented by eight heads
of government and top civil servants and business leaders. There were
about 250 participants and Malaysia was the only country outside the

region to attend and be represented by the head of the government —
Dr Mahathir. In fact, it was Dr Mahathir who often led the discussions.

This is because they saw him as an outstanding leader who did not
have to bow to the 'white man'. One of the Presidents in fact remarked
openly at the conference that he would like to be as outspoken as Dr
Mahathir is, but he could not, because his country is deeply indebted to
many powerful Western powers!

The suspicion and the resentment against the whites are quite
strong because the blacks in Africa were exploited for so long. Even
now the whites practically control the major industries in Africa. The
blacks have only a small share of the economies in Southern Africa.

This is another reason why the black leaders look up to Dr Mahathir. They see him as the leader who raised the status and socioeconomic welfare of the *bumiputeras* in Malaysia. They want to know how
they can achieve similar results for their own black people. They are
anxious to study our economic planning, our economic policies and the
techniques we used to achieve our aspirations of poverty alleviation
and the restructuring of our economy and society.

Third World countries want to find out more about our Vision
2020. Many of them have started to work on their own Vision 2020.
The Commonwealth Partnership for Technology Management
(CPTM) has been working closely with our own MIGHT to assist
some of these South-South countries, to draw up their own visionary
plans.

Our policies and practices for 'Malaysia Incorporated', Privatisation, "Look East", etc, were discussed at SAID in Botswana. I presented a paper on how to encourage greater participation of the private
sector in national economic development. My major thrust, using the
Malaysian model was that there must be the following prerequisites:
(i) strong and dedicated leadership; (ii) peace and security; (iii) reliable
fiscal and monetary policies; (iv) relatively clean government (there's
no absolutely clean government anywhere!); (v) a business-friendly
government and bureaucracy; (vi) pragmatic policies that are not fully
capitalistic or socialistic, but a practical mix of both ideologies, to suit
the national ethos; (vii) fair treatment to all communities, especially to
the most depressed ethnic groups and tribes (such as in Africa) in order for them not to feel alienated; (viii) a strong civil service that has
continuity and security of tenure; (ix) a fairly open and competitive

economy; and finally (x) a vision of shared values and aspirations, like the Rukunegara, the NEP and Vision 2020 in Malaysia.

SAID turned out to be a successful meeting. President Nelson Mandela agreed with Mr Cyril Ramaposa that "it was a 99 per cent success"! They agreed to hold SAID II in 1998.

I have to add that a group of Malaysians and friends played a significant role behind the scenes to help organise the dialogue. They were Tan Sri Omar Rahman, Tan Sri Kishu Tirathrai, Roger Bamborough, Dato' Salleh, Dr Tasir and myself. While the Botswana officials did a great deal of work to make the dialogue function smoothly, we Malaysians who were called the 'resource group' provided advice and guidance based on our earlier experiences at our own Langkawi Dialogues.

We felt good that we were able to be of service and that we were in a small way able to add on to Malaysia's good reputation at the dialogue. President Maseri of Botswana was so appreciative that he sent a few of us like Tan Sri Kishu, Roger Bamborough, Dato' Salleh and myself special letters of thanks for helping out in the preparations for the meeting at Casane. We were all touched by his kind gesture.

An African Safari

Casane, where the Dialogue was held, is situated along a broad river. The environment is rustic and almost as original as it used to be from the days of Adam and Eve. The nearest we in Malaysia have to the safari parks is Taman Negara where we have jungles that are millions of years old. The major difference is that you cannot see beyond a few feet in the jungles, whereas on the safari park one can look out to the horizon, over rolling plains and undulating grasslands, low bushes and trees. The animals roam and feed on the grass and shrubs — and other animals!

Because there is no thick foliage, it is much easier to see the animals all around you. It is very much like what we see on television of the safari parks such as in the popular programme 'Discovery'. But there is really nothing like seeing these animals at close quarters in their natural habitat, on land and in the rivers. In fact, you soon realise that in the animal kingdom, we humans are the intruders. They just walk by or keep grazing almost oblivious of our presence. I suppose they regard us as nosy tourists trying to find out how they live, just as some tourists who visit our *kampungs*, estates, new villages and aborigine settlements!

Some of us took an afternoon off just before the Dialogue began to 'go on safari'. We took a boat ride along the river. It was a small aluminum boat that could carry about eight passengers. The local boatman was very skillful. He used his motorboat to go at high speed along the open river and then slowed down and got very near to a group of hippopotamuses, rhinoceroses or huge elephants in the shallower parts along the riverbanks.

The boatmen were seasoned and brave while some of us, including myself, were uneasy. The hippos were so close that they could easily sneak under our light boat and literally lift the boat effortlessly and throw all of us into the river. We had also seen many large, long crocodiles lurking in the muddy banks and in the shade of the many little islands all along the river. What if we were playfully tipped off our little boat by these large crocodiles? What if the crocodiles came after us? In fact, it was not mere daydreaming. The possibilities were real, as some bizarre incidents had happened quite often in many parts of Africa. The boatman, however, assured us that the Botswana hippos, rhinos and crocodiles were "tourist-friendly"! But that was not much consolation when we saw some huge hippos that weighed several tons, open their gigantic jaws, as if to say, "I'm bored. I'd like to try some humans for dinner!" We soon anxiously asked the boatman to withdraw and to carry on with our journey of discovery on the African safari along the calm river.

River Safari

We went on further down the river when we came across a whole herd of enormous elephants bathing and frolicking in the river. The boatman switched off the engine and allowed the small boat to drift with the gentle breeze nearer to the elephants. We got to about 20 metres from the elephants so that we could observe them quite closely. But they were obviously observing us in return. They even seemed to be putting on a show for us as they playfully tusked each other and rolled over on their huge sides in the river to cool off. We were so engrossed with this wonderful performance that we did not realise that the elephants were getting closer and closer to us. We were rudely awakened from our reverie when the lead elephant of the herd, with its broad ears spread out, raised its long trunk and trumpeted loudly. We were all startled and then heard the engines of our flimsy motorboat restart as the alert boatman pulled away from the approaching bull elephant, one moment not too soon!

We were so relieved that we had moved off in time. The boatman however explained to us that the elephant would not have attacked us, but it was merely warning us that we had spent too much time encroaching on his herd's privacy! It struck us once again that we were in their territory and not they in ours. We were the guests who had overstayed their hospitality!

As we sped faster back to the hotel, we could see in the distant plains, the giraffes, deer and some wild cattle. We were thrilled as well as somewhat upset to see a ferocious lion racing across the plains to finally catch up and kill a gentle deer.

The image struck me as the exploitation of man by man, the rich over the poor, the strong over the weak — and the developed industrial countries over the developing countries. It made me realise that we have to be strong and even nimbler than the deer, to survive the onslaught of some avaricious powerful industrial countries that would want to dominate the developing countries! For them, globalisation could mean 'gobble-isation', like the ferocious lion that attacked and gobbled the meat of the helpless deer!

Along the way we saw hundreds of all kinds of beautiful birds, that flew freely all over the plains. They were high above the danger from predators on the ground and in the river. These birds were flying in formation, in small flocks, as the day was drawing to a close. The sun was gradually setting and it was exhilarating to witness such a grand and colourful sunset. The rivers looked like silver in areas where the sun's slanted rays hit the ripples of water. Large parts of the river shimmered in the sunshine. The horizon looked like a painted landscape of the bright colours of the rainbow. It was a glorious sight to behold, as we slowed down in our approach to the hotel and the reality of the man-made world of strife and turmoil. I pondered on how wonderful it would be if we had the best of both worlds — the rich gifts of nature and the wealth of the world, with peace all around?

The Southern African International Dialogue soon came to an end and we were all happy with its successful outcome. It surpassed our most optimistic hopes and expectations. We celebrated the success and the end of the Dialogue in traditional African style. We had a gala dinner, brisk speeches where the contribution made by Dr Mahathir was sincerely praised. After dinner we enjoyed rhythmic African music and dancing, that had a strong sentimental resemblance to our own traditional *joget*.

Almost everyone came up to dance — Presidents, Prime Ministers and other delegates. Dr Michaela Smith of the Commonwealth Partnership for Technology Management went up to Dr Mahathir and asked him for a dance. It was difficult for him to refuse her. Out of courtesy he obliged. I saw Dr Siti Hasmah sitting alone so I asked her to give me the honour. She was as gracious as her husband. Thus Dr Mahathir and his gracious wife joined other leaders briefly in a traditional dance, much to the happiness of our African hosts.

Mandela's Medal to Dr Mahathir

After the SAID meeting in Botswana, we were getting ready to return home when some of us were invited to go to Cape Town in South Africa to witness the presentation of South Africa's highest award to Dr Mahathir for his services to South Africa and socioeconomic development, especially in the Third World.

This was a rare privilege which we were honoured to accept. Tan Sri Tajuddin Ramli, the chairman of MAS, kindly offered to take us in his private jet to Cape Town, one of the world's most beautiful cities. I had been there before and I was glad to visit the picturesque city again. There is the 'Table Mountain', which is imposing in its awesome and rugged beauty. Then there is the attractive coast with fascinating old historic buildings, along the seafront and up to the Table Mountain, from where you get some of the most scenic views in the world. We had succulent seafood by the seashore and a good walk along the seafront before retiring for a well-earned restful cool night.

The next morning we set off to the Presidential Residence where President Mandela resided, to witness the ceremony for the presentation of the top South African award to Dr Mahathir. The President's official residence was like a palace. It was large, well architectured and altogether very impressive. As in most grand buildings, it was even more attractive inside. The decor was decidedly old Dutch, as could be expected. While waiting for President Mandela, Dr Mahathir and Dr Siti Hasmah, we were served good South African wine and fruit juices and enjoyed the rich ambience. I could not help observing the twist of fate and the obvious irony of the situation. Here in this palace of power of the former Apartheid regime, where cruel decisions were callously taken to suppress and exploit the black Africans in their own traditional homeland, resided the new black President Mandela! The previous Apartheid regime had incarcerated and persecuted Mandela for 27 years in prison. But now he was the undisputed leader of the whole of South Africa, ruling over both the blacks as well as his former white tormentors, in peace and harmony.

As we were admiring Mandela's official mansion, the great man himself arrived with Dr Mahathir and Dr Siti Hasmah. We could all see that everyone was close and warm with each other. Mandela shook hands with all of us, giving a kind word and a witty remark to each one of his guests. He would say, *"How are you today? Did you have a good rest? I hope you are comfortable. Have you had a drink?"* He is a very gracious host, indeed.

Mandela was revered as the "saviour of South Africa". Despite his terrible ordeal in his struggle for freedom, and his bitter experiences in prison for 27 long years, he exuded genuine warmth and sincerity. He has a wonderful charisma that is unbelievably impressive, particularly when he is observed at close quarters.

We were all soon ushered to the steps that led to beautifully manicured green lawns and a picturesque garden that overlooked the charming city of Cape Town where the Atlantic and Pacific Oceans meet at just below the Cape of Good Hope. The international press were all there to witness the award presentation ceremony.

President Mandela made a complimentary speech honoring Dr Mahathir. An impressive citation was read out praising Dr Mahathir. He then happily pinned South Africa's highest medal of honour on Dr Mahathir amid loud applause.

The international press raised a few questions for both Mandela and Dr Mahathir. CNN, BBC and other international television news agencies rolled their cameras after which we were invited for the formal lunch for only about 15 of us.

We took our seats, which were all arranged according to protocol. The long dining table was very elegantly laid out. It was a western meal. I was fortunate to sit opposite Dr Siti Hasmah, who was just two seats away from President Mandela, as she sat next to Dr Mahathir. The conversation was easy and relaxed and I was one of the few Malaysians who enjoyed the fine South African wine!

While enjoying our hearty lunch, the President called one of the black maids, and whispered in her ear. Then a sweet young lady came into the dining room. She went up to the President and respectfully greeted him. The President then introduced her to Dr Mahathir and Datin Seri as the maid's daughter, who he proudly announced, had been admitted to the university. I was impressed with his caring nature and his pride that his servant's daughter had made it to college. Such was the generosity of this great man.

I was seated between the South African Ministers of Defense and Telecommunications, and we discussed Mandela's famous book, *The Long Road to Freedom*, and their roles as freedom fighters. It was a fascinating experience. I enjoyed the conversation, but most of all, the privilege to attend such a grand occasion as President Mandela's guest — thanks to Dr Mahathir's award ceremony!

46.
MY PHILOSOPHY OF LIFE

I THINK it is only appropriate that I end my memoirs by describing my philosophy of life. I come from a simple and humble background. My family was not rich but somehow, we always had enough. There was nothing important that we lacked and we learnt to optimise on what we had.

My father was a simple man. He led a simple lifestyle. This was not only because he did not have much to spare but also because he was a plain man who was resigned to his lot in life, particularly since he had a difficult childhood, as he was orphaned early in his life. He was honest, strict in maintaining his strong principles, content with what he had and was quiet and reticent.

I am glad that I inherited many of his good qualities and absorbed them into my own philosophy of life. I believe in simplicity, thrift, good relationships and avoid being vindictive or malevolent. I tend to be close to those I like and keep a distance from those I find irksome.

I believe in hard work and try to do my best in whatever I do. I tend to be a perfectionist and to be pragmatic. My motto is:

Every day I do my best
And to God I leave the rest
I can't do better than my best
So I'll do what I can — and rest.

I always try to find the wood from the trees. When I am in charge of a project, I am concerned with the need to address not only the main issues but also the details because the details make the whole. But I would also expect those responsible at the lower levels of management to deal properly with the details. I would then scrutinise and supervise them to ensure high standards of overall performance, while I concentrated on the bigger issues.

I am a nationalist and get impatient with people who are overcritical and unduly negative. Those who are incorrigibly anti-establishment make me uneasy. I believe that one can be critical and constructive at the same time. There has to be a balanced outlook. Everything does not have to be bad. There must be some good in people, organisations and governments.

People who like to say, "Only in this country does this (bad) thing happen," put me off. It is as if they had made a complete study of the whole world situation and had arrived at that grave conclusion. Those who have not seen much of the world and the actual situation in other countries, usually make these kinds of remarks. The other groups are those who are basically biased and aggrieved and those who have migrated or intend to migrate.

My response to them is quite simple. I believe God has a purpose in placing each individual in the country of his birth. Unless there is wholesale persecution of race and religion, or anarchy, the individual has an obligation to do his best to serve the country of his birth.

There were times in my career in the civil service when I felt I was bypassed in promotions. Some of my *bumiputera* colleagues, whom I did not think were better than me, seemed to get promoted faster. But my response was to soldier on and forge ahead in the belief that in the end justice would prevail. I believe in man's basic sense of justice and fair play. I was aware that at the lower levels of government there were many who did not like to see me progress in my career. I also realised that if I got frustrated and slowed down, they would be the first to point their fingers at me and say: "There you are — he is not giving his best because he is not one of us."

So I decided not to play into their hands and undermine the goodwill and good faith of my many just and able seniors. This is where my Escalator Theory became part of my philosophy.

My lifestyle is simple but comfortable. Having grown up during the Japanese occupation, I have learnt to be hardy and financially prudent and to appreciate what God has given me and my family.

Bangsa Malaysia

My philosophy of "*Bangsa Malaysia*" has been my guiding light in my service to Malaysia. It is not based on the rejected theory of "Malaysian Malaysia" that was aggressively promoted by Mr Lee Kuan Yew when Singapore was part of Malaysia in 1963-1965. That theory contributed to resentment, suspicion and ultimately led to the dismissal or separation of Singapore from Malaysia. It reemerged recently when the Sequi movement raised its 83 demands and caused so much resentment.

I recognise the need to do more for the poor of all races and to give privileges to the underprivileged Malays. This is necessary to raise their socioeconomic levels to that of the other races, especially that of the better-off Malaysian Chinese. So, for some more time, we cannot have equal opportunities for all races. However, I believe that there is a limit to giving preferences to the *bumiputeras*, especially after they have been given good educational opportunities. If they are given special and preferred treatment right through life, then there is a danger that we will not be able to equip them to compete effectively in the new environment of liberalisation and globalisation and severe international competition. As prime minister, Dr Mahathir has said repeatedly, crutches must be removed.

Undue preferences given to preferred *bumiputeras* can also create divisiveness among the *bumiputeras* themselves. The vast majority will benefit far less than the minority of politicians and their children and the politician's limited circle of favoured friends. Thus an elitist class will be formed that may not identify closely with the aspirations of the vast majority of the people. The poor will thus progress much more slowly. This kind of trend would not be desirable and can be disturbing and damaging to socioeconomic and political stability!

To me "*Bangsa Malaysia*" (or the Malaysian race) can be defined as a concept where all Malaysians regard themselves as Malaysians first and then only their ethnicity. Anyone who believes in "*Bangsa Malaysia*" can be considered an "all-Malaysian" man or woman.

Although we have our various religions and cultures, we have many shared values such as our sense of identity, our sense of history and destiny and our common loyalty to Malaysia. We should feel proud that we are born in Malaysia, irrespective of whether our ancestors came from Indonesia, China, India, Sri Lanka or some other country. We are first and foremost Malaysians.

Hopefully, even the Malays will under the concept of *"Bangsa Malaysia"* consider themselves Malaysians first and *bumiputeras* second. This is more likely to happen when the NDP is phased out, when there will not be much advantage in calling oneself *bumiputera*. Even now, there is not much advantage in being a member of royalty, unless one is closely related to a rich, powerful or influential royal household. The same is true of the vast majority of Malays, unlike the favoured upper-middle-class *bumiputeras*.

Increasingly in the future, the premium will be on talent, competency and merit. The world of high technology and the knowledge industries will determine one's status in life, depending on how qualified we are to fit into the new world of technology and our ability to compete in it. Knowledge and the management of knowledge will be the great equalisers. No amount of privileges and preferences are going to help much. Those who are privileged and who become rich because of their family inheritance will find it difficult to maintain their status, unless they are competent and competitive themselves. There will also be growing resentment against those who became rich because of their connections.

With the Multimedia Super Corridor, Centres of Excellence would blossom all over the country and all Malaysians, regardless of their origins, would be able to develop themselves to their full potential. Then we would all have equal access to knowledge and the national goal of achieving more equality and national unity will be achieved. Only then would we achieve the status of *"Bangsa Malaysia"* in the truest sense of the term.

Religion

My religion has undoubtedly exerted a strong influence in my life. It is inherited mainly from my mother and deeply rooted in my subconscience. My father, though a good example of a man who loved God, was more informal in his observance of religion. I was born a Methodist Christian. My earliest recollections of religious practices are the times when I used to go to Sunday school at the Gospel Hall in Kuala Lumpur, near the present National Mosque. That little old prewar church is gone now. I remember that Uncle Charles Abraham used to drive his children (the Abraham cousins), Tina and I to Sunday school from Sungai Buluh when we were little.

Sunday school was something we looked forward to. We met friends from other schools and it felt good listening to Bible stories and to sing Sunday school songs. We enjoyed collecting little coloured pictures with Bible verses inscribed on them. Of course, the main motivation came from our mother. She would insist that we memorised the Sunday school texts and Bible verses. We had to recite them to her before we were allowed to go out and play on Sunday evenings.

As we grew up we joined the Methodist Youth Fellowship. That was even more exciting. We organised our own meetings and invited guest speakers to talk to us on religious and moral topics. We went for conventions and in the process learnt leadership qualities and built up our confidence in public speaking.

At the Methodist Tamil Church in Malacca Street where the headquarters of the Bank Bumiputra now stands, we had a very active Methodist Youth Fellowship chapter. There were several youth leaders like the two brothers Navarajasingam and Chelvarajasingam, the late Benjamin Niles, Sam Nalliah, the late Dr David Sarawanamuthu and the late Dr Rajah Ayadurai, who set high standards of leadership and organisation in religious, social and community activities. All of them became strong layleaders in the church in later life.

I recall attending a 'MYF Camp' at Pandamaran New Village near Klang, to help build a small wooden church. Leslie Abraham and I joined more for the fun rather than our religious conviction. However, there were Dennis Dutton and Ng Ee Lin from the Methodist Boys' School, who were very serious and prayerful even at our tender age of about 15 years. What we had in common was our enthusiasm in building the church under the supervision of the clerk-of-works. Dennis later became a bishop and a Dato', and Ee Lin became the senior superintendent of the Methodist Church. Leslie has also become a committed lay leader, while I have been less serious and formal in my religious commitment.

But I have always believed that religion is to be internalised and that it is a privilege to be shared privately between God and Man. We do not need to be expressive and formal in the observance of the ritual of regularity and even routine of going to church.

I attend the Wesley Methodist Church, Kuala Lumpur, which I have regarded as my church. Samala too enjoyed the church choir where she had taken an active part, especially when she used to give solos and conduct some of the church choir recitals. Our sons went to the Wesley Sunday School and obtained their religious training at the Wesley Church.

My Relations

Relations are an important part of my life. After all we should remember that they have been part of our lives from childhood. I draw a distinction between my immediate family and the larger extended family. I think this is only natural and fair.

As the eldest and only son, I have always felt a greater sense of responsibility to my loving parents and my four dear sisters (Tina, Angie, Julie and Georgie). My sense of duty and love for my family has been shaped by the need to protect and promote their early progress and well-being. Because our financial standing was not regarded as impressive by those who were attracted by mere social and economic status, our true worth was not sufficiently recognised in our childhood. Some misplaced self-esteem and some silly sense of self-importance, possessed some of those around us. But I think those who are like that get to know the truth at some time or other as they go through life.

Be that as it may, I am grateful that our immediate family has been greatly blessed. All my sisters have been happily married and our parents have been blessed with good grandchildren. We thank God that our dear mother Ruth Navaratnam has just celebrated her 97th birthday. We gave her a big 95th birthday party, with Angie, Julie and James coming from Australia. We pray that she will be with us for many more years to come. She generally enjoys good health and has a particularly alert mind. I owe her a great deal as I do to my late dear dad.

There are many kind and caring relatives with whom I remain close to and keep in touch. It is wonderful to have good extended families to whom you can turn to, in good and bad times, in joy and in sorrow. I try to get on well with all my relatives, especially those with whom I have a warm relationship. Despite my busy schedule I try to make time for them. Those relatives that I am less comfortable with, I see less often but nevertheless I have love for them that is founded in the past when they shared their love for me as a little boy. These are experiences we must never forget.

We are what we are largely because of the love and care of our parents, our immediate family and also the influence of the larger extended families, especially in our early years of growing up and character formation. We should be grateful for the good qualities they gave us so that we will have love and a positive attitude to them.

I would also like to acknowledge my loving gratitude to my in-laws, Albert, Kamal, James and Soren. They have regarded themselves as the 'in-laws' together with my wife Samala while I have been jovially referred to as the 'out-law', together with my sisters! I have to say that I have been really blessed with loving in-laws who have been close and caring, to me and especially to Samala, who is the only sister-in-law we have in our family.

My father- and mother-in-law, the late Mr and Mrs Dharmalingam, were always generous in their love and support. They never asked for anything, but gave of all they had. They were staunch Hindus, but never interfered in our lifestyle. We have a Christian home but they never intruded for they believed in basic grace and goodness and the universality of truth. We owe them a great debt of gratitude.

A close and loving immediate family is wonderful and I am grateful for that blessing. Good relations with the larger extended family are also important but we have to be selective and then adjust our distances in our relationships according to our compatibility. Otherwise there will be acrimony and disharmony which can be divisive and distressing. I believe I have found the balance with my extended relations and so I am at peace with them all.

47.
VISION 2020

I HAVE been impressed with Vision 2020. Tun Dr Mahathir Mohamad is a man of vision. He realised that Malaysians needed a goal to look forward to. Otherwise each community would look at each other to see what each one benefited from government policies and who got more and who got less. It is difficult to have full harmony in a complicated multiracial society, especially when the majority dominant race — the Malays — are mostly worse off than the other races. Such disparities had caused disharmony from time to time (as in the case of the race riots of 1969).

Hence it was important to give the whole country a vision of the future, a vision that would remove their preoccupation with what they have now, and to look ahead with greater confidence to the future. They had to be given a realistic dream that they could work for, a dream they could aspire for. It had to be a dream that would promise all communities a new life in a new industrial society, with greater equity, modernisation, higher technology and a better quality of life. It had to be a dream where all Malaysians would enjoy a more caring and gracious society, with religious tolerance and a pride in being Malaysian.

The Prime Minister's inspirational thoughts and concepts were developed into a new philosophy called "Vision 2020". Dr Mahathir set the nine goals. It is remarkable how this vital document has now become so successful in capturing the imagination of the whole country — right across race, religion and political affiliations. I believe that Vision 2020 will bring about a greater sense of identity and increasing well-being as Malaysia strives for greater socioeconomic growth, equity and fairness for all communities. As time marches on towards the realisation of Vision 2020, the preference given to the *bumiputeras* under the NEP and now the NDP, will gradually fade away. All differences in policy and treatment meted out to different races would hopefully slowly dissolve. And as Malaysia moves further into the realm of international competition through globalisation, there will be greater emphasis on giving priority to social needs, economic efficiency and meritocracy, and the preferential treatment that is racially based will become more economically and not ethnically grounded.

Globalisation in the 21st Century

I believe that the open competition and free trade that is developing at the MSC will gradually be extended all over Malaysia in the years ahead. As the free trade areas open up more and more, the whole country will gradually merge into the realm of globalisation where we will give 'national status' to all countries. This means that foreigners would be able to come to Malaysia and compete with us on an equal footing and vice versa.

We would have to compete with foreigners or lose out. There will be very little protection or preferences. The industrial countries will not allow special preferences for our nationals. Instead, they would gradually muscle in on us with all the pressures they can muster, to force us in the Third World to open up our industries and markets for their benefit.

The opening up of the markets will be universal. That means that we in the Third World or in the South would be given reciprocal treatment in that we will be able to trade and invest freely in the industrial countries, just as they will be able to trade and invest in our countries. But they will strongly resist the freedom in the movement of labour from poor to the rich countries!

I wonder how we will be able to match their superiority in technology and vast resources of capital and highly trained human resources in the future? We will only be able to compete and excel in areas where we have a strong comparative advantage. However, that used to be in rubber, palm oil, timber and tin. But we have lost much of these comparative advantages to more labour-intensive countries like Indonesia and now to Vietnam. Similarly, we will lose our competitive advantage in the manufacture of electronic and electrical components and air-conditioners to countries like China, India and Vietnam, where labour is much cheaper and even more skilled.

Then what will we in Malaysia be left with? Would it be manufacturing? Yes—but not for long. Since other emerging, developing countries or 'tigers' and 'dragons' will also be developing rapidly in the manufacturing industries, especially in the less-technological industrial sectors, Malaysia will invariably lose out. Malaysia would soon be caught in a trap between our rising labour costs and our low-technology manufacturing. The way out would be to go for high-technology industries and to rapidly develop the high value-added and more sophisticated service industries. This is why Dr Mahathir has had the visionary foresight to promote the development of high technology, especially information technology.

We have to move fast in IT if we are to steal a march over the other emerging or advanced developing countries. If we do not, we will be in trouble in the longer run and become 'also-rans'. We would drop out in the new world of globalisation.

Globalisation, of course, is good in the longer term. But we will have to phase into it at our own cautious pace; otherwise we will be 'gobble-ised'. Globalisation will then become 'gobble-isation'! But having adopted the new strategy of embracing information technology through the MSC, we must excel, otherwise we will fail. This could

Our sons (from left to right) Indran, Dharmen and Ravi
at our government house in Damansara in 1970

On the B.S.S. *Bernina* during a Mediterranean cruise with
Samala, Ravi, Indran and Dharmen in 1972

At the border of England and Scotland in 1986

My granddaughters Sunetra (left) and Suhanya

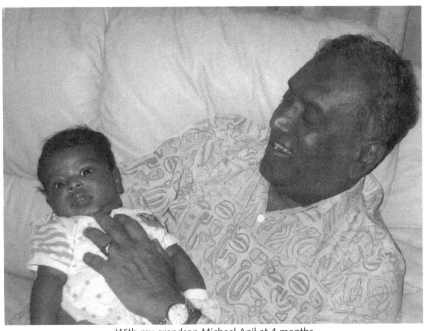

With my grandson Michael Anil at 4 months

Dharmen and my daughter-in-law Lina

Dharmen and Michael Anil Navaratnam

With my daughter-in-law Prem on her wedding day

Lina with Sarah and Michael

My mother, Ruth Navaratnam, at 95, with her six-month-old great grandson,
Michael Anil Navaratnam

Michael and Sarah with grandparents

Sharing a joke with two-year-old Suhanya

Suhanya with me in the garden at 9, Lorong Medang, Bangsar, Kuala Lumpur

Sunetra's first dance with me

Sarah at six months of age with her doting grandad

happen if Malaysians do not accept the challenge of change and take the necessary steps to move rapidly forward. We cannot take it for granted that we will change. We must work hard to change our mindsets and to innovate.

Already there are forces of resistance. This is due to ignorance, fear of the unknown, inertia and some bigotry from religious and other quarters. The government is undoubtedly aware of these problems and is taking steps to overcome them. However, the forces of change and resistance must be handled carefully yet firmly, otherwise the government's initiatives will fail.

My own experience and view of the Malaysian society is that we will have difficult times but that we will succeed. I believe that Malaysia has a great future only because I feel it is God's blessed land. We are among the few countries in the world that are free from all major natural disasters like earthquakes, tornadoes and erupting volcanoes. We have had all the man-made elements that could have made Malaysia a place of perpetual conflict and misery, but somehow we have held together. It is the Malaysian ethos and genius that I believe God has given us.

I believe Malaysia will continue to prosper in peace and harmony mainly because of the resourcefulness of all Malaysians. Our duly elected leaders, many of whom are dedicated, are also a major contributing factor. God willing, I hope I will be around for many years more to celebrate the validity of my favourable judgement and firm faith in Malaysia's steady march towards industrial-nation status by 2020!

48.
MY LATE SIXTIES

I HAVE NEVER heard of *diverticulitis*, until I suffered from it in 1997. It is the disease of the *verticuli* or protrusions in the large intestine. This condition can cause the large intestine to rupture!

One night, I had a bad stomach pain and went to see a doctor at a 24-hour private clinic in Bangsar. The doctor treated me for 'food poisoning' and I was much relieved.

A few months later, I felt the same acute stomach pain as I returned from a meeting in the afternoon. I went to see Dr Sukumaran, the company doctor for some relief. I described my history and after examining me he advised me to see a surgeon. So I went to see my close friend Dr Abel Arumugam at the nearby Subang Jaya Medical Centre. He examined me then called in surgeon Dr David Ramanathan for consultations. They decided that I should take a Barium Meal to find out what was the cause of the pain!

After examining my X-ray, they decided that I had to have surgery! I was shocked. I consulted my old university mate, Dato' Dr Jackie Metha, the chief surgeon at the General Hospital. He too agreed that surgery was necessary although he was quite confident that the 'apple core' shape of my verticulitis did not suggest cancer!

Once again Samala and our family rallied around me to give me courage and support. After all, I had had my bypass operation about only three years earlier.

I went through the operation in good faith. I believed that if my life had to end, then God would take me without pain. There was still no certainty that my intestinal growth was benign. It was only a few days after the operation that the doctors were able to confirm from the biopsy that the growth was not cancerous!

What a relief it was! I was most grateful to God for his mercy to me once again. I was also so thankful to the doctors and staff for their skill and care, especially to Dr Abel, Dr David and my university mate, anaesthetist Dr Radhakrishnan, for their concern and kindness. So life goes on and we have to make the best of it.

Dharm Marries Lina

Dharm became the best man at the wedding of one of his closest friends Lawrence Soosay, whose sister was the bridesmaid. They used to play hockey at the basketball courts at Bangsar on Saturday evenings.

After their games, Dharm would occasionally adjourn to Lawrence's house for a drink which was often served by Angelina (Lina). Dharm would also enjoy talking to Lawrence's father, Mr. Soosay, who was a longstanding schoolmaster.

Lina was a student of Samala's at the Bukit Nanas Convent in Kuala Lumpur. So she was known to our family, including Ravi and Indran who also played hockey at Bangsar.

I met Lina when she made a lovely bridesmaid at Lawrence's wedding and I was impressed with her sweet disposition. I think that wedding was the turning point in their hitherto casual relationship.

Soon they started to discuss their wedding plans. They got married at the Assumption Church at Petaling Jaya on September 26, 1998. The reception was held at the Sunway Lagoon Resort Hotel's Grand Ballroom. About 300 guests, mainly close relatives and friends were invited and they enjoyed the cosy and informal atmosphere, that is only possible when we celebrate with close relatives and friends. The staff of the Lagoon Hotel also went out of their way to make the function a real success.

I was hoping to invite my many friends, but I deferred to the couple's wish to have a relatively small reception that would be more meaningful to them. We are truly grateful that they are happily married and that Lina's family are such nice people.

Suhanya, Our First Grandchild

At sixty-three years of age, I was still without grandchildren. Our family was therefore overjoyed when Prem and Indran were blessed with the birth of their first child and our first grandchild, Suhanya.

She was born on the night of December 10, 1997 at the Subang Jaya Medical Centre. I recall seeing her for the first time as the nurse wheeled her from the lift and her eyes caught the ceiling lights. They were wide open and so bright. She stared straight at her father Indran, Samala, Ambi (Prem's mother) and me, as if to say "nice to meet you all and thanks for coming"!

We have since been blessed in 2001 with two more grandchildren. Michael Anil was born on November 16, 2001 to Dharm and Lina. Indran and Prem were blessed with their second daughter Sunetra on December 12, 2001. We are grateful for these lovely grandchildren, including a grandson, Michael Anil, who will bear my family name (God willing).

Suhanya comes home every weekday after school and Samala enjoys watching over her and teaching her. It is like a little school at our home, exclusively for Suhanya and Sunetra and at least once a week for Michael! They bring much cheer to us all and to Samala, who has rheumatoid arthritis.

Samala is quite comfortable at home, but she feels the strain when she goes out. Already Samala's condition has improved somewhat, especially after her successful hip-replacement surgery at Sunway medical Centre by Dr Lee Chong Meng and Dr Keeran's tender care.

I continue to admire Samala for her courage and faith and we pray that she will improve further.

Getting on!

At the age of 70, I still cannot get myself to retire. However, I can see the need to slow down further. I am happy and consider myself blessed that I am still quite active in public life. I continue to serve on several government and charitable committees.

A new voluntary organisation, the Community Support Network (CSN) was formed by two dedicated people, Dato' Douglas Lee and Dato' Ruby Lee. They are not only my longstanding friends but highly committed social workers who persuaded me to become an adviser to the CSN. We organised the first Great Cook Out in November 1999. We got donations of raw food and cooked tasty meals for nearly a thousand handicapped children from several 'homes' in the Klang Valley.

I have written for several years now and I still write a monthly column on economic developments in the *New Straits Times*. These articles have been rewritten, expanded and published in seven books. They are entitled *Managing the Malaysian Economy* (1997), *Strengthening the Malaysian Economy* (1998), *Healing the Wounded Tiger* (1999), *Malaysia's Economic Recovery* (2000), *Malaysia's Economic Sustainability* (2002), *Malaysia's Socioeconomic Challenges* (2003) and *Winds of Change* (2004). And with the completion of this autobiography, I feel even more fulfilled.

When I was a student at university, I never thought for a moment that I would be keen on writing that much! I believe that many of my unversity mates who knew my interests as a student would be surprised!

The proceeds from the sale of all my seven books have been committed to charity. The first donation was made to a poor 11-year-old estate boy to help finance his hole-in-the-heart surgery.

I hope to come out with my eighth book later and may not write anymore after that, as it can be quite taxing. In any case, I never thought I would write books, so I should not push my luck too far!

The award of an Honorary Doctorate of Laws to me from Oxford Brookes University in Britain on September 3, 2000, gave me more academic standing!

I have considerable satisfaction that I have finally got a golf handicap of 24! I had started many years ago with Tan Sri Sallehuddin Mohamad when we were colleagues at the Treasury. However, I did not have the sportsman's flair and therefore never got the hang of it. I also did not have the time nor patience to persist in trying to improve, so I lost interest.

However, my friends V.T. Singam and Richard Gow had more patience with me than I have for myself. Singam encouraged me to practice under his coaching at the Kuala Lumpur Golf and Country Club, near our homes. We used to adjourn for a breakfast of *thosay* afterwards on Saturdays. At the same time, Richard urged me to play with him at the Subang Golf Club, to get my handicap. Now I have enjoyed playing occasionally with Tan Sri Sheriff, my cousin Sam Bar, Richard Gow, Professor Selvanathan, my nephew Dr Surendran Thuraisingam, V.V. Nathan, Henry Selvanayagam and Dato' Teo Chiang Liang.

I also take part in public fora and present papers on economics at conferences. My participation in TV programmes has given me exposure that has been well out of proportion to my standing in society. But it has been fun to take part and to be recognised sometimes in public as someone who writes and appears on TV occasionally as a commentator on public policy!

Appointed to the NECC

I have always enjoyed participating in public debate as well as private discussion on public policy. This must be a healthy hangover from my long career in the civil service.

Thus I was glad when I was appointed by Prime Minister Dato' Seri Dr Mahathir, in his letter to me dated July 12, 1999, to become a member of the National Economic Consultative Council (NECC).

The NECC was composed of about 155 members and seven committees. Its role was to formulate policy recommendations for the socio-economic development of Malaysia for the next 10 years, i.e., the year 2001 to 2010.

I feel gratified that I have been given this privilege to continue to serve my country Malaysia, particularly in my own independent capacity. I am therefore not responsible to political parties and business and social organisations, as is the case with most other members of the NECC, who have been appointed as representatives of these organisations.

Some of my peers, like Dato' Yong Poh Kon and Dr Milton Lum persuaded me to join the Committee on Restructuring Society. This is not only a very important committee but also one of the most contro-

versial, since we discussed the sensitive issues of the NDP. I continue
to serve on the Working Groups of the National Economic Action
Council (NEAC), where we discuss globalisation issues.

As I celebrate my 70th year, I am happy and grateful that I still continue to have a full working life, without much operational responsibility. My roles are mostly advisory in nature and that's what makes life
interesting for me. Thus I have the privileges of active participation
without the responsibilities of having to make too many decisions!

49.
CONCLUSION

THE DEMISE of my brother-in-law, Albert Ramalingam, shook me.
He was stricken with cancer and we visited him in Melbourne six
months before he passed away. He was aware that he would leave us
all, but he was courageous and dignified to the very end.

I realised that despite the death of dear ones and the perpetual
prospects of imminent and sudden death for every one of us, life must
go on. We must do our best everyday so that we continue to make the
best of our lives. We must give our best and enjoy our lives to the best
of our ability until we are finally called home!

Looking back now, I am grateful to God for all His blessings on
me. I must confess that although I have not achieved that much, I am
content that I have done much better in life than I had expected.

I owe all my little successes to God and for His blessings to me of
wonderful parents, sisters and their families. My special debt goes to
my loving wife Samala and dear sons Ravi, Indran and Dharm and our
daughters-in-law Premala and Angelina and my darling grandchildren. To all relatives and friends, teachers and bosses who have given
me much kindness, consideration and encouragement all through my
ups and downs in life, I want to express my deep appreciation.

My surname 'Navaratnam' in Sanskrit means 'Nine Gems'. I have
often asked myself where my wealth has been to reflect my name. My
second name is Veerasingam which in Tamil means "Brave Lion". I
hope I have lived up to that name too, as I have always tried to be open,
frank and firm but generally polite. I am grateful that despite the many
opportunities I had to dishonestly accumulate riches in the course of
my career, I never did. I hope I have inherited and acquired other

"gems", which cannot be defined in monetary terms. They are my blessings from God.

I now feel a strong sense of fulfilment in my latter years. My only wish is to see our children happily married and to have more grandchildren. I wish they will have benefited from the values that Samala and I have instilled in them and will fondly remember that we did our best for them to fulfil God's expectations of us and them and of their own progeny in the future.

My Future

In the future, for whatever time God gives me, I hope to gradually move out of full-time work and devote more time to myself and our family, especially our loving grandchildren. I plan to do more church work, voluntary work, and carry on with public policy participation and discussion. I hope to continue doing some writing and to improve on my golf and my personal handicaps!

I have now been appointed to serve on the Human Rights Commission with effect from April 24, 2002 for four years which have been extended for a second term. I hope that I can make my full contribution to improve human rights and basic socioeconomic needs. I also hope I will not be too occupied and have enough time for myself, too! But I have been appointed in December 2004 to be an independent member of the National Higher Education Council. I wonder how much time I will have to relax!

My 70th birthday is to be celebrated on January 8, 2005, at the Sunway Lagoon Resort Hotel, with about 300 close relatives and friends. It could well be my last big celebration and I pray that God will continue to bless me and my family with good health and happiness!

I have tried my best in this autobiography to recollect and explain some of the milestones in my life in my own words and from memory as, regrettably, I never kept a diary. My purpose has been to express my own personal experiences, my thoughts and concerns — and my hopes for the future.

It is my hope that those who read this autobiography will get a general view of the times and tides that those of my generation lived through. I hope they may benefit from our experiences, our weaknesses and our strengths.

As I look back at my life, I believe that it has been a golden opportunity to serve God, King and Country, as well as my fellow beings. I pray that my immediate family, relatives, friends and colleagues will re-member me with love and affection for what I did and what I stood for, and understand and forgive me for my failings.

Now that my life's major aspirations have been attained, I feel a great sense of relief and gratitude to God. And with the completion of my autobiography, I feel fulfilled and at peace. I thank God for all His blessings on me and my dear family. I could not have asked for more.

INDEX

Rozhan Kuntum (Tan Sri), 249, 259, 264
RTD, *see* Road Transport Department

S. Samy Vellu (Dato' Seri), 260, 297, 300, 304-305
Sallehuddin Mohamad (Tan Sri), 42, 142, 185, 193, 247, 334
Samala (Samaladevi), 31-32, 34-35, 37, 39-46, 55-62, 69-71, 73-74, 76, 78, 80-81, 88-93, 106-110, 117-119, 122-123, 126, 145, 149-150, 158, 163, 196-198, 201-204, 229, 247, 266-268, 271-278, 327-328, 332, 334, 336-337
Samsuddin Osman (Tan Sri), 209
Sarawanamuthu, David (Dr), 326
Sekher, B.C. (Tan Sri), 83
Selvaratnam, David, 229
Shanmugalingam, M. (Dato' Dr), 126
Sheriff Kassim (Tan Sri), 182, 195, 335
Sidhu, Jagjit Singh (Dr), 302
Siti Hasmah Mohd Ali (Tun Dr), 286, 320-321
Smart partnership, 163, 173, 285, 287, 313-315
Smith, Michaela (Dr), 312, 320
Sreenivasan, Lolitha, 34
Suhanya, 333
Sukarno (President), 63-64, 71-72
Sulaiman Abdullah (Dato'), 50, 99
Sulaiman Sujak (Dato'), 237
Sunetra, 333
Sunway College, 269, 281, 292

Tallala, Bertie (Dato'), 123
Tan Cheng Lock (Tun), 131

Tan Chye Mian, 102-103
Tan Siew Sin (Tun), 72, 80, 102, 105, 107, 127-128, 131, 133, 136
Tan Tock Seng Hostel (Singapore), 28
Tan, K.L. (Dato'), 269
Tharumagnyanam, T. (Tan Sri), 52
Thillainathan, R. (Dr), 245, 248, 263, 298-299
Thomasio, Bernard, 223, 226-227
Thong Yaw Hong (Tan Sri), 65-66, 88, 96, 99, 101-102, 140
Thuraisingam, Clough (Dato'), 25
Tik Mustapha (Dato'), 128
Tina (Christina), 2, 10-11, 16-17, 21-22, 37-38, 47, 56, 64-65, 177-178, 273, 328-329
Tirathrai, Kishu (Tan Sri), 189, 293-294, 322
Toh Ah Bah (Dato'), 99, 104-105
Toh Boon Hwa, 19, 198

UMNO, *see* United Malays National Organisation
UNCTAD, *see* United Nations Conference on Trade and Development
Ungku A. Aziz (Professor), 313
United Malays National Organisation, 134, 167, 170
United Nations Conference on Trade and Development, 83, 85, 88, 119

VI, *see* Victoria Institution
Victoria Institution (VI), 3, 18-20, 24, 196-197, 200
Vision 2020, 69, 160, 239, 296, 316-317, 328-329